Key Concepts in
Journalism
Studies

BOB FRANKLIN, MARTIN HAMER,
MARK HANNA, MARIE KINSEY AND
JOHN E. RICHARDSON

Key Concepts in
Journalism
Studies

SAGE Publications

London • Thousand Oaks • New Delhi

First published 2005

SAGE Publications Ltd
1 Oliver's Yard
55 City Road
London EC1Y 1SP

SAGE Publications Inc
2455 Teller Road
Thousand Oaks, California 91320

SAGE Publications India Pvt Ltd
B-42 Panchsheel Enclave
Post Box 4109
New Delhi 110 017

British Library Cataloguing in Publication data

A catalogue record for this book is
available from the British Library

ISBN 1 7619 4481 8
ISBN 1 7619 4482 6 (pbk)

Library of Congress Control Number: 2005924233

Typeset by M Rules

Printed in Great Britain by The Cromwell Press Ltd, Trowbridge, Wiltshire

contents

V

vii

X

acknowledgements

We would like to thank Annie Franklin for volunteering editorial assistance with compiling the various sections of this book during the summer of 2004. Thanks also to Julia Hall for her suggestion that we might write this book and her belief it might prove useful to students and teachers of journalism studies. Jamilah Ahmed and the editorial and production staff at Sage also deserve a vote of thanks for their support and skill in bringing the book to fruition.

Journalism Studies

note on the text

At the end of each entry, the initials of the contributor are shown:

Bob Franklin	BF
Martin Hamer	MGH
Mark Hanna	MNH
Marie Kinsey	MK
John Richardson	JER

Each concept includes cross-references guiding readers to other related concepts and institutions. References in **bold** are to other journalism studies concepts; references in *italics* relate to institutions/organizations.

introduction

Key Concepts in Journalism Studies is designed for students of journalism, media and communications studies and aims to provide them with an accessible, authoritative but preliminary guide to the central concepts informing the innovatory and burgeoning field of journalism studies. Perhaps away from the gaze of students, academics and teachers will also find the book a useful source of up-to-date information about contemporary journalism; as might working journalists in search of a more theoretical evaluation and explanation of their daily professional practice. Members of the broader reading public will also hopefully find something of interest here in the discussion of agony aunts, cartoons, Gonzo journalism, readers' letters, spin doctors and media scrums.

Written by experienced academics, journalists and teachers, the book identifies, analyzes and presents key concepts in journalism studies, explores their interconnections and offers recommendations for further reading and study. The book examines journalism across all media platforms embracing print, radio, television and online journalism. An initial question is obvious: how is this field of journalism studies to be understood? Others soon follow. What parameters define its limits? How does this fledgling discipline connect to the concerns of other arts and social science subjects such as media studies, sociology and linguistics? Browse through the alphabetical listing of concepts and page 128 delivers one answer to these questions and outlines the essential features of journalism studies. Contrary definitions of the field undoubtedly exist: so much the better. It is contested accounts rather than unwarranted certainty that prompt further reflection and intellectual development.

Journalism studies is the multidisciplinary study of **journalism** as an arena of professional practice and a subject focus for intellectual and academic inquiry. More specifically, it entails the critical analysis of the various processes involved in gathering, evaluating, interpreting, researching, writing, editing, reporting and presenting information and comment on a wide range of subjects (including business, fashion, news, politics, sport and travel), that are disseminated via an expansive range of mass **media** (including the **Internet**, magazines, newspapers, **radio** and **television**) to diverse **audiences** (distinguished by culture, identity and intellectual interests) resident in local, regional, national and international settings.

Sources, of course, are invaluable to journalists and central to journalism studies; they are also important to students of journalism studies. Routinely or one-off, sources provide journalists with possible stories, exclusive insider information and authoritative quotations. Whistleblowers, leaks and spin-doctors' press briefings have the added advantage that they come for free, but they bring their own dangers. The growth in chequebook journalism, moreover, means that journalists increasingly need to dip into their back pockets and expense accounts to access sources' deep well of information.

But sources' real value for journalists depends on how they are used. Journalists need to reflect on the information which sources provide, assess its accuracy and relevance, interpret its meaning, adjudicate between contested and contradictory information delivered by different sources, consider the relationship between them and, finally, use a diverse range of sources to construct a balanced and even-handed argument or account of events. The same requirements should steer the use of this book by students of journalism, media and communication studies who are also reliant on sources.

Open the book at the entry for **Sources** and that message is underscored. Sources are 'the people, places and organizations that supply journalists with ideas and general information for news stories and features . . . Cuttings, archival material, broadcast recordings and a variety of documents and websites provide further useful sources of information.' All these sources of information, data and documentation are available in *Key Concepts in Journalism Studies*.

The health warnings posted in the same entry about journalists' use of sources, apply with equal force to readers' use of this book. Journalists, for example, risk their independence being 'compromised by an over-reliance' on sources or their use of 'a limited number of news sources'. Journalists' reliance on significant and authoritative sources, moreover, may offer the latter too great an influence on 'how stories are reported and debated'. The dangers of getting too close to sources should be as apparent to journalists as students of journalism studies. But readers of *Key Concepts in Journalism Studies* differ markedly from journalists concerning the 'need to protect the identity of sources'. Journalists traditionally guarantee their sources absolute anonymity while the protocols of scholarly research and writing insist on openness and honesty in the use of academic sources.

What connects the ways that readers should use the sources of information in this book with journalists' use of sources of news is the simple observation that these 'key concepts', like journalists' sources, are intended to provide the starting point, not the terminus, of any inquiry. Their purpose is not to serve as a surrogate for further reading or critical reflection: unattributed sources to be 'glued' together into an ill-considered and intellectually inadequate pastiche. *Key Concepts* is not a simple dictionary that delivers uncontested 'meanings' or a précis of complex ideas.

On the contrary, each concept should trigger thoughtful reflection about its meaning, prompt readers to explore the cognate concepts and, where meanings and interpretations collide, to strive for and achieve some new synthesis and understanding. Like journalists, readers, who wish to maximise the benefit to be derived from the sources provided here, should consult the widest possible range of sources, follow the recommendations for further reading which accompany entries and use the extensive bibliography to explore more widely, but in closer detail, the literature of this field of scholarly inquiry. See how useful this book can be?

The book has been clearly structured into two broad parts to facilitate readers' access to information and source materials. Part I contains the substantive listing of key concepts in journalism studies, which is ordered alphabetically. Entries range from **absence** and **agenda setting** through to **uses and gratifications** and **yellow journalism**. Along the way **censorship**, **discourse analysis**, **news values** and **tabloid** journalism are discussed and analysed. Entries embrace consideration of both theoretical and practical concerns and, where appropriate, try to reconcile differences arising from this mix of theory and practice. The book makes explicit the interconnections between key concepts and highlights them by using bold type 'hyperlinks' across the alphabetically listed entries, but also seeks to whet readers' appetites for further reading by providing extensive and explicit bibliographical guidance to a wide range of primary and secondary literature to facilitate further study. Articles in newspapers, academic journals, books and a range of online sources offer readers opportunities to follow up particular interests. We have tried to include every concept which is relevant and useful, but if we have missed anything, please write to us c/o Sage, and we will attempt to make good the omission in any subsequent edition.

Part II offers a listing of journalism organizations and institutions selected according to two criteria: first, their significance to the structures and processes of journalism; second, the extent to which they illustrate

XVII

the institutional form through which particular concepts find organizational expression in the UK or European setting. Consequently, the discussion of the key concept **regulation** in Part I finds a complementary and companion discussion in the entries in Part II on the *Press Complaints Commission, Ofcom* and the *BBC Board of Governors*. Concepts such as **news management** and **agenda setting** will similarly find institutional illustration through the entries concerned with the *Government Information and Communication Service (GICS)* and the *Central Office of Information (COI)*. Organizations identified for inclusion range across a broad spectrum including regulatory bodies (*Ofcom*), press agencies (*Reuters*), trade unions (*National Union of Journalists, NUJ*), journalists' professional organizations (*Women in Journalism*), government news management organizations (the *Government News Network, GNN*) and journalism educational organizations (*Broadcast Journalism Training Council, BJTC*).

Towards the end of the book, there is a glossary listing key technical terms and phrases commonly used in print, broadcast and online journalism. Entries here include actuality, copy taster, corpsing, freelance and piece to camera.

The book also explores the complex relationship between journalism studies and the connected disciplines of media, communication and cultural studies, seeking to resolve boundary disputes where they break out. The various entries also indicate the multidisciplinary character of journalism studies and the degree to which it builds on the traditional social science and humanities disciplines of sociology, politics, economics, history, psychology, literature and linguistics.

Key Concepts in Journalism Studies illustrates the plurality and range of theoretical frameworks which deliver explanatory accounts of structures and processes in journalism studies, as well as identifying the characteristic methodological approaches which inform the knowledge base of the discipline and steer further research inquiries. It also introduces readers to the significant debates within the discipline, by outlining the arguments and positions of key protagonists and by offering summaries and evaluations of academics' and journalists' critical assessments of recent developments in journalism studies.

Finally, *Key Concepts in Journalism Studies* outlines the impact of recent policy developments on the organizational structures, financial arrangements and regulatory environment of the media within which journalism is conducted as well as their consequences for journalism products.

These are giddy ambitions. We hope we have achieved some of them.

---

introduction

One measure of our success will be the extent to which readers find this publication valuable and engaging: typical benchmarks of success in journalism. We have tried to provide a useful but critical source of information and ideas about journalism studies. Use it wisely. To get the best from the book, readers, like journalists, must approach this source with appropriate scepticism, an open mind, a genuine spirit of inquiry and a desire to learn. Return to the entry on **Sources** on p. 248. Remember always to avoid the dangers involved in getting too close to a source or becoming overly reliant on a single source. But also remember that sources provide an extremely valuable fund of ideas, information and authoritative quotations. Significantly, they provide the starting point for an inquiry, but it is for the reader to evaluate, compare and reflect on the information and ideas delivered by multiple sources to arrive eventually at the terminus of that inquiry. Have a good trip!

Bob Franklin
Martin Hamer
Mark Hanna
Marie Kinsey
John E. Richardson
October 2004

xix

PART I

Concepts

Absence

For a significant period in the development of journalism and communication studies, analysts proceeded with the assumption that the only important aspects of journalism to study are the 'who says what to whom and with what effect' of Lasswell's (1949) formula. In fact, textual meaning is communicated as much by *absence* as by presence; as much by what is 'missing' or excluded, as by what is remembered and present. Though it's perhaps slightly ironic to start this glossary with such an entry, it is important (although rather difficult) to consider what/where/who is *not* included, as well as what/where/who is included, in reporting.

Absence can occur in two inter-related ways: first, absence of content, by which an individual, group, idea, etc. is totally excluded from a report, leaving no reference or discernible trace. Van Leeuwen (1996) refers to this as *suppression* and its importance to the study of journalism is clear: under current reporting practices, access to the news is a power resource *in itself* and the frequency of inclusion provides us with an index of social power.

Second, absence of form or expression, wherein an individual (or group, or idea, etc.) is not explicitly named or referred to, but their presence may nevertheless still be inferred. This absence in expression can occur through **presupposition**, through euphemism, or by a syntactic transformation (see **transitivity**) such as active agent deletion. The work of critical linguists (Fowler et al., 1979; Kress, 1994) argues that while certain syntactic structures play an important role in the ideological (re)construction of social reality, they are ignored by **content analysis** since their importance lies in textual absence.

JER

Accessibility

Businesses and organizations in many countries are legally obliged to ensure that their services can be accessed by everybody, including disabled people. The Royal National Institute of the Blind says: 'Producing information in such a way that all your customers can read, makes **good business sense**, is the **law** and is **fair**' (Royal National Institute of the Blind, 2004, bold emphasis in original).

3

Providing accessible content has become increasingly important on the Internet, too. The inventor of the **world wide web**, Tim Berners-Lee, insists: 'The power of the Web is in its universality. Access by everyone regardless of disability is an essential aspect' (World Wide Web Consortium, 2004). He says this is 'irrespective of hardware or software platform, network infrastructure, language, culture, geographical location, or physical or mental impairment' (Schofield, 2003).

Certain design and content features can help to make **websites** globally available to anyone regardless of ability or disability. To be more accessible, for example, website designs can accommodate the use of tools such as screen readers, which read text to blind users, and be navigable with only a keyboard, allowing people with restricted movement to navigate via **hypertext** links using the tab key rather than a mouse. The degree of accessibility, which is closely related to website **usability**, depends on many factors including, for example, whether descriptive and meaningful alternative (alt) text tags are used for graphical elements like images and navigation buttons (Royal National Institute of the Blind, www.rnib.org.uk). The alt text appears when the cursor moves across an image, etc, allowing it to be read out by the screen reader.

The *World Wide Web Consortium* (*W3C*), of which Berners-Lee is a director, has laid down universal standards in its Web Accessibility Initiative (WAI) which has published the Web Content Accessibility Guidelines (World Wide Web Consortium, 2004). The WAI, working with organizations around the world, pursues web accessibility through five main areas of work: technology, guidelines, tools, education and outreach, and research and development. The EuroAccessibility Consortium is one such organization (EuroAccessibility Consortium, 2004).

4

Further reading

Schofield J. (2003), Decorators With Keyboards', *Guardian Unlimited*, available at www.guardian.co.uk/online/story/0,3605,999218,00.html

MGH

Accountability

In a democracy, media organizations and the journalists who work in them are accountable to their **audience** and to wider society in various ways.

They are accountable to the law courts, for example, if they **libel** someone or commit **contempt of court**.

In Britain, the Office of Communications (*Ofcom*) has responsibility for the statutory **regulation** of the broadcast sector. Its scope includes programme quality and **ethics**.

Journalists in the *BBC*, a **public service broadcaster**, are accountable to the *BBC Board of Governors*. The BBC itself is accountable, in some respects, to *Ofcom* and ultimately, despite structural safeguards to protect its day-to-day independence, to the British Government under the terms of the BBC Agreement.

The British Press (the newspaper and magazine section) is not accountable to any statutory regulator (except in the field of **competition,** i.e. proposed takeovers or mergers of newspaper companies). In ethical matters, the press is governed by **self-regulation,** administered by the *Press Complaints Commission,* which holds editors accountable by means of its ability to ensure critical adjudications are published.

Media organizations stress that they are also held accountable by their audiences (and advertisers). Readers, viewers or listeners can be lost if there is adverse public reaction to particular conduct or content. Various factors usually stop consumer action being effective (Gibbons, 1998: 46–54). However, in 1989 the *Sun* lost thousands of Merseyside readers outraged because of inaccurate coverage of the Hillsborough football stadium disaster (Chippindale and Horrie, 1992: 276–93).

In recent years some British newspapers have each appointed a senior executive to be the 'readers' editors' or 'an ombudsman', to bolster their accountability to readers or anyone else aggrieved by particular coverage, with such executives having power to publish corrections and adjudications (Sanders 2003: 155–8). The term 'media accountability systems' has been coined to describe the variety of means and methods – including press councils, ombudsmen, training in ethics, readership surveys – which can encourage ethical conduct in the media (Bertrand 2000, 2003). Critics of the British media – for example, the *Campaign for Press and Broadcasting Freedom* and *MediaWise* – argue that the huge expense of libel and privacy litigation, weaknesses in the regulatory and self-regulatory systems, the market dominance of a concentrated number of powerful media corporations, and the reluctance of successive governments to attempt radical reform in these fields, mean that journalists are not sufficiently accountable to the public.

With rare exceptions (e.g. the BBC, which is a purely public service broadcaster, and the *Guardian* and *Observer* newspapers, which are owned by a trust), media corporations are also accountable, structurally,

5

to their shareholders to make good profits.

Further reading
Sanders, K. (2003) *Ethics and Journalism*. London: Sage.

MNH

Accuracy

Irrespective of the extent to which any piece of journalism can be held to exhibit **objectivity**, or otherwise pay heed to the wider contexts in which **news** occurs, it can be judged at a basic level on matters of accuracy.

At this level, the term accuracy means, for example, that the names of those featured in the piece are spelt correctly, that quotes are reproduced in direct form, or in *précis* which preserves their meaning, and that events are clearly related. The term encompasses the ethical principle that a news journalist should take all reasonable steps to corroborate any version of events likely to be disputed, if he/she has not witnessed those events, and indicate, in what is published, any such dispute. If the **public interest** merits it, the airing of uncorroborated facts is ethically justifiable, but the lack of corroboration must be made explicit.

The term 'accuracy', if used in isolation, is of limited value. Journalism usually involves summarizing events or arguments. Good journalism exhibits **fairness** in the summary.

British law, when conferring 'privilege', i.e. protection against **defamation** lawsuits, on certain types of media reports – for example, coverage of court cases, council meetings or Parliamentary proceedings – specifies such protection will only exist if the reports are accurate and fair (Welsh and Greenwood, 2003: 259–72).

The statutory **regulation** of broadcasting in Britain requires, under the terms of licences to be awarded by *Ofcom,* and those awarded by predecessor bodies, that news be presented 'with due accuracy', fairness and **impartiality**, and this requirement is reflected in codes of **ethics**, issued by those bodies, and in the *BBC*'s **Producers' Guidelines**.

Clause 1 of the Code of Practice used by the *Press Complaints Commission* concerns accuracy, fairness and the need for prompt corrections. The majority of complaints ruled on by the PCC – e.g. 53 per cent of its rulings in 2003 – concern alleged breaches of Clause 1.

MNH

Adversarial journalism

The achievement which gradually uncovered the **Watergate** scandal led to renewed enthusiasm in American newsrooms for **investigative journalism**. But there was also increased soul-searching about **ethics.** Some commentators began to warn that reporters who were overly-hostile to and cynical about politicians, public institutions and business risked alienating the public from journalists, or could erode public faith in democracy. In 1982 Michael J. O'Neill, then editor of the *New York Daily News*, condemned the increase in 'adversarial mindset' among journalists. Despite these concerns, research suggests only a small minority of American journalists consider they have an adversarial mindset (Weaver and Wilhoit, 1996: 134–5, 139–40).

A survey in the 1990s suggested that, compared to their US counterparts, British journalists are more likely to declare an adversarial scepticism of the pronouncements of public officials and businesses. This is a reflection, perhaps, of the tougher legal environment, in terms of **defamation** and the culture of official secrecy, in which British journalists operate (Henningham and Delano, 1998: 153).

The terms 'adversarial' and 'hyperadversarial' have also been used, negatively, in Britain and America to describe journalistic interviewing techniques deemed aggressive and dramatic which, though they may help inflate the interviewer's ego, are essentially ritualistic, and superficial in terms of helping the public consider social issues (Keeble 2001: 4 and 6).

Adversarial journalism is sometimes compared unfavourably with **public journalism** or **civic journalism.**

7

Further reading

Fallows (1997) *Breaking the News: How the Media Undermine American Democracy.* New York: Vintage Books.

Lloyd, J. (2004) *What the Media Are Doing to Our Politics.* London: Constable.

McNair, B. (2000b) 'Journalism and Democracy: A Millennial Audit', *Journalism Studies*, 1(2): 197–211.

MNH

Advertising

Revenues are crucial to newspapers, magazines and commercial broadcasting media. They provide a large part of the income of these media and, in the case of newspapers and magazines, offset the purchase cost for the consumer. Tabloid newspapers receive approximately 30 per cent of their income from advertising while for broadsheets it rises to 70 per cent (Baistow, 1985: 33). The figures for local daily (60 per cent) and weekly newspapers (80 per cent) are similarly high while local **free newspapers** are wholly reliant on advertising revenues for their income (Franklin, 2005).

Levels of advertising expenditure in UK media are considerable and expansive. In 2002, advertising revenues for UK media totalled £13,666 million. **Television** digested the largest portion (26 per cent or £3553 million) of the advertising cake with local and regional newspapers in second place with 21 per cent (£2870 million) of aggregate advertising income. National newspapers (14 per cent or £1913 million), magazines (13 per cent or £1776 million), **radio** (4 per cent or £546 million), cinema (1 per cent or £136 million), and the Internet (1 per cent or £136 million) displayed varying degrees of reliance on advertising revenues to fund their activities (ibid.). Different media sectors face highly variable prospects with national press advertising revenues declining by 14.5 per cent between 2000 and 2002 while local newspaper revenues expanded by 3.9 per cent across the same period. In the USA levels of advertising income are predictably higher with television ($47 billion) leading newspapers ($43 billion), magazines ($15 billion) and radio ($13 billion) (Applegate, 2000: 285–6).

Competition for these considerable advertising revenues is fierce and newspapers' reliance on advertising impacts significantly on all aspects of their production and distribution. Free local newspapers simply would not exist without it. The expansion of colour supplements in Sunday newspapers in the 1970s, the development of supplements in the Saturday broadsheets in the 1990s, the expansion of pagination and the variability of pagination across the news week, along with the growth in financial sections in the 1990s each reflect the impact of advertising revenues (Franklin, 1997: 93–4). The most controversial aspect of the relationship between advertisers and newspapers is the suggestion that advertisers might influence editorial content.

Although McGregor's Press Commission argued for little advertiser influence on the press, academics like James Curran have demurred, suggesting 'successive Royal Commissions on the Press have failed to identify adequately the different ways in which advertising shapes and influences the Press' (Curran, 1978: 230–1). Advertisers exert pressure on journalists, although quantifying how often this happens is difficult. The issue is seldom aired in the UK. But some advertisers, when lobbying for favourable publicity in news coverage, remind journalists of past and potential advertising patronage. Threats to withdraw advertising are made in efforts to suppress unfavourable coverage. At UK national newspaper and broadcast network level, such pressure – although it does occur (see Willcock, 1999; Robertson and Nicol, 2002: 640) – should be easily resisted because of the dominant market position of these media. Advertiser threats are more likely to be effective when made to the local/regional media.

But advertiser influence is typically subtle. A publication's news agenda is influenced by its need to target a particular **audience** for advertisers. A relationship between a niche publisher and advertisers can be so financially symbiotic that **self-censorship** is likely to dilute journalistic principles; fashion magazines, for example, are unlikely to campaign vigorously against the high prices of top brand perfumes. But if a media organization is too readily supine to advertisers in editorial matters, it risks compromising its credibility with its audience. In America, research reveals that most journalists did not perceive advertiser pressure as a major problem (Pew Research Center, 1999) although varying degrees of self-censorship were admitted (Pew Research Center, 2000).

Advertiser pressure is usually inimical to good journalism, but not always. The sacking of Mike Gabbert as editor of the *Daily Star* in 1987 was attributed, at least in part, to British supermarket chains withdrawing their advertising after he plumbed new depths of salaciousness in the tabloid's news agenda (Chippindale and Horrie, 1992: 226–7). Advertising may, moreover, be seen historically as the bulwark of the free press, freeing it from economic dependence on the state, though this view is open to challenge (Curran and Seaton, 1997). **Alternative media** campaigning against multinational companies, of course, do not expect to receive advertising revenues from such sources.

Further reading

Applegate, E. (2000) 'Advertising in the United States: Past, Present and Future', *Journalism Studies*, 1(2): 285–303; Curran, J. (1978)

Curran, J. and Seaton, J (1997) *Power without Responsibility*, 6th edn. London: Routledge.

Fleetwood, B. (1999) 'The Broken Wall: How Newspapers Are Selling Their Credibility to Advertisers', *Washington Monthly*, September http://www.washingtonmonthly.com.

Franklin, B. (1997) *Newszak and News Media*. London: Arnold.

Franklin, B. (2005) 'McJournalism: The McDonaldization Thesis and the UK Local Press', in Allan, S. (ed.) *Contemporary Journalism: Critical Essays*. Milton Keynes: Open University Press. pp. 137-151.

Herman, E. and Chomsky, N. ([1988] 1994) *Manufacturing Consent: The Political Economy of the Mass Media*. New York: Pantheon.

Kennedy, P. (2002), 'People's Champ Leaves NoW in Censorship Row', *Press Gazette online*, 24 January.

Meyer, P. (1987) *Ethical Journalism*. Lanham, MD: University Press of America.

Porter, C. (2002) 'The Truth about Mags and Ads', *Guardian*, 15 November. http://www.guardian.co.uk/style/story/0,3605,840390,00.html.

BF and MNH

Advertising codes

The largely self-regulatory system, used by the mass **media** industries, to ensure that any advertising they include is 'legal, decent, honest and truthful' (Radio Authority www.radworth.org.uk: 7). There are four main codes which offer guidelines on advertising practice: the British Codes of Advertising, Sales Promotion and Direct Marketing (the CAP Code) covering non-broadcast advertising such as the press; the ITC Advertising Standards Code, covering **television** advertising; the Radio Authority Advertising and Sponsorship Code, covering **radio** advertising; and the Direct Marketing Association Code of Practice, covering direct marketing. Although the *Radio Authority* and the *ITC* have now been superseded by the Office of Communications (*Ofcom*), the RA and ITC Codes remain in operation.

With all broadcast media, it is the responsibility of the broadcasters to ensure the advertising they transmit complies with both the spirit and the letter of the relevant Code – although broadcasters are entitled to request copy clearance for specific adverts from the Broadcast Advertising Clearance Centre (BACC) or the Radio Advertising Clearance Centre (RACC). Fundamentally, the Codes demand 'There must be a clear distinction between programmes and advertisements' (ITC, www.ofcom.org.uk/codes: 12). Therefore, advertising must not 'use a situation, performance or style reminiscent of a programme in a way that might confuse viewers as to whether they are watching a programme or an advertisement' (ibid.). Further, the Codes contain detailed and specific guidance, including the products and services which it is unacceptable to advertise (for example, tobacco, pornography and 'bodies with political objectives'), misleading advertising (for example, on the use of the word 'free' or 'environmentally friendly') and avoiding offence and harm, particularly to children.

Compliance with broadcast Codes is now enforced by Ofcom, though day-to-day responsibility for regulating broadcast advertising content is, since November 2004, overseen by the Advertising Standards Agency (ASA). Under this new system, an 'advertising industry committee – BCAP (Broadcast Committee of Advertising Practice) – will be responsible for setting, reviewing and, if necessary, revising the broadcast advertising Codes. The ASA will receive and respond to complaints about television and radio commercials [while] adjudications will be by a new legal entity, ASA(B)' (www.cap.org.uk).

JER

Advertorial

This is a hybrid of **advertising** and editorial. More specifically, it is a paid advertisement masquerading as editorial which risks misleading readers into the belief that they are reading a straight news story or feature rather than an advertisement (Franklin and Murphy, 1998: 13, 245–7). For the company or individual buying the advertising space, the advertorial has the advantage of conferring the authority and truth claims associated with news on the advertisement. For the newspaper selling the space, advertorial allows the editor to allocate a greater part of the paper to advertising copy which typically generates up to half the newspaper's revenues (for **free local newspapers** which are wholly reliant on advertising, advertorial assumes an even greater economic significance). Advertorials have become increasingly popular in the past two decades (Eckman and Lindlof 2003: 66) with one study revealing that advertorial revenues in USA print media doubled in the second half of the 1980s to more than an estimated US$200 million in annual profits (Cameron et al. 1996). In summary, advertorial reflects 'the rising pressure to find new ways of getting cash from advertisers' but significantly and worryingly, 'the once sacred split between editorial and advertising is now being sewn together' (Smallman, 1996: 11). Advertorial is evident in both the local and national press: in both settings, the format of these advertising features is highly stylized. In a local newspaper, for example, advertorial may feature a local business which is perhaps celebrating a centenary or opening new premises. A formulaic article applauds the company's achievements (typically in rather glowing terms) while the newspaper, on the strength of the article, solicits further advertising, usually in the form of good wishes messages, from the company's major suppliers and

11

customers (Morley and Whitaker, 1986: 11). In the national press, a broadsheet paper may publish a special edition/supplement focusing on a particular African or Middle Eastern country, for example, and surround the text with advertisements from major companies and contractors.

Further reading

Cameron, Ju-Pak, K. and Kim, B. H. (1996) 'Advertorials in Magazines', *Journalism and Mass Communication*, 73: 722–33.

Eckman, A. and Lindlof, T. (2003) 'Negotiating the Gray Lines: An Ethnographic Case Study of Organisational Conflict Between Advertorials and News', *Journalism Studies*, 4(1): 65–79.

Franklin, B. and Murphy, D. (1998a) 'Changing Times: Local Newspapers, Technology and Markets', in Franklin, B. and Murphy, D. (eds) *Making the Local News: Local Journalism in Context*. London: Routledge, pp. 7–23.

Morley, D. and Whitaker, B. (1986) *The Press, Radio and Television: An Introduction to the Media*. London: Commedia.

Smallman, A. (1996) 'Telling the Editorial from the Adverts', *Press Gazette*, 10 May, p. 11.

BF

Agenda setting

12

The basic premise of agenda-setting theory is that the way in which news media report particular issues influences and helps to shape public awareness and debate (McCombs and Shaw, 1972). In much the same way that a committee agenda ranks items to reflect their significance, with the least consequential matters receiving only scant attention or not being discussed at all, media agendas reflect a process of selection (prioritizing) with certain issues enjoying sustained and prominent coverage in news reports while others are relatively marginalized or ignored (Weaver et al., 1981; McCombs et al., 1997). In this sense, agenda-setting theory has clear affinities with news **framing** and **media effects**. But in agenda setting, the influence claimed for the media is less certain than in some theorizing of media effects and eschews implications of **propaganda**. In a classic formulation of agenda setting, the suggestion is that while the media do not tell us what to think, they may tell us what to think about.

Agenda setting, however, does not posit a simple uni-directional model in which news media set the priorities for public debate, but suggests that typically a number of contesting agendas vie for prominence. Extensive research on agenda setting during election periods, for example, has illustrated the distinctive agendas which politicians and journalists bring to the electoral process, characterized as a battle between the 'earnest and the determined' (Blumler et al., 1989). Similarly, a study of local press coverage of the 2001 general election in West Yorkshire illustrated the extent to which journalists and political parties (both committed to an electoral agenda which emphasized local issues, such as local schools, local services and local candidates) were starkly at odds with newspaper readers whose election agendas were overwhelmingly informed by national concerns such as Europe and taxation (Franklin and Richardson, 2002).

Further reading

Blumler, J. G., Gurevitch, M. and Nossiter, T. (1989) 'Earnest Versus the Determined', in Crewe, I. and Harrop, M. (eds) *Political Communications: The General Election Campaign of 1987*. Cambridge: Cambridge University Press, pp. 157–75.

Franklin, B. and Richardson, J. (2002) 'A Journalist's Duty? Continuity and Change in Local Newspapers' Coverage of Recent UK General Elections', *Journalism Studies*, (2002) 3(1): 35–52.

McCombs, M. and Shaw, D. (1972) 'The Agenda-setting Function of the Mass Media', *Public Opinion Quarterly*, 36: 176–87.

BF

Agony aunt

Prurience or a public service? Tonic or titillation? Probably all of them. The agony aunt and her male equivalent, the agony uncle, are a mainstay of newspapers, magazines, radio and television and there are thousands on the Internet. Their trenchant advice to the lovelorn and generally wretched on emotional, sexual and health problems, as well as much else has poured out in the past 50 years or so.

Advice columns have been around since the 1930s, but the term itself did not gain currency until the 1970s, with the first citation in the *Oxford English Dictionary* in 1975. One of the best-known columns, Ann Landers, was in the *Chicago Sun-Times*. According to her obituary in the *Chicago Tribune*, 'Dear Ann' began running in the early 1950s and by 1993 was appearing in 1,200 newspapers around the world with an estimated 90 million readers.

But the relatively tame columns of the 1950s and 1960s gave way to a new breed of agony aunt with the launch of a new wave of womens' magazines such as *Cosmopolitan*. These columns pulled few punches in the way they dealt with stories of sexual angst and emotional dysfunction.

In Britain the doyenne of agony aunts was Marje Proops, who wrote a column in the *Daily Mirror* and died in 1996. Until the mid-1990s, agony aunts were mainly found in the tabloids and womens' magazines, but Virginia Ironside became the first broadsheet agony aunt for the *Independent*.

Further reading
Anderson, J. (2002) 'Advice Columnist Ann Landers Dead at 83', *Chicago Tribune*, 22 June.

MK

Alternative media

This blanket term is used to describe various forms of publication, containing news, general information and features, which are not produced or distributed by the mainstream, corporate media organizations, but by individuals, or by small, non-hierarchical collectives. These seek not profit but to represent particular interest groups – e.g. community or sub-cultural or political – who feel their ideas, concerns and viewpoints are neglected, marginalized or suppressed by the institutionalized news agendas of professional journalists in the mainstream.

Thus, the term 'alternative' can be used of the community-based, investigative newsletters published in British cities in the 1970s to challenge local politicians and expose corruption; pioneering magazines written by feminists, e.g. *Spare Rib* and/or gay rights activists; the music 'fanzines' which flowered with punk rock; the irreverent, grass-root soccer fanzines which scrutinize British professional football clubs; SchNEWS, the 'direct action' collective embracing a wide range of protest and campaign causes, including ecological, anti-racist and anti-globalisation groups, which has a website but also distributes news on A4 paper and by email (see http://www.schnews.co.uk)

Chris Atton, in his 'typology of alternative and radical media', lists several elements including 'politically radical, socially/culturally radical content'; de-professionalization of journalism and printing, e.g. use of voluntary labour and photocopiers to achieve cheap production; transformed roles and responsibilities, e.g. readers are encouraged to become writers; and horizontal networks of research and distribution, rather than the vertical 'top-down' processes of the mainstream media (2002b: 27). He takes issue with John Fiske's assertion that much of the alternative media 'circulates among a fraction of the same educated middle classes as does official news' (ibid.: 13).

Because they usually lack financial capital, are heavily reliant on the enthusiasm of those who produce them and, usually, on informal

14

distribution networks, most alternative media are relatively short-lived, ceasing publication as those creating them suffer burn-out, move to more conventional jobs, or cannot afford to subsidize them when demand falls (Harcup, 1998: 114). But the grass-root nature of their experiences and contacts, their specialized pool of knowledge and unconventional 'take' on the world mean those involved in alternative media sometimes uncover scandals or raise broad issues subsequently pursued by mainstream media. The Internet has greatly aided alternative publishers to reach **audiences** cheaply.

Further reading

Atton, C. (2002a) 'News Cultures and New Social Movements: Radical Journalism and the Mainstream Media', *Journalism Studies*, 3(4): 491–505.

Doig, A. (1997) 'Decline of Investigatory Journalism', in Bromley, M. and O'Malley, T. (eds) *A Journalism Reader.* London: Routledge, pp. 189–213.

Franklin, B. and Murphy, D. (1998a) 'Changing Times: Local Newspapers, Technology and Markets', in Franklin, B. and Murphy, D. (eds) *Making the Local News: Local Journalism in Context.* London: Routledge, pp. 7–23.

Harcup, T. (1998) 'There Is No Alternative: The Demise of the Alternative Local Newspaper', in Franklin, B. and Murphy, D. (eds) *Making the Local News: Local Journalism in Context.* London: Routledge.

Harcup, T. (2003) 'The Unspoken – Said: The Journalism of Alternative Media', *Journalism: Theory, Practice and Criticism* 4 (3): 356–76.

MNH

Ambient news

A phrase used by Ian Hargreaves in his book *Journalism: Truth or Dare?* to signal that the availability of relatively cheap digital technology, combined with the growing economic, political and cultural value of information, have made news more accessible to **audiences**, to the point where it is omnipresent or 'ambient' (Hargreaves, 2003: 3).

Audiences' greatly enhanced access to news reflects: (1) the increased number of media platforms, especially the development of the **Internet**; (2) access to approximately 250 digital radio and television channels with the consequent increase in news provision; (3) the greater range of news and depth of journalistic analysis offered by the Internet and online newspapers; (4) the availability of news for 24 hours each day instead of being limited to the set times of the evening television news bulletins or the publishing schedules of newspapers; and (5) the relatively cheap cost – and widespread use – of information technologies such as personal computers and mobile phones.

15

The cumulative consequence of these changes is 'the age of ambient news' where the prevalent assumption is that 'news is something available free of charge and even free of effort' (Hargreaves and Thomas, 2002: 5). 'News which was once difficult and expensive to obtain,' Hargreaves argues, 'today surrounds us like the air we breathe. Much of it is literally ambient: displayed on computers, public billboards, trains, aircraft and mobile phones' (2003: 3). But, paradoxically, because so much news is available, people are not always able to discriminate between the good and the bad. The perception that news is 'free', moreover, means that audiences tend to value it less and certain forms of costly, resource intensive journalism may be undermined. While 'we have more news and more influential journalism . . . than at any time since the birth of the free press in the eighteenth century . . . journalism is also under widespread attack from politicians, philosophers, the general public and even from journalists themselves' (ibid.: 2).

Further reading

Hargreaves, I. (2003) *Journalism: Truth or Dare?* Oxford: Oxford University Press.
Hargreaves, I. and Thomas, J. (2002) *New News, Old News*. London: ITC/BSC.

BF

Apologies

16

With the dramatic headline 'Sorry. We Were Hoaxed' on 15 May 2004 the *Daily Mirror* joined a select group of publications to make a front page apology. And it lost an editor in the process. Two weeks previously, the paper had printed photographs it claimed showed British soldiers abusing prisoners in Iraq. The front page of that Saturday edition admitted they were fakes. 'So to you today we apologise for publishing pictures which we now believe were not genuine.'

Apologies feature in both press and **broadcasting** codes of practice but there's nothing in either that directs offenders on when an apology should be given. Much, however, is said about how quickly something should be corrected. And printing or broadcasting a correction doesn't necessarily go hand in hand with an apology. Increasingly newspapers are appointing **readers' editors** who are responsible for ensuring that mistakes are corrected quickly, and they're sometimes brought together in a particular section of the paper.

In the case of broadcasters, the regulator *Ofcom* has the power to direct broadcasters to publish a correction, or all of its adjudication in cases where complaints are upheld. It can also direct the broadcast of an apology, as it did with Central Television over the **reconstruction** in the **documentary** *The Connection* (1996). Its **radio** code says apologies should be broadcast 'where appropriate'. Clause 1 of the *Press Complaints Commission* Code of Practice asks for prompt corrections and an apology if appropriate when it is recognized that 'a significant inaccuracy, misleading statement or distorted report has been published'. It asks that such corrections are given 'due prominence'. As in the case of the *Mirror*, sometimes they are.

The decision to apologize is never taken lightly, particularly if libel either has been or could be involved. They are carefully worded, finely crafted and stick in editors' throats.

MK

April fool

Putting a fake story in newspapers and broadcast news on 1 April each year has a long and honourable history.

According to a 2002 study of such hoaxes by Alex Boese, a 1957 spoof by the respected BBC news programme *Panorama* tops the list of all-time greats. With his characteristic genial gravitas, presenter Richard Dimbleby reported that thanks to a mild winter and the virtual elimination of the dreaded spaghetti weevil, Swiss farmers were enjoying a bumper spaghetti crop. Hundreds of viewers rang in asking how to grow the trees and were advised 'place a sprig of spaghetti in a tin of tomato sauce and hope for the best' (BBC, 2002). In fact, cameraman Charles de Jaeger, while working on another story, had draped 20 pounds of cooked spaghetti on a cluster of laurel bushes and then filmed the locals apparently 'harvesting' them. Even the BBC's then director general Sir Ian Jacob admitted he'd consulted three different reference books before being reassured it was a hoax (Lindley, 2002: 50).

The *Guardian* is credited with firing the enthusiasm of the newspapers for April Foolery with its 1977 seven-page supplement marking the tenth anniversary of San Seriffe, a small republic located in the Indian Ocean made up of several semi-colon-shaped islands. Articles described its geography and culture; how its two main islands were called Upper Caisse and Lower Caisse, its leader was General Pica and the capital Bodoni. Not everyone spotted that everything was named after printing terms.

Then there was the well with the power to make hair grow (BBC *Nationwide*, 1977), the hot-headed naked ice borer (*Discover* Magazine,

17

1985), the Japanese marathon runner who thought he had to run for 26 days not 26 miles (*Daily Mail*, 1981), smellovision (BBC, 1965), changing the value of pi (New Mexicans for Science and Reason, 1998) and the man who flew by his own lung power (*Berliner Illustrierte Zeitung*, 1934). Over to you.

Further reading

Boese, A. (2002) *The Museum of Hoaxes*. London: E.P. Dutton.

MK

Audience

At bottom there is an assumption by most journalists that **news** is *for* people, that out there are readers, viewers and listeners. **Editors**, circulation managers and advertisers care greatly about the number of people who buy a publication, listen or watch at particular times. They also care about whether they're reaching the **target audience** and worry greatly about **audience fragmentation** and **audience segmentation**.

Audience measurement has become more sophisticated in the past 20 years. Not only are numbers gathered by the *Audit Bureau of Circulations* (for newspapers and magazines), *BARB* (for television) and *RAJAR* (for radio), but surveys and **focus groups** also generate information on the profile of the audience; their age, their interests, their habits. Measurement systems carefully define words such as 'listener', 'viewer' and 'reader' (Kent, 1994).

The relationship between **journalists** and their audience has been described in several different ways with many writers (Gans, 1980; Schlesinger, 1987; Harrison, 2000) observing that at grass-roots level journalists have little knowledge of their audience and may not even be very interested. Harrison (2000: 116) notes that when asked about audience, individual television journalists didn't respond with numbers, but with a more 'organic and emotional' view, referring to types of people. Allan (1999: 109–10) makes the same point about newspaper journalists and also that audience feedback seems to have little impact as it is deemed to come from cranks. But he also suggests that the appointment of **readers' editors**, or **Ombudsmen**, is developing the relationship between the news providers and the news consumers.

The growing awareness of who is listening, watching or reading has meant a more sophisticated visualization of Mr, Mrs or Ms

Listener/Viewer/Reader drawn from marketing and advertising information. This has led to **newsrooms** trying to make their news service more distinctive by running the types of stories they think the audience want.

Journalists, however, are acutely aware that they ignore their audience at their peril, as the *Sun* found to its cost on 19 April 1989. Under the banner headline 'The Truth' the paper reported that anonymous police officers were accusing Liverpool football fans of 'robbing the dead and attacking rescue workers' during the Hillsborough disaster, in which 95 Liverpool fans died. Chippendale and Horrie (1992) described how all over the city copies of the paper were ripped up, banned in pubs and from newsagents. Sales crashed by a third. And memories are long. Fifteen years later, on 9 July 2004, Merseysiders were outraged when former Everton footballer Wayne Rooney sold his story to the *Sun* and the paper tried to apologize for its previous story.

Further reading

Allan, S. (1999) *News Culture*. Buckingham: Open University Press.
Gans, H.J. (1980) *Deciding What's News*. London: Constable.
Harrison, J. (2000) *Terrestrial TV News in Britain: The Culture of Production*. Manchester, Manchester University Press.
Schlesinger, P. (1987) *Putting Reality Together*. London: Methuen.

MK

Audience fragmentation

19

The division of the available **audience** between ever increasing numbers of **media** options. Faced with more and more choices, the audience has a tendency to disperse among the different media options, leaving each option with a smaller share of the audience. And, since the amount that advertisers are willing to pay is directly linked to audience share, the fragmentation of audiences has a knock-on effect, reducing revenue and resources.

Audience fragmentation has not affected all news media equally. **Television** is particularly affected, with hundreds of channels, in many different languages, now available via satellite, digital and cable in addition to domestic analogue transmission. In contrast, the share of the readers is relatively stable across and between newspaper titles, due in part to the costs inherent in launching and establishing a new paper and in part to the bounded distribution of specific titles. This stability has led John

Honderich, the publisher of the *Toronto Star*, to claim 'more and more, newspapers are becoming the sole mass medium, particularly for advertising' (www.mediainfo.com).

Drawing these two points together, the worry is that greater fragmentation of the television audience will adversely affect programme quality. Simply put, advertisers will not subsidize a channel without an audience. This pushes broadcasters towards either increasing light, entertaining programmes at the expense of more weighty (and expensive) documentaries, or towards attracting a wealthy audience segment at the expense of poorer viewers. But not everyone offers such a pessimistic evaluation. Indeed, Janeway (2000) claims that 'audience fragmentation also means, for those prepared to think about it, a new niche, however modest in size, for quality, for seriousness of purpose'. Early reports suggest that the greater corporatization of news media, particularly in the USA, has pushed audiences towards 'alternative' news providers on the Internet, such as Common Dreams, Democracy Now, FAIR and Z-Net (Hightower, 2004).

JER

Audience segmentation

This is the more worrying corollary of **audience fragmentation**. While audience fragmentation occurs 'bottom-up' as a result of increased choice between media options, audience segmentation occurs 'top-down' when media producers attempt to corral a **target audience** (defined by age, gender, **ethnicity**, class or some other group characteristic) in order to attract advertising revenue. Of course, advertisers are not interested in the size of an **audience** per se, nor in the share (or 'fragment') of the total audience that a newspaper or television station attracts. Certain products only sell to certain segments of the population and hence only need to be advertised to these segments: BMW cars need only be advertised to the rich, while dodgy loan companies need only be advertised to the poor. News organizations that conform to the 'marketing requirements of advertisers', producing news that can be shown to attract (or *generate*) a desired target audience, obtain large external subsidies which they 'can then spend on increased editorial outlay and promotion in order to attract new readers' (Curran and Seaton 1997: 37).

Schement (1998: 93) argues that 'in the calculus of modern media, ethnicity has emerged as a potent determinant for organising media segments'. In every Western country, without exception, Black communities are significantly over-represented in the impoverished and ill-educated social strata. Media organizations earn more money by supplying a product that attracts the richer strata of the audience and therefore 'content of interest to smaller, or minority, audiences will not be produced in amounts that will satisfy the preferences of that minority' (Gandy, 2000: 47). And, while racial or ethnic identity can never be used as a fail-safe basis for predicting wealth and status, it remains true that '[m]edia produced for the poor folks at or near the bottom of the racial hierarchy will be of the lowest quality, and will most often be financed by the sale of dangerous, debilitating or worthless goods and services' (Gandy, 2001: 10).

Further reading

Gandy, O. Jnr (2000) 'Race, Ethnicity and the Segmentation of Media Markets', in Curran, J. and Gurevitch, M. (eds) *Mass Media and Society*. London: Arnold, pp. 44–69.

JER

Bad News

This was the title of the first book, in a pioneering series of books, produced by the **Glasgow Media Group** which explored the way in which television journalists reported contemporary industrial relations (GMG, 1976). The *Bad News* studies (*Bad News*, 1976; *More Bad News*, 1980; *Really Bad News*, 1982; *War and Peace News*, 1985; and *Bad News from Israel*, 2004) rejected the 'common-sense' view that television news coverage of the economy, industrial relations and war was balanced or neutral, arguing that news was simply an artifice which systematically articulated a partial viewpoint reflecting the special status and credibility afforded to certain sectional interests (Eldridge, 2000: 114).

The *Bad News* series, which aimed 'to examine how news bulletins were organised and constructed in general' as well as 'in particular . . . what it meant in practice to treat a controversial matter [industrial relations] in a way that claimed to be impartial' (Eldridge, 2000: 116), suffered a hostile reception from news organizations such as *ITN* (which funded Martin Harrison's alternative study *Whose Bias?* (1985)) and the *BBC* (Hoggart, 1993: 258).

The *Bad News* research was unprecedented in scope, analyzing all television news content for five months: its conclusions were highly

21

critical. The study revealed similarities, rather than differences, between BBC and ITN news bulletins, in terms of the frequency and ordering of items, the selection of stories, the use of **sources** and the **news values** reflected in news programming. In brief, the study identified a common journalistic culture with shared routines of news production. The study also cast doubt on the widely held assumption that television news was in some way 'objective', offering a yardstick against which to measure 'bias'. The redefined task became to reveal what was produced 'in the name of objectivity and impartiality and to consider what evaluation could be made of that product' (Eldridge, 2000: 115). Significantly, the research posed a crucial question: 'does the way television news is constituted help to explain and clarify events in the world or does it mystify and obscure them?' The response was highly critical, claiming that news production was 'a process of mystification' with the media researcher fulfilling the function of 'dispelling illusions'. Moreover, 'since there is a distinction between illusion and reality this was one reason for calling the work *Bad News* . . . the implication was that bad news could be better' (ibid.: 115).

Further reading

Eldridge, J. (2000) 'The Contribution of the Glasgow Media Group to the Study of Television and Print Journalism', *Journalism Studies*, 1(1): 113–27.

Glasgow Media Group (1976) *Bad News*. London: Routledge and Kegan Paul.

Glasgow Media Group (1980) *More Bad News*. London: Routledge and Kegan Paul.

Glasgow Media Group (1982) *Really Bad News*. London: Writer and Readers.

Glasgow Media Group (1985) *War and Peace News*. Milton Keynes: Open University Press.

Harrison, M. (1985) *Whose Bias?* Berkshire: Policy Journals.

Hoggart, R. (1993) *An Imagined Life*. Oxford: Oxford University Press.

Philo, G. and Berry, M. (2004) *Bad News from Israel*. London. Pluto Press.

BF

22

Balance

Like its close relations, **impartiality** and **fairness**, the notion of balance lies at the heart of British **broadcasting**. Newspapers are not bound in the same way, although they would certainly claim to take a balanced approach to reporting. References to 'unbalanced reporting' underpin many complaints to broadcasters. But while the emphasis these days has shifted to 'due impartiality' in all *Ofcom* radio and television news codes of practice and the *BBC* **Producers' Guidelines**, balance seems to serve a purpose in defining impartiality itself.

The narrowest interpretation is that balance simply means saying 'on the one hand x and the other hand y', an even-handedness of approach. There is also the 'stop-watch' definition (Wilson, 1996; Harcup, 2004) which means 30 seconds for one view, 30 seconds for its opposite. The Ofcom television news code is clear on this point: 'While broadcasters should deal even-handedly with opposing points of view in the arena of democratic debate, it does not mean that "balance" is required in any simple mathematical sense or that equal time must be given to each opposing point of view' (Ofcom, 2003). Similarly for radio: 'Whilst balance, in a mathematical sense of equal time, is not always necessary, programmes should not be slanted by the concealment of relevant facts or by misleading emphasis' (ibid.).

And while impartiality in news broadcasting is a legal requirement, enshrined in the Broadcasting Acts of 1990 and 1996, balance doesn't feature in the same way, although it could be argued that impartiality entails balance. For Wilson (1996: 45), balance means 'exploring issues in an uncommitted way so that viewers, listeners and readers appreciate all the important arguments, including the weight of support they enjoy'.

Further reading

Harcup, T. (2004) *Journalism: Principles and Practice*. London: Sage.
Ofcom (2003) *Programme Code*, Section 3.7. London: Ofcom.
Wilson, J. (1996) *Understanding Journalism*. London: Routledge.

MK

Bandwidth

23

In electronic **communication** terms, bandwidth is the difference in the range of frequencies used on a particular transmission channel. Signal frequency is measured in hertz, which is the number of cycles of change per second (searchNetworking.com, 2004).

Bandwidth is also used in computer terminology as the amount of digital data, measured in bits (short for binary digits) per second (J. Hall, 2001: 247), that can be transmitted along a network. It ranges from narrowband (the conventional dial-up method on a computer) to high-speed delivery known as broadband which allows users to view pages on the **world wide web** faster, send and receive **emails** without delay, download files quicker and always-on access to the **Internet** (BBCi, 2003).

Feldman and De Wolk both use the common analogy of a pipe when discussing bandwidth – the width of the pipe determines how much information can be sent and at what speed; the fatter the pipe, the greater the bandwidth, hence the larger amount of information that can be conveyed at a higher speed. Digital information can also be compressed to fit more into the same physical space, effectively widening the width of the pipe (De Wolk, 2001: 94; Feldman, 1997: 7).

The various types of broadband Internet access include an Asymmetric Digital Subscriber Line (ADSL), using existing telephone networks, and cable, wireless or satellite connections, although all these vary in availability, the quality of service and cost (BBCi, 2003; Whittaker, 2000: 29).

The first decade of the world wide web did not witness extensive use of **multimedia** content by the major **news** providers like the BBC and CNN, due almost entirely to capacity issues relating to bandwidth (De Wolk, 2001: 94; J. Hall, 2001: 17–18; Ward, 2002: 22; Whittaker, 2000: 64).

See *Digitization*

Further reading

De Wolk, R. (2001) *Introduction to Online Journalism*. Boston: Allyn and Bacon.
Feldman, T. (1997) *An Introduction to Digital Media*. London: Routledge.
Ward, M. (2002) *Journalism Online*. Oxford: Focal Press.
Whittaker, J. (2000) *Producing for the Web*. London: Routledge.

MGH

Bias

24

'Pure bias' was NUM leader Arthur Scargill's description of television news bulletin's coverage of the 1984 miners' strike (*Guardian*, 28 August 1984, cited in Harrison, 1985, Introduction). Scargill's certainty in recognizing and denouncing media bias is typical of the term's more frequent usage in popular and public, rather than academic, discussions of the alleged distortions and misrepresentations in media content; especially news and current affairs.

The notion of bias is significant and enjoys affinities with the cognate concepts of **objectivity**, **impartiality**, **balance** and truth, but there is no reference to bias in the BBC's **Producers' Guidelines** which set out the 'editorial and ethical principles that drive the BBC' (BBC, 1994, Introduction). But in everyday use, bias implies that the 'real world' constitutes an objective reality which the media persistently fail to represent accurately.

The *Shorter Oxford English Dictionary* reveals the word's origins in the game of bowls where it describes the 'bias' a player places on the bowl to make it 'swerve from the right line'. But in popular use, bias has come to mean a particular 'inclination, predisposition, leaning or bent' (1973: 188). Typically the disposition or leaning that triggers complaints of bias is political. Throughout the 1980s, for example, the disposition of the Murdoch press (especially the *Sun*) to favour successive Conservative administrations in the paper's political coverage was widely recognized. (Franklin, 2004: 142–3). A number of journalists and editors similarly acknowledged the extensive influence of Rupert Murdoch's political principles in shaping editorial even in papers of record such as *The Times* (Evans 1984: 4; Neil 1996). Since 1997, the Murdoch press has supported Labour (Franklin, 2004a: 130–2). Alternatively viewers and readers may complain about the metropolitan dominance or bias of news and other programming, despite the existence of regional centres of broadcasting in ITV and BBC and recent emphases on 'regionalizing' editions of national newspapers (McNair, 2004: 206).

Bias may be conscious, reflecting journalists' undue emphasis on a particular interpretation of events or their marginalizing or neglect of certain stories or sections of opinion and interest. But such crude and deliberate bias is rare; typically bias is attributed to structural or systemic relations and factors (Glasgow Media Group, 1976, 1980). McNair, for example, suggests 'there is a link between the power structure of a society and its journalistic output; that journalism is part of a stratified social system; part of the apparatus by which that system is presented to its members in terms with which they can be persuaded to live' (2003: 46). This structural bias is functional. In the words of the Glasgow Media Group, it secures 'the cultural legitimation of the consensus and the status quo' (1976: 15).

Further reading

BBC (1994) Producer Guidlines. London: BBC.
Evans, H. (1984) *Good Times, Bad Times*. London: Coronet.
Franklin, B. (2004) *Packaging Politics: Political Communications in Britain's Media Democracy*. London: Arnold.
Glasgow Media Group (1976) *Bad News*. London: Routledge and Kegan Paul.
Glasgow Media Group (1980) *More Bad News*. London: Routledge and Kegan Paul.
Harrison, M. (1985) *Whose Bias?* Berkshire: Policy Journals.
McNair, B. (2004) *News and Journalism in the UK*. London: Routledge.

BF

Bi-media

In the cost- and efficiency-conscious BBC of 1990 the idea that journalists could work for both **radio** and **television** had an irresistible appeal. Working practices within both media were becoming more multi-skilled and this was part of the same process. The idea was simple: whatever story a journalist was working on, they could file for both radio and television.

The concept was first rolled out in the regions, with a swathe of appointments of specialist correspondents in areas like health, business and local government. The brief was to break stories, cover them for both regional television news programmes and for **local radio** in a particular area.

Critics pounced on the idea, saying it didn't take into account the fundamental differences between radio and television reporting. There were fears that radio would be ignored as the more glamorous and time-consuming television hogged the journalists. Radio risked becoming a 'bit part player' (Karpf, 1996 in Franklin, 1997: 137).

Many journalists themselves found the sheer practicalities of the job unwieldy and the conflict was more between meeting the on-air demands of several outlets and finding time to break stories, rather than the inherent differences of the media.

Bi-media journalism stayed and developed. BBC World Affairs Correspondent John Simpson (2002) describes how he covered the eviction of the Taliban from Kabul for radio and television. BBC network **reporters** move between both media. Within ITN, journalists will file material for both the television news bulletins and the radio news service IRN. Similarly at Sky.

But if bi-media was the buzz word of the 1990s, tri-media and multi-skilling are those of the early twenty-first century. With the growth of on-line reporting and technological advance, increasing numbers of **journalists** find themselves needing to pat their heads and rub their stomachs at the same time.

Further reading

Franklin, B. (1997) *Newszak and News Media*. London: Arnold.
Simpson, J. (2002) *News from No Man's Land: Reporting the World*. London: Macmillan.

MK

26

Broadcasting

Broadcasting can lay claim to being the most significant revolution in communication of the twentieth century, along with the invention of the internal combustion engine and the telephone. It changed the relationship between what had been thought of as 'private' and what was 'public' and brought a new social dimension to communication which is still developing.

But the innovators of the late nineteenth and early twentieth century could not have foreseen the social impact of their early experiments in the recording, playback and transmission of sound and pictures.

The first developments in what came to be called **radio** – wireless telegraphy and wireless telephony – tried to send messages from one fixed point to another, a feat accomplished by the Italian-born scientist Guglielmo Marconi in 1901. At first it was seen as a means of communicating between individuals and the idea that it could be used as a way of talking to large groups, and that the medium had social possibilities, was relatively slow to take hold. The idea that the **audience** might like to talk back was an even later phenomenon and had to wait for further technological advances.

In Britain in 1922, the body responsible for the control of wireless telegraphy, the Post Office, drew for the first time a distinction between technology that could allow communication between individuals and technology that 'addressed all and sundry' (Crisell, 1994). Between 1909 and 1927 broadcasting began to establish itself all over the world.

Radio was an instant hit. It gripped the public imagination with its ability to bring events, people and music into the home. By 1928 British audiences were as high as 15 million (Black, 1972: 26). But it was nothing compared to the impact of **television** which brought the pictures as well as the sound.

The box in the corner of the room had been in development since the 1880s and no single person can be said to have 'invented' it. Test transmissions were underway in the late 1920s in America and Britain, but television broadcasting really took off after the Second World War.

While radio is not television without pictures, television is not radio with pictures. But both address a perceived audience and Briggs (1965: 6) identified the relationship between the broadcaster and the audience as key to understanding broadcasting.

Further reading

Black, P. (1972) *The Biggest Aspidistra in the World*. London: British Broadcasting Corporation.

Briggs, A. (1965) *The History of Broadcasting in the United Kingdom*, Vol. II: *The Golden*

Age of Wireless. Oxford: Oxford University Press.

Crisell, A. (1994) *Understanding Radio*, 2nd edn. London: Routledge.

MK

Broadloid

A neologism, coined by Alan Rusbridger (the current editor of the British **broadsheet** newspaper the *Guardian*) to describe a growing tendency of broadsheet newspapers to adopt the stories and styles of **tabloid** reporting. Franklin (1997) argues that this transformation is observable in four principal ways: first, broadsheets now 'contain less news, especially foreign news, parliamentary news and investigative stories' (ibid.: 7), preferring photographs to these expensive reporting formats. Second, 'views have increasingly replaced news' (ibid.: 8), with broadsheets choosing to fill the pages emptied of international and investigative reporting with engaging opinion from **columnists**. Third, Franklin suggests that broadsheets are increasingly 'allocating a high news priority to stories which until recently would have been dismissed and disdained as merely tabloid stories' (ibid.: 9). Thus, coverage of the Royal Family (particularly Diana, years after her death), stories recycled from the tabloids, celebrity tittle-tattle and pop-culture musings now regularly find their way into the main 'news' sections of broadsheet newspapers. Fourth, broadsheets are increasingly likely 'to include many editorial features which previously were the exclusive preserve of the tabloids' (ibid.: 9), such as problem pages (suitably disguised of course). Indeed, whole supplements have been designed and introduced with an eye to including formats more typical of tabloid reporting. Sticking with the *Guardian*, Peter Preston (editor 1975–95) has described the daily G2 tabloid section of the paper, which he introduced, as an opportunity for a change of pace.

> No more indigestible broadsheet pages dominated by a single picture and piles of text. Natural opportunities for what we call 'furniture' – the little bits of fun such as Note and Queries. . . The ability to take important subjects and run them on and on across spreads. . . Tabloids, I knew from my travels, didn't equal dumbing down. On the contrary, many of Europe's finest papers were tabloid. (Quoted in Cole, 2002: 55–6)

This quote suggests a number of objections to the critics of 'broadloid newspapers'. Franklin's (1997) critique implicitly, and at points explicitly, suggests that tabloid reporting is inferior reporting and that the inclusion of 'tabloid stories' or 'tabloid formats' represents a degradation of the broadsheet newspaper. Preston disagrees with this argument and points to the 'quality tabloids' of the continent such as *El País*: a tabloid format and tabloid (popular) styles by no means denote **dumbing down**. Second, the introduction of daily tabloid supplements may arguably have protected the serious reporting and punditry, since they allow the more irreverent, popular (tabloid?) content to be siphoned off into a separate section. Third, and related to this point, we need to consider the space afforded to journalists within the modern broadsheet newspaper. Franklin's third and fourth criticisms lament the increasing inclusion of tabloid stories and tabloid styles. Assuming that this is accurate, does this content replace more traditional broadsheet content or sit side by side with it? Increased pagination in both main section and tabloid supplements have offered journalists the opportunity to write at length on a range of subjects 'from the inconsequential celebrity talking point to the human take on an international tragedy. A writer could be sent out to "live on the minimum wage" or to explore the Israeli-Palestinian conflict' (Cole, 2002: 56). From such a perspective, the broadloid newspaper represents a democratized rather than dumbed-down news agenda.

Further reading

Franklin, B. (1997) *Newszak and News Media*. London: Arnold.

JER

Broadsheet

A broadsheet is a large format newspaper, written and distributed for a national audience on the basis of a national news agenda. (The many local newspapers printed in a broadsheet format are therefore rightly categorized as 'local' rather than 'broadsheet papers'.) Broadsheet news values traditionally favour a mix of politics-plus-diplomacy-plus-war with sport on the back page; broadsheets aim at in-depth and comprehensive coverage; and are written using moderate and emotionally controlled language (assumedly) typical of the middle classes. Broadsheets tend to lead on the 'issue', or the substantive consequences, of a story rather than first-hand human interest approach more typical of **tabloids**; they tend to be 'print heavy' rather than the more pictorial tabloids; and are less inclined to use more ethically dubious reporting practices, such as door-stepping or paying sources for stories.

Further, the **readership** profiles of broadsheet newspapers are heavily skewed in favour of society's more powerful middle and upper classes. In the case of British broadsheet newspapers, Worcester has claimed: 'Hardly anything so divides the British by class as does their newspaper reading habits. [In] 1993, of the middle class households, eight in ten (79 per cent) read the so-called "quality" papers and only one in five (21 per cent) working class adults did' (1998: 41). As a consequence of their coverage, tone and readers, broadsheet newspapers have historically been regarded, both by journalists and readers, as the epitome of journalistic excellence.

Further reading

Sparks, C. (1999) 'The Press', in Stokes, J. and Reading, A. (eds) *The Media in Britain*. Houndsmills: Macmillan.
Worcester, R. (1998) 'Demographics and Values', in M. Bromley and H. Stephenson (eds) *Sex, Lies and Democracy*. London: Longman, pp. 39–48.

JER

Calcutt

The late 1980s was a time of feverish competition between national tabloid newspapers for sensational stories which resulted in a heightened concern among British Members of Parliament about press behaviour; including intrusion into the **privacy** of individuals.

In 1989 the Conservative Government formed an advisory group, the Committee on Privacy and Related Matters, to inquire whether reforms, regulatory or otherwise, were needed to further protect privacy and improve, for ordinary citizens, rights of recourse against the press. The eminent lawyer, David Calcutt QC, chaired it and it became known as the Calcutt Committee.

Later in 1989 the then Home Office Minister David Mellor, referring to the mood of some MPs that new laws were needed to curb press excesses, made his famous remark on Channel 4's *Hard News* programme: 'I do believe the press – the popular press – is drinking in the Last Chance Saloon'. (Snoddy, 1993: 101)

The Committee's report, published in June 1990, recommended, inter alia, the abolition of the discredited *Press Council* and its replacement by a more streamlined body, to be called the *Press Complaints Commission* (Calcutt, 1990). This would administer a complaints system which remained self-regulatory. But the report also recommended that if such reforms failed to curb Press excesses within a probationary period (eventually set at 18 months), then the industry should be made subject to statutory **regulation**. The Press, to blunt this threat of new legislation, quickly scrapped the Press Council, replacing it on 1 January 1991 with a Press Complaints Commission, though the PCC it created – and the Code of Practice on which its adjudications were to be based – differed in some key respects from the system proposed by the Calcutt Committee.

Subsequently the government asked Sir David Calcutt – this time without a committee, but with a knighthood – to consider the probationary performance of the PCC. In his review he was scathing about the effectiveness of the PCC, and said it was unable to command public confidence (Calcutt, 1993). He recommended a statutory tribunal should replace it. However, the government was by then unpopular because of economic downturn and the involvement of Conservative Ministers in financial and adultery scandals exposed by the press, e.g. the married Mr Mellor's affair with an actress. Despite further proposals for statutory controls, this time made by backbench MPs in the National Heritage Committee in 1993, the government decided not to risk antagonizing editors with an election looming, and – in the report *Privacy and Media Intrusion*, published in July 1995 – rejected the idea of proceeding with statutory regulation of the press (Department of National Heritage, 1995).

The Calcutt Committee report of 1990 is sometimes referred to as Calcutt I and Sir David's 1993 Review as Calcutt II.

See *Accountability, Ethics, Self-regulation.*

Further reading

Gibbons, T. (1998) *Regulating the Media*, 2nd edn. London: Sweet and Maxwell.
Lord Chancellor's Department (1993) *Infringement of Privacy*, consultation paper. London: Lord Chancellor's Department.
National Heritage Committee (1993) Fourth Report, *Privacy and Media Intrusion*, Parliamentary Paper 294 of Session 1992–3. London: HMSO.
O'Malley, T. and Soley, C. (2000) *Regulating the Press*. London: Pluto Press.
Robertson, G. and Nicol, A. (2002) *Media Law*. 4th edn. London: Penguin.
Sanders, K. (2003) *Ethics and Journalism*. London: Sage.
Shannon, R. (2001) *A Press Free and Responsible: Self-regulation and the Press Complaints Commission 1991–2001*. London: John Murray.
Snoddy, R. (1993) *The Good, the Bad and the Unacceptable: The Hard News about the British Press*. London: Faber and Faber.

MNH

31

Cartoons

Cartons offer a special kind of editorial comment: they are 'editorials in pictures' (Seymour Ure, 2003: 230). Similar to editorials, newspaper cartoons tend to be a regular size and routinely located on the same page in each edition. Their presence in newspapers is relatively recent. In the eighteenth century, the age of Hogarth, cartoons were typically published as prints, while during the nineteenth century magazines such as *Punch* provided the setting for the satirical cartoon. The first newspaper cartoonist Francis Carruthers Gould (FCG) was appointed in 1888 by the *Pall Mall Gazette*, but the cartoon quickly became established as an editorial format alongside the emergence of a national popular press exemplified by Harmsworth's *Daily Mail* in 1896. By the 1930s the *Daily Mail*, the *Daily Express* and the *Daily Herald* enjoyed circulations in the millions and their proprietors wanted their papers to be entertaining and well illustrated.

Cartoons fall into two broad categories. First, there is the humorous cartoon strip which features in tabloid rather than **broadsheet** newspapers and which typically revolves around a central character such as Andy Capp (*Daily Mirror*). The humour of these cartoons derives from the sideways glance they offer on the everyday lives of the paper's readers. Second, there is the explicitly political cartoon which features in both tabloid and broadsheet papers but predominates in the latter: in 1998, for example, of the 1,635 cartoons published in the national press, 1,132 featured in broadsheets with 503 in tabloids (Seymour Ure, 2003: 235).

The presence of cartoons in newspaper is paradoxical in three ways: they are essentially graphic in a verbal medium; they exaggerate and distort while newspapers typically stress factual accuracy and **impartiality**, and, finally; they often play on readers' emotions while journalists and editorial offers evidence and reasoned argument. Consequently, the cartoon sticks out like 'a sore thumb' among standard newspaper editorial formats (Seymour Ure, 2001: 333).

The 'cartoonist's armoury' (Gombrich, 1978) is crammed with the weapons of exaggeration, distortion, simplification, caricature and ambiguity. This last is useful since it allows cartoonists to be more critical 'in pictures' than law and editorial judgement allow in words. 'My get out clause' cartoonist Martin Rowson claims 'will always be that anyone who doesn't like it "can't take a joke"' (Rowson, 2000: 26). Steve Bell's caricature of John Major illustrates the point. In 1990, shortly after he became Prime Minister, Bell caricatured Major in a two-page spread as an incompetent superman ('super-uselessman') replacing the original superman briefs with a pair of cellular underpants (Bell, 1999: 112–13). Later, Bell took this image one step further and began to draw Major with his pants worn outside his trousers and 'proceeded to flog the motif for all it was worth' (ibid.: 111) and to 'devastating effect' (Plumb, 2004: 436). Such imagery can prove tenacious in the public mind and serve as an instantly recognizable symbol for the politician. In 2002 when Edwina Currie disclosed details of her long-standing affair with John Major, the front cover of *Guardian* 2 featured a Bell cartoon of Currie with a pair of 'John Major' pants over her head.

Three final points about cartoonists. First, they have traditionally been very well paid. In 1933, for example, Beaverbrook doubled George Strube's salary to £10,000 to prevent him being 'headhunted' from the *Express* to the *Daily Herald*, while Vicky at the Daily Mirror was earning 'a great deal of money' (Cameron, 1967: 45). Second, they begin young. Scarfe was 24 when he began working for the *Evening Standard*: Gibbard started at the *Guardian* at 24. Finally, cartoonists work long and tend to stay loyal to a single paper. Cummings, for example, retired at 77 having worked for the *Daily/Sunday Express* for 47 years (Bryant, 2000); Trog (short for troglodyte, a name given to clarinet player Wally Fawkes by Humphrey Lyttleton, reflecting his love of playing in cellars) retired from the *Daily Mail* at 72 after 35 years drawing the Flook cartoon strip (Melly, 2004).

Further reading

Bryant, M. (2000) *Dictionary of Twentieth Century Cartoonists and Caricaturists*. Aldershot: Ashgate.
Melly, G. (2004) 'The Jazzman Cometh', *British Journalism Review*, 15(2): 31–5.
Seymour-Ure, C. (2003) *Prime Ministers and the Media: Issues of Power and Control*. Oxford: Blackwell.

BF

Censorship

Woolmar defines censorship broadly to include

> the control of information that is given out . . . censors are not just people with big black pens cutting out information which they don't like from books or letters, or with scissors chopping out bits of film or video. As well as government officials, they can be owners of publications, judges, editors, advertisers or even the writers themselves. Nor are they always in far-off countries ruled by dictatorships. (Woolmar, 1990)

Woolmar's definition highlights three interesting features of censorship. First, censorship is usually understood negatively to involve the withholding or limiting of information, whereas Woolmar's phrase 'control of information that is given out' implies censorship may involve the distribution as well as restriction of information. The 'over-provision' of information as much as its restriction can be used as a strategy in information and **news management**. According to an apocryphal story, a KGB officer commented to a CIA agent, 'We keep our people in the dark by telling them nothing, you keep yours in the dark by telling them everything.'

Second, censorship is not limited to governments and public authorities but can result from the actions of private individuals and organizations: indeed, journalists' **self-censorship** illustrates precisely this. Political economy theorists like Herman and Chomsky, moreover, argue that the corporate and monopoly ownership of media institutions, along with the actions of powerful advertisers, serve not only to limit the diversity of expressed views but construct a 'manufactured consent' among readers and viewers, although such media are not officially censored (Herman and Chomsky [1988] 1994, Chapter 1).

Finally, Woolmar's definition notes that censorship is a function of *all* governments no matter how Liberal, especially in times of war (Miller, 2003). In the UK context, such censorship involves the system of **D Notices** (www.dnotice.org.uk/system.htm, and Sadler, 2001), the restrictions imposed by the **Official Secrets Act** (Ponting, 1988: 15) and, occasionally, the formal censorship of news agencies forbidding them from reporting particular events and processes such as the political problems and paramilitary campaigns in Northern Ireland.

On 19 October 1988, the Home Secretary announced that 11 political and paramilitary groups in Northern Ireland, including the legally constituted party Sinn Fein, were to be banned from television and radio but, curiously, not from newspapers (Article 19, 2000). Notices were issued to the BBC and the IBA requesting that they 'refrain at all times from sending any broadcast matter which consists of or includes any words spoken . . . by a person who . . . represents an organisation specified . . . below, or when the words support or solicit or invite support for such an organisation.' The ban applied retrospectively and resulted in the absurdity of broadcasters having to re-edit educational programmes to remove footage of the Nationalist politician Connelly. The ban was eventually lifted in 1994.

Further reading

Miller, D. (2004) *Tell Me Lies: Propaganda and Media Distortion in the Attack on Iraq.* London: Pluto.

Sadler, P. (2001) *National Security and the D Notice System.* Aldershot: Ashgate.

BF

Chequebook journalism

The practice of journalists paying for information or for exclusive interviews dates from the earliest origins of the modern press. Exclusive stories have a market value in circulation wars, or in battles for television ratings.

When pursuing major stories, tabloid newspapers and popular magazines will authorize journalists to produce cheques on door-steps and carry contracts to sign up the individual concerned. Reporters may become 'minders', hiding the contracted individual at a secret location to thwart rival journalists. Britain's regional press is usually too mean to make such payments, leaving it scope to take a high moral stand against them.

The ethical argument against such payments is that they may encourage people to lie or embellish facts to gain money, or impede the free flow of information by limiting journalistic access to that interviewee (Sanders, 2003: 115). They may also induce people to breach others' **privacy**, e.g. in 'kiss and tell' sexual revelations. But since retired politicians sell rights to their autobiographies, and celebrities sell details of their private lives, there is, in general, no moral case to prevent other citizens, e.g. victims of crime or tragedy, doing the same.

The sums involved can be substantial. In 2001 two national newspapers, a magazine and TV programme reportedly agreed to pay £350,000 to the parents of the conjoined twins Gracie and Rosie Attard (Rosie died in surgery) (Hall, S., 2001). But most deals are for much smaller sums. Unethical reporters do not always honour promises of payment (Taylor, 1992: 414).

In recent decades publicity about chequebook journalism has made members of the public much more likely to ask for payment. Sometimes there is strong **public interest** for making them. *The Sunday Times'* famous campaign for victims of the Thalidomide drug was aided by information it bought from a pharmacologist (Knightley, 1997: 161). Payment by the *News of the World* to a former associate of Jeffrey Archer, formerly a leading Conservative politician, led to Archer's conviction for perjury (Hodgson, 2001; Kelso, 2001). Surveys suggest British journalists are more relaxed than those in America about paying for important stories (Henningham and Delano, 1998: 156).

The derogatory term 'chequebook journalism' gained currency in the 1960s after controversy over payment to vice-girl Christine Keeler in coverage of the Profumo scandal (Levy, 1967: 384–97, 438–47, 484–8).

35

In Britain, the most serious controversies concerning chequebook journalism have concerned payments offered to witnesses in pending, major trials. Such 'buy-ups' could pollute the trial evidence (Hanna and Epworth, 1998). The Code of Practice used by the *Press Complaints Commission* was amended in 2003 to improve safeguards concerning such payments, after the government threatened to pass a law to ban them (Press Complaints Commission, 2003). This code and the BBC **Producers' Guidelines** also have restrictions on when payment can be made to children or their parents.

MNH

Circulation

The number of copies of an edition in a particular print medium (e.g. a newspaper, a magazine, a book, etc.) sold or otherwise distributed. In the USA, the largest daily newspaper is *USA Today*, with a circulation of around 2,200,000; the largest Australian daily is the *Herald Sun* (nicknamed the Hun) with a circulation of 553,000; in France, the largest is the regional newspaper *Ouest France* with a circulation of around 872,000; while in Britain, the largest circulating daily has for some time been the *Sun*, at around 3,250,000 copies.

Various organizations count and assess national circulations, primarily 'to provide useful and timely information about the circulation of printed media for advertisers, advertising agencies, publishers and general use' (www.ojd.es). This job is performed by the OJD in France (Office de justification de la diffusion des médias) and Spain (Oficina de Justificación de la Difusión); by the ABC (Audit Bureau Circulations) in the USA and Australia; while in Britain, bought newspapers are monitored by ABC and **free newspapers** by VFD (Verified Free Distribution). Recently, ABC in Britain announced that 'publishers will be able to report readership figures digital editions', such as downloadable replicas, alongside print circulation (Kiss, 2004). Four new rules will govern this audit: 'readers must have opted to receive the e-publication; proof of reader registration or subscription; the audited edition must have been available during the audit period; subscribers must have been notified about particular categories of additional, free publications' (ibid.).

Bare circulation figures of print editions often conceal the fact that a newspaper can be bought in ways other than active reader purchase. In the face of year-on-year decline in circulation figures, newspaper marketing and distribution departments devised a variety of cut-price schemes, including bulk sales and discounted copies, to attempt to stem plunging sales – particularly when losses threatened significant benchmarks, such as the *Daily Telegraph*'s historic million copies a day. In Britain, this practice of 'padding' circulation is now on the decline. The **advertising** industry prefer 'clean and transparent circulation figures' (www.newspapersoc.org.uk) and the British newspaper industry has responded by attempting to reduce bulk sales and discounted copies. The Newspaper Society claims that 99 per cent of newspapers are now actively purchased compared with 96 per cent four years ago, and three-quarters of local and regional papers have stopped bulk sales entirely, posting 100 per cent actively purchased circulations (ibid.).

See *Media.*

JER

Civic journalism

See *Public journalism.*

Codes of practice

See *Advertising codes, Ethics of journalism.*

37

Collocation

Collocations are patterns or consistencies in language use, which create an expectancy that a word, phrase or even the mention of an individual or group, will be accompanied by other specific words. According to the frequently cited maxim of the British linguist, J.R. Firth, 'you shall know a word by the company it keeps'. In other words, the function and meaning of a word are fixed, from a range of possibilities, by the words which surround it. Examples of collocations are legion: for example, though 'blonde' is a colour, we expect it to be followed by 'hair' and not alternative nouns such as 'flower'. So too, we expect 'writhe' to be collocated with 'pain' rather than 'pleasure', and perhaps even with 'ground'. With many words the predictability of a collocation is weaker, since they have multiple referents (e.g. 'ball' – a spherical object or a posh party?).

While this is mildly diverting when discussing made-up examples such as those above, when considered in relation to the real world, and journalism in particular, collocations may have sizeable political significance. A quick game of *Blankety Blank* (a British quiz show based on the fun of collocation!) should illustrate this. Fill in the blank: 'Muslim _' (I wonder how many people initially thought of 'fundamentalist/ism' or 'terrorist/ism'); now think of a collocate for 'Christian _ ' (here, 'worship', 'Ministry' and 'Democrat' are usually popular choices). Games such as this illustrate the way in which collocation is implicated in, and can be used to study, the binding of words and ideology (Krishnamurthy, 1996). The Collins CoBuild Wordbanks *Online* English collocation library – a corpus composed of 56 million words drawn from British and American books, newspapers, magazines and transcribed speech – is but one attempt to chart the occurrence and changes in collocation in the English language.

Further reading

Krishnamurthy, R. (1996) 'Ethnic, Racial and Tribal: The Language of Racism?', in Caldas-Coulthard, C.R. and Coulthard, M. (eds) *Texts and Practices: Readings in Critical Discourse Analysis*. London: Routledge, pp. 129–49.

JER

38

Columnist

'Great columnists make the difference great sauces make', claims Bernard Shrimsley (2003: 23) in reference to those writers who assume personalities, sometimes fictitious, to opine to an **audience** to whom they appear familiar and friendly (Silvester, 1997: xi). The column, sometimes categorized as 'personal **journalism**', is a natural development and refinement of the traditional essay and belongs to the age of mass newspaper consumption. Columns, which tend to respond to contemporary events and shared experiences, usually appear regularly in the same publication (ibid.). Both **broadsheets** and **tabloids** are addicted to columnists (Shrimsley, 2003: 25).

The role of the columnist has been varied and may change, according to one historian, 'from teacher or entertainer to the passive onlooker who records the pleasantries of everyday life' (Silvester, 1997: xiv). MacArthur insists that the best definition of a column is that it is a 'good read': they 'set us up for the day, help to define our views . . . or they utter thoughts we might agree with but are ashamed to own up to . . . or we read them because we can't stand them' (2004: 39).

The golden age of columnists was between the two world wars, although the United States still produces engaging writers of this genre; Britain has also delivered a respectable crop of columnists down the years, but now has too many second-rate performers in this field (Silvester, 1997: xxv). One of the reasons for this is that in the USA, being a columnist is a life-long job while it tends to be just one of several roles for a British **journalist** (ibid.: xiv).

American Eugene Field is recognized as the first writer to achieve nationwide fame as a columnist, his 'Sharps and Flats' (a mixture of light verse and essay humour) featured in the *Chicago Daily News* in the 1980s. Two new types of columnist appeared between the wars: the syndicated Washington (political) correspondent, Walter Lippmann being a prime example, and the Broadway columnist, typified by Walter Winchell's slang style. The same period saw the emergence of several prominent newspaper columnists in Britain, including Tom Driberg's 'William Hickey' column for the *Daily Express*, while others have been spawned by weekly magazines (Silvester, 1997: xiii). Other great British columnists include Cassandra, Alan Watkins, Ian McKay, G.K. Chesterton, Robert Lynd, J.B. Morton, George Orwell, Bernard Levin, Peter Jenkins, Auberon Waugh, Nigel Dempster and Keith Waterhouse. Bill Connor, who wrote as Cassandra in the *Daily Mirror* from 1935 to 1942 and from 1946 to 1967, was voted the greatest British columnist of all time in a poll conducted by the *British Journalism Review*. The *Daily Mail*'s Keith Waterhouse was adjudged by his peers to be Britain's 'most admired contemporary columnist' (MacArthur, 2004: 39).

'Columnists! Love 'em or hate 'em, you can't ignore 'em' (Shrimsley, 2003: 26).

Further reading

MacArthur, B. (2004) 'Ego Trips Full of Passion that Set the Tone for Newspapers', *The Times*, 27 February, p. 39.

Shrimsley, B. (2003) 'Columns! The Good, the Bad, the Best', *British Journal Review*, 14(3): 23–30.

Silvester, C. (ed.) *The Penguin Book of Columnists*. London: Penguin Books.

MGH

Commercial radio (Independent local radio/ILR)

The Conservative Party election manifesto of 1970 contained a commitment to introduce competition into **radio** for the first time. It had been a long political battle. Ten years earlier, the Pilkington Committee (1962) had concluded that a radio system funded by advertising revenue was incompatible with the needs of a local **audience**. Harold Wilson's Labour Government was opposed to the concept and the idea took hold that the spectrum for radio broadcasting was finite (Crook, 1998: 261). The runaway success of pirate radio, many of which had something of a local identity, demonstrated the existence of an audience who wanted something other than the *BBC* (Harris, 1970). So did the existence and success of European-based stations like Radio Luxembourg and Radio Normandie.

But it was an experiment in the Isle of Man that finally convinced the then Conservative Government that commercial radio might work. On 29 June 1964, broadcasting from a caravan on a windy hilltop, Manx Radio went on air as a pilot project under the General Managership of John Grierson (not of **documentary** association). Grierson, who was also the station's first presenter, described himself as the 'pioneer of licensed UK based commercial radio' (2003). Manx Radio was an instant hit, grabbing more than 80 per cent of the available audience within six months.

The 1971 White Paper *An Alternative Service of Broadcasting* established ILR along **public service** lines, with a remit to provide a service that could become a real alternative to the BBC. There were to be no national commercial stations – at least at first.

A year after the Sound Broadcasting Act of 1972, in basement studios off Fleet Street, the all-speech **local radio** station for London LBC went on air at 6 a.m. on 8 October 1973. It was followed a week later by the all-music station for London, Capital Radio. At the same time, and sharing LBC's premises, *Independent Radio News* began providing a national and international **news** service to the new stations, an alternative to the BBC way of doing **journalism.**

Progress was initially slow. Some 19 stations were on the air by the end of 1976. A second phase began in 1980 with another thirty stations launched by the end of 1984. But expansion gathered pace again after the election of the Thatcher Government in 1979 with its commitment to deregulation and competition. The Broadcasting Act of 1990 set the scene for even more rapid growth and now there are more than 260 independent local radio stations across Britain. However, relaxation in the rules of media ownership means that these stations are owned by 15 main groups, of which the biggest is Capital Radio (Peak, 2002).

The first years of local commercial radio were marked by cash crises, technical innovation and a pioneer spirit fondly remembered by those involved. Some stations, particularly in the larger cities outside London, found making a profit relatively easy as advertisers rushed to grab a share of the new audiences. Others, particularly LBC and Capital in the early days, stumbled financially through underestimating overheads and running costs (Franklin, 1997: 131).

Regulation and licensing of commercial radio was handed to *The Radio Authority* as a result of the Broadcasting Act 1990 and in 2003 to *Ofcom*.

See *Independent national radio, Promise of performance.*

Further reading

Barnard, S. (1989) *On the Radio: Music Radio in Britain*. Milton Keynes: Open University Press.
Crook, T. (1998) *International Radio Journalism, History, Theory and Practice*. London: Routledge.
Franklin, B. (1997) *Newszak and News Media*. London: Arnold.
Peak, S. (ed.) (2002) *Guardian Media Guide 2003*. London: Guardian Books.

MK

Communication

41

The system and processes through which meanings are shared. Hence, communication is fundamentally a social phenomenon. And though communication is not particular to humans – cats meow and hiss, dogs bark, growl and bare their teeth, etc. – studies have repeatedly failed to demonstrate that any other species shares the human capacity for language. That is, no other species shares our capacity to communicate through systems of external **signs** and symbols. Such signs and symbols can make up part of a larger message or argument, which may in turn form part of a **text**. Should this text then be disseminated, via mass **media**, to an **audience** wider than the original participants, then the process is more accurately described as **mass communication**.

JER

Communication Act 2003

This Act followed the White Paper *A New Future For Communications* (DTI and DCMS 200), and received royal assent on 17 July 2003 (www.culture.gov.uk/broadcasting). The Act reflects successive governments' policy commitment to **deregulation** of both programme contents and media ownership which has been evident since the *Peacock Committee* report in 1986 (Franklin, 2001: 53–9). It is a complex piece of legislation divided into five parts and 411 sections.

The Act makes a number of specific provisions. Undoubtedly most significant is the recommendation to establish a new Office of Communications (Ofcom), operational since 15 December 2003, which assumes the regulatory responsibilities of the previous five regulators: the Independent Television Commission (ITC), the Office of Telecommunications (Oftel), the Broadcasting Standards Commission (BSC), the Radiocommunications Agency (RA) and the Radio Authority (RA) (Part 1, Section 2). Its first Chairman is Lord Currie; its Chief Executive is Stephen Carter.

The Act provides Ofcom with new powers to impose sanctions and financial penalties on the BBC for breaches of taste and decency, any failure to meet independent production quotas (set at 25 per cent for BBC1 and BBC2) and unfair commercial competition. The BBC Governors were intended to retain responsibility for the BBC **public service** remit although this was hotly contested (Part 3, Chapter 1, Section 198) and in the March 2005 Green paper on broadcasting, this role was given to a newly constituted public trust. Ofcom also has a content board, chaired by Richard Hooper to monitor and regulate programmes in accordance with the requirements of the Act to ensure broadcasters' compliance with their public service remits (Part 1, Sections 12–13). An early task for Ofcom was a review of the current provision of public service broadcasting on all terrestrial channels. Its report in April 2004 alleged a decline in serious programming, reflecting the arrival of multichannel television in the UK and set out ten 'propositions' which questioned whether the BBC's role was too wide, whether the licence fee should be distributed more widely among broadcasters and whether the present scale of regulation and funding would be necessary once all households enjoyed access to digital television (Wells 2004: 9; ofcom.org.uk/consultations/current/psb/).

The Act made a number of provisions concerning the deregulation of media ownership. The restriction preventing a non-EU company from owning ITV has been abolished, along with the regulation prohibiting an ITV company from enjoying more than a 15 per cent share of **audience**, paving the way for a single owner of the ITV network (in truth the Act merely legitimated the existing merger between Carlton and Granada). But the restriction that prohibits an organization with a 20 per cent share in a national newspaper from owning an ITV company remains intact. Channel 5, however, may be purchased by such a company (whether UK or overseas-owned) subject to the new **plurality test** if Ofcom judges the purchase meets the new **public interest** requirements reflecting Lord Puttnam's amendment to the Communications Bill (Part 3, Chapter 5, Sections 348–56). Restrictions on radio ownership have been similarly relaxed allowing foreign companies to own British radio interests and permitting greater concentration of ownership in regional radio. The Act also requires broadcasters to subtitle 60 per cent of their output within five years moving to 80 per cent within ten years (Part 3, Chapter 4, Section 303).

Further reading

Communications Act 2003 (2003), DTI and DCMS (2000) *A New Future for Communications*. London: The Stationery Office.
Franklin, B. (2001) *British Television Policy: A Reader*. London: Routledge.
Wells, M. (2004) 'Serious Shows Turn Off Viewers', *Guardian*, 22 April, p. 9.

BF

Competition

Most democracies value plurality in the media. Consequently, they employ **regulation** to prevent individuals or corporations gaining monopolistic proprietorial control in the various media sectors of press and broadcasting, which might militate against free competition. In the UK, *Ofcom*, the Secretary of State for Trade and Industry, the Office of Fair Trading and the Competition Commission have statutory roles in the regulation of media competition.

In the UK, a regulatory regime to oversee newspaper mergers was introduced in 1965, following the Report of the Royal Commission of the Press (1962) and subsequently a law was enacted with detailed rules to regulate broadcast and cross-media mergers (Department of Trade and Industry, 2004: 9). But ownership of national and regional newspapers (as well as broadcast media) in the UK has become increasingly concentrated with a consequent decline in competition; regulatory powers are rarely used to curb this trend.

Critics argue that the statutory **public interest** tests, phrased to guard against monopolies, to ensure **accuracy** in news presentation, to encourage free expression of opinion and (in TV and commercial radio sectors) to safeguard, **impartiality, public service broadcasting** and other quality programming, appear historically subject to ready reinterpretation by corporations and politicians. In the UK, media policy has tended to be controlled by Prime Ministers, rather than subject to wider governmental scrutiny (Tunstall, 1996: 377–90). The governmental permission for Rupert Murdoch's News International to take over *The Times* group in 1981 is regarded as a prime example of political considerations weighing uppermost in the regulatory process (Evans, 1983: 80–153).

In broadcast media, the discussion of competition invariably triggers a discussion about choice and quality. The title of the Conservative Government's 1988 White Paper captures this trend: *Broadcasting in the '90s: Competition, Choice and Quality.* Competition elevates the role of 'consumer sovereignty in shaping broadcasting services' (Franklin, 2001: 6) and has a similarly decisive role in determining programme quality. The *Peacock Committee* (1986: 133, cited in Franklin, 2001: 6) argued that broadcasting should rest on 'a system which recognises that viewers and listeners are the best judge of their own interests which they can best satisfy if they have the option of purchasing what they require from as many alternative sources of supply as possible'.

But this emphasis on competition and markets generates at least three difficulties. First, many citizens' ability to be 'consumers' is limited by poverty, resulting in their viewing preferences being sidelined or ignored completely. Second, the economic logic of the system pushes broadcasters towards **minimax programming**, which third, almost inevitably results in a rise in prurient subject matter, **'dumbed down'** programming and (depending on definitions) a decline in quality.

At this point, the regulatory regime for broadcast media steps in to attempt to square the circle of 'consumer choice' and 'quality'. Since the Communication Act 2003, Ofcom has enforced television regulation.

Further reading

Barendt, E. (1995) *Broadcasting Law: A Comparative Study.* Oxford: Clarendon Press.
Feintuck, M. (1999) *Media Regulation, Public Interest and the Law.* Edinburgh: Edinburgh University Press.
Franklin, B. (2001) *British Television Policy: A Reader.* London: Routledge.
Gibbons, T. (1998) *Regulating the Media*, 2nd edn. London: Sweet and Maxwell.

Humphreys, P.J. (1996) *Mass Media and Media Policy in Western Europe*. Manchester: Manchester University Press.

Ofcom (2004a) 'Ofcom Publishes Guidance on Media Mergers Public Interest Test', press release, 7 May. http://www.ofcom.org.uk/media_office/latest_news/nr1_20040507.

Ofcom (2004b) 'Ofcom Guidance for the Public Interest Test for Media Mergers'. http://www.ofcom.org.uk/codes_guidelines/broadcasting/media_mergers/.

Paraschos, E.E. (1998) *Media Law and Regulation in the European Union: National, Transnational and US Perspectives*. Ames: Iowa State University Press.

Robertson, G. and Nicol, A. (2002) *Media Law*. 4th edn. London: Penguin.

BF, MNH and JER

Contempt of court

Britain's legal system includes trial by juries drawn from the general public, or by lay magistrates. Such people are not as experienced as lawyers or judges, and are therefore regarded as potentially influenced by any bias in media coverage of cases before them.

British contempt of court laws include those drawn up to prevent prejudice to fair trials. They place considerable legal duty on the media to limit what is published about arrested suspects or defendants in criminal proceedings.

Proceedings in any eventual trial can usually be reported by the media contemporaneously, but until any verdict it is legally dangerous for the media to publish additional information about a defendant's character, or speculation about the evidence.

If prejudicial matter is published by mistake or misjudgement, this can ruin a journalist's reputation and career, because British media organizations face large fines if convicted of contempt, and great embarrassment if their coverage causes a major trial to be abandoned. In 2002 the *Sunday Mirror* was fined £75,000 after an article led to the halting of the first trial of two professional footballers accused of assault. The Attorney General's office estimated the cost of the aborted trial at more than £1 million (Welsh and Greenwood, 2003: 183). The paper's editor Colin Myler resigned because of the error.

Restrictions of media coverage of British civil law proceedings were eased after *The Sunday Times*, in its campaign to publish the plight of victims of the Thalidomide drug, successfully challenged contempt law in an appeal to the European Court of Human Rights in 1978 (Evans, 1983: 58-79).

The 1981 Contempt of Court Act was an attempt to codify the law.

But interpretation of it by judges and the Attorney General remains controversial. Some commentators call for greater use of it to prevent tabloid 'trial by media'. Journalists complain that it can hinder publication of **investigative journalism**.

In America, which also has juries, media reports of arrests and of pending court cases are much more extensive, protected by the **First Amendment** to the US Constitution.

British journalists who refuse to reveal their **sources** of information when ordered to do so in court cases risk being fined or jailed for contempt.

Further reading

Crone, T. (1997) 'Public Are the Losers from this Shameful Travesty', *Press Gazette*, 25 July.
Crone, T. (2002) *Law and the Media*, 4th edn. Oxford: Focal Press.
Robertson, G. and Nicol, A. (2002) *Media Law*. 4th edn. London: Penguin.

MNH

Content analysis

Content analysis is a research method aimed at recording the salient features of texts using a uniform system of categories. The content analyst designs and employs categories which are directed towards producing (usually quantitative) data in response to specific research questions or hypotheses. These data are then used to summarize and describe any patterns in the texts. Berelson offers a definition which has subsequently been widely adopted as *the* definitive description of traditional content analysis: 'Content analysis is a research technique for the objective, systematic and quantitative description of the manifest content of communication' (1952: 263).

From this definition, Berelson outlines four requirements of content analysis, which we feel should be quoted here at length since they accurately specify the requirements needed for the completion of successful content analysis:

1 The *requirement of objectivity* stipulates that the categories of analysis should be defined so precisely that different analysts can apply them to the same body of content and secure the same results (ibid.: 263).
2 The *requirement of system* contains two different meanings. In the first place it states that *all* of the relevant content is to be analyzed in terms

of *all* the relevant categories . . . The second meaning of a 'system' is that analyzes must be designed to secure data relevant to a scientific problem or hypothesis (ibid.: 263).

3 The *requirement of quantification* [is] the single characteristic on which all the definitions agree . . . Of primary importance in content analysis is the extent to which the analytic categories appear in the content . . . In most applications of content analysis, numerical frequencies have been assigned to occurrence of the analytic categories (ibid.: 263).

4 And, finally, Berelson defines the actual content which should be the object of this objective and systematic quantification: content analysis is ordinarily limited to the manifest content of the communication and is not normally done directly in terms of the latent intentions which the content may express nor the latent responses which it may elicit. Strictly speaking, content analysis proceeds in terms of what-is-said, and not in terms of why-the-content-is-like-that (e.g. 'motives') or how-people-react (e.g. 'appeals' or 'responses') (ibid.: 263).

Of course, the methodology underpinning this research method makes several assumptions, all of which continue to be regularly interrogated. First, that there is a relationship between communicative intent and content, or that the motivations of the communicators are reflected in their outputs. Second, that the analysts' record of the 'manifest content' of the selected texts is valid – in other words, that the content which the analyst is counting (or otherwise recording) is the content which all other readers recognize. Third, that the counting of content is meaningful – in other words, that frequency of appearance is an important aspect in communication, or that it matters that certain themes or actors or words are present in reporting more frequently than others. The corollary of this third assumption is that content is defined by what is there. **Absences** must necessarily be ignored, even when these absences are systematically under-used alternatives.

Further reading

Berelson, B. (1952) 'Content Analysis in Communications Research', in Berelson, B. and Janowitz, M. (eds) (1966), *Reader in Public Opinion and Communication*. New York: Free Press, pp. 260–6.

Deacon, D. et al. (1999) *Researching Communications: A Practical Guide to Methods in Media and Cultural Analysis*. London: Arnold.

Gerbner, G. (1958) 'On Content Analysis and Critical Research in Mass Communication', in Dexter, L.A. and Manning, D. (eds) (1964) *People, Society and Mass Communications*. New York: Free Press, pp. 476–500.

JER

Context

The situation(s) in which a message is conveyed and received, or in which a **text** is produced and consumed. More specifically, context is a term employed in three principal ways: first, it can be used in an interpersonal way to refer to the immediate location in which a speaker and listener interact. Location has a profound effect on communication, shaping not only who speaks but also when they speak and even how and what they will say. Regarding journalism for example, reporters are not allowed to take sound or video recording equipment into a British courtroom, compelling them to rely on shorthand notes or memory. This reporting context therefore has a fundamental influence on the texts eventually produced.

Second, context can be used as a synonym for 'background'. Thus, a reporter may contextualize a **story** by providing certain facts, by referring to prior episodes of this same story or by summarizing the conduct (past and present) of the people involved. Context in this sense is information additional to the basic 'who, what, when, where and how', provided in order to aid the **readership**'s understanding of the reported event. Third, context may be used to refer to the wider social, political, historical (etc.) circumstances that the reported event may be part of, or in which a story is made meaningful. At this level of analysis we need to consider a text's 'words, images and themes *in juxtaposition* to . . . the broader social, cultural and political context' (Daniels, 1997: 142), since it is only within social contexts that reporting has any social significance.

JER

Contextualized journalism

Journalists have always sought to place **stories** into a more complete **context**. However, the practical limitations (of time and space) of traditional **media** have meant stories being truncated and told from a single point of view rather than the whole truth behind the **news** being presented (Pavlik, 2001: 23).

Pavlik describes a new form of news emerging in the online (electronic) world as contextualized journalism, which is multi-dimensional and can produce more engaging reporting and more complete information, in the process benefiting democracy by better informing a global citizenry (ibid.: 4, 23).

'Whether achievable or not, **objectivity** and truth can best be pursued through a storytelling medium that supplies the texture and context possible in an online, **multimedia**, and interactive environment,' says Pavlik (ibid.: 25).

This new media genre, which is transforming the nature of storytelling and news content, has five aspects to it: (1) breadth of **communication** modalities (multimedia); (2) hypermedia (or **hypertext**); (3) heightened **audience** involvement (**interactivity**); (4) dynamic content (breaking and constantly updated news); and (5) customization (or personalization) of content (ibid.: 4–22). Linking to related **websites** 'can help readers understand an issue in depth' (Kovarick, quoted in Dimitrova et al., 2003: 403).

The twenty-first century journalist will need to be a more skilful storyteller and act as a guide in linking the news with a wider set of contextualizing events and circumstances. Editing skills will also be placed at a premium due to the enormous amount of information available online (Pavlik, 2001: 217–218).

Further reading

Dimitrova, D.V., Connolly-Ahern, C., Williams, A.P., Kaid, L.L. and Reid, A. (2003) 'Hyperlinking as Gatekeeping: Online Newspaper Coverage of the Execution of an American Terrorist', *Journalism Studies*, 4(3): 401–14.
Pavlik, J.V. (2001) *Journalism and New Media*. Columbia, NY: University Press.

MGH

Convergence

The blurring of the distinctions between telecommunications, computers, radio, television and newspapers has been made possible by digital technology. Caught up in the fallout from this exciting and confusing upheaval are journalists who as a result, can no longer rely on one set of skills to see them through a career and need to be more technologically adept than ever before. **Journalism** itself became a global enterprise and a 'two way street' (Hargreaves, 2003: 242) as the **Internet** dispensed with national boundaries. Almost anyone can join in and there is unprecedented interactivity between journalist and **audience**.

It is what Crisell (2002: 286–7) describes as the 'interchangeability' of media that is allowing all the various media platforms to take on some of the characteristics and functions of others. Computers can offer a form of **radio** and **television**. Mobile phones have picture and text functions and can take on some of the characteristics of computers and radio. Radio programmes become interactive through referring listeners to their website. Newspapers print the email addresses of their journalists and have on-line versions. The television itself has some functions of the computer. An increasing number of television programmes invite viewers to 'press the red button' if they want more information on a story.

Some of the consequences of this technological media revolution are reflected in the creation of *Ofcom*, a single regulatory body for media and telecommunications, where once there were five. The implications for working practices are just as great. Some organizations, particularly in America, already have news centres that are home to television and radio stations as well as newspapers and online publications (Thelan et al., 2003). Newsgathering is sometimes shared, leading to fears that convergence is a way of producing and presenting news more cheaply.

Further reading

Crisell, A. (2002) *An Introductory History of British Broadcasting*. London: Routledge.
Hargreaves, I. (2003) *Journalism: Truth or Dare?* Oxford: Oxford University Press.
Thelan, G., Kaplan, J. and Bradley, D. (2003) 'Convergence', *Journalism Studies*, 4(4): 513.

MK

Conversation analysis

A qualitative research method which focuses on the sequential progression of talk-in-interaction. Taking 'naturally occurring' data (transcribed from tape recordings) as the focus of study, conversation analysis (CA) assumes that conversations are negotiated collaborations between cooperative participants (see Heritage, 2001). CA argues that the study of conversation should be directed at uncovering the organizing practices and procedures which manage interaction between individuals, and (crucially) that the analysis of the linguistic and interpersonal aspects of conversation can take place without reference to wider social (political, historical, etc.) **contexts**.

The bulk of studies concentrate on informal conversations between 'equals' (for example, telephone conversations) (Cutting, 2002), but other studies have been completed on media and journalistic **discourse**, particularly the radio phone-in and the news interview (Heritage, 1985; Greatbatch, 1998). Here, research has illuminated the 'ground rules' of interviewing – specifically, turn-taking, the use of semi-formalized sequences and the violation of question–answer adjacency pairs, particularly when politicians ignore an interviewer's question and talk about something they regard as more important.

However, while CA can strengthen analysis of broadcast media language through its close and detailed accounts of the organization of talk-in-interaction, at the same time it ignores – indeed, consciously disregards – many features which a full analysis of journalistic discourse should take into account. Fairclough, for example, points out that while Heritage (1985) 'emphasises the normative side of news interviews, what news interviews have in common', he misses the fact that the news interview 'is not a unitary genre: there is considerable, culturally patterned, variation not only historically . . . but also in contemporary broadcasting, depending upon the medium, type of programme, and particular style of interviewer' (Fairclough, 1995: 22–3).

Further reading

Greatbatch, D. (1998) 'Conversation Analysis: Neutralism in British News Interviews', in Bell, A. and Garrett, P. (eds), *Approaches to Media Discourse*. Oxford: Blackwell, pp. 163–85.

Heritage, J. (2001) 'Goffman, Garfinkel and Conversation Analysis', in Wetherell, M., Taylor, S. and Yates, S.J. (eds), *Discourse Theory and Practice*. London: Sage.

JER

Culturological approaches

A manner of studying journalism which suggests that the 'determinants of news [lie] in the relations between ideas and symbols' (Schudson, 1989: 16) rather than in the material circumstances of production and consumption. In the words of Alasuutari (1995: 71), news reporting represents the modern manifestation of the culturally signified and culturally significant **story**. By this approach, cultural understandings and cultural practices are the *key* factors in understanding the form and content of journalism because culture is inter-woven with all social practices.

Goffman argues that since 'our understanding of the world' precedes the stories in the press, it determines 'which ones reporters will select and how the ones that are selected will be told' (Goffman, 1986, cited in van Ginneken, 1998: 22). The central determinant shaping the *selection* of news is, according to Fowler (1991: 16), 'a preoccupation with countries, societies and individuals perceived to be like oneself'. Thus,

51

events which reflect and resonate with shared social values are more likely to be reported as news. From such a perspective, news about crime, for example, is 'a main source of information about the normative contours of a society. It informs us about right and wrong, about the parameters beyond which one should not venture' (Cohen and Young, 1973: 431).

The telling, or form, of news is similarly culturally determined. There are certain key 'assumptions about **narrative**, storytelling, human interest and the conventions of photographic and linguistic presentation that shape the presentation of all the news that the **media** produce' (Schudson, 1989: 20). We can all recognize a Cinderella ('rags to riches') story, or 'a tragedy', or 'a heroic victory' because of their heavily encoded **mythic** status in (our) culture (Lule, 2001). Each of these story-forms places demands on the content of the texts which, in part, explains why it is almost impossible to find a news story about a cancer victim who wasn't brave. Similarly, Darnton (1975, in Bird and Dardenne, 1988) recalls the influence which the archetypal form of the 'bereavement story' had over the content of his own crime reporting:

> When I needed such quotes, I used to make them up, as did some of the others . . . for we knew what the 'bereaved mother' and the 'mourning father' should have said and possibly even heard them speak what was in our minds rather than what was in theirs. (cited in Bird and Dardenne, 1988: 338)

52

The culturological approach maintains that journalists use 'culturally embedded story values, taking them from the culture and re-presenting them to the culture' (Bird & Dardenne, 1988: 344). In this way, a news story 'is not just a happening in the world; it is a relation between a certain happening and a given symbolic system' (Sahlins, 1985: 153).

See *News values.*

Further reading

Bird, S.E. and Dardenne, R.W. (1988) 'Myth, Chronicle and Story: Exploring the Narrative Qualities of News', in Berkowitz, D. (ed.) (1997), *Social Meanings of News: A Reader.* Thousand Oaks, CA: Sage.

Cohen, S. and Young, J. (eds) (1973) *The Manufacture of News: Social Problems, Deviance and the News Media.* London: Constable.

Lule, J. (2001) *Daily News, Eternal Stories: The Mythical Role of Journalism.* New York: Guilford Press.

JER

Cyberspace

This futuristic term, commonly accepted as being introduced by William Gibson in his 1984 science fiction novel, *Neuromancer*, is often used as another, trendier, name for the **Internet**. However, it relates more specifically to the conceptual space connecting **virtual communities** of people who use computer-mediated communications (CMC) to interact without the need for physical proximity (Rheingold, 1994: 5). Associated words include cybercafé, a café with computer equipment providing (usually for a fee) public access to the Internet (Word Reference.com, 2003).

Further reading
Rheingold, H. (1994) *The Virtual Community* London: Minerva.

MGH

D notice, DA notice

A Defence Advisory notice, formerly called a D Notice (Defence Notice), is part government guidance, and in part informal warning, to the British media and book publishers to encourage them to exercise **self-censorship** on sensitive matters of national security.

There are currently five standing DA notices, phrased in general terms, covering military operations; nuclear and non-nuclear weapons; ciphers and secure communications; sensitive installations and home addresses; security and intelligence services, and special forces (such as the SAS).

Such notices are approved by, and can be read on the website of, the Defence, Press and Broadcasting Advisory Committee, chaired by the Permanent Under-Secretary of State for Defence, on which sit 13 media representatives, nominated by newspaper and magazines employers' associations, the Press Association, the BBC, ITN, ITV and Sky TV. The committee meets twice a year. Its secretary – paid as a senior civil servant – or her/his deputy is available at all times to offer pre-publication advice to editors. The committee's advice and notices have no legal standing. Its supporters argue that, by encouraging voluntary negotiation between the government and the media, it helps journalists make moral judgements on what detail of national security should be aired. But journalists who publish in contravention of advice know, in some circumstances, they may risk criminal prosecution under the **Official**

53

Secrets Act, though it is more likely the government would try to use injunctions to restrain publication.

Critics of the notice system – created in 1912 and shrouded in secrecy itself for its first 40 years – argue that it continues to permit the Government to exert 'secret pressures and persuasions' on editors, and to gain advance warning of embarrassing disclosures (Robertson and Nicol, 2002: xiii, 577–88). See also http://www.dnotice.org.uk

Further reading

Hodgson, J. (2001a) 'A Gentleman's Agreement: Is the D Notice Committee an Archaic Leftover or Vital to National Security?' *Guardian*, 1 October.
Hooper, D. (1988) *Official Secrets: The Use and Abuse of the Act*. Sevenoaks: Coronet.
Liberty and Article 19 (2000) *Secrets, Spies and Whistleblowers*. London: Liberty and Article 19.
Robertson, G. and Nichol, A. (2002) *Media Law*, 4th edn. Harmondsworth: Penguin.
Sadler, P. (2001) *National Security and the D Notice System*. Aldershot: Ashgate.
Welsh, T. and Greenwood, W. (2003) *McNae's Essential Law for Journalists*, 17th edn. London: LexisNexis.

MNH

Decoding

The process through which a reader/viewer draws meaning from a **text** (Hall, 1980). In the words of Condit (1989: 494): 'viewers and readers construct their own meanings from texts. **Audiences** do not simply receive messages; they decode texts.'

Although the meaning(s) which a journalist intends an article to have (*encoded meaning*) and a reader's interpretation of this same article (*decoded meaning*) may not be the same thing, decoding is not entirely 'free' either: encoding produces *preferred meanings* which limit some of the parameters within which decoding takes place (Hall, 1980: 57). Hall lists three positions which the reader may take in relation to these preferred meanings: the *dominant-hegemonic* position, where the reader 'is operating inside the dominant code' (ibid.: 59) and adopts the encoded message in full. Second, the *negotiated* position in which the reader 'accords the privileged position to the dominant version of events while reserving the right to make a more negotiated application to "local conditions"' (ibid.: 60). For example, a reader may agree with the conclusion 'We should invade Iraq' but disagree with the offered justifications ('Iraq has illegal weapons'); or else agree with the justification that 'Iraq has illegal weapons' but disagree with the conclusion 'We should invade Iraq'. And third, the *oppositional* position in which the reader understands a text but decodes it in an entirely contrary way. For example, every time President Bush refers to a 'War on Terror', the reader decodes this as a 'War for the New American Empire'. Hall argues that the meanings produced through encoding and decoding, and specifically how identical they are, depend on the degree of asymmetry between the codes of 'source' and 'receiver' at the moment of transfiguration into and out of the discursive form. What are called 'distortions' or 'misunderstandings' arise precisely from the lack of equivalence between the two sides in the communicative exchange (ibid.: 54).

Texts whose messages are open to different readings are necessarily complex, inviting the possibility for wrongful interpretation. O'Sullivan et al. (1994) therefore suggest a fourth position: the *aberrant* reading, in which the encoded meaning of a text is not understood and the reader interprets it in an unusual or deviant way.

Further reading

Hall, S. (1980) 'Encoding/Decoding', in Marris, P. and Thornham, S. (eds) *Media Studies: A Reader.* Edinburgh: Edinburgh University Press. pp. 51–61.

JER

Defamation

55

Defamation is the communication of a statement which ruins or diminishes the reputation of an individual or organization. An allegation that someone is dishonest or a hypocrite or adulterous is always likely to be defamatory. If a defamatory allegation is made in a permanent form (e.g. sent to a third party in a letter or email, or published in a newspaper, magazine or on a website) the defamed person can sue the writer and publisher for libel in the civil courts. Unless the allegation can be proved true, or there is legal 'privilege' or other legal defence, the court will declare it to be libellous, which means the defamed person or organization will be awarded financial damages, to be paid by the writer and publisher, for loss of reputation. Statements broadcast on radio or television are also deemed permanent in libel law. Slander is the term used for defamatory statements made verbally, e.g. in a conversation or speech, which can also provoke lawsuits.

Legal precedent means that some public bodies, including local councils, cannot sue for libel. But individuals within them – e.g.

councillors – can sue if the defamatory statement identifies them in some way.

It is also possible in British law for a journalist to libel someone without intending to, if the published matter has an unforeseen meaning.

British defamation law is regarded by journalists as the harshest in the Western world, because of potentially massive legal costs, high amounts awarded for libel damages (which can run into six figures) and the unpredictability of the juries who sit in many, but not all, libel trials. The legal costs of a fortnight's trial could be £750,000 for each side (Robertson and Nicol, 2002: 76). The loser of a trial pays both sides' costs. A media organization may prefer to offer damages in a pre-trial settlement rather than risk such costs, even if it believes what it published is true. It is argued such laws have 'a chilling effect' deterring **investigative journalism**, particularly in the local and regional press, and that many scandals therefore remain unexposed.

The *Guardian's* editor Alan Rusbridger has campaigned for Parliament to introduce a 'public figure' defence, such as that enjoyed by American journalists, arising from the **First Amendment** to the US Constitution. This defence enables US journalists, if they have no malicious motive and have made all reasonable checks, to safely publish, in the **public interest**, allegations of improper conduct by politicians and other public figures, even if the truth is not clear.

In 1999 a House of Lords judgment in a libel action brought by Albert Reynolds (a former premier of Eire) against the *Sunday Times*, extended the defence of qualified privilege, so shifting British law a little towards a 'public interest' defence, though the newspaper's unfair treatment of Reynolds meant it could not benefit from the judgment (Robertson and Nicol, 2002: 128–35).

The British media, while complaining of the law's harshness, benefits from the fact that most people cannot afford to sue for libel, though some law firms do offer a 'no win, no fee' service.

Further reading

Crone, T. (2002) *Law and the Media*, 4th edn. Oxford: Focal Press.

Harding, L., Leigh, D. and Pallister, D. (1997) *The Liar: The Fall of Jonathan Aitken*. London: Penguin.

Leigh, D. and Vulliamy, E. (1997) *Sleaze: The Corruption of Parliament*. London: Fourth Estate.

Rubenstein, S.M. (1992) 'The Flow and Ebb of US Libel Law', *British Journalism Review*, 3(3): 47–56.

Rusbridger, A. (1997a) 'The Freedom of the Press and Other Platitudes', in Stephenson, H. (ed.) (2001) *Media Voices: The James Cameron Memorial Lectures*. London: Politicos, pp. 246–280.

56

Rusbridger, A. (1997b) 'Why Are We the Libel Capital of the World?' *British Journalism Review*, 8(3): 25–31.

Vick, D.W. and Macpherson, L. (1997) 'An Opportunity Lost: The United Kingdom's Failed Reform of Defamation Law', *Federal Communications Law Journal*, 49(3). http://www.law.indiana.edu/fclj/pubs/v49/no3/vick.html.

Welsh, T. and Greenwood, W. (2003) *McNae's Essential Law for Journalists*, 17th edn. London: LexisNexis.

MNH

Deregulation

This is the opposite of **regulation** and therefore implies the weakening or ending of the various statutory or non-statutory controls and restrictions on the ownership and the contents of news media (Franklin, 2001).

In the UK different traditions have characterized the regulation of print and broadcast media. Newspaper content – what actually appears in newspapers – is subject to self-regulation, since 1991, by the *Press Complaints Commission* (PCC) (Frost, 2004) but is subject to statutory (i.e. legal) controls concerning libel and other statutory wrongs. Regulation of press ownership is guaranteed by monopolies and competition legislation although since December 2003, press mergers must comply with the **plurality test** embodied in the new **Communication Act 2003**: the new regulator *Ofcom* makes a recommendation about the degree of compliance but the *Department of Trade and Industry* (Dti) makes the final decision about the acceptability of the merger proposal.

Broadcast media are subject to statutory regulation. The *Board of Governors* regulates the *BBC* while the commercial sector, regulated by the Independent Television Commission (ITC) between 1991 and 2003, has been regulated by Ofcom since 2003.

From the early 1980s, successive UK governments have followed a policy of deregulation of broadcast media in terms both of their contents and their structures of ownership. In proposing the 1990 Broadcasting Act, the then Home Secretary Douglas Hurd, argued that in the more competitive market ushered in by the 1990 Act, broadcast media should be regulated with 'a lighter touch': consequently, the ITC was considered a less rigorous regulator than its predecessor the Independent Broadcasting Authority (IBA). In terms of broadcast media ownership, the Broadcasting Acts of 1990, 1996, and the more recent Communication Act of 2003, have reduced the restrictions limiting the concentration of

57

media ownership and loosened restrictions on cross-media ownership: the 2003 Act, for example, made provision for a single company to own the entire *Channel 3* network. Granada and Carlton had announced their intention to merge three months previously.

Deregulation has proved a contentious policy especially with advocates of **public service broadcasting** who argue that it will diminish the quality of programming (*Campaign for Press and Broadcasting Freedom* 1996) and accelerate a process of **dumbing down** and the tabloidization of media (*Campaign for Quality Television* 1998): others believe that deregulation is an inevitable consequence of developments in digital technology, media convergence (Smith, 1999) and a multi-channel, broadcasting system. Governments and other advocates suggest that deregulation provides viewers and listeners with greater choices of programmes and services; allows programme-makers greater freedom; encourages competition and innovation among programme providers (Dti and DCMS, 2000); reduces the potential for paternalism by governments and programme-makers, and prompts the efficient use of resources in programme production and broadcasting.

Further reading

Franklin, B. (2001) *British Television Policy: A Reader.* London: Routledge.
Frost, C. (2004) *Media Ethics and Self-regulation.* London: Longman.

BF

De-unionization

58

The de-unionization of the British media was the process by which, as part of a general trend across all industry, the power of trade unions was challenged and largely removed by employers. Most key disputes occurred in the 1980s when the Conservative Governments led by Prime Minister Margaret Thatcher gave legislative and other encouragement to employers to renounce 'collective bargaining' agreements with their workforces over manning levels, working conditions and wages. Media employers could then take full advantage of the flexibility and cost-saving potential of **new technology**, including computerization. In the television sector, the weakening of production unions – whose restrictive practices had been a particular bugbear for Mrs Thatcher (Thatcher, 1995: 634) – helped make news-gathering cheaper and more flexible. Market-friendly **regulation** policies, including programming quotas for independent producers, led to increasing casualization of the TV workforce.

In the **national press**, where the readiness of printers to strike to protect high wages, gross over-staffing and – in some cases – morally indefensible practices, had long held employers to ransom, the printing unions' power was broken in the bitter 1986 dispute with Rupert Murdoch's News International corporation after it switched production of its national newspapers to a new plant at Wapping (Heren, 1988: 237–61; Melvern, 1986). Other employers also took advantage of the new climate, to secure greater profits, or to launch new national papers (including the *Independent*) (Glover, 1993).

Regional press employers, too, cowed the printers' unions, heralding an enduring era of mammoth corporate profit (Gall, 1998). The National Union of Journalists, which historically had never been able to consistently replicate, or gain much from, the militancy of other media unions, was de-recognized by most employers. The wages offered to trainee reporters, never high, have since sunk to pitiful levels on local papers (NUJ 2003a, 2003b).

Further reading

Barnett, S. and Seymour, E. (1999) *A Shrinking Iceberg Travelling South: Changing Trends in British Television – A Case Study of Drama and Current Affairs*. London: Campaign for Quality Television.

Chippindale, P. and Horrie, C. (1992) *Stick It Up Your Punter: The Rise and Fall of The Sun*. London: Mandarin Paperbacks.

McNair, B. (2003) *News and Journalism in the UK*. London: Routledge.

Shawcross, W. (1992) *Rupert Murdoch: Ringmaster of the Information Circus*. London: Chatto and Windus.

Tunstall, J. (1996) *Newspaper Power: The New National Press in Britain*. Oxford: Clarendon Press.

MNH

59

Diary, Off-diary

Information kept by newsdesks/picture desks, to assist forward planning, about news events due to occur later that day, month or year, e.g. court cases, council meetings, film premieres, Royal visits, scheduled press conferences. A 'diary **story**', therefore, is predictable in so far as its timing is concerned and usually depends on official sources for much of its content.

An 'off-diary' story is one originated by a journalist's own idea, or suggested by or discovered through his/her informal contacts or non-official **sources**, or generated by a tip-off to the newsdesk. Off-diary work, therefore, if it yields an end-product, is more likely than a diary story to produce an exclusive.

Job adverts for journalists often stress that the ability to generate 'off-diary' stories is essential. However, in under-staffed newsrooms, a **news editor** will hesitate to permit much off-diary work (which includes **investigative journalism**) because the diary provides the comfort of predictable, regular news flow.

MNH

Digitization

Probably the most far-reaching technical innovation in **journalism** since the first efforts to reproduce and transmit words, sound and pictures. It revolutionized **newsroom** practices, destroyed the print trade unions, gave more control to the **journalist**, led to a completely new publishing platform, the **Internet** and paved the way for **convergence**.

Digital technology reduces information to a stream of data expressed in zeros and ones. The spectacular growth of computer technology meant that by the early 1960s American newspapers were using basic machines in the production process. It spread, slowly at first, through Europe and by the mid-1980s in Britain hot-metal printing was a thing of the past (Hodgson, 1998). The flight of Rupert Murdoch's News International from central London to 'fortress Wapping' in Docklands in 1986 'proved that it was possible to produce two mass circulation newspapers without a single member of his existing print force, without using the railways and with roughly one fifth of the numbers he had been employing before' (Wintour, in McNair, 1999: 143).

Journalists were now sitting at keyboards, writing and sub-editing newspaper stories, making up pages and effectively setting the newspaper in type themselves with the pages printed on web-offset presses. The development of more sophisticated software systems such as QuarkXpress made the process even more flexible and speedy. (Hodgson, 1998). Add the mobile phone, the laptop, digital cameras and digital telephone lines and journalists can produce in seconds what used to take days.

In broadcasting, the digital revolution had consequences in two distinct areas, in working practices and in **broadcasting** itself. The advent of digital recording and playback equipment, on-screen audio and video editing in the mid-1990s had just as fundamental an effect on working practices in broadcasting as in print by giving the journalist more control. **Radio journalists** had always worked with recording and editing equipment, particularly in commercial radio, but in **television**, there had been less direct contact with the technology. The development of lightweight digital cameras and computer-based editing led to experiments with **video journalists**, who shoot, edit and write their stories single-handedly.

The big changes came in the potential for an expansion of the industry 'which would make all previous expansions seem paltry.' (Crisell, 2002: 264) and which were heralded by the Broadcasting Act of 1996. Radio and television transmission had historically been based on analogue technology – one station for one channel. Digitization meant a single multiplex could accommodate more channels, each offering digital quality audio and video, hence the possibility of hundreds more radio and television stations.

Further reading

Crisell, A. (2002) *An Introductory History of British Broadcasting.* London: Routledge.
Hodgson, F.W. (1998) *New Subediting.* Oxford: Focal Press.

MK

Discourse

One of the most over-used, and some would say misused, concepts in the social and human sciences. Discourse is a highly contested field, with authors offering widely different accounts of what discourse is (and isn't) and how it should be studied (see van Dijk, 1997, 1998). Only three approaches to discourse are introduced here: the formalist and functionalist definitions used in linguistics (Schiffrin, 1994b); and the Foucauldian notion of 'orders of discourse'. First, we can define discourse as a particular unit of language, specifically, as a unit of language 'above', or larger than, the sentence. As Cameron (2001: 10–11) illustrates:

> [linguists] 'treat language as a 'system of systems', with each system having its own characteristic forms of structure or organization . . . If discourse analysis deals with 'language above the sentence', this means that it looks for patterns (structure, organization) in units which are larger, more extended, than one sentence'.

Since such an approach to discourse focuses on the form which language takes – and specifically how discourse attains the quality of being unified

61

and meaningful – it is usually called the formalist or structuralist definition of discourse. Theorists who adopt this first definition of discourse tend to focus on more formal questions such as: how do we know that a series of sentences is a 'text' and not just a collection of unrelated fragments? In answering such questions, researchers have adopted the methods of **conversation analysis** and focused on aspects such as the orderliness of broadcast talk and cohesion and coherence in news texts.

Second, the functionalist definition, which holds that discourse should be studied as 'language in use' (see Brown and Yule, 1983). Cameron suggests that theorists who adopt this definition of discourse are interested in '*what* and *how* language communicates when it is used *purposefully* in particular instances and *contexts*' (2001: 13; emphases added). Language is used to *mean* something and to *do* something and that this 'meaning' and 'doing' are linked to the context of its use – that is, the immediate context of speaker–text–**audience** and also the wider socio-political context which bounds the communicative act. Thus, in order to properly understand discourse, we need to do more than analyze the meanings of sentences, their inter-relations and how they hang together as a cohesive text. To properly interpret, for example, a press release, or a newspaper report, or an advert, we need to work out what the speaker or writer is *doing* through discourse and how this 'doing' is linked to the context of its usage. Such an approach has been adopted most fruitfully by researchers within Critical **Discourse Analysis** (CDA).

Third, and developing the social contexts and consequences of discourse further, there is the Foucauldian notion of 'orders of discourse', wherein discourse*s* are viewed as 'practices which systematically form the objects of which they speak' (Foucault, 1972: 49). In other words, discourses show how language use is always interrelated with other social, political and institutional practices. The pluralization – discourses – is notable and important. Foucault considers discourses to be flows of knowledge/power through society and time which create 'the conditions for the formation of subjects and the structuring and shaping of societies' (Jäger, 2001: 35). Discourses are the means through which institutions shape and define both subject positions and relations between social subjects. These institutions, and their discourses, are often in conflict with each other; they offer different and sometimes opposing claims to truth and, through feeding on past and other current discourses, produce 'domains of objects and rituals of truth' (Foucault, 1979: 194). Thus, we may speak of medical discourse, legal discourse, political discourse, academic discourse, etc.

Imagine, for example, you were to write a news item about (illegal) drug addiction. (Prior to the selection of a subject, your story would already be the product of a series of discourses including the differentiation between illegal and legal drugs and why legal drug addiction is less newsworthy.) For an expert source, you could locate and quote a medical doctor, who may describe drug addiction as a sickness or, less judgementally, as a physiological dependency. Or you could quote a psychologist who may explain drug addiction via habitual social use, or perhaps to fill an emotional need borne of alienation. Or you could quote a Police officer, who may describe drug addicts as criminals and social deviants who need to be locked up. Each account is supported by a body of evidence, by an internal system of verification – by *discourse* – which gives it form, strength and effect. Each of these discourses: define 'the problem' (here, medical-pathological, psychological and criminological); position the addict; and dictate the manner in which the problem should be solved (by drug rehabilitation, by counselling or by incarceration, respectively). By drawing on one or other of these discourses in contextualizing or explaining a story, journalists do not simply 'reflect' reality; rather, they help to *construct* it (Riggins, 1997: 2). In this case, the outcome of these choices may be a story 'about' either health, mental health or crime – three themes with significantly different connotations and potential repercussions for the addict him/herself.

Further reading

Brown, G. and Yule, G. (1983) *Discourse Analysis*. Cambridge: Cambridge University Press.

Cameron, D. (2001) *Working with Spoken Discourse*. London: Sage.

Foucault, M. (1972) *The Archaeology of Knowledge and the Discourse on Language*. New York: Pantheon.

van Dijk, T. A. (ed.) (1997) *Discourse as Structure and Process*. London: Sage.

JER

63

Discourse analysis

Literally, the analysis of **discourse**. More specifically, discourse analysis (DA) is the analysis of what people *do* with **text** and talk. Methodologically, the field of discourse analysis is extremely diverse (see Wodak and Meyer, 2001; Weiss and Wodak, 2003), and Woods and Kroger suggest that DA should be approached 'not just as an object, but as a way of treating language' (2000: 3). Principally, DA assumes

key concepts

that language exists in a dialogue with society: that 'language simultaneously *reflects* reality ('the way things are') and *constructs* (*construes*) it to be a certain way' (Gee, 1999: 82). Thus language represents and contributes to the production and *re*production (which discourse analysts usually label 'the (re)production') of social reality. This dialectic (two-way) relationship is observable at a number of different levels of analysis: semiotically, through the (re)production of **signs** (see Kress and van Leeuwen, 1996); institutionally, through the (re)production of corporate activities (see Fairclough, 1993; Wodak and Iedema, 1999); politically, through the (re)production of power, status and their supporting **ideologies** (see Foucault, 1973; Laclau and Mouffe, 1985; Fairclough, 1995b); and socio-culturally, through the (re)production of knowledge, values and identities (see: Antaki and Widdicombe, 1998; Wodak et al., 1999).

Recent years have seen the ascendance, and arguably the pre-eminence of Critical Discourse Analysis (CDA), 'whose overall aim has been to link linguistic analysis to social analysis' (Woods and Kroger, 2000: 206). Critical discourse analysts argue that if we accept the general principle of DA – that language use contributes the (re)production of social life – then, logically, language must play a part in producing and reproducing social inequalities. In response, 'CDA sees itself as politically involved research with an emancipatory requirement: it seeks to have an effect on social practice and social relationships' (Titscher et al., 2000: 147), particularly relationships of disempowerment, disenfranchisement, dominance, prejudice and/or discrimination.

In seeking to accomplish these goals, CDA investigates, and aims at illustrating, 'a relationship between the text and its social conditions, ideologies and power-relations' (Wodak, 1996: 17–20, cited in Titscher et al., 2000: 146). Critical analysis of this kind may be focused 'at different levels of abstraction from the particular event: it may involve its more immediate situational context, the wider context of institutional practices the event is embedded within, or the yet wider frame of the society and the culture' (Fairclough, 1995b: 62). Previously analysts have focused on racist rhetoric (Reisigl and Wodak, 2001), **racism** in the press (van Dijk, 1991, 2000), the representation of Muslims in **broadsheet** newspapers (Richardson, 2001a, 2004), the discourse of New Labour (Fairclough, 2000), the rhetoric of the new capitalism (Fairclough, 2003), discourses on unemployment in the EU (Muntigl et al. 2000) as well as more general studies of media discourse (Fairclough, 1995b).

Further reading

Fairclough, N. (1995b) *Media Discourse*. London: Edward Arnold.

Gee, J.P. (1999) *An Introduction to Discourse Analysis: Theory and Method*. London: Routledge.

van Dijk, T.A. (ed.) (1991) *Racism and the Press*. London: Routledge.

van Dijk, T.A. (ed.) (2000) 'New(s) Racism', in S. Cottle (ed.), *Ethnic Minorities and the Media*, Buckingham: Open University Press. pp.33–49.

Weiss, G. and Wodak, R. (2003) *Critical Discourse Analysis: Theory and Interdisciplinarity*. London: Palgrave.

Wodak, R. and Meyer, M. (eds) (2001) *Methods of Critical Discourse Analysis*. London: Sage.

JER

Documentary

The term was first coined in 1926 by John Grierson, the man widely thought to be one of the founding fathers of documentary and who went on to make the classic *Night Mail* in 1936. He defined it as 'the creative treatment of actuality' (in Kilborn and Izod, 1997: 12).

But Winston's critique of the form (1995: 11) points out: 'The supposition that any "actuality" is left after "creative treatment" can now be seen as being at best naïve and at worst a mark of duplicity.' Nevertheless, all forms of documentary, in **radio** and **television**, within drama-documentary and docu-soaps have at their heart some form of relationship to the real world. Corner (1996) suggests that documentary is now seen as a form of extended **journalism**.

Some documentarists themselves dislike the term, 'I think it smells of dust and boredom' (Sussex, 1975, in Winston, 1995: 12), 'a dry approach to a dull subject' (Diamond, 1991: 30), and the oft-suggested decline of the traditional television documentary seems to suggest that viewers can find them a turn-off.

Documentary has its roots in film and radio and even earlier in nineteenth-century photography. Early cinema of the 1880s, like the work of the French Lumiere brothers, showed scenes of everyday life. The film makers of the 1920s including the likes of Grierson and, in the then Soviet Union, Dziga Vertov, believed documentary was a tool in cultural or educational enlightenment.

In the rapidly developing world of radio in the 1930s, the Manchester Group under Archie Harding with Olive Shapley, D.G. Bridson and others were among the pioneers of radio documentary. Shapley herself (1996) describes how she used new recording technology to get to the

65

voices of ordinary people. Her colleagues made witness-testimony programmes about the industrial north, e.g. *Steel* (1934).

But the impact of television on documentary has been profound, both in determining the types that are made and the form they appear. Devices are myriad: the telling of factual stories in dramatic format (*Cathy Come Home*, BBC, 1966; *Hillsborough*, ITV, 1996), fly on the wall (*The Family*, BBC, 1974), **reconstruction**, (*Crimewatch UK*, BBC), personal testimony (*Video Diaries*, BBC), and reality programming (*Big Brother*, C4).

Further reading

Corner, J. (1996) *The Art of Record: A Critical Introduction to Documentary*. Manchester: Manchester University Press.
Diamond, E. (1991) *The Media Show: The Changing Face of the News 1985–1990*. Cambridge, MA: MIT Press.
Kilborn, R. and Izod, J. (1997) *An Introduction to Television Documentary: Confronting Reality*. Manchester, Manchester University Press.
Shapley, O. (1996) *Broadcasting a Life: The Autobiography of Olive Shapley*, Scarlet Press.
Winston, B. (1995) *Claiming the Real: The Documentary Film Revisited*. London: British Film Institute.

MK

Dumbing down

The 1990s witnessed a significant and controversial development in contemporary journalism which continues to generate a lively debate, namely, the alleged shift in the editorial values of journalists which has prompted media academics (Sampson 1996), as well as print (Engel, 1996) and broadcast journalists (Cronkite, 1998; Humphrys, 1999; Clarke, 2003), to criticize national and local media for 'dumbing down', being subject to a process of 'tabloidization' and offering trivial **infotainment** rather than 'high quality' programming as well as news and current affairs.

The dumbing down phenomenon is judged to be global in reach, prompting an academic and journalistic literature in America (McManus, 1994a; Fallows, 1996), the UK (Franklin, 1997); the 'new democracies' of Central and Eastern Europe (Sparks and Tulloch, 1999; Coman, 2000); Australia (Langer, 1998), Africa (Berger, 2000) and Sweden (Djerff Pierre, 2000).

The evidence to support the dumbing down thesis is hotly contested. Winston (2002) compared television news contents and formats from the *Bad News* studies of 1975 with an equivalent sample of broadcast news during 2000–2001 but noted no significant shifts. By contrast, Barnett and Seymour's (1999) study of television across 20 years (1977–97), observed striking changes, especially the decline in the foreign news components of current affairs programming.

Newspaper editors such as Alan Rusbridger have counter-argued for a 'dumbing up' of news and a retreat from reports of celebrities and reality TV. For their part, academics have suggested that recent developments signal the extent to which mainstream understandings of 'quality' news have too frequently been gendered (Costera Meijer, 2001) or the degree to which there has been a 'dumbing down of the workforce' in certain key respects (Ursell, 2003). Others have made a plea for extending journalistic repertoires to embrace a *public quality* approach to broadcasting which rejects the binary polarities of popular and quality news (Costera Meijer, 2003).

See *Newszak, News values.*

Further reading
Clarke, N. (2003) *The Shadow of a Nation.* London: Weidenfeld and Nicholson.
Djerf Pierre, M. (2000) 'Squaring the Circle', *Journalism Studies*, 1(2): 239–60.
Franklin, B. (1997) *Newszak and News Media.* London: Arnold.
Humphrys, J. (1999) *Devil's Advocate.* London: Hutchinson.
Sparks, C. and Tulloch, J. (2000) *Tabloid Tales: Global Debates over Media Standards.* Lanham, MD: Rowman and Littlefield.

BF

Editor

The life of a newspaper editor can be a chequered one. At its best, it is a prestigious and highly-paid job with responsibility for a publication which may have millions of readers and involves a social life mixing with celebrities and politicians. At its worst, the position is high-pressured and a continuous battle trying to strike a fine balance between the editorial and commercial elements, while being personally accountable for legal problems which may lead to imprisonment. Editors may also face interference from the proprietor in the running of the paper; many such power struggles are dotted throughout the history of the **media**.

Basically, the editor is the person in charge of the content of a newspaper. He or she has overall responsibility for the editing of the paper, ensuring it is published on time (Hodgson, 1996: 68). The modern-day editor also has the added commercial pressures of controlling aggressive marketing in sales and **advertising**, with editorial costs coming under close scrutiny and a new emphasis on efficiency and accountability (ibid.: 71). 'Editors who fail to get at least two of the three apples on the fruit machine lined up – **circulation**, editorial budget and advertising revenue – do not last' (Sanders, 2003: 133). Editors work long hours but generally get well paid for their efforts. They will also usually have, particularly in the **national press,** a hierarchy of editors below them, including possibly a deputy editor, assistant editors, **news editor**, night editor, chief sub-editor, features editor, sports editor, political editor, foreign editor, city editor and others. At the highest level, there may be editorial directors and managing directors, although the nature of these roles and those containing the words 'associate' and 'executive' can vary between publications. There are different types of editors, including those who try to do everything themselves, down to writing headlines, some who delegate everything, which can result in confusion over duties, and caretaker ones who keep the seat warm for the next incumbent (Hodgson, 1996: 68–9).

Harold Evans, the only person to have edited both *The Sunday Times* (1967–81) and *The Times* (1981–82), was the clear winner of a combined poll run by *British Journalism Review* and *Press Gazette* to find the greatest newspaper editor of all time. Of the 20-plus editors to receive at least one vote, none were female and seven dominated; these included second-placed C.P. Scott (*Manchester Guardian*, 1872–1929); David English (*Daily Sketch*, 1969–71 and *Daily Mail*, 1971–92) and Kelvin MacKenzie (*The Sun*, 1981–1994), who were joint third; Hugh Cudlipp (*Sunday Pictorial* and *Daily Mirror*), Arthur Christiansen (*Daily Express*, 1932–56) and Larry Lamb (first editor of the modern *Sun*, 1968-81) finished together in fifth, with Thomas Barnes (*The Times*, 1817–41) close on their heels (Hagerty, 2002: 6). Other legendary editors include John Delane (*The Times*, 1841–77) and W.F. Deedes (*The Daily Telegraph*, 1974–86), while Evans himself put forward (in addition to Barnes) W.T. Stead, the nineteenth-century editor-campaigner of *The Northern Echo* who invented the big-time newspaper **interview** and who 'went to jail on a malicious technicality' (Evans, 2002: 13–14).

Among the great **stories** uncovered under Evans' editorship were the injustice of the thalidomide compensation and the case for urgent reform in Ulster (ibid.: 11). Evans appreciates only too well the dilemmas facing editors: 'Is it more important to change the world or the front page? . . . If you lend one ear to staff and the other to **readership**, where do you find the third ear for **ownership**?' As a national newspaper editor, he felt he should stay independent from government and business. On the marriage between editor and ownership/management, he believes the best results are 'where both agree on the core identity of the newspapers and its resources, and then leave the editor to do his best, mistakes and all' (ibid.: 11–12). But this has clearly not always been the case. In *Good Times, Bad Times*, Evans says Parliament and the Thomson ownership asked Rupert Murdoch to give guarantees to honour editorial independence under his proprietorship of *The Times*. Among the guarantees were that 'editors would have control of the political policy of their newspapers . . . that instructions to journalists would be given only by their editor . . . in my years as editor of *The Times*, Murdoch broke all these guarantees' (Evans, 1994: 461). In contrast, Andrew Neil, editor of *The Sunday Times* for more than a decade, said that Rupert Murdoch 'kept to the letter of his promises to Parliament of editorial independence when he bought Times Newspapers in 1980', saying he only once tried – and failed – to influence the paper's editorial line (Neil, 1997: 203).

Hodgson believes editors are freer from proprietorial interference compared with 25 or 50 years ago, due to a new shift in ownership (Hodgson, 1996: 69–71), but recent newspaper history has featured many clashes between owners and editors, usually ending with the departure of the 'non-compliant editor' (Franklin, 1994: 37). Even the most independent editors have to operate within the established position of their newspaper (Wilson, 1996: 34).

Female editors have been few and far between in the history of the national press. Rebekah Wade has been the most prominent in the new millennium, relinquishing the editorship of the *News of the World* to become the first female editor of the *Sun* in January 2003 (Byrne, 2003).

69

Further reading

Byrne, C. (2003) '*Sun*'s Yelland in Shock Depoarture', *Guardian Unlimited*. http://www.media.guardian.co.uk/presspublishing/stpru/0,7495,873980,00.html.
Evans, H. (1994) *Good Times, Bad Times*, 3rd edn. London: Phoenix.
Evans, H. (2002) 'Attacking the devil', *British Journal Review*, 13(4): 6–14.
Franklin, B. (1994) *Packaging Politics*. London: Edward Arnold.
Hagerty, B. (2002) 'Editorial', *British Journal Review*, 13(4): 6.
Hodgson, F.W. (1996) *Modern Newspaper Practice: A Primer on the Press*. Oxford: Focal Press.
Neil, A. (1997) *Full Disclosure*. London: Pan Books.
Sanders, K. (2003) *Ethics and Journalism*. London: Sage.
Wilson, J. (1996) *Understanding Journalism: A Guide to Issues*. London: Routledge.

MGH

Email

Electronic mail, usually shortened to email, or e-mail, has revolutionized communication and many people wonder how they managed before it came into common use. It is an informal but extremely popular – and quick – method of sending and receiving messages on the **Internet**. Many emails contain just text, but images, graphics and other **multimedia** files can also be included with the message – these are known as attachments. The astonishing speed of email (it usually takes only seconds to reach its destination, although this depends, among other things, on the size of any attachments) has resulted in the traditional physical transportation of postal letters being described as 'snailmail' (Webopedia, 2003). Email can involve one-to-one communication, but it also supports one-to-many transmissions in which the same message can be sent to lists of people (Reddick and King, 2001: 24). There are different types of mailing lists by which people can receive and contribute free, up-to-date and sometimes expert information on a specific subject (The Living Internet, 2003). A **world wide web**-based browser or a specific mail application like Outlook Express can be used to view email.

There are several parts to an email address; first there is the name of the user (or something which represents him/her); then there is the @ symbol which represents the word 'at'; this is followed by his/her company or Internet Service Provider; there are also usually abbreviated domain details indicating the user's subject area and, sometimes, country (Reddick and King, 2001: 64; Ward, 2002: 91). This information alone will often tell a **journalist** something about the person behind the email, although the name may not necessarily represent the person who actually sent the message (Ward, 2002: 90).

Email allows **interactivity** between journalist and his/her **audience**. For example, some reporters give their email addresses at the bottom of their stories, allowing the reader/user to either comment on the article or maybe offer some information which may help to develop the storyline. Journalists could also interview information **sources** or check facts and quotes, as well as communicate with their colleagues, by email. In the United States of America, email correspondence is considered part of the Public Record, meaning journalists can view messages sent by government officials (Reddick and King, 2001: 62, 79). **Media** organizations can also send newsletters by email to a target audience (Hall, J., 2001: 29).

Emails can be used for mass marketing purposes, although not always in a positive way if it is junk mail, also known as spam. These are messages sent, sometimes anonymously, by an individual or company to a list of recipients, most of whom probably did not request the mailing. Such emails are often unsuitable for the receiver as they may contain links to pornographic material or make get-rich-quick promises. Email accounts can often become full and unusable due to the amount of unsolicited mail (Whittaker, 2000: 20). Emails can also be used in a mischievous way for sending viruses, programmes intended to interfere with the normal operation of a computer (Reddick and King, 2001: 75).

Further reading

Hall, J. (2001) *Online Journalism: A Critical Primer*. London: Pluto Press.
Reddick, R. and King, E. (2001) *The Online Journalist: Using the Internet and Other Electronic Resources*, 3rd edn. Orlando, FL: Harcourt Brace and Company.
Ward, M. (2002) *Journalism Online*. Oxford: Focal Press.
Whittaker, J. (2000) *Producing for the Web*. London: Routledge.

MGH

Embargo

The practice of telling **newsrooms** they can't run a story until a particular time is both a gift and a constraint. It highlights the often fraught relationship between people and organizations who think they have a **story** to tell and the journalists who want to tell it.

Embargos appear on some **news releases** instructing journalists that the information may not be published until a prescribed time – usually midnight on a particular date. For example: 'Embargoed until 0001 Friday July 25'. On forward planning desks which are looking for scheduled material to include in future editions or programmes, embargoed material can be a godsend. The story can be covered, quotes and interviews obtained before the embargo and the piece completed and published. Space or airtime is filled with minimum fuss. The Queen's New Year's Honours List is a good example. The information goes to the newsroom in advance and local angles can be followed up ready for publication or broadcast when the embargo is lifted.

For the organization placing the embargo, the advantages are straightforward. If an embargoed release goes out to newspapers, radio and television, the organization hopes to maximize the amount of coverage and the impact of the story by getting it on as many outlets as possible on the same day, rather than it trickling out over a few days.

It sounds a fairly innocent practice and in some circumstances

71

relatively harmless. But it can encourage news manipulation (Wilson, 1996: 154). Bad news could be held back because a more favourable event is known to be coming up. UK government press officer Jo Moore lost her job after she was reported to have put in an email that 11 September 2001 was a good time to release bad news because it would be lost in the coverage of the twin towers disaster.

At bottom, very few worthwhile embargoed stories stay that way for long. Journalists will wheedle to run the story early if there's a good reason for it – and if they think they can get away with it. And report authors will often trail the story in pre-release interviews, again to maximize the impact.

See *Agenda setting, News Management.*

Further reading
Wilson, J. (1996) *Understanding Journalism: A Guide to Issues.* London: Routledge.

MK

Embedded journalist

A new term for an old concept. Indeed, '[t]he tradition of the "embed" is well established, from the earliest correspondents in the nineteenth century through to . . . the Second World War and Vietnam' (Freedman, 2004: 67–8). In the words of the US Government, embedded journalists 'live, work and travel as part of the units with which they are embedded to facilitate maximum, in-depth coverage of US Forces in combat' (www.militarycity.com). Recognizing that 'media coverage of any future operation will, to a large extent, shape public perception of the National Security environment', the US Government recently acknowledged that 'our people in the field need to tell our story' (ibid.). Embedded journalists are viewed as the best way to achieve this **propaganda** aim.

During the 2003 invasion of Iraq, around 900 journalists were embedded with troops (Miller, 2003). The embedding relationship implemented during this war controlled the **representation** of the fighting in a number of ways. First, it was the US Assistant Secretary of Defense for Public Affairs who granted permission to who was allowed in and who wasn't, resulting in potentially 'awkward' journalists being largely excluded. Following the *modus operandi* established during the Falklands War, journalists from countries not involved in the fighting were denied

72

access almost completely. Of the 136 journalists embedded with British forces, only eight came from outside of the UK (ibid.). Second, embedded journalists had to sign a contract with their military 'hosts', accepting a number of ground rules. Central to this contract was the requirement that journalists 'follow the direction and orders of the Government related to such participation . . . The media employee acknowledges that failure to follow any direction, order, regulation or ground rule may result in the termination of the media employee's participation in the embedding process' (www.militarycity.com).

These ground rules included a list of stories and categories of information that were always out of bounds (principally those that would 'endanger operational security') and the procedures that were to govern journalist-troop relations. For example, the agreement stated that 'Unit commanders may impose temporary restrictions on electronic transmissions for operational security reasons', which resulted in journalists having their mobile phones blocked. Such restrictions ensured that journalists effectively 'missed the war' since they were only allowed 'a fragmented view' of what was going on (*Journalist*, 2003: 10). The US 'rules of engagement' were also included as a 'non-releasable' category of information. In other words, journalists were forbidden to report who the USA thought were legitimate targets, the methods the troops used to distinguish between legitimate targets and innocent civilians and the ways that soldiers were 'engaging with' legitimate targets. Such 'rules of engagement' became quite significant in the later stages of the invasion when US troops started to be accused of being more than a little trigger happy.

Perhaps understandably, these rules put journalists on their toes. Simply put, their continued presence in Iraq depended on leaving out 'the wrong kind of details'. In order to ensure that they weren't ejected, some journalists practically integrated themselves with the military command structure. In the words of Richard Gaisford, a BBC embed:

> We have to check each story we have with them [the military]. And if they're not at the immediate level above us – that's the Captain who's our media liaison officer – he will check with the Colonel who is obviously above him and then they will check with Brigade headquarters as well. (*BBC News 24*, 28 March 2003, cited in Miller, 2003)

Therefore, Miller (2003) argues, in exchange for access to the fighting, the use of transport, accommodation and military protection, embedded journalists 'agree to give up most of their autonomy'.

See *self-censorship.*

Further reading

Freedman, D. (2003) *Television and the Labour Party, 1951–2001.* London: Cass.
Miller, D. (2004) *Tell Me Lies: Propaganda and Media Distortion in the Attack on Iraq.* London: Pluto.

JER

Ethics (of journalism)

Journalism ethics are the moral principles, reflected in rules, written or unwritten, which prescribe how journalists should work to avoid harming or distressing others, e.g. when gathering information; when deciding what to publish; when responding to complaints about their work. Consideration of ethics also helps define journalism's wider social purpose, and therefore a journalist's duty in any particular assignment, e.g. when he/she decides whether it is in the **public interest** to destroy someone's **privacy** or (false) reputation.

Though rules may be collated into written, ethical codes – drawn up collectively by journalists, employers' organizations or individual employers – each media institution or newsroom may have its own distinct ethical, or unethical, culture in unwritten traditions. It then becomes a basic, ethical matter for a journalist to decide whether he/she can work there with a clear conscience. National cultures also influence journalism ethics (Weaver, 1998: 469–73).

Ultimately conscience must be the ethical well-spring in situations where formal codes give no clear guidance or morality dictates that such guidance is not appropriate. The more experienced a journalist is, the more readily he/she should recognize that such codes are not all-inclusive.

If followed, codes usually offer the public greater protection, from unethical journalism, than the law does, e.g. in the UK the code used by the *Press Complaints Commission* states that rape victims, even in rare cases when UK law permits them to be named, should not have their identities revealed without adequate (ethical) justification.

Adherence to ethical duty may place a journalist in conflict with the law, when he/she refuses to reveal the identity of a confidential **source**, in defiance of a court order (Welsh and Greenwood, 2003: 327–51).

See *Accuracy, Audience, Contempt of court, Fairness, Right of reply*.

Further reading

Frost, C. (2000) *Media Ethics and Self-regulation*. London: Longman.
Harcup, T. (2004*) Journalism: Principles and Practice*. London: Sage.
Keeble, R. (2001) *Ethics for Journalists*. London: Routledge.
Meyer, P. (1987) *Ethical Journalism*. Lanham, MD: University Press of America.
Sanders, K. (2003) *Ethics and Journalism*. London: Sage.

MNH

Ethnicity

Derived from the Greek *ethnos*, meaning people or nation, an ethnic group is a cultural phenomenon in which tradition, language, religion, custom and common experience form the salient traits. Although recent years have seen 'ethnicity' being increasingly used as a polite (or perhaps euphemistic) alternative to 'race', the two concepts are significantly different. In the broadest of terms: 'race' is a socio-biological marker of difference in which genetic or phenotypic characteristics are ascribed social significance; ethnicity is a socio-historical, or socio-cultural concept in which *cultural* characteristics are used as a marker of difference.

That said, the two concepts *are* linked, in as much as ethnicity arose from the inadequacy of 'race' to account for differences between groups. How do you use 'race' to explain the differences in the social values between British Pakistani and White communities when, by most racial typologies, they are part of the same 'Caucasian race'? Ethnicity stepped into the breach left by the departure of 'race' and, because of this, the adjective 'ethnic' was, for a considerable period, applied solely to non-white groups. Cashmore (1988: 98), for example, argues that an ethnic group 'stands for the creative response of a people who feel somehow marginal to the mainstream society'. Later in his definition he even uses the term 'non-ethnics' (ibid.: 100) to describe empowered White communities. Such an account, wherein the core 'whiteness' of society is considered non-ethnic while those on the periphery *are* 'ethnic' (just as previously They had a 'race' and We did not) is now considered at best inaccurate and at worst encouraging a patronising exoticism. White people are ethnic too – the central importance of ethnic identity in Belgium to the (White) Dutch-speaking Flemish and the (equally White) Francophone Walloons is testament to this fact (Blommaert and Verschueren, 1998).

Developing this point, and given that ethnicity approaches identity as 'culturally fluid, internally contested and politically engaged' (Cottle, 2000: 219), ethnicity is a useful concept to account for differences *within* 'racial' groups. In the words of Cottle: 'The earlier and strategic political mobilization of "the essential black subject" (Hall, 1988, in Cottle, 2000) here gives way to an acknowledgement of important ethnic minority differences and the multiple subject positions found within and between these' (ibid.).

Further, Sreberny (2000) has argued that the proliferation of research on **racism** suffered by racial and ethnic minorities threatens to underestimate the importance of contemporary **media** in invoking cultural memories, maintaining attachments to countries and places of importance and hence supporting ethnic cultural identities. The boundaries and identities of ethnic groups, and specifically their intermingling and flux, are increasingly intertwined with the production and consumption of mass media. On this point, Gillespie (1995, 2000) illustrates how national *and* international media (satellite television and international press) interact to form and sustain identities of the British South Asian communities.

Further reading

Blommaert, J. and Verschueren, J. (1998) *Debating Diversity: Analysing the Discourse of Tolerance*. London: Routledge.
Gillespie, M. (1995) *Television, Ethnicity and Cultural Change*. London: Routledge.

JER

Fairness

Throughout the world, **ethics** codes for journalists allude to the need to be fair to the subjects of their journalism (Keeble, 2001: 14). Fairness and **accuracy** are mutually-dependent qualities. Codes differ in the extent to which they prescribe how journalistic fairness should be achieved. But the term is usually taken to mean there should be no distortion of fact or in selection of quotes; that fact should be distinguishable from comment; that all sides in any dispute being aired should be given the chance to comment; and that any unfairness or significant mistake in what is published should be promptly corrected, if necessary by offering a **right of reply** to any affected party.

Such ethical procedures, if followed, should go some way to ensure fair treatment of individuals or organizations in the news. But, as regards coverage of public issues, the code used by the British Press's organ of **self-regulation**, the *Press Complaints Commission,* insists that newspapers and magazines are 'free to be partisan'. Partisanship is a manifestation of **plurality** and **press freedom,** and adds vibrancy to public debate, but also frequently leads to unbalanced, sloppy journalism polluting such debate.

Britain's radio and television journalists must comply with stricter notions of fairness and **impartiality**, in that their codes reflect the requirements of statutory **regulation**. But these broadcast codes acknowledge the complexity of reporting politics and social issues, permitting fairness in these contexts to be achieved over a series of programmes, rather than just in one.

MNH

Fallacy

A fallacy is a significantly or seriously defective argument, judged in terms of either the content (reasoning) of the argument or the approach and personal conduct of the arguer. Since Aristotle (1984; 1991), scholars of argumentation have attempted to compile lists of the ways in which an argument may be viewed as inherently flawed and as such fallacial – Aristotle originally suggested there were 13 such fallacies; more recent attempts put the number at 20 (Hansen and Pinto, 1995). Broadly speaking, however, Whately's (1848) distinction between formal and informal fallacies is now largely accepted. The formal fallacies are errors in the argumentative reasoning, in which an inadequate proof is intentionally or accidentally presented or disguised as an adequate proof. Informal fallacies are errors of argumentative strategy and can occur when arguers use an inappropriate argumentative approach or introduce irrelevant issues. Thus, fallacies may occur as either errors in the argumentative product or errors in the argumentative process (see Tindale, 1999: 157–83).

However, one of the more interesting aspects of fallacies is that they display both vice and virtue (Powers, 1995): although they are incorrect ways of arguing (either in the sense of 'presenting' or 'having' an argument), they often *appear* to be correct and hence to be persuasive. For example, the *post hoc ergo propter hoc* fallacy (meaning: 'after this, therefore caused by this') is a *formal* fallacy in which a correlation is mistakenly presented as a causal relationship. This fallacy is frequently used in persuasive discourse and often with great effect. The *argumentum ad populum*, or appeal to popular opinion, is an example of an *informal* fallacy, in which the opinion of some (usually large) number of people is incorrectly used to support the acceptance of a standpoint. For example:

> Most British taxpaying citizens of every age, gender, colour, country or origin or religious persuasion are increasingly worried by the inability of the Government to keep a check on the number of immigrants . . . This is an important issue which must come under scrutiny. (Reader's letter, Halifax *Evening Courier*, 26 May 2001)

The above statement characterizes the form which the appeal to popular opinion usually takes: even assuming that the first claim is true (that 'most Britons *are worried* about X') the implied inability of the government to limit immigration ('X') is neither proved nor disproved. The arguer tries to use the apparent popularity of public perception to convince us that what the public perceives does in fact exist – and that is a fallacious move.

Although very little research has been completed on the presence and use of fallacious reasoning in journalism, their potential importance in evaluating journalistic discourse (particularly more argumentative genres such as editorials and **readers' letters**) should not be under-estimated.

Further reading
Aristotle (1984) *'Sophistical Refutations'* (trans. Pickard-Cambridge, W.A.), in Barnes, J. (ed.), *The Complete Works of Aristotle*. Princeton, NJ: Princeton University Press.
Hansen, H.V. and Pinto, R.C. (1995) *Fallacies: Classical and Contemporary Readings*. University Park, PA: Penn State University Press.

JER

Fifth estate

The phrase 'fifth estate' was coined by Tom Baistow in his classic text *Fourth Rate Estate: An Anatomy of Fleet Street* to describe the expansive **public relations** industry in the UK and what he believed to be the undesirable consequences of such growth (Baistow, 1985: 67–76). Drawing on the idea of the press and news media as a **fourth estate** of the realm, an indispensable critic and watchdog holding government publicly accountable for its actions, Baistow claimed that a fifth estate of public relations and marketing specialists was being deployed by political and economic elites to obscure and offset the critical oversight which journalists previously provided to protect the public interest. 'Everyone from the Prime Minister to the latest rock star, and not least big business, has something they want to sell, from ideas and personal images to consumer goods and services', Baistow argued and the result is a 'media's non-stop flow of **Newszak**' (ibid.: 67–8).

While Baistow's claim about the political functions of the public relations industry remain contentious, his assertions concerning the growth of the industry are indisputable. Franklin estimates the number of practitioners working in the private and public sectors of public relations, including central and local government public relations, to be approximately 25,000 (Franklin, 1997: 19): Michie confirms this number and suggests this trend is 'deeply undemocratic' (Michie, 1998: 17). Other academic observers have recently offered support to Baistow's more contentious arguments concerning the fifth estate (Miller and Dinan, 2000), with Davis claiming, 'the liberal description of the fourth estate media, based on an image of independent autonomous journalists seeking out news, has been severely undermined by the growth of the PR sector' (2002: 173). The expansive use of public relations and **news management** techniques by central government has prompted growing concern among the public, journalists (Oborne, 1999) and academics (Franklin, 1994) about **spin** and **spin doctors**.

Further reading

Davis, A. (2002) *Public Relations Democracy: Public Relations, Politics and the Mass Media in Britain*. London: Sage..

Franklin, B. (1994) *Packaging Politics*. London: Edward Arnold.

Miller, D. and Dinan, W. (2000) 'The Rise of the PR Industry in Britain, 1979–98', *European Journal of Communication*, 15(1): 5–35.

Michie, D. (1998) *The Invisible Persuaders*. London: Bantam Press.

BF

Fillers or 'COIs'

This is the industry term for the pre-recorded tapes produced by the *Central Office of Information* (COI) as part of its various publicity, information and **news management** campaigns. Fillers are distributed free to local radio and regional television journalists and constitute the broadcast equivalent of the news releases issued to local newspapers (Gardner, 1986; COI, 2001: 13).

The content is typically formatted as an interview, often with a minister who is discussing a contentious issue or legislative proposal, with the role of the interviewer adopted by an information officer (civil servant). The tapes provide local radio with a free 'filler', a publicly funded **information subsidy**. Fillers were used extensively during the Conservative Government's campaign to promote the poll tax which targeted local news media (Golding, 1989: 6). Take-up rates tend to reflect the station's journalistic resources: the COI acknowledges that 'commercial stations [i.e. less well staffed news outlets] are more adventurous and less likely to dismiss our output as establishment material' (Gardner, 1986). But one independent station conceded that up to 70 per cent of the tapes it received were broadcast (Cobb, 1989: 12).

Given the market pressures under which local radio stations increasingly operate, it is perhaps unsurprising that these 'fillers' have enjoyed expansive air time (Franklin, 1997: 129–30). In 1985, the COI distributed more than 400 tapes to **local radio** stations (Gardner, 1986) but by 2001 the COI annual report claimed that 'over the past year they [fillers] have been transmitted 708,000 times. That's 11,800 hours of donated airtime – the same as 151 years of episodes of *EastEnders*' (COI, 2001: 13).

Further reading

Cobb, R. (1989) 'PR has Radio Taped', *PR Week*, 20 April, pp. 12–13.
COI (2001) *Annual Reports and Accounts 2000–1* HC53. London: HMSO.
Franklin, B. (1997) *Newszak and News Media*. London: Arnold.
Gardner, C. (1986) 'How They Buy the Bulletins', the *Guardian*, 17 September.
Golding, P. (1989) 'Limits to Leviathan: The Local Press and the Poll Tax', paper presented to the Political Studies Association Annual Conference, University of Warwick, 6 April.

BF

80

First Amendment

The First Amendment to the American Constitution reads: 'Congress shall make no law respecting an establishment of religion, or prohibiting the free exercise thereof; or abridging the freedom of speech, or of the press; or the right of the people peaceably to assemble, and to petition the Government for a redress of grievances.'

The amendment (drafted by James Madison) went into effect in 1791, part of the Bill of Rights which amended the original US Constitution (ratified in 1788) by making explicit guarantees of essential freedoms. Thus the US states, founded originally by (white) settlers, including many seeking escape from religious and class oppression in Europe, took care to define the human rights of these citizens with regard to free expression.

Subsequent American laws and judgements, therefore, were

constructed on these constitutional guarantees, though judicial acceptance that the Amendment bans not only any prior restraint of **press freedom**, but also – in most circumstances – any subsequent punishment for what is expressed, is a comparatively modern common law development.

The Amendment's creation of a legal presumption in favour of freedom of expression means that, in key respects, US media law differs greatly from that of the UK. The American media can safely speculate on the likely verdicts in pending criminal trials, whereas in Britain such speculation could land journalists in jail for **contempt of court**. In 1964 Judge William Brennan, in his famous *New York Times* vs Sullivan judgment (376 U.S. 254 (1964)) relied on the First Amendment when creating the 'public figure' libel defence, whereby the US media, provided they make professional effort to check facts, and publish without malice, cannot be successfully sued for **defamation** of public figures, including politicians and the police, even if allegations aired turn out to be untrue. The First Amendment culture also led to America's freedom of information and 'sunshine laws', which encourage the press to inspect and scrutinize government and state official records. Though these access freedoms are not perfect, they have long been the envy of British reporters battling against a culture of official secrecy in the UK. **Investigative journalism** in the USA therefore has fewer legal inhibitions than in the UK. Surveys suggest awareness of their greater power makes US journalists more strait-laced as regards **ethics** (Henningham and Delano, 1998: 157).

Further reading

Braithwaite, N. (ed.) (1996) *The International Libel Handbook*. London: Butterworth-Heinemann Ltd.

Rubenstein, S.M. (1992) 'The Flow and Ebb of US Libel Law', *British Journalism Review*, 3(3): 47–56.

Rusbridger, A. (1997a) 'The Freedom of the Press and Other Platitudes', in Stephenson, H. (ed.) (2001) *Media Voices: The James Cameron Memorial Lectures*. London: Politicos, pp. 246–280.

MNH

81

Fleet Street

This most legendary of London roads has been synonymous with **journalism** for more than 500 years, although what was once known as the 'street of adventure' is now virtually deserted of the hundreds of

journalists who used to work and socialize in its famous buildings.

Situated in EC4 between the Strand and Ludgate Circus, and just a stone's throw away from the instantly recognizable St Paul's Cathedral, Fleet Street was home to the British **national press** until the mass exodus in the 1980s when the **newspaper** titles were relocated from their historic properties to cheaper sites elsewhere in the capital housing **new technology**, particularly to riverside locations such as Wapping and Canary Wharf. In 1989, a national newspaper rolled off a Fleet Street-based printing press for the last time (Curran and Seaton, 1997: 101–2).

Fleet Street's links with journalism began with the arrival in 1500 of London's first printing press based next to St Bride's church which itself has a long and proud association with the **media**. The trend of newspapers being established on the street was started by the arrival there of London's first daily newspaper, *The Courant*, in 1702 (*Talking Cities*, 2004) and in time nearly every national and many provincial titles had set up offices and printing presses in the area (Ezzard, 2003).

The street's two most dominating, Art Deco buildings are those which housed the *Daily Telegraph*'s headquarters and the *Daily* and *Sunday Express*, although both are now facades for a merchant bank. Other well-known landmarks included Mac's Café, the printers' and journalists' greasy spoon that supposedly never closed, and the Cheshire Cheese pub which contains a plaque commemorating Dr Johnson's completion of the first English dictionary there in the mid-eighteenth century. There is also the Press Club in close proximity to St Bride's, although this is nowhere near as busy as it once was (ibid.).

After the national newspapers' exit, the **news agencies** also started to leave the famous street. The *Press Association* moved its London offices to Victoria in the 1990s and the imminent departure of its former co-occupant *Reuters* would mean there was no longer a national English-language **news** organization in Fleet Street. The London offices of Dundee publisher DC Thomson and AFP, the French news agency, are the only media organizations left there (Ezzard, 2003).

Further reading

Curran, J. and Seaton, J. (1997) *Power without Responsibility*, 5th edn. London: Routledge.

Ezzard, J. (2003) '500 Years of History Ends for Fleet St', the *Guardian*, 24 September.

MGH

Focus groups

These have become a significant research device for studying media **audiences**. Their growing prominence reflects the rise of reception studies in media research, which stress the different ways in which audiences *interpret* media messages rather than trying to establish **media effects** on audiences (Kitzinger and Barbour, 1999). The method involves 'bringing together a group or series of groups of individuals to discuss an issue in the presence of a moderator' (Gunter, 2000: 42). Groups are carefully structured with members selected to represent distinctive demographic and sociological characteristics appropriate to the particular study; six to ten members is judged the ideal group size. The moderator stimulates discussion and keeps it on track, without steering it and discussions are typically recorded for later transcription (Hansen et al. 1998: 264–83).

In his classic essay 'The Focused Interview and Focus Groups: Continuities and Discontinuities' (1987), Robert Merton traces the origins of focus groups back to the 1940s, his own work with Paul Lazarsfeld at the University of Columbia, but especially the use of focus groups by military psychologists to establish the effectiveness of radio programmes designed to boost army morale (Gunter, 2000: 42). Focus groups were largely neglected by subsequent social scientists, however, but developed and used extensively by commercial marketing and research organizations (Hansen et al., 1998: 259). Morley's study of audience responses to the television programme *Nationwide* is often credited with re-establishing scholarly interest in focus groups.

Morley showed the same two episodes of the programme to 27 focus groups, varying between 3 and 13 in number and structured to reflect a 'wide range of ages as well as educational, occupational, social, cultural, ethnic and geographical backgrounds' (Morley, 1980: 37–8). Morley's analysis of group discussions illustrated how groups with divergent socio-demographic backgrounds made distinctive readings of the *Nationwide* text. The readings fell into one of three broad categories: dominant, oppositional or negotiated readings (see **decoding**). Morley's study of *Nationwide*, Philo's analysis of television coverage of the 1984/5 miners' strike (*Seeing and Believing*), as well as Kitzinger's studies of media reporting of HIV/AIDS, have developed and established the utility of focus group-based research for audience studies. As well as conducting and recording group discussion, the Glasgow researchers developed the 'News Game', which involved focus group members writing news stories, in the style of a news item, based on still photographs taken from mainstream television news footage of the miners' strike or HIV/AIDS coverage (Philo, 1990; Kitzinger and Barbour, 1999: 272–4; Philo and Berry, 2004).

The advantages claimed for using focus groups rather than individual interviews or surveys to explore audience research are that: (1) group discussions are social rather than solitary and reflect typical conditions of television viewing; (2) discussion uses the everyday terms and language of the group members rather than any imposed vocabulary; and (3) group discussion helps members crystallize their perspective. Critics, however, allege that (1) more passive members will be dominated by more articulate colleagues and (2) group discussion inevitably generates consensus which may marginalize dissident views (Hansen et al. 1998: 263; Gunter, 2000: 44–5).

Further reading

Gunter, B. (2000) *Media Research Methods*. London: Sage.

Hansen, A., Cottle, S., Negrine, R. and Newbold, C. (1998) *Mass Communication Research Methods*. Basingstoke: Macmillan.

Merton, R.K. (1987) 'The Focused Interview and Focus Groups: Continuities and Discontinuities', *Public Opinion Quarterly*, 51: 550–66.

Mosley, D. (1980) *The Nationwide Audience*. London: BFI.

Philo, G. (1990) *Seeing and Believing: The Influence of Television*. London: Routledge.

BF

Fourth estate

Classical liberal theory views the press as a defender of **public interests** and a 'watchdog' on the workings of government. The term originated in the eighteenth century, gained ground during the nineteenth and even now generates debate.

It is derived from the notion of 'estates of the realm'. The traditional three are the Lords Spiritual (clergy that sit in the House of Lords), the Lords Temporal (other peers) and the House of Commons. It's been attributed to several thinkers and writers including Edmund Burke, Richard Carlyle and the nineteenth century *Times* leader writer Henry Reeve. In October 1855 Reeve wrote in an article in the *Edinburgh Review* 'journalism is now truly an estate of the realm; more powerful than any of the other estates' (in Boyce et al., 1978).

The argument runs that the press plays a central but unofficial role in the constitution because it helps to inform the public of issues, articulates public opinion and therefore can guide and act as a check on government. (O'Malley, 1997). But it can only fulfil that function if it is independent and free from censorship.

Described as arrogant and grandiose by some, and satirised in an 1855 novel *The Warden* by Anthony Trollope, the notion refuses to lie down and die. As one of the ways of expressing the relationship between **journalism** and society, it still has ideological resonance. As recently as 2001, the BBC's political editor Andrew Marr wrote in the *Independent* 'If people don't know about power and let their attention wander completely then those in power will take liberties.'

Further reading

Boyce, G., Curran, J. and Wingate, P. (eds) (1978) *Newspaper History from the 17th Century to the Present Day*. London: Constable.

O'Malley, T. (1997) 'Labour and the 1947–49 Royal Commission on the Press', in Bromley, M. and O'Malley, T. (eds) *A Journalism Reader*. London: Routledge.

MK

Framing

When people have little direct knowledge of events, they become increasingly reliant on news media for information, but also an understanding or interpretation, of those events. The claim of framing theorists is that the media frame reality for their **audiences**: 'how people think about an issue,' the argument runs, 'is dependent on how the issue is framed by the media' (Semetko and Valkenburg, 2000: 94). The result is 'a "media-constructed" version of reality' (Callaghan and Schnell, 2001: 184). In this sense, framing theory forms part of a broader literature on **media effects**.

Gamson and Modigliani define a media frame as 'a central organizing idea or story line that provides meaning to an upholding strip of events . . . The frame suggests what the controversy is about, the essence of the issue' (1987: 143). According to Entman, to frame means 'to select some aspects of a perceived reality to make them more salient, thus promoting a particular problem definition, causal interpretation, moral evaluation, and/or treatment recommendation' (1993: 52).

Iyengar (1991) differentiated between *episodic* and *thematic* media frames with the former depicting public issues as instances or specific events that are the results of actions by individuals. Thematic frames, by contrast, report systemic problems in society on a more abstract level and

85

in the form of general outcomes. Iyengar argues, moreover, that these distinctive forms of media framing connect with audiences' attribution of responsibility. Consequently, choosing thematic over episodic frames may shift the attribution of responsibility for events from personal to abstract societal causes (Iyengar, 1991).

Research studies have typically focused on the ways in which news stories, and the frames within them, help to define public discourse around political issues, but other work has focused on social and welfare policy. Haller and Ralph (2001), for example, analyzed the reporting of disability issues, especially the controversial issue of 'physician-assisted suicide' in the *New York Times* and the *Guardian* across 1996 and 1998. They identify six news frames within press coverage of physician-assisted suicide and argue that their aggregate consequence is to systematically ignore or devalue disability issues. They also argue that the US disability rights movement has generated an oppositional news frame to those in mainstream media, which suggests that physician-assisted suicide has been 'presented' to disabled people as part of a cultural view that disabled people are 'not worth keeping alive' (Haller and Ralph, 2001: 407).

Further reading

Entman, R. (1993) 'Framing: Toward Clarification of a Fractured Paradigm', *Journal of Communication*, 43 (4): 51–8.

Gamson, W.A. and Modigliani, A. (1987) 'The Changing Culture of Affirmative Action', in Braungart, R.G. and Braubgart, M. (eds) *Research in Political Sociology*. Greenwich, CT: JAI Press, vol. 3, pp. 137–77.

Haller, B. and Ralph, S. (2001) 'Not Worth Keeping Alive? News Framing of Physician-Assisted Suicide in the United States and Great Britain', *Journalism Studies*, 2(3): 407–21.

BF

Franchise auction

The Broadcasting Act 1990 (Part 1, Chapter 2, Sections 15–17), which aimed to introduce greater competition into the commercial sector of broadcasting, proposed a new procedure for the allocation of licences to broadcast in the 15 geographical regions of the commercial Channel 3 network and the franchise for Breakfast programming: the proposal had its origins in the *Peacock Committee* Report of 1986 (Davidson, 1992: 11).

Companies competing for the various franchises were required to tender 'blind' bids to the Independent Television Commission (ITC) in a two-stage franchise auction. At the first stage, applicants submit programming proposals and business plans to establish whether the individual bid meets the **quality threshold** specified by the legislation (Part 1, Chapter 2, Section 16 (2)). Second, the licence to broadcast is awarded to the highest cash bid apart from cases where 'exceptional circumstances' prevail. The Broadcasting Act judges it 'appropriate to award the licence to an applicant who has not submitted the highest bid . . . where the quality of the service proposed . . . is exceptionally high' (Part 1 Chapter 2, Section 17 (4) (a)). This 'exceptional circumstance' amendment was introduced to the original Bill by the then Home Secretary David Mellor, to allay the loudly voiced concerns of broadcasters that the innovatory auction protocols might adversely affect the quality and range of programming on Channel 3 (Franklin, 2001: 63).

But when the ITC announced the results of the first auction round in November 1991, the initial ambition to increase competition in broadcasting markets seemed thwarted in a number of respects. First, three of the most lucrative franchises, including Central Television, were awarded uncontested for the statutory minimum bid of £2000. Second, there were fewer applicants for the licences than during previous franchise rounds. Third, the auction prompted overbidding by companies anxious to retain their licence but leaving them short of cash for programme provision. Finally, the franchise resulted in uncertainty about whether 'quality of programming' or the 'highest bid' was the criterion for success in the auction since only 5 of the 16 franchises went to the highest bidder. The auction for the Channel 5 licence, advertised in May 1995, generated the same problematic outcomes with the franchise being awarded to Channel 5 Broadcasting Limited which tendered the second highest bid of £22 million: £14 million behind the bid offered by UK TV Developments Limited.

Further reading

The Broadcasting Act 1990 (1990) London: HMSO.
Davidson, A. (1992) *Under the Hammer: Greed and Glory inside the Television Business* London: Mandarin Books.
Franklin, B. (2001) *British Television Policy: A Reader*. London: Routledge.

BF

Free newspaper

There was a significant proliferation during the 1970s and 1980s in the number of free community or regional newspapers, known as 'freesheets', which were funded entirely by **advertising** income (McNair,

1999: 15), although the growth has stalled and even gone into reverse since the 1990s (Franklin, 1998: 125). Some free newspapers are standalone newspapers containing local or national **news**, while others contain a sprinkling of stories, the publisher's aim being that the reader will be tempted to buy the paid-for equivalent. Franklin discusses the 'double paradox' in that they are called newspapers despite the fact they report little, if any, news (ibid.). Local free newspapers are usually delivered directly to homes weekly and include numerous advertisements for local businesses and services. The **circulation** of free newspapers is monitored in the UK by VFD (Verified Free Distribution).

The daily *Metro* is a city-based free newspaper drawing on an idea which originated in Sweden but which has been increasingly adopted in both the UK and the USA. An example of a *Metro* is the *Washington Post Express*, a 20-page, 15-minute read of which 125,000 copies are distributed free at bus and subway stations (Preston, 2003a). And while newspapers in general appear to be in terminal decline, Associated Newspapers' *Metro*, the morning paper given free to commuters in six of Britain's most populous regions, is expanding into more cities (Greenslade, 2004b: 7).

Aided by the introduction of **new technology**, independent publishers like Eddie Shah set up many of the early free newspapers, but the quality of the **journalism** was derided by the competing regional publishing establishment, although the latter began to set up free titles themselves as 'complementary, rather than threatening' to existing paid-for newspapers. Free and paid-for regional newspapers have since co-existed relatively comfortably and the investment which has come from their successful integration has led to stable **circulation** and an overall improvement in the editorial standard of free newspapers (McNair, 1999: 201–3), many of which were increasingly owned by the major chains, accelerating the growth of local press concentration in the UK (Curran and Seaton, 2003: 78, 291).

Debate rages over the quality and purpose of the *Metros*, described at worst as a **'dumbed down** publication . . . [produced] by people who can't write for people who won't read'. Others see them as 'an advertising solution to the problem of declining circulation. They've more to do with business than journalism' (Preston, 2003a). The emergence of the *Metro* would appear to have had a detrimental effect on the sales of paid-for newspapers (McNair, 1999: 203; Preston, 2003a), while free newspapers in general have taken up a sizeable share of the advertising revenue in the regional press based on the claim that they have a 100 per cent penetration of households in a particular locality (McNair, 1999: 200–1).

Free newspaper

Franklin argues that one of the major reasons for the decline of local and regional newspapers was the rapid expansion of free newspapers (1997: 103).

Further reading

Curran, J. and Seaton, J. (1997) *Power without Responsibility*, 5th edn. London: Routledge.

Franklin, B. (1997) *Newszak and News Media*. London: Arnold.

Franklin, B. (1998b) 'No News Isn't Good News: The Development of Local Free Newspapers', in Franklin, B. and Murphy, D. (eds) *Making the Local News: Local Journalism in Context*. London: Routledge.

Greenslade, R. (2004b) 'Metros on the March', *MediaGuardian*, 19 January, p. 7.

McNair, B. (1999) *News and Journalism in the UK*, 3rd edn. London: Routledge.

Preston, P. (2003a) 'The Regeneration Game', *Observer*, 14 September.

MGH

Freelance

Those **journalists** who have no fixed employer but rather work for (usually) more than one **media** organization are known as freelances. Effectively being self-employed means they have the freedom and flexibility to work for who they want when they want, but it can be a 'life of hard work, often for little reward and without any security'. The perfect freelance is a 'jack of all trades' who has multi-skills, specialist knowledge and a stunning book of contacts (Van den Bergh, 1998: 196–7).

Freelances (or casuals as they are sometimes termed) are often journalists who like the excitement and diversity of working for different publications or broadcasters, the prospect of working from home, plus an escape from office politics and daily routine, but some find themselves in that position more by necessity than choice (Franklin, 1997: 53). Indeed, a host of industrial factors, including the arrival of cross-media **ownership** and **new technology**, has resulted in fewer staff positions and a record number of freelances in **journalism**, some of who are fresh out of college or university. Television companies commission **independent producers** to make some programmes, thus employing less full-time staff (Van den Bergh, 1998: 196). This general trend towards more freelances in the industry is known as casualization (Franklin, 1997: 53). In many countries, the majority of journalists are freelances (International Federation of Journalists, 2003).

There is a view that new technology is starting to give freelance journalists an advantage over their full-time counterparts, the **Internet** in particular providing benefits like flexibility (for example, being able to work from virtually anywhere) and increased productivity, with women in particular making the most of the new-found opportunities (Meek, 2003).

Rates of pay vary on the type of organization, with **local newspapers** paying on a lineage basis by which the freelance gets paid according to the number of lines (about four words per line) published. Freelance work is usually commissioned first by an **editor** to ensure the story will be suitable and of sufficient quality (Van den Bergh, 1998: 200). Every two years, the *National Union of Journalists* (NUJ) publishes details of recommended rates for freelance journalistic work across all media. The guide also provides advice on a freelance's rights and other issues (National Union of Journalists, 2003). As in other professions, the freelance has to manage his or her own financial affairs. They also get none of the holiday and sickness benefits usually enjoyed by permanent staff. Some freelances work for local or national **news agencies** (Van den Bergh, 1998: 196–197).

Copyright can be a grey area for freelances who legally retain the rights on all their work unless they sign them away or sell them; editors usually buy first rights only to the work unless a specific deal is agreed, although some media organizations try to insist on buying all rights as they can also use material on electronic media (ibid.: 204). Journalists have moral rights, which include being credited for their work, although some newspapers adopt a policy of not by-lining freelances (ibid.: 202, 204).

Further reading

International Federation of Journalists: www.ifj.org/default.asp?Issue=FREELANCE& Language=EN.

Meek, C. (2003) 'Internet Is a Boon for Freelancers' (14 October) *dot Journalism*: www.journalism.co.uk/news/story60.html.

National Union of Journalists: www.nuj.org.uk/front/inner.php?docid=SS.

Van den Bergh, P. (1998) 'The Business of Freelance Journalism: Some Advice from an Old Friend', in Franklin, B. and Murphy, D. (eds) *Making the Local News*. London: Routledge.

MGH

90

Gallery reporters

Along with **sketch writers** and **lobby** correspondents, gallery reporters represent the three main traditions of parliamentary reporting in the UK. Gallery reporters gather political news by taking accurate shorthand notes of proceedings in the House and writing them up verbatim and without commentary. They also provide digests of debates and accounts of ministerial statements, Question Time and a broad range of Parliamentary events.

Gallery reporters' 'official' recognition dates back to 1803 when the Speaker ruled that seats in the public gallery must be reserved for reporters, although the earliest reports of Parliament predate this ruling by almost two centuries. Journalists' reports were initially very popular and by the end of the eighteenth century 'several British newspapers were launched largely in response to public demand for reports from Parliament' (Sparrow, 2003: 3). But by the early 1990s, the gallery tradition was suffering a serious decline: indeed it 'largely died out' (ibid.: 4). Some journalists delighted in speaking ill of the dead and of their complicity in the demise. Simon Jenkins, ex-editor of *The Times*, for example, confirmed that it had been his decision 'to stop parliamentary reporting' since he 'couldn't find anyone who read it except MPs' (Franklin, 2004a): other newspapers followed suit.

Reasons cited for the collapse of gallery reporting include: (1) a more general malaise afflicting journalistic standards, triggered by **deregulation** and competitive media markets, which has prompted a '**dumbing down**' of political coverage (McKie, 1999); (2) the burgeoning coverage provided by other news media – especially **television** and the Internet (Straw, 1999); (3) individual MPs' self-promotional publicity and **news management** strategies which have prompted the media to bypass the House (Negrine, 1998); (4) the 'downgraded' status of Parliament in the British political system which means it is 'no longer the central arena of politics' (Riddell, 1999: 29); and (5) the declining reader interest in Parliament alleged by Simon Jenkins and other journalists. By the mid-1990s the 'sharp and universal' decline of gallery reporting (ibid.: 29) prompted the BBC's then political correspondent John Cole, to joke that 'if you want to keep a secret make a speech about it in the House' (John Cole, quoted in Franklin, 1996: 13).

Further reading

Franklin,B. (1996) 'An Obituary for the Press Gallery', *Parliamentary Brief*, 4(4): 13–15.
Negrine, R. (1998) *Parliament and the Media: A Study of Britain, Germany and France*. London: Pinter.
Riddell, P. (1999) 'A Shift of Power and Influence', *British Journalism Review*, 10(3): 26–33.
Sparrow, A. (2003) *Obscure Scribblers: A History of Parliamentary Journalism*. London: Politicos.

BF

Gatekeeper

Developed in the seminal American studies of the 1950s (White, 1950; Carter, 1958), a gatekeeper is an individual who filters out and disregards unwanted, uninteresting and/or unimportant information or stories and attends to information of more import. Adopted from the work of social psychologist Kurt Lewin, 'gatekeeping' was developed in these early studies to include not just individuals *attending to* but also *imparting* information, and applied to the study of journalism. White shows that the subject of his study, *Mr Gates*, 'received approximately 12,400 inches of press association news from the AP, UP and INS during the week [studied]. Of this he used 1,297 column inches of wire news, or about *one tenth* in the seven issues we measured' (1950: 65). White argued that the criteria 'Mr Gates' used to filter this copy were 'highly subjective' and 'reliant upon value judgments based upon the gatekeeper's own set of experiences, attitudes and expectations' (ibid.).

Later studies suggested that this explanation was overly individualized, divorcing the editor from organizational and professional considerations. Gieber, for example, shows that the 16 wire editors of his study were 'preoccupied with the mechanical pressures of his work rather than the social meanings and the impact of his work' (1964: 175), and were more 'concerned with goals of production, bureaucratic routine and interpersonal relations within the newsroom' than with their own personal evaluations of the copy they received (ibid.).

Gatekeeper research has not gone uncriticized and is now usually dismissed as a little simplistic, for two principal reasons. First, although the metaphor of a gatekeeper is an interesting one, it lacks clarity at a number of stages. For example: what kind of story passes through the gate? What kind of story does not pass through the gate? By way of deduction, what parameters does the gatekeeper use to distinguish the two? And perhaps most importantly, do these parameters change? Second, the metaphor seems to suggest a binary opposition between selection and acceptance which glosses over the complexities of the situation. News is not simply selected, but rather constructed through a complex set of interactions between reporter and source, reporter and sub-editor/editor, editor and proprietor, newspaper and **audience**/consumer, all within a socio-economic **context**. Information, or whole stories, may be doctored (or 'spun') in order to maximize their appeal. Thus, news is shaped through the *perceived criteria of acceptance* at the different stages of production, be they real or imagined, as well as *direct contact* with others.

Further reading

Gieber, W. (1964) 'News is What Newspapermen Make It', in Dexter, L.A. and Manning, D. (eds), *People, Society and Mass Communications*. New York: Free Press, pp. 173–82.

White, D.M. (1950) 'The "Gatekeeper": A Case Study in the Selection of News', in Berkowitz, D. (ed.) *Social Meanings of News: A Reader*. Thousand Oaks, CA: Sage, pp. 63–71.

JER

Glasgow Media Group

This is the best-known, longest-established university-based group of academics committed to researching and publishing scholarly work in the field of **journalism**, media and communication studies.

Established in 1974, Glasgow Media Group's (GMG) founding members included Brian Winston (Director of Research) John Eldridge, Paul Walton, Greg Philo, Peter Beharrell, Howard Davis, John Hewitt and Jean Oddie. The opening paragraph of GMG's first major publication *Bad News*, announced the group's basic and contentious assumption that 'Contrary to the claims, conventions and culture of television journalism the news is not a neutral product. For television news is a cultural artifact: it is a sequence of socially manufactured messages, which carry many of the culturally dominant assumptions of our society' (GMG, 1976: 1).

Developing new methods of content analysis, the Group's early studies focused on television news coverage of the economy and industrial relations. The *Bad News* series of books alleged a systematic skew in media reports, which reflected broader power relations within society and favoured managers and owners of industry against workers, but specifically against those who engage in industrial action. During the 1980s and 1990s innovative research methods, employing focus groups and techniques such as the 'news game' – which involves giving members of **focus groups** images taken from television news and inviting them to write news stories – explored and analyzed **audience** reception of issues such as HIV/AIDS, child sexual abuse, mental health, famines in Africa, food scares and most recently the media reporting of war (Philo, 2002: 173–86).

In more recent times, the GMG has become a 'looser' organizational grouping, no longer located solely at Glasgow University and this latter research reflects the work of Jenny Kitzinger, David Miller, Kevin Williams, Paula Skidmore, Lesley Henderson and Jacquie Reilly; John

93

Eldridge and the GMG Director Greg Philo remain at Glasgow.

Further reading

Eldridge, J. (2000) 'The Contribution of the Glasgow Media Group to the Study of Television and Print Journalism', *Journalism Studies*, 1(1): 113–27.
Glasgow Media Group (1976) *Bad News*. London: Routledge and Kegan Paul.
Philo, G. (2002) 'Television News and Audience Understanding of War, Conflict and Disaster', *Journalism Studies*, 3(2): 173–86.

BF

Globalization

Conventionally, globalization is taken to refer to 'both the compression of the world and the intensification of the consciousness of the world as a whole' (Robertson, 1992: 9). But to suggest there is much unity in the way in which globalization is either conceptualized or assessed would be particularly misleading. Held and McGrew (2000) argue that a basic split is discernible between globalists, who see globalization as a new trend and are largely supportive of it, and 'sceptics' who view the present as 'a continuation of trends that developed in the period of European colonial expansion' (Schirato and Webb, 2003: 16). By this second approach, globalization is simply 'imperialism [which] has acquired a new form as formal empires have been replaced by new mechanisms of multilateral control and surveillance, such as the G7 and World Bank' (ibid.).

Less critically, Waters (1995: 3) argues that globalization is 'a social process in which the constraints of geography on social and cultural arrangements recede'. He suggests that evidence of globalization is discernible in increasingly global dimensions of three inter-related areas of social life, each of which is characterized by a form of exchange. First, the economy, characterized by the international exchange of material goods and wealth; second, the polity, characterized by political exchange; and third, the culture, characterized by the symbolic exchange of information, ideas, entertainment, **propaganda** and **advertising**. The news **media** straddle all three of these globalized exchanges, being involved in the transference of information and entertainment, political influence and money.

It should also be pointed out that 'the constraints of geography on social and cultural arrangements', suggested by Waters (1995), do not *naturally* 'recede' but are being dissolved in ways which illustrate the inter-related character of these three arenas of social life. For example,

94

cultural imperialism does not rest solely 'on the power to universalise particularisms linked to a singular historical tradition' (Bourdieu and Wacquant, 1999: 41), it also requires: the financial collateral of media giants such as CNN or Disney or the BBC; and pressure from institutions such as the World Bank and the IMF to **deregulate** and fragment national media markets to facilitate corporate expansion. Hence, Mohammadi (1997: 3) argues media communications are 'a major factor in the globalization of the market'.

Further reading

Mohammadi, A. (ed.) (1997) *International Communication and Globalisation*. London: Sage.
Schirato, T. and Webb, J. (2003) *Understanding Globalisation*. London: Sage.

JER

Gonzo journalism

A style of **journalism** inextricably associated with the late American writer Hunter S. Thompson and more broadly with the New Journalism of the 1960s, exemplified by Tom Wolfe and Norman Mailer, which applied the techniques of fiction to non-fiction writing and aspired to write journalism 'that would read like a novel' (Wolfe, 1977: 21–2). Contra the conventions of standard journalism practice, gonzo journalism features a bold, exaggerated, irreverent, hyperbolic and extremely subjective style of writing, which positions the author at the centre of the narrative.

Gonzo journalism debuted in a classic essay by Thompson entitled 'The Kentucky Derby is Decadent and Depraved' which offered a scathing critique of the 'bigoted, chauvinistic and caste-bound culture' of his native Louisville and was published in *Scanlon's Monthly* in 1970. But it was his autobiographical search for the American dream in *Fear and Loathing in Las Vegas: A Savage Journey into the Heart of the American Dream*, which delivered the classic exemplar of gonzo. The book was a great success and subsequently Thompson made both the word and the style his own.

Definitions of gonzo abound, with one scholar reporting a Google search locating more than 597,000 references to gonzo, including gonzo theology: assessments of gonzo journalism range from the complimentary to the contemptuous. (Hirst, 2003: 1). In the words of one biographer of

95

Thompson, gonzo places 'the reporter and the quest for information as the focal point. Notes, snatches from other articles, transcribed interviews, verbatim telephone conversations, telegrams – these are all elements of a piece of gonzo journalism' (McKeen, 1991: 36). But at the centre of all definitions is the requirement for the gonzo journalist to write in the first person and to become the dominant participant in the narrative. 'True gonzo reporting needs the talents of a master journalist, the eye of an artist/photographer and the heavy balls of an actor,' Thompson wrote on the cover notes of his classic essay 'because the writer must be a participant in the scene, while he's writing it – or at least taping it, or even sketching it. Or all three' (Jacket blurb for *Fear and Loathing in Las Vegas*).

Further reading

Thompson, H.S. (1971) *Fear and Loathing in Las Vegas: A Savage Journey into the Heart of the American Dream*. New York: The Modern Library.
Wolfe, T. (1977) *The New Journalism*. London: Picador.

BF

Guard dog theory of journalism

An approach to the study of the news suggested by Donohue, Tichenor and Olien (1995), the guard dog theory was intended as a development of (but distinct from) the **lapdog** perspective. The guard dog model suggests that journalism is characterized by three features. First, the news media act as protector of particular groups within the power elites. Second, the focus and approach of the news media are shaped according to who is being protected and who is defined as the threat (external/internal, political/racial, etc.). Third, in times of political conflict and/or scandal it is common for the guard dog to turn on one of the masters.

On the basis of this model of journalism, Donohue et al. suggest a number of hypotheses for further testing of journalists' performance (another shortcoming of the lapdog model, they suggest, is its inability to predict reporting patterns). The first of these reads: 'the intensity of press reporting and editorialising about a public issue is directly proportional to the degree to which top power positions are uncertain as a result of organized challenge' (ibid.: 125). In other words, reported political conflict is a reflection of conflict between political elites, and when two power blocs (e.g. separate political parties, factions or powerful individuals within a party) are in conflict, different media will always side 'with one or the other, but without adopting a third, or innovative, position' (ibid.). Thus, while in 'the lapdog view, the only media role in conflict would be the defence of the powerful against outside intruders . . . in the guard dog perspective occasions would arise that entail reporting of conflicts between dominant powers of power blocs' (ibid.: 120). The model therefore has a dynamic element, reflecting the dynamic nature of media influence and **agenda setting**.

Further reading
Donohue, G.A. Tichenor, P.J. and Olien, C.N. (1995) 'A Guard Dog Perspective on the Role of the Media', *Journal of Communication*, 45(2): 115–32.

JER

Hard news

The collapse of the twin towers in New York, the first man on the moon, the assassination of John F. Kennedy, income tax goes up by a penny. All these are examples of a hard news story. All journalists recognize a hard news **story** the minute they hear one, but it's less easy to generalize than you might think.

News itself has been defined in a variety of memorable ways. 'The first rough draft of history,' according to Ben Bradlee, former editor of the *Washington Post*; 'anything that makes a reader say "Gee Whiz!"', according to Arthur McEwen; 'something someone, somewhere doesn't want you to print' (Anon) or more prosaically as 'that which is new, interesting and true'. Importance, significance, relevance and immediacy also play their part and generally, the more important, significant, relevant and immediate something is, the better the story and the stronger its claim to being hard news. The classic joke headline of a *Times* sub-editor 'Small earthquake in Chile – not many dead' was meant to be everything news is not. Except if you live in Chile, where undoubtedly this would be classified as a hard news story.

A 1973 study by Gaye Tuchman pointed out how difficult journalists themselves find it to categorize news because often stories will fall into more than one. In a two-year project in a television and print newsroom, journalists voluntarily contrasted hard news and **soft news**: 'hard news concerns events potentially available to analysis or interpretation and consists of "factual presentations" of events deemed newsworthy' (Tuchman, 1973, in Berkowitz, 1997: 176). Andrew Boyd (2001) invokes

97

newsroom staffer Harry Hardnose, created by cartoonist Steve Bell. Harry's a hack of the old order and for him hard news is simple: 'information of importance to the listener'. In other words, something that will have a material impact on people's lives. But woe betide any journalist who fails to develop a nose for news. Of whatever sort.

Further reading

Boyd, A. (2001) *Broadcast Journalism: Techniques of Radio and Television News*, 5th edn. Oxford: Focal Press.
Tuchman, G. (1973) 'Making News by Doing Work: Routinizing the Unexpected', in Berkowitz, D. (ed.) (1997) *Social Meanings of News: A Text-Reader*. London: Sage.

MK

Hegemony

The process in which a ruling class persuades all other classes to accept its rule and their subordination (Gramsci, 1971). With the successful institution of hegemony, the subordinate classes consent to the leadership of the ruling class and the dominance of their institutions and values. In short, this equates with consenting to unequal class relations. When successful, the ruling class can implant its values with the minimum of force since the ruled acquiesce to the power and political legitimacy of the rulers. In the words of Gramsci:

> The 'normal' exercise of hegemony . . . is characterized by the combination of force and consensus which vary in their balance with each other, without force exceeding consensus too much. Thus it tries to achieve that force should appear to be supported by the agreement of the majority, expressed by the so-called organs of public opinion – newspapers and associations. (*Quaderni del Carcere*, p. 1638, cited in Joll, 1977: 99)

Thus, a hegemonic ruling class is one which gains support for itself from other classes. This is achieved, first, by the ruling class taking into consideration 'the interests and tendencies of the groups over which hegemony is to be exercised' (Gramsci, 1971: 161). Second, any concessions to public demands should be publicized in order to 'demonstrate' probity of the ruling class and hence their moral and political leadership. Of course, 'such sacrifices and such compromises cannot affect what is essential', that is, the maintenance of economic privilege of the ruling class (ibid.). Third, hegemony is maintained by the

98

ruling class teaching their ideas and their values in the general public, particularly their central claim to political legitimacy.

Education therefore lies at the heat of hegemony – indeed, Gramsci argues, '[e]very relationship of hegemony is necessarily a pedagogic relationship' (ibid.: 350) – a process spear-headed by 'public intellectuals' working in ideological cultural agencies such as journalism. Although relatively autonomous (indeed, their autonomy is a necessary condition of domination through consent), journalists mediate the relationship between ruling class **ideology** and news content (Murdock, 2000) and support the hegemony by naturalizing, or taking for granted, the inequalities of contemporary capitalism (Gitlin, 1979; Tuchman, 1983). Further, by 'perpetuating as commonsensical notions of who ought to be treated as authoritative, [news] routines help the system maintain control without sacrificing legitimacy' (Reese, 1990: 425) and hence play an essential role in maintaining the class authority within the political system.

Further reading

Gramsci, A. (1971) *Extracts from the Prison Notebooks*. London: Lawrence and Wishart.

JER

Hierarchy of influences

A theoretical framework, developed in Shoemaker and Reese (1996), which examines news media in relation to 'levels of analysis' and investigates the way factors which influence the production of news operate 'both separately and in conjunction with each other' (Reese, 2001: 178). The helpful text-reader by Berkowitz (1997) was also organized in accordance to this approach, with chapters grouped into sections which 'focus on different degrees of social aggregation – individual, organizational, institutional and societal' influences on journalism and news production (ibid.: xiii).

Taking each of these levels of analysis in turn: news can first be studied as the product of (individual) journalists. In the words of Gieber (1964), 'news is what newspapermen make it' and this approach is perhaps best embodied in early **gatekeeper** studies (White, 1950; Carter, 1958). Second, we should consider the norms and values of journalism as a profession, including the central importance of **news values** (Galtung and Ruge, 1965; Harcup and O'Neill, 2001), routines (Schlesinger, 1978) and

99

objectivity (Tuchman, 1972). Third, given that news is produced in institutional settings, the 'newsroom culture' of the news organization should be considered (Eliasoph, 1988; Harrison, 2000). Fourth, many news organizations have close (some would say *overly* familiar) relations with other institutions within the 'political economy' and hence we need to consider 'their relationships to other systems such as markets' (Gerbner, 1958: 488) and the way that this influences news production (Bagdikian, 1987; Herman and Chomsky, [1989]1984; Klaehn, 2003). Fifth, the very 'cultural air which we breathe' influences journalism, selecting that which is culturally resonant (to both journalist and **audience** alike) and ignoring that which is not (see Hall, 1973; Hartmann and Husband, 1973; Molotch and Lester, 1974).

Common to all these news paradigms is the *social constructed* nature of news, considered at different levels of analysis. The hierarchy of influences approach suggests that analysis should demonstrate how 'these forces operate simultaneously at different levels of strength in any shaping of media content' (Reese, 2001: 179).

Further reading

Reese, S.D. (2001) 'Understanding the Global Journalist: A Hierarchy-of-Influences Approach', *Journalism Studies*, 2(2): 173–87.
Shoemaker, P. and Reese, S. (1996) *Mediating the Message: Theories of Influence on Mass Media Content*. White Plains, NY: Longman.

JER

Himalayan option

The emergence of a multi-channel broadcasting environment in the mid-1990s, posed a programming dilemma for the BBC as the dominant **public service** broadcaster. Expressed broadly, should the BBC try to compete for **audiences** with the burgeoning commercial television channels or attempt to define a distinctive programming identity?

The government Green Paper *The Future of the BBC*, suggested that one option for the BBC would be to specialize in news and current affairs, arts and science programmes, religious programmes and 'programmes which are unlikely to be broadcast by other organizations'. The BBC would also 'broadcast few general entertainment programmes, but more programmes for minority audiences, so increasing the overall diversity and choice' (Department of National Heritage, 1992, para. 4.5).

Communications scholar Jay Blumler rejected the view that public service broadcasting could, or should, be defined by the programming omissions of commercial sector broadcasters (Blumler, 1993: 30). The BBC's response, *Extending Choice: The BBC's Role in the New Broadcasting Age* (1992), was similarly unequivocal and rejected what quickly became dubbed as the 'Himalayan option'. The then Director General John Birt claimed that colonizing the 'high ground' of programming in this way would simply consign the BBC to 'a cultural ghetto' with inconsequential minority audiences, which was the experience of public service television in America (BBC, 1992: 8). In later policy publications (*Responding to the Green Paper* 1993, and *People and Programmes* 1995), the BBC confirmed its rejection of the Himalayan option and its intention to provide a broad range of quality programmes and sustain 'a strong bond of understanding with our audience' (BBC, 1995). Crucially, the BBC 'should maintain regular contact with all viewers and listeners and deliver programming which appeals to them . . . but they should do so in a way which places the greatest importance on developing services of distinction and quality rather than on attracting a large audience for its own sake' (BBC, 1992: 24).

Further reading

BBC (1992) *Extending Choice: The BBC's Role in the New Broadcasting Age*. London: BBC.
BBC (1993) *Responding to the Green Paper*. London: BBC.
BBC (1995) *People and Programmes*. London: BBC.

BF

Human Rights Act

101

The 1998 Human Rights Act came into force in October 2000 and adopted the 1950 European Convention on Human Rights into UK domestic law (ECHR 2003). Previously the Convention's influence on UK law had been very limited, although since 1966 British subjects had been able to petition the European Court of Human Rights if appeals failed in the British courts (Robertson and Nicol, 2002: 36).

For the UK media, the Convention's incorporation directly into domestic law was welcome since Article 10 upholds freedom of expression, and therefore **press freedom** to a greater extent than earlier common law (i.e. case law) made by British judges (Nicol et al., 2001: 7; Robertson and Nicol, 2002: ix).

Article 10 should therefore, as new case law develops, help deter the

British legal authorities from making any over-zealous use of the **Official Secrets Acts**, and help protect the media's confidential **sources** of information from legal action to expose their identity. However, the tabloid media, in particular, are wary of the effect of the Convention's Article 8, which upholds **privacy**.

Further reading

Nicol, A., Millar, G, and Sharland, A. (2001), *Media Law and Human Rights*. London: Blackstone Press.
Robertson, G. and Nicol, A. (2002) *Media Law*. 4th edn. London: Penguin.
Rozenberg, J. (2004) *Privacy and the Press*. Oxford: Oxford University Press.

MNH

Hutton Inquiry

At lunchtime on 27 January 2004, *BBC* director general Greg Dyke sat down in his office to read the report of the Hutton inquiry into the circumstances surrounding the death of government scientist Dr David Kelly.

Forty minutes later he walked into an adjoining meeting room where the then BBC **News** director Richard Sambrook, his deputy Mark Damazer and business manager Magnus Brooke were doing the same. As he recalls: 'They tell me I said something like, "Well, boys, we've been fucked, so what are we going to do about it?"' (Dyke, 2004: 4). On 28 January BBC Chairman Gavyn Davies resigned. On the 29th, so did Greg Dyke.

Over the hot summer of 2003, journalists – and much of the public – were fixated by the unfolding drama of the Hutton inquiry and the implications it might hold for the way **journalists** work. It had been called under the chairmanship of Lord Hutton, a former Lord Chief Justice of Northern Ireland, to examine the circumstances surrounding Dr Kelly's death. Dr Kelly was an expert on biological warfare and a senior weapons inspector in Iraq. He'd been named as a **source** used by BBC journalist Andrew Gilligan in the infamous **two-way** broadcast on the *Today* programme on 29 May 2003. In the broadcast Gilligan suggested the government had 'sexed up' a dossier on Iraq to include the claim that the Iraqi military were able to deploy chemical or biological weapons within 45 minutes of an order to use them, when the government probably knew that the 45-minute figure was wrong (Hutton, 2004). On 15 and 16 July Dr Kelly was called to give evidence to the Foreign Affairs Committee

102

and the Intelligence and Security Committee. On 19 July he was found dead in woods near his home.

Hutton concluded that Dr Kelly had taken his own life, but the shockwaves from the report came from the unexpectedly serious criticism of the BBC's **journalism**. It said Andrew Gilligan's claim was unfounded, Dr Kelly wasn't authorized to meet Gilligan, the broadcast had impugned the government's integrity and that the BBC's editorial system was defective in that editors didn't see or approve a script for the two-way. They didn't check Gilligan's notes of his meeting with Dr Kelly or whether the notes supported the allegation made in the broadcast. And the BBC governors themselves should have done more to check the **accuracy** of the claim.

Jaw-dropping incredulity greeted the report's formal publication on 28 January 2004. Much of the press was sceptical, with the *Independent*, among others, describing it as one-sided (*Independent*, 2004) in that most of its firepower was directed at the BBC and not the government. Lord Hutton himself was described as naïve, knowing little of the characters and events he was required to confront (Aaronovitch et al., 2004: viii). At the BBC Greg Dyke's departure sparked unprecedented scenes of staff support, with demonstrations outside BBC buildings and Dyke himself mobbed outside BBC Television Centre in London. But there was also a period of intense reflection leading to the Neil Report of 23 June 2004, which examined the 'lessons to be learned' from Hutton, and promised 'substantial changes in how the BBC will execute its commitment to impartial and **fair** journalism' (Neil, 2004). It led to increased emphasis on training, particularly in the area of note taking, and an overhaul of the internal complaints procedure. But it restated five journalistic values already expressed in the corporation's **Producers' Guidelines**: truth and accuracy, serving the **public interest**, **impartiality** and diversity of opinion, independence and accountability. Changes are planned to the role of the governors in **regulating** the BBC.

That the corporation's confidence was knocked in the run up to the important Charter review is not in doubt. The impact on its journalism is far harder to gauge. In the 2004 McTaggart Lecture, *Today* presenter John Humphrys insisted he personally had not been leant on by his bosses in the wake of Hutton to go easy on interviewees. 'We should not be fearful of standing up to those in power. That is our job: to be fearless in the face of power. It is our job in a pre-Hutton, a mid-Hutton . . . a post-Hutton era. In any era' (Humphrys, 2004).

103

Further reading

Dyke, G. (2004) *Inside Story*. London: HarperCollins.

Hutton (2004) *Report of the Inquiry into the Circumstances Surrounding the Death of Dr David Kelly, CMG*. London: The Stationery Office. HC247 at http://www.the-hutton-inquiry.org.uk.

Neil, A. (2004) *The Neil Report*. Available at: http://www.bbc.co.uk/info/policies/neil report.

Whittaker, R. (2004) 'How Could He Have Got It So Wrong?' *Independent*, 1 February.

MK

Hypertext (hypermedia, hyperlink)

There are many hypertext systems in use, the earliest of which can be traced back to 1945 (Nielsen, 1995: 33), their main characteristic being that they cross-reference information presented in non-linear ways. A hyperlink, which can be represented by a word, phrase, image or other object, is the most essential element of electronic hypertext systems, which include the **Internet** and the **world wide web**. A clickable point on a web page or other electronic document, a hyperlink – more commonly known simply as a link – takes the user, upon being clicked, to another (usually associated) page or image within the same **website** or document (internal) or a separate document or website (external). 'The power to link lies at the heart of the web' (Ward, 2002: 141).

Hyperlinks can be used as a main navigational tool on a website, the same button or graphic being present on every page and linking through to a specific page indicated by that icon. Or they could be used to develop or supplement a story. Hyperlinks are presented in different ways, but usually in a different colour to the rest of the text (blue and underlined has been the general convention during the early years of the world wide web, although this is not universally followed); they are usually best identified by the arrow changing to the image of a hand when the cursor passes over the link.

The term hypertext was coined by author and designer Theodore Nelson in the mid-1960s, although the first system of its kind was proposed by Vannevar Bush 20 years earlier (Nielsen, 1995: 37). The development of hypertext links connecting information stored on different computers became known as hypermedia (Reddick and King, 2001: 35). Hypermedia and hypertext are therefore often used interchangeably, although the former could specifically be applied to a **multimedia** system rather than one just using text (Nielsen, 1995: 5).

Hypertext is a major feature of **online journalism** in that it can be used to add context to a story, for example, connecting it via hyperlinks to related articles and other **sources** of information, like background about the major figures or events mentioned. These links can be placed within the text or at the end or alongside text. It is being seen as a 'new form of journalism that places stories in a much richer historical, political, and cultural context' (Pavlik, 2001: 16). The process of hyperlinking demands that the reader think 'about the text in a way that print or broadcast texts do not . . . each one that is encountered by the reader forces a decision as to whether to follow the link or stay with the anchor text' (Hall, J., 2001: 68–9). The decision relating to which hyperlinks to include and which not to include gives web **news editors** an additional **gatekeeper** role (Dimitrova et al., 2003: 402).

Further reading

Dimitrova, D.V., Connolly-Ahern, C., Williams, A.P., Kaid, L.L. and Reid, A. (2003) 'Hyperlinking as Gatekeeping: Online Newspaper Coverage of the Execution of an American Terrorist', *Journalism Studies*, 4(3): 401–14.
Hall, J. (2001) *Online Journalism: A Critical Primer*. London: Pluto Press.
Nielsen, J. (1995) *Multimedia and Hypertext: The Internet and Beyond*. London: Academic Press.
Pavlik, J.V. (2001) *Journalism and New Media*. Columbia, NY: University Press.
Reddick, R. and King, E. (2001) *The Online Journalist: Using the Internet and Other Electronic Resources*, 3rd edn. Orlando, FL: Harcourt Brace and Company.
Ward, M. (2002) *Journalism Online*. Oxford: Focal Press.

MGH

Icon

One of Charles Peirce's three categories of **sign**, an icon is a sign which is determined by what it represents. In general, words not only appear dissimilar to what they represent, the relationship between a word and what it refers to (or what it *means*) is arbitrary. In contrast, an icon 'possesses some of the properties of the thing represented' (Peirce (1939) cited in Hall, 1980: 55). For example: the word 'cow' 'possesses *none* of the properties of the thing represented, whereas the visual sign [for example, a photograph of a cow] appears to possess *some* of those properties' (Hall, 1980: 56). Television images are iconic; so too, though to a lesser extent, are onomatopoeic words like 'buzz' or 'mumble'.

Further reading
Hall, S. (1980) 'Encoding/Decoding', in Marris, P. and Thornham, S. (eds) *Media Studies: A Reader*. Edinburgh: Edinburgh University Press, pp. 51–61.
Peirce, C.S. (1931–58) *Collected Papers*. Cambridge, MA: Harvard University Press.

JER

Ideological state apparatuses

French Marxist Louis Althusser argued that the perpetual class war between the bourgeoisie and proletariat required the capitalist state (and all predecessor states in class societies), to be an essentially repressive organization: an orthodox Marxist contention. But Althusser argued that the repressive state apparatuses (RSAs), which corresponded closely to Marx's conception of the state and included the courts, prisons, police, army and the legislative and executive branches of government – indeed, all those organizations and institutions which sustained order by their claim to the legitimate use of coercion and physical force – constituted only one element in a twofold system of repression.

The ideological state apparatuses were private institutions located in civil society, which enjoyed relative autonomy from the state and the dominant class. ISAs included the education system, the Church, trade unions and the media of mass communication but, in contrast to the RSAs, contributed to the maintenance of social order by disseminating the dominant ideology and securing the compliance and consent of subordinate classes by representing class relations built on exploitation as natural and immutable. In this way, Althusser believed, the dominant class was blinded *by* its interests while the subordinate classes were blinded *to* their interests. Consequently, ISAs reflected the institutional expression of ideology in particular class formations of social systems (see also Poulantzas, 1973: 195–224).

Althusser believed that social order was secured by a carefully achieved, but historically shifting, balance between coercion and consent, although ideological dominance via the ISAs was the preferred and typical mechanism in class societies. It followed logically, he believed, that any use of force by the state was an articulation of the weakness, rather than the strength, of the dominant class since capitalist rule was typically secured through **hegemony** or rule by consent and ideology. Althusser also suggested that the relative importance of the ISAs changed across distinctive modes of production with their differing ideological and cultural systems. In feudal society, for example, the Church had been the prominent ISA whereas the establishment of capitalist societies witnessed the ascendancy of education and the media as the most significant ISAs.

Further reading

Althusser, L. (1971) 'Ideology and Ideological State Apparatuses', in *Lenin and Philosophy and Other Essays*. London: New Left Books.

Poulantzas, N. (1973) *Political Power and Social Classes*. London: New Left Books.

BF

Ideology

An essentially contestable concept and, as such, it makes little point to describe what it 'really' means. Instead we should trace the history of the concept and how it is used. Ideology was coined originally by Antoine Destutt de Tracy in the years after the French Revolution to refer to 'a new science of ideas, an idea-logy, which would be the foundation of all other sciences' (Gee, 1990: 4). Destutt de Tracy argued that the ideas we hold are not the product of God or nature but are generated by our social environment as perceived through our physical senses. Hence, ideology refers in this first instance to the 'study of how ideas are formed based on experience' (ibid.).

Marx developed this approach to ideology, arguing that 'the history of ideas demonstrate[s] that the products of the intellect are refashioned along with material ones' (Marx, [1848] 1998: 27). However, the relation between ideas and experience is further refined and focused in Marx's account, to reveal that our ideas and beliefs are not the product of 'experience' *per se*, but rather 'alter according to their *economic* circumstances' (ibid. emphasis added) and therefore stand as a reflection of these circumstances – as a reflection of social relations. More specifically, they stand as a reflection of the circumstances of the *ruling* class and their desire to maintain their class privilege. As Gee (1990: 6) points out, ideology under Marx:

107

is an 'upside-down' version of reality. Things are not really the way the elite and powerful believe them to be: rather, their beliefs invert reality to make it appear the way they would like it to be, the way it 'needs' to be if their power is to be enhanced and sustained.

Accordingly, '[t]he ideas [or *ideology*] of the ruling class are in every epoch the ruling ideas, i.e. the class which is the ruling material force in society is at the same time its ruling intellectual force' (Marx and Engels, 1974: 64).

Therefore, contrary to the psychological (and, in Marxist terms, bourgeois) perspective of Destutt de Tracy, Marx illustrated that ideology is more than individual ideas formed through experience: ideology and its **signs** develop 'through the process of social interaction, [and are] defined by the social purview of the given time period and the given social group' (Vološinov, [1929]1973: 21). Certain cruder interpretations of Marx's position suggest that such ideological work is one-way traffic: that the economic relations of society *create* false ideas which are held often contrary to people's true interests. Such interpretations fail to realise how ideology does 'not just reflect 'reality' but partially help[s] to create, to constitute it' (Gee, 1990: 8). The question of *how* this occurs – *how* ideological ideas help produce and reproduce (inequitable) social realities – have been most fruitfully broached by two neo-Marxist scholars: first, by Gramsci and his theory of **hegemony**; and, second, through the work of Althusser (1971).

Althusser held that ideology acts, first, as a body of ideas existing 'to dispel contradictions in lived experience. It accomplishes this by offering false, but seemingly true, resolutions to real problems' (Storey, 1993: 113). Second, ideology exists as a material practice – in other words, in the form of behaviours – shaped and (re)produced through the **ideological state apparatuses** (ISA) and enforced by repressive state apparatuses (RSA) like the police. The news media, as examples of the ISA, contribute to the dominance of ruling-class ideology in several ways, most notably by a twin process of *neutralizing* dissent and *naturalizing* elite dominance. Journalists, having internalised news routines, values and 'commonsensical notions of who ought to be treated as authoritative' (Reese, 1990: 425), 'accept the frames imposed on events by officials and marginalise the delegitimate voices that fall outside the dominant elite circles' (ibid.) In short, elite ideological dominance arises 'as a property of the system of relations involved, rather than as the overt and intentional biases of individuals' (Hall, 1982: 95).

Althusser, L. (1971) 'Ideology and Ideological State Apparatuses', in *Lenin and Philosophy and Other Essays*. London: New Left Books.

Hall, S. (1982) 'The Rediscovery of Ideology: Return of the Repressed in Media Studies', in Gurevitch, M., Bennet, T., Curran, J. and Woollacott, J. (eds), *Culture, Society and the Media*. London: Methuen,.pp. 56–90.

JER

Impartiality

Broadcasters are bound by law and their own guidelines to be impartial. Newspapers are not. At its simplest, expressed in the former *Radio Authority*'s code of practice, it means not taking sides. But as Wilson (1996: 43) points out, 'It is in the class of understanding which says the elephant is difficult to describe but easy to recognize'.

The notion goes back to the earliest days of broadcasting. When the *British Broadcasting Company* began **radio** news bulletins in 1922, they were compiled by and credited to a consortium of news agencies. So nervous were newspaper proprietors about the impact of this new medium that bulletins could go out only after 7pm so it wouldn't damage sales, and the coverage of 'controversial' matters was prohibited. In 1924 John Reith, then managing director of the company, wrote a letter to the government requesting 'permission to handle controversial subjects, provided we can guarantee absolute impartiality in the act' (cited in Allan, 1999: 28).

Reith was refused then but the BBC's reporting of the General Strike of 1926 was pivotal and paved the way for the creation in 1927 of the British Broadcasting Corporation *(BBC)* governed by a Royal Charter, the annex to which enshrined the principle of 'due impartiality'.

In 1954, the Churchill Government passed the Television Act which set up the Independent Television Authority, which in turn established *Independent Television News (ITN)*. Clause Three of the act (cited in Allan, 1999: 37) imposed a series of requirements, including 'that any news given in the programmes (in whatever form) is presented with due accuracy and impartiality'. ITN's second editor, Geoffrey Cox (1995) saw in the Act a way of winning more autonomy. These ideas were restated in the Broadcasting Acts of 1990 and 1996 and underpin the BBC's **Producer's Guidelines**, and the codes of practice of the former *Independent Television Commission* and the Radio Authority.

Pinning down the notion of what it is to be impartial is more difficult.

109

All the codes speak of 'even-handedness', '**balance**', '**fairness**' and 'dispassionate reporting' and interpret it as something to be achieved over a period of time on a particular issue rather than in a single programme or news bulletin. In interviewing, impartiality means editing words so that the final version fairly represents the views of the interviewee. In political reporting it means giving a fair amount of time to each noteworthy opinion.

But, as Wilson points out (1996: 43), the achievement of complete impartiality is unattainable. Journalistic judgements are inevitably affected by personal perceptions, ignorance, or insight, whether intended or not. He describes it as 'an ideal to be aimed for, best regarded in the spirit in which honest programmes are made, an approach that tries to be fair in very complex conditions'.

See *Fairness*

Further reading
Allan, S. (1999) *News Culture*. Buckingham: Open University Press.
Cox, G. (1995) *Pioneering Television News*. London: John Libbey.
Wilson, J. (1996) *Understanding Journalism: A Guide to Issues*. London: Routledge.

MK

Independent national radio (INR)

The Broadcasting Act 1990 sanctioned the creation of the Radio Authority which, under the next wave of expansion, was to license three independent national radio stations by the middle of the decade, as well as a host of new local stations. These new stations were subject to a 'lighter' regulatory regime than had existed before and their eight-year licences were retained through honouring their '**promise of performance**'. But unlike the '**quality threshold**' which then operated in the television licensing system, the licences would go to the highest cash bidder in a blind auction.

Classic FM, the UK's first Independent National Radio station (INR1), began broadcasting a classical music service in September 1992. In April 1993, *Virgin 1215* (INR2) went on-air with a rock music service. In February 1995, *Talk Radio* (INR3) began a speech-based service. *Talk Radio* re-launched as *talkSPORT* in January 2000 with sports-focused programming.

There is an 'unauthorized' national station, *TEAMtalk*, which broadcasts from the Irish Republic, putting it beyond the reach of the 1990 Act. It began life as the music station *Atlantic 252* before being sold in December 2001.

Independent national radio, including *TEAMtalk*, has a weekly **reach** of 26 per cent of the available **audience** and takes a listening share of 9.5 per cent (Boon, 2003).

MK

Independent producers

There are around 151,000 people working in broadcasting in the UK, of whom a little less than 10 per cent (13,300) work in over 1,000 independent production companies. Some of these companies are quite large, for example Hit Entertainment, with about 400 employees, though most are small and medium-sized enterprises (SMEs) and employ 10–40 people (from www.prospects.ac.uk). Under the terms of the Broadcasting Act (1990) and now the **Communication Act 2003**, British broadcasters are required to meet a quota of outputs sourced from independent and European producers. Margaret Thatcher stated explicitly that this was intended to weaken 'the monopolistic grip of the **broadcasting** establishment' (1993: 53). Like so many of Thatcher's policies, the Blair Government has since backed the quota system, on the grounds that it encourages 'competition and economic growth' and ensures that 'citizens receive a diverse range of content from a plurality of sources' (Government Consultation, cited in Barnicoat and Bazalgette, no date).

The Communication Act 2003 shifted the relationship between independent programme-makers and broadcasters, aiming to bring about 'a significant transfer of control and value of intellectual property rights back to independent producers' (PACT, 2004). Under the terms of the Guidelines, 'producers should retain rights in their programmes unless these are explicitly sold to broadcasters' (*Ofcom*, para 14.) The Act also redefined what it means to be 'independent'. Under the new rules, 'a UK producer cannot be regarded as independent if it is more than 25 per cent owned by a broadcaster, or by a company which controls or is an associate of a broadcaster, even where that broadcaster does not broadcast in the UK' (Barnicoat and Bazalgette, no date). What this means is that certain large production companies, such as Endemol UK (owned, through its parent company Endemol Entertainment, by the Spanish telecoms giant

111

Telefonica) are no longer defined as 'independent' and hence lose out on lucrative contracts associated with 'independent producer status'. Endemol UK feel aggrieved by this change, and argue that the rules 'force independent producers to choose between their independent status and their ability to grow via upward investment' (ibid.). Given that the restriction hampers the government's stated desire 'to encourage a dynamic market' (para 1.11 of the Consultation), it seems unlikely that it will remain for long.

Further reading

Barnicoat, T. and Bazalgette, P. (no date) 'Endemol UK: response to the consultation on media ownership rules', available at: www.culture.gov.uk/PDF/media_own_endemol.PDF

JER

Information architecture

The essential structure of a **website** upon which all things – including form and function – are built, Information Architecture (IA) is the 'foundation for great web design . . . initiating the IA process is the first thing you should do when designing a site' (Shiple, 2003). IA has several working definitions, including the organization, labelling and navigation of information (including search systems), and the structural design involving varying levels of granularity like sentence, paragraph and article (Rosenfeld and Morville, 2002: 4–5). The extension brief also features defining the site's mission and vision, and determining its content and functionality (Rosenfeld and Morville, [1998]2002: 11).

Nielsen says a site should be structured to mirror the users' tasks rather than to reflect the company's structure (2000: 15). The better the information architecture of a website, the more enhanced will be the **usability** experience for the user.

Further reading

Nielsen, J. (2000) *Designing Web Usability*. Indianapolis: New Riders Publishing.
Rosenfeld, L. and Morville, P. ([1998]2002) *Information Architecture for the World Wide Web*, 2nd edn. Sebastopol, CA: O'Reilly and Associates.
Shiple, J. (2003) 'Why's Information architecture so important?' available at: http://hotwired.lycos.com/webmonkey/98/28/indexOa.html.

MGH

112

Information subsidies

A concept developed by American scholar Oscar Gandy in his influential book *Beyond Agenda Setting*, which explores the rise of specialist information professionals (special advisers) within government structures in the United States. Gandy argues that, 'at every level of government [state and federal] . . . there are information specialists whose responsibility is to ensure that the nation's public media carry the desired message forward to the general public, other government officials and key corporate leaders' (1982: 74).

The successful functioning of this system rests on what Gandy terms information subsidies which include a wide range of strategies and mechanisms deployed by information professionals to minimize the costs of information which journalists require to construct, publish and report particular news stories. This provision and control of information subsidies (including news releases, press conferences, the distribution of government reports and official statements by politicians such as the '**fillers**' provided by the COI) are significant because they confer on information providers the possibility for agenda building and **agenda setting** in news media.

Subsequent studies have revealed the extent to which this provision of information subsidies can prove highly effective in enabling information professionals, such as public relations specialists and government information and press officers, to influence and manage the news agenda in: press coverage of local/state politics in both America and Britain (Franklin and VanSlyke Turk, 1988); reports in national and local newspapers of government policy initiatives such as the poll tax (Deacon and Golding, 1994); local newspaper reporting of UK general elections (Franklin, 1989); press reporting of devolution in Northern Ireland (Fawcett, 2001); local and regional news media reporting of local government (Fedorcio et al., 1991) and many other areas of news coverage.

Some scholars believe that the provision of information subsidies and their successful deployment by information professionals working within state structures, has become so endemic to modern systems of governance that it is appropriate to speak of Britain as 'a public relations state' (Deacon and Golding, 1994: 4) or a 'public relations democracy' (Davis, 2002).

113

Further reading

Davis, A. (2002) *Public Relations Democracy: Public Relations, Politics and the Mass Media in Britain*. London: Sage.

Deacon, D. and Golding, P. (1994) *Taxation and Representation: The Media, Political Communication and the Poll Tax*. London: John Libbey.

Franklin, B. and VanSlyke Turk, J. (1988) 'Information subsidies: agenda setting traditions', *Public Relations Review*, Spring: 29–41.

Gandy, O. (1982) *Beyond Agenda Setting: Information Subsidies and Public Policy*, New York: Ablex.

BF

Infotainment

A neologism combining the two words 'information' and 'entertainment' to suggest the tendency for the content of news and current affairs programming to blend entertainment with information in order to make factual programmes more accessible and increase **audience** size and reach (Franklin, 1997: 4). Consequently, the term 'infotainment' appears routinely in discussions about the **dumbing down** debate, tabloidization and **newszak**. The Chief Executive of the ITC, for example, declared his disappointment and regret that 'factual programming is on a downward path towards the triumph of infotainment above both information and entertainment' (Glencross, 1994: 7–8), while American journalist James Fallows argues that 'the most influential parts of the [US] media have lost sight of . . . the essence of real journalism . . . which is the search for information of use to the public' (1996: 6–7).

Market pressures are typically identified as the culprit driving the development of infotainment, although such an argument rests on the contentious and unsubstantiated assumption that moving 'downmarket' editorially will increase rather than diminish **audiences** and readerships. This has not been the experience of the British tabloid press, especially the Sunday tabloids, whose growing reliance on infotainment as an editorial feature has accompanied plummeting circulations, while the **broadsheets** have largely sustained their **readerships** across the last decade.

Further reading

Fallows, J. (1997) *Breaking the News: How the Media Undermine American Democracy*. New York: Vintage Books.

Franklin, B. (1997) *Newszak and News Media*. London: Arnold.

Glencross, D. (1994) 'Superhighways and Supermarkets', a speech to the *Royal Television Society*, 8 March.

BF

114

Interactivity

A process involving the multi-directional flow of information between agents, which might include computers, the **media** and the **audience**, is seen as interactive. The non-linear qualities and technological capabilities of the **world wide web** have given interactivity a new dimension with almost unlimited potential. Traditionally, the consumption of books, newspapers and magazines has mostly been a one-way engagement of reading: 'The online experience is two-way, allowing readers to contribute via e-mail, bulletin-board discussion, and all matter of annotation as they navigate the Web', having a democratizing effect (Levinson, 1999: 38). Many newspapers put a reporter's **email** address at the end of an article, so readers can email him or her directly.

Ward uses three different models of **mass communication** to illustrate the varying levels of interactivity. The traditional model (newspapers and broadcasters) does not involve any input from the (predominantly passive) audience, i.e. it is all one way, while the two-way model gives the user a choice in the information they want to consume and an opportunity to contribute. The (triangular) three-way model might involve users sharing information and possibly **news** with other users, with the **journalist** acting as a user as well as a provider (Ward, 2002: 144–8). This final dimension begins to challenge the journalist's traditional role as the sole **gatekeeper** of news and raises important issues including accuracy and veracity (ibid.: 25).

Pavlik says that interactive storytelling embraces a wide range of communication modalities, including using different forms of media like text and graphics, which 'offers possibilities for extraordinary customization and heightened audience involvement' (Pavlik, 2001: 1). Text becomes more interactive when readers can restructure it to their own needs using a range of hierarchical entry points, as with the use of **hypertext** links which can set a news piece in context as well as guiding its readers through it (Hall, J., 2001: 49). Archives and search engines are other examples of interactivity online which offer extremely useful resources to the journalist.

Special scripts can be inserted into the coding of web pages to make them interactive; basic online examples include simple animation, games and guestbooks.

Interactive television has also provided viewers with a range of extra options and additional features. For example, people watching terrestrial

115

channels BBC1 and BBC2 during the 2004 Athens Olympics got up to 18 hours a day of coverage of the event; interactive viewers, who could switch between up to four different sports using the red buttons on their remote controls, could get a further 1,000 hours during the fortnight's coverage. Statistics monitoring the habits of those with access to interactive TV showed that sports fans wanted to 'editorialize' their own viewing experiences (Timms, 2004).

Further reading

Hall, J. (2001) *Online Journalism: A Critical Primer*. London: Pluto Press.
Levinson, P. (1999) *Digital McLuhan*. London: Routledge.
Pavlik, J.V. (2001) *Journalism and New Media*. Columbia, NY: University Press.
Timms, D. (2004) 'Record numbers follow Olympics via web and interactive TV'. 20 August, *Guardian Unlimited*, available at: http://media.guardian.co.uk/broadcast/story/0..1287620.00.html.
Ward, M. (2002) *Journalism Online* Oxford: Focal Press.

MGH

Internet (intranet, extranet)

It is almost easier to say what the Internet is not, rather than what it is. Not to be confused with the **world wide web**, although the two are very closely linked, the Internet is a global network of networks linking up millions of computers (and the data stored on them) by telephone lines, cables, satellites and radio waves. This huge information infrastructure hosts a variety of applications, including the world wide web and electronic mail (**email**). It uses a set of rules such as TCP/IP (Transmission Control Protocol/Internet Protocol) and FTP (File Transfer Protocol) which govern the exchange of information and allow computers of different types to communicate with each other (Whittaker, 2000: 8–9).

Two adaptations of Internet technology, the intranet (a private network usually used to share corporate information and computing resources among employees) and the extranet (part of an intranet that is made available to users outside a company), also use the TCP/IP protocol (SearchWebServices.com, 2003). Networks can be 'local area' (LAN) or 'wide area' (WAN).

The Internet, particularly through the world wide web, constitutes 'a shared global resource of information, knowledge, and means of collaboration, and cooperation among countless diverse communities' (Internet Society, 2003). Particularly through the world wide web, the Internet has revolutionized **journalism** in many ways, changing what is reported and how it is reported, being a virtually endless **source** of information as well as a far-reaching communications medium which can present all kinds of content in many different formats (Reddick and King, 2001: 241).

The origins of the Internet, a word often shortened to Net and also known as **cyberspace**, can be traced as far back as 1957 when Russia launched Sputnik, the first artificial satellite, which was to herald the beginning of the global communications era. After the launch of Sputnik, the Advanced Research Projects Agency (ARPA), funded by the US Department of Defense, began conducting both military and academic research. These included projects to develop an experimental computer network which would function even if parts of it had been destroyed in a war. This involved messages being split into small packets of information which would be reassembled at its destination. As the packets might travel by different routes, this method would ensure that significant amounts of the information would be successfully sent even if several of the connected computers were out of action. An experimental network named ARPANET was launched in 1969 involving four universities, and within two years a sizeable group of North American governmental and academic institutions were linked up to each other, being expanded to include European connections by 1973.

Exponential growth in the use of the Internet started in the late 1980s with the launch by the National Science Foundation of NSFNET, a high-speed network which linked up five newly-established supercomputing centres and a series of regional networks, forming the basic, multi-layered structure of the Internet which was fully established by 1990, the year ARPANET ceased to exist. At around the same time, the then US Senator Al Gore was popularizing the concept of an 'information superhighway', a term sometimes used as a synonym for the Internet. The birth of the world wide web in the early 1990s introduced a graphic user interface and a protocol for hyperlinking (see **hypertext**) information stored on different computers, meaning access for millions and effectively taking the Internet into the **public sphere** (Whittaker, 2000: 8–9; Hall, 2001: 10–11, 26; Reddick and King, 2001: 21–2).

The basic architecture of the Internet is a client-server model in which servers are accessed by client software operating on different (remote) computers (Whittaker, 2000: 13). People mostly pay an *Internet Service Provider (ISP)* such as AOL (America Online) to give them access to various applications, including email and the world wide web. When you are connected to the Internet, you are online (BBCi, 2003).

The Internet is not an institution, nor is it owned by anybody; and nobody controls it or takes responsibility for it (Reddick and King, 2001: 17), although an Internet Code of Conduct can be found at the *Internet Society* **website** (2003). It has become a public and self-sustaining facility using part of the total resources of the public telecommunication networks (SearchWebServices.com, 2003). The growth and success of the Internet can be measured by the number of host computers and number of users linked to the network, although precise figures are difficult to gauge due to its decentralized structure (Reddick and King, 2001: 21). Figures suggest that more than 500 million people worldwide had Internet access at the end of 2002 and that this would double by the year 2005 (Nua.com, 2003).

A new, more advanced Internet network is currently being developed. Internet2, a consortium of academia, industry and government, is working on advanced applications and technologies in an effort to create a leading edge network capability for the national research community (Internet2, 2003).

Further reading

Hall, J. (2001) *Online Journalism: A Critical Primer*. London: Pluto Press.
Reddick, R. and King, E. (2001) *The Online Journalist: Using the Internet and Other Electronic Resources*, 3rd edn. Orlando, FL: Harcourt Brace and Company.
Whittaker, J. (2000) *Producing for the Web*. London: Routledge.

MGH

Intertextuality

The concept of intertextuality is founded on the notion that **texts** cannot be viewed or studied in isolation since texts are not produced or consumed in isolation. All texts exist, and therefore must be understood, in relation to other texts. As Leitch noted, not only do 'prior texts reside in present texts', 'no text itself is ever fully self-present, self-contained or self-sufficient; no text is closed, total or unified' (1983: 98). Thus, intertextuality may be understood across two inter-related axes: in terms of text-internal and text-external intertextualities. Both these characteristics are of significant importance to the study of journalism. Taking the text-internal characteristics first: all texts (and perhaps news reports in particular) consist of, or are composed of fragments or elements of previous texts. A news report 'Z' may therefore contain elements of a press release 'Y', or a press conference 'X', or a evaluative comment 'W', or all three of these genres (see Fairclough, 2003). An awareness of this text-internal relationship between utterances and prior texts is particularly important given the ability of powerful individuals and groups to shape reporting agendas.

Second, texts are only fully intelligible (or, rather, their detailed, more complete meaning is only revealed) when contextualized and 'read' in relation to other texts and other social practices. Thus, in Montgomery's (1999) analysis of Tony Blair's televised tribute to Princess Diana following her fatal car accident in 1997, he finds it impossible to analyze Blair's rhetorical performance in isolation. Not only must the speech be viewed in relation to other speeches made by Blair, and his (staged) informal style more generally, it also needs to be viewed within the broader social **context**: as a British Prime Minister articulating a collective response to the accident on behalf of 'the British nation'. Thus, texts must be viewed in context – in other words, in relation to the **audience**'s (awareness of) particular **narrative** or discursive models which serve to provide a frame of knowledge or values through which texts are made understandable.

Further reading

Fairclough, N. (2003) *Analysing Discourse: Textual Analysis for Social Research*. London: Routledge.

Leitch, V.B. (1983) *Deconstructive Criticism: An Advanced Introduction*. New York: Columbia University Press.

JER

Interview

119

The interview, the basic active ingredient of **news** and features involving the asking of questions and recording of answers either in writing (preferably using shorthand) or on tape depending on the medium (Harcup, 2004: 95), has been the mainstay of reporting for the past 100 years. Face-to-face and telephone have been the main methods of inquiry in order to obtain quotes, which can add authority and drama (ibid.: 103), **email** now being another technique (Reddick and King, 2001: 79). The interview can be a brief telephone conversation, a lengthy chat over a meal, a live talk (pre-arranged or otherwise) or some questions answered by fax or email (Harcup, 2004: 95). It could be a 'doorstep', which involves waiting at the home of a person in the news, or a 'death knock', calling on a bereaved family seeking information (ibid.: 101). **Radio** (and **television**) interviews can be the straightforward informative kind (see also **two-way**), the emotional type or personality-driven ones; the latter concern the person rather than the event (Gage, 1999: 50–1).

Interviews have been described as 'pseudo-events' (a way of making the news) and initially they were viewed as contrived encounters and invasions of **privacy** (Harcup, 2004: 94). Winston says: 'The introduction of the interview marks a sort of corruption of the idea of the **reporter** as mere observer and the newspaper as nothing more than a chronicle . . . the interview was not absorbed into everyday journalistic practice without misgivings as to its validity as news' (2005). Despite the early misgivings and hostility, the interview was established in the USA and then Europe as a recognized way of gathering journalistic material (Boorstin, in Harcup, 2004: 94).

Similar approaches to interviews, including applying the news writing framework of needing to know the five Ws (Who? What? Where? When? Why?) and how? of **journalism**, will be taken by **journalists** irrespective of the **media** platform or topic (Boyd, 2001: 117; Harcup, 2004: 99–100). Reporters should avoid asking closed questions and opt for more open-ended questions unless a yes or no answer is specifically required (Boyd, 2001: 118; Harcup, 2004: 100). However, there are some fundamental medium-based differences. For example, there is often a strong element of performance about interviews in **broadcasting**, for many of which the questions are central – they tend to be invisible to the reader in print journalism (Harcup, 2004: 99). Additionally, much of what is said in most print interviews will not be directly quoted but rather become part of reported speech, which raises ethical concerns in terms of what is selected (ibid.: 97). If the subject has made 'off the record' comments, a journalist should not attribute them to the interviewee (ibid.: 100).

Planning is seen as important to the success of an interview as it should help the reporter or presenter to remain in control. The preparation will include thinking of some set questions or a script which will depend on the type and length of interview, the **audience** and the **news angle** being pursued, although the journalist should be prepared to be flexible (Boyd, 2001: 112–13; Harcup, 2004: 95). Pre-chat gives the reporter an opportunity to establish a rapport with the subject (Boyd, 2001: 115).

Eye contact and body language in face-to-face interviews are seen as important while the journalist, who must be appropriately dressed (in broadcasting, this will depend on the station's policy), should be 'polite yet assertive but never aggressive' (ibid.: 114–15). Some interviews, like the 'set-piece studio slanging match or the doorstep challenge to a rogue', are clearly of an adversarial nature (Harcup, 2004: 100). Conversation – listening as well as talking – is seen as the key to good interviewing, with

120

tone of voice and the introductory words particularly important on the telephone where there are no visual clues. Interviews by fax or email are clearly even more difficult and are not recommended unless they are the only way of gleaning information from a **source** as it is difficult to establish a rapport and you cannot be sure who is replying, although they can be advantageous for several reasons, including contacting experts in different time zones and questionnaire-style celebrity quizzing (2004: 98). Email can also be used to contact sources, clarify information, as an enhancement for personal interaction, for doing the groundwork for face-to-face interviews and, occasionally, for sending questions in advance if required. In some cases, email correspondence is deemed to be part of the public record (Reddick and King, 2001: 79).

Famous interviewers include David Frost, the late Sir Robin Day and Jeremy Paxman, the *Newsnight* presenter who asked Home Secretary Michael Howard the same question 14 times without getting an answer (Harcup, 2004: 99). Research on televised political interviews showed how face management had significant implications for the evaluation of the performance of the interviewer (Bull, 2003: 170).

Sir Robin Day said he felt the 'big set-piece television interview' had been hijacked by the politician and ceased to be as effective in counteracting the 'artificial professionalism of politics' (Crewe and Harrop, 1989: 129–30). Interviewees like politicians and celebrities (backed up by **public relations** companies or agents) are probably more media-literate and schooled in the art of **spin** than previously (Harcup, 2004: 95). The public has been increasingly used as interrogator (for example, the *BBC*'s *Question Time*) and this has produced some fascinating confrontations, like Diana Gould's questioning of Margaret Thatcher about the sinking of the *Belgrano* during the Falklands War (Crewe and Harrop, 1989: 135).

See *Ethics*

Further reading

Boyd, A. (2001) *Broadcast Journalism: Techniques of Radio and Television News*, 5th edn. Oxford: Focal Press.

Bull, P. (2003) *The Microanalysis of Political Communication: Claptrap and Ambiguity*. London: Routledge.

Crewe, I. and Harrop, M. (eds) (1989) *Political Communications: The General Election Campaign of 1987*. Cambridge: Cambridge University Press.

Harcup, T. (2004) *Journalism: Principles and Practice*. London: Sage.

Reddick, R. and King, E. (2001) *The Online Journalist: Using the Internet and Other Electronic Resources*, 3rd edn. Orlando, FL: Harcourt Brace and Company.

MGH

121

Journalism Studies

Inverted pyramid

The inverted pyramid (also known as the 'climax first' or the 'top-heavy form') is a standardized format for writing a **hard news** story which places the most important information at the head of the story and uses the lead paragraph to answer the five 'W questions': Who? What? Why? Where? and When? The subsequent paragraphs then unravel the details of the story in declining order of significance, so that any necessary editing of the story can be achieved by simply 'cutting' paragraphs from the bottom of the copy until the desired story length is achieved. This style of writing, pioneered by American journalists in the nineteenth century, replaced the older narrative style according to which journalists reported events in a chronological order: in much the same way as oral story telling proceeds.

There are four widely accepted explanations for the emergence of the inverted pyramid as a professional format at the time of the American Civil War (1861–65), reflecting: (1) the unreliability of the new technology of the telegraph (technological factors); (2) the information policy of the Union (political); (3) the increasing competition between publishers (economic); and, finally, (4) editors and publishers' increasing use of illustrations, headlines and other formats and editorial devices to increase the comprehensibility of their products – in brief 'the professional effort to strengthen the communicative quality of news' (Pottker, 2003: 501).

In a fascinating study which involved analysing the contents of the *New York Herald* and the *New York Times* between 1855 and 1920, journalism scholar Horst Pottker revealed that the inverted pyramid did not emerge as a standard news format in these newspapers until the 1890s, more than two decades later than previous research suggested (Pottker, 2003: 507–10).

Further reading

Pottker, H. (2003) 'News and its Communicative Quality: The Inverted Pyramid – When and Why Did It Appear?', *Journalism Studies*, 4(4): 501–11.

BF

Investigative journalism

The term 'investigative journalist' smacks of pretension, and has few ardent adherents among practitioners. But it helps denote the self-motivation, the experience and knowledge, the methodology and the set of skills which sustain a journalist through a complex, lengthy assignment. The investigative journalist's intent usually embraces the need to (justifiably) defame some person or an organization to expose a scandal and/or speed up institutional or legislative reform. Though British journalists generally face less personal hazard than those in totalitarian or gun-infested nations, the financial stakes of investigative journalism in Britain are very high because of strict **defamation** laws. Even if they provoke no libel claim, investigations are expensive, because of staff time and research outlay, yet may not uncover anything to publish.

Campaigning journalism and press exposure of rogues began in the nineteenth century. But investigative journalism first became a distinct genre in Britain's upmarket press and on the nation's television in the 1960s. Its stimulus was a young generation of reporters who adopted the exposure methods of the popular press, but were more prepared to relate the suffering or dishonesty of individuals to wider social contexts, and to tackle institutional corruption. Better technology made gathering evidence easier (Doig, 1992, 1997) Some of this generation still rank among Britain's best-known journalists.

But the widespread perception in media and academic circles is that investigative journalism has declined, in quality and quantity, since 1970s heydays. Cost-cutting, to facilitate massive profits, in the regional press means many reporters who aspire to investigations can rarely free themselves from mundane tasks. Cost-cutting, and a more competitive market, have also affected the news-gathering operations of national newspapers (Tunstall, 1996). A study by the *Campaign for Quality Television* group has stated that a more 'ratings-driven environment' in TV favours a more emotional and picture-led approach to current affairs at the expense of more analytical or investigative programmes, and that a downward pressure on programme budgets has reduced 'original investigative journalism' (Barnett and Seymour, 1999).

But there are voices which challenge or seek to qualify the dominant perception of decline. De Burgh (2000: 316) argues that pessimism about the future of investigative journalism can seem exaggerated, pointing out that 'new types of outlet are developing and information [e.g. on the **Internet**] is more readily available and testable'.

In the 1990s, the *Guardian* newspaper emerged as a torchbearer of investigations, after its success in investigating 'sleaze' among Conservative politicians (Harding et al., 1997; Leigh and Vulliamy, 1997). And Britain's popular press, however much its content is dominated by stories of celebrities, can still rise to the investigative heights too – not least in the *News of the World*'s skewering of Jeffrey Archer, former deputy chairman of the Conservative Party, leading to his jail term for perjury (Kelso, 2001).

See *Adversarial journalism, Alternative media.*

Further reading

Hanna, M. (2000) 'British Investigative Journalism: Protecting the Continuity of Talent through Changing Times', paper presented at the Professional Education section of the International Association for Media and Communication Research, 22nd General Assembly and annual conference, Singapore.

Linklater, M. (1993) 'An Insight into Insight', *British Journalism Review*, 4(2): 17–20.

Marks, N. (2000) 'Uncovering the Secrets of "Real" Journalism', *Press Gazette*, 14 January, p. 15.

Northmore, D. (1996) *Lifting the Lid: A Guide to Investigative Research.* London: Cassell.

Spark, D. (2000) *Investigative Reporting: A Study in Technique.* Oxford: Focal Press.

MNH

Journalism

At its most basic, journalism consists in finding things out then telling people about them via newspapers, **radio, television** or the **Internet**. It's not a product, but a process, one that used to be seen as a one-way street but more recently has been conceived as involving an **audience** which will filter messages through its own experiences and understanding (Harcup, 2004) and arrive at its own reading.

The notion that journalism has a social role runs throughout many discussions of what it is. According to McNair (2002: 9), it is 'an account of the existing real world as appropriated by the **journalist** and processed in accordance with the particular requirements of the journalistic medium through which it will be disseminated to some section of the public'. McQuail (2000) describes it as paid writing, or the audio-visual equivalent, for public media that refers to current events of public relevance.

But the idea of a social role in the sense that journalism helps people understand the world around them and make informed decisions has mutated. As the structure of the media industries has changed, so, maybe, has journalism. Franklin picks up Malcolm Muggeridge's neologism '**Newszak**' as identifying a retreat from investigative journalism and **hard news** reporting to lighter, softer and more celebrity-driven news. 'The task of journalism has become merely to deliver and serve up what the customer wants; rather like a deep-pan pizza' (Franklin, 1997: 5). Curran and Seaton (1997: 259) say **news values** are becoming less about news in the social sense and 'more about scandals and attracting audience attention'.

Some writers distinguish between types of journalism, for example, gossip journalism, **tabloid** journalism, 'new' journalism, **investigative journalism** and journalism of record (McQuail, 2000). For Randall (2000), there are only two sorts of journalism: good or bad.

Then there are the more colourful definitions. 'Journalism largely consists in saying "Lord Jones Dead" to people who never knew that Lord Jones was alive' (G.K. Chesterton). 'Journalism is a refined version of the instinct that makes people slow down and crane their necks at the scene of a road accident.' (Simpson, 2002: 21). 'Writing for pay about matters of which you are ignorant' (Leslie Stephen, father of writer Virginia Woolf).

Further reading

Curran, J. and Seaton, J. (1997) *Power without Responsibility*, 5th edn. London: Routledge.
Franklin, B. (1997) *Newszak and News Media*. London: Arnold.
Harcup, T. (2004) *Journalism: Principles and Practice*. London: Sage.
McNair, B., Hibberd, M. and Schlesinger, P. (2002) 'Public Access Broadcasting and Democratic Participation in the Age of Mediated Democracy', *Journalism Studies*, 3(3): 407–22.
McQuail, D. ([1987] 2000) *Mass Communication Theory*. London: Sage.
Randall, D. (2000) *The Universal Journalist*. London: Pluto.
Simpson, J. (2002) *News from No Man's Land: Reporting the World*. London: Macmillan.

MK

Journalism of attachment

125

An approach to reporting, born of the war in former Yugoslavia, which argues that journalists should record the human and emotional costs of war rather than acting as 'transmission vehicles' for governmental or military **sources** (Bell, 1996). The journalism of attachment argues that 'reporters cannot remain detached or neutral in the face of modern evils like genocide in Bosnia or Rwanda, but must side with the victims and demand that something-must-be-done' (Hume, 1997: 4). This mantle has been taken up by various **reporters** – Martin Bell who coined the term (1998), Ed Vulliamy, Maggie O'Kane, Jonathan Steele in the UK, Roy Gutman in the USA – and is summarized impeccably by Christiane Amanpour of CNN:

I have come to believe that **objectivity** means giving all sides a fair hearing, but not treating all sides equally. Once you treat all sides the same in a case such as Bosnia, you are drawing a moral equivalence between victim and aggressor. And from here it is a short step to being neutral. And from here it's an even shorter step to becoming an accessory to all manners of evil. (from *Quill* (April, 1996), cited in Hume, 1997: 6)

Thus, the rejection of journalistic neutrality is justified as a consequence of a moral imperative to stand up to wickedness which its proponents see as an indispensable aspect of good journalism (Tumber and Prentoulis, 2003). To adopt the familiar canine metaphor, the attached journalist is a kind of *guide dog*, leading not only the gaze of the audience but also their understanding of, and emotional response to, the **story**.

The movement has not been without its critics. First, 'attached reporting' depends upon conflicts being depicted as battles between the 'Good' and 'Bad', and calls upon journalists to appoint themselves as judges of who to cast in these two polarized roles. On this point, McLaughlin (2002) argues that attached journalism encourages unacceptable self-righteousness and moralizing. Second, once 'guilt' is established, a journalist's responsibility to print all the facts may 'come a poor second place to broadcasting what is considered to be the morally correct line' (Hume, 1997: 4). Thus, uncorroborated stories from the 'good guys' may be reproduced blindly due to their adherence to accepted/acceptable truths, while the un*think*able (regardless of factuality) is avoided.

Third, we must look not only at the problematic issues related to journalists acting as moral arbiters, but also their demands that 'something must be done'. What type of 'something' does attached journalism demand? With wars being reduced to a clash between the forces of Good and Evil, 'it becomes easy to turn the West into the political saviour of the "uncivilised" world and to demand more [military] intervention against the forces of darkness' (Hume, 1997: 15). From such a perspective, Tumber and Prentoulis' suggestion that the events of 11 September 2001 have accelerated 'a trend in which attachment and emotion eventually become fully embraced into the culture of journalism' (2003: 228) sounds like a worrying prospect.

Further reading

Bell, M. (1998) 'The Journalism of Attachment', in Kieran, M. *Media Ethics.* London: Routledge, pp. 15–22.

JER

Journalism education

The term refers to teaching programmes in higher education (mainly in universities) which are a mixture of vocational training in journalism skills (e.g. news-gathering, news writing, broadcast techniques), **ethics** and academic exploration in **journalism studies**. The ratios of the ingredients in this mix, and the extent to which journalism students have access to or must study other disciplines, e.g. the liberal arts or communications, vary between institutions and nations.

Journalism education had begun to establish itself securely in the American academy in the early twentieth century (Johansen et al., 2001: 471) but the British media industry was, for more decades, resistant to the idea of universities offering journalism qualifications. Some British employers believed that a traditional degree – in, say, English literature or politics – provided a more suitable, broader education for journalists (Cole, 1997). Others were mercenarily anti-intellectual, believing any type of graduate would want more pay and shorter apprenticeships, and preferred to send school-leaver apprentices to, or recruit only from, strictly vocational courses at technical or further education colleges (Boyd-Barrett, 1970). Postgraduate courses in journalism did not gain a firm foothold in British universities until the 1971 launch of a diploma at the University of Wales, Cardiff (Melville, 1998). But these pioneering courses quickly produced trainees respected by employers. Undergraduate journalism degrees began to be launched in Britain in the 1990s, and met similar initial suspicion from some quarters of the press, but are now major providers of recruits for the industry. As these undergraduate courses are popular with students, administrators relish them as a source of income. They have proliferated. Some have too many students. They vary greatly in quality.

Further reading

Bromley, M., Tumber, H. and Zelizer, B. (2001) 'Editorial', *Journalism: Theory, Practice and Criticism*, 2(3): 251–4.

Delano, A. and Henningham, J. (1995) *The News Breed: British Journalists in the 1990s.* London: The London College of Printing and Distributive Trades.

Holtz-Bacha, C. and Frolich, R. (eds) (2003) *Journalism Education in Europe and North America: An International Comparison.* Cresskill, NJ; Hampton Press.

Phillips, A. (2003) 'A Question of Degree', *British Journalism Review*, 14(1): 71–5.

Reese, S.D. and Cohen, J. (2000) 'Education for Journalism: The Professionalism of Scholarship', *Journalism Studies*, 1(2): 213–27.

Splichal, S. and Sparks, C. (1994) *Journalists for the 21st century* Norwood, NJ: Ablex.

MNH

Journalism studies

This is the multidisciplinary study of **journalism** as an arena of professional practice and a subject focus for intellectual and academic inquiry. More specifically, it entails the critical analysis of the various processes involved in gathering, evaluating, interpreting, researching, writing, editing, reporting and presenting information and comment on a wide range of subjects (including business, fashion, news, politics, sport and travel), that are disseminated via an expansive range of mass **media** (including the **Internet**, magazines, newspapers, **radio** and **television**) to diverse audiences (distinguished by culture, identity and intellectual interests) resident in local, regional, national and international settings.

Consequently journalism studies does the following:

- adopts an international and multidisciplinary approach to journalism;
- explores both academic and professional concerns and attempts to meld theoretical with practical concerns;
- is attentive to the full range of journalistic specialisms including sport and fashion journalism as well as **hard news** journalism, **photo journalism**, **cartoons** and **agony aunts**;
- considers the divergent media contexts within which journalism is conducted as well as the distinctive patterns of media ownership, finance and journalistic cultures which characterize the different media;
- is international in focus, but addresses local and national media as well as issues arising from the emergent global **newsroom** and the global market for journalism and its products.

BF

128

Journalist

Muck-raking scumbag or noble seeker after truth? Journalism seems to accommodate both stereotypes with the same ease it embraces lurid allegations of the latest celebrity infidelity alongside exposure of serious institutional or individual wrongdoing or serious political and social analysis.

Certainly in the rankings of trustworthiness, journalists regularly feature somewhere around the bottom, along with politicians, used car salesmen and estate agents. Yet scratch a journalist and you'll often find some intriguing mix of idealism and scepticism. You'll always find a passion for the job and a belief, often well hidden, that **journalism** matters.

According to *BBC Newsnight* presenter Jeremy Paxman, journalists are members of the 'awkward squad'. They're not there to be loved or to be popular, but to ask questions some would prefer not to answer. Veteran BBC foreign correspondent John Simpson describes them as, like actors, instantly recognizable to each other if not the rest of the world. 'There tends to be a certain unkempt quality about all journalists . . . a hint of vagueness strangely allied to a driving force which can at times be obsessional, the otherness of a confirmed outsider' (Simpson, 2002: 23) Curran and Seaton (1997: 277) say 'Part of their job is to translate untidy reality into neat **stories** with beginnings, middles and denouements.'

Then there's the passion for writing, for telling people things (preferably first), coupled with an uneasy fear that what they write or tell lacks any serious value. There are the crazy working patterns, the neglected home life.

But if that's *what* a journalist is, *who* are they? A survey by the Journalism Training Forum (Skillset, 2002) found a profession equally split between male and female, mostly under the age of 40, four out of ten are single, widowed or divorced and three-quarters have no dependent children.

Journalism is often seen as a way of informing society about itself, in all society's diversity. Yet the same survey found that 96 per cent of Britain's 70,000 journalists are white and that new journalists are coming from an ever narrower section of society, almost entirely middle class and wealthy enough to get through further education and unpaid work experience. Only 3 per cent of new entrants come from families headed by someone in a skilled or semi-skilled job. As Ray (2003: 167) puts it: 'Can a workforce like this properly reflect and understand society as a whole when it is made up of such a narrow section of it?'

Further reading

Curran, J. and Seaton, J. (1997) *Power without Responsibility*, 5th edn. London: Routledge.
Ray, V. (2003) *The Television News Handbook*. London: Macmillan.
Simpson, J. (2002) *News from No Man's Land: Reporting the World*. London: Macmillan.
Skillset (2002) *Journalists at Work: Their Views on Training, Recruitment and Conditions.* London: The Journalism Training Forum.

MK

Lapdog theory of journalism

Intended as a play on journalists' self-proclaimed 'watchdog' responsibility, the lapdog model suggests that news media are a conduit for the agenda of the society's elites, supporting and perpetuating the exploitation and social inequalities on which they profit (see Golding and Murdock, 2000). More specifically, the lapdog theory can be summarized in the following three assumptions. First, the news media display a lack of independent power, being reliant upon government, corporate and elite sources for both information and economic support (Bagdikian, 1987). Second, journalists show neither understanding nor interest in the opinions, attitudes and information requirements of any other group other than those of society's elite establishment. Third, and consequently, the news media are characterized by a consistent argumentative and political bias to the benefit of these social and corporate authorities to the extent that they appear to act as their trained pooch. In some theorists' views, this deference amounts to a total submission to authority.

A number of criticisms may be levelled at this characterization of the news media; we cite only two here. First, in explaining reporting outcomes, lapdog theory can over-emphasize the overt intensions of individuals to the detriment of more structural or professional explanations. Although journalistic routines and practices are frequently referred to (especially in more structurally founded research such as Herman and Chomsky's (1994) **propaganda model**), the inclination of 'lapdog research' is to return to the beliefs, outlook and motivations apparently shared between journalists and social and economic elites to explain reporting outputs. Second, the model assumes that consensus exists within social and economic elites and hence they may be conceptualized as a united class, sharing beliefs and motivations and acting as a 'class for itself'. This ruling class then mobilize the press to act at their behest. However, conflicts do exist and are reported, and with a moment's thought, numerous examples of 'the bloody victims of press exposure and critique' (Franklin, 1997: 31) can be recalled. The lapdog model has difficulties in explaining the frequently reported conflicts between elite individuals and groups, and is particularly unsuccessful at explaining concerted and sustained media attacks against political leaders. This second criticism forms the *raison d'être* of the '**Guard dog**' theory.

130

Further reading

Bagdikian, B.H. (1987) *The Media Monopoly*. Boston: Beacon Press.

JER

Libel

See *Defamation.*

Licence fee

This is the annual fee paid by everyone who owns a television set to finance the provision of *BBC* radio, television and web-based programmes and services: the government sets the level of the fee.

The significance of the licence fee is that it constitutes a central element of **public service broadcasting**, intended to guarantee the independence of broadcasters from economic (corporate/commercial) and political (especially government) interests and influences (The Sykes Committee 1923 and The Crawford Committee 1925, cited in Franklin, 2001: 218). But, in truth, the licence fee has been used as a lever by governments of all political hues, to try to influence programming and policy at the BBC: famously by Prime Minister Harold Wilson who, dissatisfied with coverage of the Labour Government, confronted a senior BBC executive claiming that 'hell will freeze over before you get a licence fee increase unless we get a better deal out of you' (cited in Franklin, 1994: 82).

Critics of the licence fee claim: (1) it constitutes a regressive, flat-rate fee which takes no account of the ability of particular viewers to pay (Mrs Thatcher described the licence fee as a 'regressive poll tax'); (2) it is unfair since viewers may choose to watch only commercial channels; (3) it is expensive to administer; (4) it encourages evasion of payment; (5) it makes it impossible to assess consumer satisfaction with the service provided, and (6) it implies some degree of political control since the fee level is set by the government. Critics have proposed privatizing the BBC (Hargreaves, 1993), abolishing the licence fee (Boulton, 1991), its eventual replacement by a system of **subscription** (Peacock, 1986, 12.6, paras 671–701), but following an extensive review of alternative funding mechanisms, the Department of National Heritage concluded in favour of the licence fee on the rather uncertain grounds that 'No-one has devised an obviously better system' (1992: 31).

In defence of the licence fee, even the *Peacock Committee*, established to investigate replacing the fee with paid advertising on BBC services, claimed: (1) it provided a secure form of financing for the BBC; (2) it preserves the independence of the BBC; and (3) it enables the BBC to produce programmes of high quality (Peacock, 1986). This last is significant. From the beginning of commercial broadcasting in 1955, the licence fee has been defended on the ground that funding of programmes by **advertising** or a **market-driven**, profit-seeking broadcasting structure, would lead inevitably to a decline in the quality of programmes and the **dumbing down** of standards.

In 1999 an independent review panel, chaired by Gavyn Davies, considered the desirability of establishing a digital licence top-up fee to be levied on owners of digital televisions, to help the BBC unravel its new digital services. But the issue proved so contentious with commercial broadcasters and some politicians, that the then Secretary of State Chris Smith decided against the new top up fee (*The Future Funding of the BBC*, 1999).

The licence fee continues to prove contentious and, as government policy and technological developments nurture a multichannel broadcasting environment which delivers 40,000 hours of broadcast television programming to viewers each week, the BBC may find it increasingly difficult to articulate a legitimate rationale for the continued levying of the licence fee in the context of a declining audience share. Indeed, Ofcom's report on the communication's market revealed that subscription (£3.3 billion) had overtaken both advertising (£3.24bn) and the licence fee (£2.3bn) as the major income source funding television programming (*Ofcom*, 2004c), but the most recent Green Paper on broadcasting (March 2005) confirmed the licence fee as the main source of funding for the BBC until 2012.

132

Further reading

Department of National Heritage (1992). *The Future of the BBC*. London: HMSO;
Franklin, B. (2001) *British Television Policy*. London: Routledge.
Hargreaves, I. (1993) *Sharpter Visions*. London: Demos.

BF

Lobby

The Lobby or Parliamentary lobby has its origins in 1884 when, because of civil disorder, the members' lobby of the House of Commons was closed to the public and access was restricted to political journalists whose names were kept on a list compiled by the Sergeant-at-Arms. The Lobby is a cartel for the provision of political information: in the words of one critic, 'a self-perpetuating elite with written rules, whose members accord government ministers and spokespersons with anonymity in return for privileged access to political information' (Horgan, 2001: 259). It is the formal association of the 220 or so newspaper, radio and television journalists based at the Palace of Westminster who deliver the majority of authoritative political news deriving from briefings by senior politicians and spokespeople (McNair, 2000a: 43–4). This 'elite' expanded in 2003 to include London-based foreign correspondents. Consequently, the daily morning briefings by the **Prime Minister's Press Secretary (PMPS)** (or Official Spokesperson, PMOS) are now conducted at the Foreign Press Association rather than the basement at No. 10: the 4 p.m. briefing is still conducted in the lobby room in the House.

The Lobby has been criticized: (1) because of the secrecy which characterize its operations (Hattersley, 2001: 234); because (2) it packages political news for journalists, and 'produces lazy journalism undertaken by lazy journalists' (Kellner, 1988: 281); (3) because it is used to 'fly kites' allowing politicians to gauge public responses to potential policies (Gaber, 2000: 67); and (4) because it promotes half-truths, lies and gossip (Franklin, 2004a: Chapter 3).

Advocates of the Lobby system argue that: (1) journalists are too diverse in their political affiliations, journalistic backgrounds and understandings of politics to be duped by politicians and official spokespersons; and (2) that criticisms fail to understand how the Lobby works: an official briefing is rarely more than the start for a journalist's story, and rarely the terminus (Barnett and Gaber, 2001: 41).

The lobby, moreover, has changed radically in recent years: (1) since 1997, journalists have been allowed to identify the Prime Minister's Official Spokesperson in their reports; (2) on 11 February 2000, the government launched the Number 10 website (http: //www.Number-10.gov.UK) containing edited extracts from the previous day's lobby briefing; (3) Michael Cockerell's film *News from No 10*, broadcast in July 2000, shattered the tradition of secrecy concerning the lobby by featuring unprecedented footage of a lobby briefing including the arrival of Alastair

Campbell with his advisers and supporters from the *Government Information and Communications Service* (GICS); (4) in July 2000, *Guardian* editor Alan Rusbridger announced that the *Guardian* would adopt a stricter code for journalists to 'encourage reporters to be as specific as possible about the source of any anonymous quotation' (Rusbridger, 2000), in order to prevent the anonymity of lobby briefings being used to attack critics of the Prime Minister; (5) and, finally, on 2 May 2002, Alastair Campbell announced that the 11 a.m. lobby briefings were no longer to be confined to the Westminster-based correspondents, but opened to all journalists, including London based foreign correspondents, to question officials, government experts and sometimes even ministers: since that date some briefings have been televised and the Prime Minister has requested the Phillis Inquiry to consider the desirability of televising all lobby briefings.

BF

Further reading

Barnett, S. and Gaber, I. (2001) *Westminster Tales: The Twenty-first Century Crisis in Political Journalism.* London: Continuum.

Hattersley, R. (2001) 'The Unholy Alliance: The Relationship between Members of Parliament and the Press', James Cameron Lecture 1996, reprinted in Stephenson, H. (ed.) *Media Voices: The James Cameron Memorial Lectures,* London: Politicos, pp. 227–45. http://www.Number-10.gov.UK.

Local newspaper

A local, or regional, newspaper (also known as provincial if based outside London) is described by The Newspaper Society as

> any publication in written form on newsprint or similar medium, published . . . at regular intervals not exceeding seven days, and available regionally rather than nationally (i.e. not available throughout all or most of the British Isles). It should contain **news** and information of a general nature, updated regularly, rather than being devoted to a specific interest or topic. (The Newspaper Society, 2004)

The larger regional newspapers have daily editions, morning or evening – or both. Added to this could be the fact that online editions of local newspapers can potentially reach a national – and global – **audience** and be updated constantly.

Among the traditional 'parish pump' roles of a local newspaper include campaigning on behalf of its **readership** on important issues and championing various causes (The Newspaper Society, 2004). Local newspapers should articulate the history and concerns of a local community and be central to local democracy by providing a forum for public debate' (Franklin, 1997: 114).

The local newspaper was established during the eighteenth century, although the prototypes, primitive in design and content, had to survive attempts by a hostile government to undermine them. The provincial weekly press contained little local **news**, its main function being to amuse as much as to inform (ibid.: 76). The nineteenth century saw the real growth of the provincial press (ibid.: 77). Leading industrialists bought many of the new local dailies which 'encouraged positive identification with the local community and its middle-class leadership' (Curran and Seaton, 1997: 38).

The local daily press provided the majority of working-class people with local, national and international news up until the inter-war period, since when it has undergone much structural change and suffered considerable instability. Franklin and Murphy state seven significant factors for this radical change: a steady decline in the number of local newspaper titles and **circulations**; the arrival of **free newspapers**; increasing use of **advertorials** rather than news; **new technology**; the casualization of the industry; the tabloidization in both size and content of local newspapers – a **dumbing down** which could be described as **McJournalism** (Franklin, 2005); and changes in **ownership** patterns (Franklin and Murphy, 1998a: 7–9). Another reason for this decline is the growth of alternative **sources** of **news** provided by local **radio** and regional **television** services, while multi-skilling means the local **journalist** now performs tasks previously performed by specialist colleagues, for example, subbing as well as writing; this has led to job losses and a decline in quality. In addition, television and radio have become for many the primary sources of news, replacing national and, to a lesser extent, local newspapers (Franklin, 1997: 104, 107, 108).

For more than a century, the typical British newspaper was owned by a local company or local family, and reported the local court and council. Most have now been incorporated into large multinational corporations (for example, Trinity International), a process also involving an increasing overlapping of the national and local press (ibid.: 1997: 108). The few book-length studies of local newspapers include Anne Hayes' *Family in*

135

Print (1996) and *Attacking the Devil: 130 Years of The Northern Echo* by Chris Lloyd (1999).

Added to this grim picture was the demise of the alternative local press (which was born in the 1960s, flourished during the 1970s and 1980s, but died in the 1990s – due among other things – to a lack of capital and new technology resources). These local newspapers adopted a magazine format and combined an alternative news agenda (supporting minorities and focusing on environmental matters) with an events guide within their circulation area. They had a tradition of investigative journalism and were a breeding ground for some of the best, radical journalists such as Duncan Campbell. The closure of the once-successful *Northern Star* (an alternative newspaper published and circulated in West Yorkshire for 20 years and whose history is recounted in Tony Harcup's *A Northern Star: Leeds' Other Paper and the Alternative Press 1974–1994*), signalled the end of local alternative newspapers (Franklin, 1997: 109–11).

The market has been the dominant force overseeing the dramatic change in the local press whose **watchdog journalism** role as part of the democratic process looks bleak (Franklin and Murphy, 1998a: 22).

See *Advertising, Investigative journalism, Media, Press baron, Public relations.*

Further reading

Curran, J. and Seaton, J. (1997) *Power without Responsibility*, 5th edn. London: Routledge.

Franklin, B. (1997) *Newszak and News Media*. London: Arnold.

Franklin, B. and Murphy, D. (1998a) 'Changing Times: Local Newspapers, Technology and Markets', in Franklin, B. and Murphy, D. (eds) *Making the Local News: Local Journalism in Context*. London: Routledge, pp. 7–23.

Franklin, B. (2005) 'McJournalism: The McDonaldization Thesis and the UK Local Press', in Allan, S. (ed.) *Contemporary Journalism: Critical Essays*. Milton Keynes: Open University Press.

Harcup, T. (1994) *A Northern Star: Leeds' Other Paper and the Alternative Press, 1974–1994*. Upton: The Campaign for Press and Broadcasting Freedom (North) MNH.

Hayes, A. (1996) *Family in Print*. Dursley: Bailey Newspaper Group Ltd.

Lloyd, C. (1999) *Attacking the Devil: 130 Years of The Northern Echo*. Darlington: The Northern Echo.

The Newspaper Society (2004) www.newspapersoc.org.uk/home.html.

MGH

Local radio

In the beginning, UK **radio** was local, but because the technology was in its infancy, not because it was planned that way. When the Marconi Company began broadcasting as 2LO in November 1922, it was only to London because the transmitter wasn't powerful enough to reach any further. Over the next two years, the newly created British Broadcasting Company opened 18 more transmitters in other cities, but again their reach was only local.

The Beveridge Report of 1949 first proposed the introduction of local radio as we presently understand it. Former BBC war correspondent Frank Gillard and BBC manager Maurice Ennals are widely credited as the founding fathers of the modern format. The vision came from a visit to America by Gillard, who noted the informality of US radio and the way stations were part of the community (Crisell, 1994). His report went to the BBC in 1954, but it wasn't until the advent of VHF transmitters in 1955 that local broadcasting became technically viable. Experiments finally began in 1963.

There is some evidence to suggest that the BBC was also under pressure from the success of offshore pirate radio (Crisell, 1994) By the mid-1960s, pirate radio audiences were estimated to be over 24 million (Harris, 1970) and **television** was sweeping all before it. With the pirates forced off the air under the Marine Broadcasting (Offences) Act in August 1967, the BBC set about trying to regain some of the audience share it had lost. According to Anthony Smith (1974a), there was a growing feeling that radio and **broadcasting** should become a means of 'two-way' communication.

Nineteen sixty-seven was a year of radical change. The *BBC* launched Radios 2, 3 and 4 to replace the Light Programme, the Third Programme and the Home Service, and radio went properly local. On 8 November of that year, BBC Radio Leicester went on air, broadcasting four hours of locally made programmes aimed at local people each day. It was less than a year before the phone-in, the mainstay of local radio programming, was first heard on BBC Radio Nottingham.

But the BBC didn't have local broadcasting to itself for long. By the late 1960s the Conservative Party had swung behind the idea of competition in radio in response to lobbying from the Local Radio Association and Commercial Broadcasting Associates (Crook, 1998). The runaway success of Manx Radio on the Isle of Man, which began broadcasting as an experiment in **commercial radio** in 1964, also played

137

an influential role. The election manifesto of 1970 contained a pledge to let the commercial sector in.

There are now 38 BBC local radio stations in Britain which take nearly 11 per cent of audience share (*RAJAR*, 2003). They are typically on air about 18 hours a day and speech content can be as high as 80 per cent (Chantler and Harris, 1997). Nearly 260 local commercial stations take over 37 per cent of audience share (RAJAR, 2003). Typically local commercial stations broadcast different music programming on medium wave and FM 24 hours a day and will eventually be available digitally.

See *Independent National Radio, Promise of performance.*

Further reading

Chantler, P. and Harris, S. (1997) *Local Radio Journalism*. Oxford: Focal Press.
Crisell, A. (1994) *Understanding Radio*, 2nd edn. London: Routledge.
Crook, T. (1998) *International Radio Journalism, History, Theory and Practice*. London: Routledge.
Harris, P. (1970) *When Pirates Ruled the Waves*. London: Impulse Books.
Smith, A. (ed.) (1974a) *British Broadcasting*. Newton Abbott: David and Charles.

MK

Macrostructure

The hierarchical organization of meaning in texts. Used most prominently in van Dijk's (1988a; 1988b) analyses of international news stories, macrostructures are a concept developed within the **discourse** analytic tradition of journalism studies. 'The point of macrostructures', van Dijk (no date) argues, is that '**texts** not only have local or microstructural relations between subsequent sentences, but that they also have overall structures that define their global coherence and organisation.' Macrostructures are derived from three rules: 'by eliminating those propositions which are not relevant for the interpretation of other propositions (deletion), by converting a series of specific propositions into a more general proposition (generalisation) and by constructing a proposition from a number of propositions in the text (construction)' (Tomlin et al., 1997: 90). Texts are easier to comprehend when the macrostructure is clearly defined (ibid.).

In terms of news discourse, macrostructures can be useful in analyzing: the very specific non-chronological thematic/topic structure of news stories; the inter-relations between headline, lead paragraph and the information, claims and argumentative moves included lower down an article; and how audience members comprehend and remember news stories. In defining the gist or 'most important information', macrostructures necessarily delete dissenting or counter-factual information, or else generalize it out of the picture. Macrostructures therefore offer one explanation of how a news article can offer a subjective (or even biased) version of an event while simultaneously meeting the requirements of 'an objective report'.

Further reading
van Dijk, T.A. (1988a) *News as Discourse*. Willsdale, NJ: Lawrence Erlbaum Associates.

JER

Market-driven journalism

A phrase associated with John McManus, American media scholar and author of *Market Driven Journalism* (1994a). McManus's thesis is that US journalism no longer reports news in the public interest but is increasingly driven by market considerations which require broadcasters to make rational calculations about the relative financial advantage to be achieved from maximizing income while minimizing costs. He illustrates this general thesis with a detailed examination and analysis of local television news: on McManus's account, news has become a commodity while viewers have metamorphosed into consumers (1992: 799).

McManus argues that this requirement for the lowest possible production costs, combined with the widest possible audience reach, leads to the prominence of certain programme formats in the schedules: typically, repeats, low budget quiz shows, animation and soaps. The implications for the production of news are especially critical and damaging.

Journalistic and economic requirements do not necessarily clash and some events deemed newsworthy by journalistic norms also meet the purely financial considerations of this broadcasting market. Examples here include 'tragedies such as train or airliner crashes, a fatal fire in a tenement building and a mud-slinging debate among political candidates' (McManus, 1994a: 87). But 'if the goal of journalism is public enlightenment, there is potential for conflict with the business goal of maximizing benefit for investors at each stage of news production' (ibid.:

139

88). McManus identifies three such stage of news production: (1) uncovering potentially newsworthy issues and events. Here the most significant news is often the 'most expensive to discover because powerful interests want it hidden' (ibid.); (2) choosing among issues and events selected at stage 1. Here market and journalism norms may collide if 'important stories are dull – such as economic trends or apportionment debates' (ibid.); (3) reporting the story. Journalism requires disinterested, well-rounded reporting of significant sources, context for the story and the checking of any dubious facts. But these processes are expensive because they consume reporters' time and 'if a station seeks to maximize profit, less care may be taken with information. And just as the interesting topic may replace the merely important, the interesting source and quote may replace the informative source and quote' (ibid: 89).

McManus argues that this identification of news as a commodity, produced and sold in a market place, as part of a relentless pursuit of profit (often termed 'bottom line journalism'), inevitably results in a growing tabloidization of news and a perpetual process of **dumbing down**.

See *Minimax programming.*

Further reading

McManus, J. (1992) 'What Kind of Commodity is News?', *Communications Research*, 19(6): 780–812.
McManus, J. (1994a) *Market Driven Journalism*. London: Sage.

BF

Mass communication

Mass communication is the 'technologically and institutionally based mass production and distribution' of symbols, images and messages (Gerbner, 1967: 51) to a heterogeneous and (largely) non-interactive **audience** – in other words, communication through the mass **media**. This only becomes possible 'when technological means are available and social organisations emerge for the mass production and distribution of messages' (ibid.: 50). Only *modern* mass-mediated communication is defined as such, excluding prior forms of *public* communication involving large groups of audience members, such as public speaking, plays and town criers.

Modern mass communication is not only *technologically* different to prior forms of public communication, it is also conceptually and

ideologically different. First, there is no assurance that a mass (e.g. TV or radio) broadcast is even attracting an audience or, if they are, what this audience is like. Objective knowledge of the audience is replaced by assumption and expectation in the mass communicator's decisions of how to monitor what is said (Bell, 1991: 92), occasionally resulting in communicators causing offence. Second, the audience is heterogeneous, creating real difficulties of who to assume is watching/listening and hence how to pitch your communication. On this point, McQuail (1969: 79, cited in Bell, 1991: 90) argues: 'whatever assumptions the communicator makes [about the audience] are bound to be of an imprecise and limited kind'.

Third, mass communication is largely one-way traffic: the 'speaking rights belong to the mass communicator alone' and the audience is rarely involved in providing any direct input or feedback (Bell, 1991: 87). Even **readers' letters** columns and audience participation programmes preserve this imbalance, with the mass communicator holding all the power to include or 'cut off' participants. Fourth, the audience is not only separate from the communicator, they are also (in the main) separate from each other. Mass communicators may attempt to *reduce* this atomization, for example, by recording in front of a studio audience to give the illusion of a shared experience; or they may *engage* with it, by importing aspects of direct inter-personal communication into their mass-mediated products. For example, women's magazines generally speak to their readers as individuals through the direct and singular 'you', and adopt a personal and informal tone of address in order to contrive a sense of intimacy between mass communicator and audience members (Iedema, 1997; Machin and Thornborrow, 2003).

Hence, all the characteristics of mass communication – 'multiple originators, a mass simultaneous audience, a fragmented audience, absence of feedback, and general accessibility to the public' – have a profound effect on media production, 'on audience's ability to understand media content, and on communicators' ability to make themselves understood' (Bell, 1991: 2).

Further reading
Bell, A. (1991) *The Language of News Media*. Oxford: Blackwell.

JER

McDonaldization and McJournalism

In 1993, George Ritzer neologized the term McDonaldization to characterize the highly controlled, bureaucratic and dehumanized nature of contemporary, particularly American, social life. For Ritzer, it is 'the process by which the principles of the fast-food restaurant are coming to dominate more and more sectors of American society as well as the rest of the world' (1993: 1; Schlosser, 2002).

The fast-food restaurant built on principles of efficiency, calculability, predictability and control, where quantity and standardization replace quality and variety as the indicators of value, serves as a highly suggestive metaphor for the general mania for efficiency. Increasing areas of social life are subject to McDonaldization including the contemporary university (Ritzer, 1998: 151–63), and shop and hotel chains (Ritzer, 1993: 88). Some scholars have found it irresistible to add to this list the increasingly standardized **local newspapers** articulating an evident corporate style, the uniform formats of television **journalism** characterized by a preoccupation with going live, conducting **two ways** and the growing obsession with journalists talking to journalists, as well as the banality and homogeneity of the scripted docu-soaps, which are intended to serve as adequate surrogate for genuine documentary (Franklin, 2005). McJournalism has allegedly arrived. Consequently Ritzer nicknames the American paper *USA TODAY*, 'McPaper', while the short pithy articles it publishes are known as 'News McNuggets'. When *USA TODAY* launched a television programme modelled on the paper, some began to call it 'News McRather' (Ritzer, 1993: 4).

The principles of calculability and predictability are crucial to this process. Calculability implies an emphasis on what can be counted and quantified: *quantity*, rather than *quality*, becomes the measure of value (Ritzer 1993: 62–82). So there are 'Big Macs' rather than tasty Macs, large fries but not delicious fries, double and even triple-decker burgers but not wholesome burgers. Big newspapers with expansive pagination and large circulations or VFDs assume a greater significance than quality of editorial. In broadcast journalism the preoccupation with ratings overwhelms and becomes definitive.

Predictability implies standardization. In McDonald's, the settings, the food and the behaviour of the staff are identical (Ritzer, 1993: 83–9): and across time and space. The Big Mac eaten today will be identical to the one eaten yesterday, as well as the one to be bought tomorrow: whether purchased in Wigan, Wakefield or Whitby. Corporate ownership, centralized subbing, slip editions and agency copy guarantee the standardization of the local press. In broadcasting, the rip 'n' read, the *IRN* feed, a move from local to regional newsrooms to achieve cost savings and expansive advertising revenues, increasingly deliver McJournalism over the airwaves. McJournalism guarantees predictable journalism not quality journalism. Viewers get the papers they expect: McJournalism offers few surprises.

Further reading

Franklin, B. (2005) 'McJournalism: The McDonaldization Thesis and the UK Local Press', in Allan, S. (ed.) *Contemporary Journalism: Critical Essays*. Milton Keynes: Open University Press.
Ritzer, G. (1998) *The McDonaldization Thesis*. London: Sage.

BF

Media

Literally, the plural of medium, or the channel in and through which messages are communicated, whether by written, spoken or otherwise semiotic means. Therefore, in contrast to an increasingly unwelcome trend, we write: 'the news media *are*' not 'the news media *is*'; and 'the news media *have*' not 'the news media *has*'.

When people refer to the media more often than not they are in fact referring to the mass media. Mass media are the impersonal – in other words institutionalized – means of **mass communication** through which messages are transmitted to an audience. They are characterized by 'a mechanism of impersonal reproduction' (Klapper, 1949: 3) which acts as a go-between, connecting a speaker and relatively large, heterogeneous and non-present **audience**. Mass media therefore include **radio**, **television**, newspapers, pamphleteering, Party manifestos, magazines, books, cinema films, **advertising**, the **Internet** and mass distributed music, and exclude media such as letters, phone calls and even public speeches, *unless* such communicative messages are reproduced and made available to an audience wider than their immediate participants.

JER

143

Media effects

The phrase media effects implies that media messages have a direct and significant effect on the knowledge, attitudes and even behaviour of members of the audience. In one sense, of course, the claim for media effects is a truism. Even watching the weather forecast will increase viewers' knowledge of the short-term forecast and may even influence their behaviour, encouraging them to take a brolly with them if rain is forecast. But the extent and character of any media effect has been hotly contested (Barker and Petley, 1997: 1–12; Philo and Miller, 1999: 21). It remains the area in mass communications about which 'there is least certainty and least agreement' (McQuail, 1987: 251) with some authors expressing their scepticism about media effects in book titles such as *The More You Watch, The Less You Know* (Schechter, 1997).

Significantly, the effects which it is believed that television and other media can induce are largely *negative*, prompting media theorists to suggest that news portrayals of criminality, sexual behaviour and violence are sufficient to trigger similar socially disruptive behaviour in the audience (Belson, 1978). Following what the press described as 'race riots' in Toxteth, St Pauls, and other urban centres in the early 1980s, politicians tried to prevent broadcast coverage of these events in order to prevent 'copy cat riots' (Tumber, 1982). This belief in media effects is long-standing. Victorian moralists, for example, expressed great concern about the impact of 'penny dreadfuls' on the morals of their young readers, while the judge in the James Bulger case speculated that the child murderers Thompson and Venables had been influenced by watching the video *Child Play III*. These alleged media effects are at the heart of **moral panics** about mugging, sexual permissiveness, HIV/AIDS, alcohol and drug abuse and other anti-social behaviours which envisage media as cause and catalyst in triggering such behaviour (Critcher, 2003).

The phrase 'media effects' also describes a particular tradition in the analysis of the effects of media on audiences: what is sometimes termed the 'hypodermic model', which was later contested by the **two-step flow** and **uses and gratifications** approaches to audiences. The model assumed that media were like needles which injected messages directly into viewers, and with discernible and uniform effects (Kraus and Davis, 1976: 115). But the media effects tradition of audience research has been subject to growing criticism for its assumption of a passive and uncritical audience, which is highly receptive to media messages with little ability to select or make independent judgements about them. Gauntlett has

144

criticized the model as 'inadequate in numerous respects from broadest paradigm assumptions to specific methodological issues' (1996: 7–8; 1997). The emphasis on media effects in audience research has been replaced by reception studies which try to establish how audiences interpret media messages rather than assessing their impact on them.

Further reading

Barker, M. and Petley, J. (1997) *Ill Effects: The Media/Violence Debate*. London: Routledge.
Critcher, C. (2003) *Moral Panics and the Media*. Maidenhead: Open University Press.
Gauntlett, D. (1996) *Video Critical: Children, the Environment and Media Power*. London: John Libbey.
Gauntlett, D. (1997) 'Ten Things Wrong With the "Effects" Model', in Dickinson, R., Harindranath, R. and Linne, O. (eds), *Approaches to Audiences*. London: Arnold.
Philo, G. and Miller, D. (1999) 'The Effective Media', in Philo, G. (ed.), *Message Received*. London: Longman, pp. 21–33.
Schechter, D. (1997) *The More you Watch The Less You Know*. New York: Seven Stories Press.

BF

Media mogul

A person who owns and operates major **media** companies in a personal or eccentric manner, while taking business risks, can be categorized as a media mogul (Tunstall and Palmer, 1991: 105). Those proprietors, traditionally known as **press barons**, are now largely referred to as media moguls as a result of cross-media **ownership**.

The twentieth-century trend towards more concentrated ownership of national (and regional) newspapers means that the power of the press has increasingly been in the hands of a few individuals like Australian-born Rupert Murdoch, owner of News Corporation, with global business interests across a range of media which include a host of national newspapers, and substantial stakes in the Fox Entertainment Group and British Sky Broadcasting (*BSkyB*). These media moguls have often acquired their monopolies as a result of takeovers and mergers, while many also have non-media interests (Franklin, 1997: 95–100). Murdoch was the first – and so far most successful – of this new generation of press barons who were 'ideologically committed and politically interventionist, but also a hard-headed pragmatist, ready to change horses when he feels that the time is right' (McNair, 1999: 146).

One effect of cross-media and concentrated ownership by media

145

moguls is said to be a reduction in editorial autonomy and journalistic standards due to economic and political influence from proprietors; several **editors** under Murdoch have told how he interfered with production and content (Franklin, 1997: 97–100). Andrew Neil, former editor of *The Sunday Times*, recalls that Murdoch's editorial control was subtle although he adds: 'He expects his papers to stand broadly for what he believes' (Neil, 1997: 202, 204). Franklin says: 'Editors have never proved effective in subduing their proprietors' journalistic ambitions' (1997: 99).

There have been claims that Murdoch's influence has extended to governments (Franklin, 1997: 99–100). Indeed, former *Sunday Times* editor Harold Evans says: 'The secret of Murdoch's power over the politicians is, of course, that he is prepared to use his newspapers to reward them for favours given and destroy them for favours denied' (Evans, 1994: xx). Murdoch is arguably the world's only real media mogul having concluded, towards the end of 2003, a takeover of America's largest satellite pay-TV channel (Wolff, 2004: 3), becoming television's non-terrestrial overlord in the process (ibid.: 4).

See *Proprietorialism*

Further reading

Evans, H. (1994) *Good Times, Bad Times*, 3rd edn. London: Phoenix.
Franklin, B. (1997) *Newszak and News Media*. London: Arnold.
McNair, B. (1999) *News and Journalism in the UK*, 3rd edn. London: Routledge.
Neil, A. (1997) *Full Disclosure*. London: Pan Books.
Tunstall, J. and Palmer, M. (1991) *Media Moguls*. London: Routledge.
Wolff, M. (2004) 'And Then There Was Murdoch', *Media Guardian*, 5 January.

MGH

Media scrum

The drive to get the story first, to get the right quote, the right interview, the right pictures are at the heart of daily journalism and in the white heat of a breaking story, **reporters** are very often chasing the same person. And at the same location. So it's your question, your microphone, your camera that's fighting everyone else's.

The ability to elbow your way to the front and a loud voice are two essentials for journalistic success in a media scrum. Favourite locations are outside courts at the close of a big trial, outside the house of a celebrity or politician, or impromptu press conferences.

For ordinary people who are thrust unexpectedly into the limelight, the sea of television cameras, microphones and popping flashguns is unnerving. Less so for those who court publicity or who are used to celebrity.

But there have been occasions where the pack instincts of journalists and the necessity of covering a story have led to intrusion and the kind of behaviour which gives journalism a bad name. After the Zeebrugge ferry disaster of 1987 an article in *UK Press Gazette* described how there had been incidents of reporters and photographers scuffling with relatives in hospital wards.

By the time it came to the Dunblane shootings in Scotland in 1996, when 15 primary school children and their teacher were shot dead in a school gym, some lessons appeared to have been learnt. Richard Sambrook, then editor of BBC television newsgathering, told the *Guardian* newspaper that editors, film crews and reporters had been briefed that 'there was to be no doorstepping and no close-ups of grieving families' (Boyd, 2001: 208).

MK

Further reading

Boyd, A. (2001) *Broadcast Journalism: Techniques of Radio and Television News*, 5th edn. Oxford: Focal Press.

Hammond, J. (1987) 'Ashamed of the Press', *UK Press Gazette*, 23 March, reproduced in Boyd, A. (2001), *Broadcast Journalism, Techniques of Radio and Television News*. Oxford: Focal Press.

Metaphor

147

A familiar concept to most, a metaphor, in the most general sense, involves perceiving one thing in terms of another. More specifically, a metaphor is a condensed analogy, in which the meanings (direct and implicit) of a person or object are superimposed upon another person or object in the following form: 'some physical, behavioural or ideational quality/characteristic of X is comparable to a corresponding physical, behavioural or ideational quality of Y'. Take the economy, for example. We can talk about an economy being 'overheated' or 'stagnating', 'tiger economies', 'peaks' and 'troughs' in production, 'a financial boom', the 'bubble bursting' or a range of other metaphors which are employed in order to understand financial affairs in terms of something else.

Certain types of metaphor are associated with specific genres of journalism. Metaphors of war are frequently, indeed ubiquitously, employed in sports reporting, for example, the *Daily Mirror*, a British tabloid, described rugby player Dan Luger as 'a strike weapon England need in their armoury' (3 January 2003). The choice of metaphor can also be socially significant, with metaphors used to 'negativize' people, personal characteristics and/or political positions. To this end, metaphors drawing upon disease/germs, natural disasters (floods and fires) and (dirty or unattractive) animals are frequently employed to refer to and represent foreigners or ethnic and 'racial' minorities. For example, when describing one particular area of Cairo, the *Guardian* suggested Imbaba 'is a breeding ground for Islamic fundamentalists' (4 October 1997). Here the paper applies a metaphor of uncontrolled biological growth, implying that the 'Islamic fundamentalists' in this area of Cairo are comparable to germs, or perhaps animals.

Further reading

Montgomery, M., Durant, A., Fabb, N., Furniss, T. and Mills, S. (2000) *Ways of Reading: Advanced Reading Skills for Students of English Literature*. London: Routledge.
Reisigl, M. and Wodak, R. (2001) *Discourse and Discrimination: Rhetorics of Racism and Anti-Semitism*. London: Routledge, pp. 45–54.

JER

Metonym

A figure of speech in which one word, phrase or object is substituted for another from a semantically related field of reference. Metonymy differs from **metaphor**, in that metaphors operate through transference of similar characteristics while metonymy operates through more direct forms of association: in other words, something associated with X is substituted for X. Reisigl and Wodak (2001: 56–8) detail a number of metonymic replacements:

- the cause or creator is replaced by the product, e.g. 'the Anti-terrorism, Crime and Security Act 2001 criminalizes Muslims';
- the user of an object replaced by the object, e.g. 'the trains are on strike';
- people replaced by a place in which these people work/are staying, e.g. 'The White House declared'; 'the detention centre erupted into violence';
- events replaced by the date on which these events occurred, e.g.

'September 11th must never be allowed to occur again';
- a country, or state, replaced by (certain) people living in this country, e.g. 'We cannot let the evil of ethnic cleansing stand. We must not rest until it is reversed' (Tony Blair, 22 April 1999, cited in Fairclough, 2000: 148).

Metonyms assume and require a basis of shared knowledge. For example, if we were unaware of the terrorist events of 11 September 2001, we would either not understand the metonym above or else believe that the speaker was proposing to erase a date from the calendar. More significantly, 'metonyms enable the speakers [or writers] to conjure away responsible, involved or affected actors (whether victims or perpetrators), or to keep them in the semantic background' (Reisigl and Wodak, 2001: 58). Occasionally, therefore, metonyms may be intentionally employed to background uncomfortable information or knowledge.

Further reading

Reisigl, M. and Wodak, R. (2001) *Discourse and Discrimination: Rhetorics of Racism and Anti-Semitism*. London: Routledge, pp. 45–54.

JER

Minimax programming

The emergence of the 'minimax' programming philosophy reflects the increasingly competitive markets in which television and radio broadcasting operate, which foster a relentless search for audiences and, in the commercial sector, advertisers (Golding and Murdock, 1973).

When competition was limited to the *BBC* and *ITV* (the 'comfortable duopoly' which preceded the emergence of *Channel 4* (1982) and *BSkyB* (1989)), broadcasters believed competition would serve to enhance programme quality, i.e. competition would oblige broadcasters to raise their game. But in the deregulated, multi-channel broadcasting ecology of the new millennium, competition has the opposite effect and encourages a minimax programming philosophy in which the broadcasting of low budget popular programmes such as quizzes, bought-in American sit-coms and repeat programmes, *minimizes* programmes costs while *maximizing* potential audiences and advertisers. As American scholar John McManus observed, 'when the business goal of maximising profits dominates . . . rational organizations will offer the least expensive mix of contents that garners the largest audiences that advertisers will pay to reach' (1992: 799).

149

This minimax programming philosophy has fairly severe implications for the presentation of news in such a 'market-driven' (McManus, 1994a) broadcasting environment, since news and current affairs programming is expensive to produce but relatively unpopular with viewers. Consequently, the journalistic and economic ambitions of a news organization may conflict and, McManus argues, in such circumstances the minimax commitments of the organization suggest that financial considerations will trump journalistic concerns. 'Given the actual news market and the particular nature of news as a commodity', McManus argues, 'the logic of maximising [economic outcomes] often conflicts with the logic of maximising public understanding' (1992: 800). The provision of a comprehensive news service arguably requires broadcasters to adopt a 'maximin' approach to programming and to incorporate **public service** commitments into their calculations concerning programme provision.

Further reading

Golding, P. and Murdock, G. (1973) 'For a Political Economy of Mass Media', in Miliband, R. and Saville, J. (eds) *Socialist Register*. London: Merlin, pp. 205–34.
McManus, J. (1992) 'What Kind of Commodity is News?', *Communications Research*, 19(6): 780–812.
McManus, J. (1994a) *Market Driven Journalism*. London: Sage.

BF

Modality

The counterpart of **transitivity**, modality refers to comment and attitude in language, and the degree to which a speaker or writer is committed to the claim s/he is making. Modality is usually indicated via the use of modal verbs (such as *may, could, should, will, must*), their negations (*may not, couldn't, shouldn't, will not* and *must not*) or through adverbs (*certainly*). A regular feature of more 'opinionated' genres of journalism such as the editorial, the letter and the op/ed page, modality may be expressed in two principal forms: truth modality; and obligation modality. Truth modality varies along a scale of options from the absolutely categorical ('This war *will* be stopped if the people intervene in the political process') through to varying degrees of hedging ('*We believe* that this war *can* be stopped if the people intervene in the political process') and reduced certainty ('*We believe* that this war *might* be stopped if *only* the people intervene in the political process'). Categorical modal truth claims (*will, was, certainly*, etc.) appear more authoritative than hedged claims and therefore tend to be used more frequently in argumentative **discourse**.

Obligation modality refers to future events, and specifically the degree to which the speaker/writer believes that a certain course of action, or certain decisions *ought* or *should* be taken. Again, this modality can be expressed in categorical terms ('children's rights *must* take precedence over the profit motive of private-sector companies') or more cautiously ('children's rights *ought to* take precedence over the profit motive of private-sector companies').

Modal choices are an indication of the attitudes, judgements or political beliefs of the writer/speaker. They therefore provide a window into the political functions, and the potential political effects, of the language of journalism.

Further reading

Fairclough, N. (2000) *New Labour, New Language?* London: Routledge.
Fowler, R. (1991) *Language in the News: Discourse and Ideology in the Press.* London: Routledge and Kegan Paul.

JER

Modern mainstream

This was the phrase chosen by *Channel 5* to describe its early programming philosophy and output. Launched on 30 March 1997, but progeny of the Broadcasting Act 1990, Channel 5 was never given a clear identity or programming remit by the legislation (Franklin, 1997: 198). The application bid to the *ITC* by Channel 5 Broadcasting, which was eventually awarded the licence, was more than a little ambiguous about its programming intentions. Channel 5 would 'cater for a variety of tastes' and 'respond to public demand' without always following the 'wishes of the majority' by offering 'a user friendly schedule of programmes for everyone' (Channel 5 Broadcasting, 1995: 2).

Dawn Airey, programme director for the infant channel, inaugurated a new programming philosophy. Contra Reith's suggestion that broadcasting's mission should be to 'educate, inform and entertain', Airey announced that Channel 5, programming would focus on the 3 fs: in her infamous phrase, Channel 5 would specialize in 'football, films and fucking'. The approach proved successful and substantially improved audiences and reach, but Airey's departure in 2003, combined with a reduced emphasis on soft pornography in late night schedules, saw audiences for Channel 5 dropping. Current audience share seems immobile at 6.5 per cent reflecting the modest programming budget which was a mere £153 million in 2003: approximately one-quarter of *Channel 4*'s programme budget (Brown, 2003: 6).

Further reading

Brown, M. (2003) 'Now – Can Five Maintain its Momentum?', *Guardian* 14 July, pp. 6–7.
Franklin, B. (1997) *Newszak and News Media*. London: Arnold.

BF

Moral panic

A concept first used by Cohen (1973) to describe orchestrated and mass mediated public campaigns aimed at generating fear of visibly identified 'folk devils'. Moral panics are directed at bringing about changes in law, policy or current practices (which are represented as being lax or too lenient) in order to protect the public from the identified threat. However, we should be careful not to suggest that a moral panic is an actual 'thing'. Rather, as Critcher (2003: 2) suggests, a moral panic is 'a model of a process' displaying several key characteristics. These characteristics do not necessarily manifest themselves sequentially as moral panics tend to have a 'circular and amplifying' structure rather than a linear development (Cohen, 1973: 24). Nevertheless, six processes can be identified (Critcher, 2003), which usually first appear in the following order.

First, some thing or a group of people is identified as a threat to safety, values or interests. Here, the 'enemy' (real or putative) is identified, the good and the bad are separated and the public are informed of the danger they are assumed to face. Second, the threat is distilled, simplified and depicted in an easily recognizable form by the mass **media**. This simplification usually involves a *distortion* of 'the problem'; *prediction* that such events will recur; and *symbolization*, such that (for example) all youth (sub)culture becomes criminalized or all sex crime becomes paedophilic (Critcher, 2003: 12).

Third, there is a rapid build-up of public concern, or at least there is a construction and exaggeration of public concern by **primary** and secondary **definers** of the panic. If the object of the moral panic has yet to produce negative social effects, then the mass media may emphasize not so much what did happen as what *could* have and may still happen

(Cohen, 1973: 53–4). Fourth, the elevation of the panic and accompanying demand that 'something needs to be done' elicit a response from 'moral entrepreneurs', opinion makers and 'other right-thinking people' (ibid.: 9) which, fifth, provokes governmental or legal authorities into implementing a way of coping with the problem. In the words of Goode and Ben-Yahuda (1994: 82), 'legislation or law enforcement' – the creation of new penalties or the more forceful application of current penalties – 'are two of the most obvious and widely resorted to efforts to crush a putative threat during a moral panic'. Sixth, and finally, the panic results in some form of (real or ostensible) social change and goes into remission.

As Critcher (2003: 17–18) illustrates, the model produces as many questions as answers. Most notably, in the emergence phase: 'In what form does the "problem" emerge? What is perceived as novel about it?' Later, when the panic has developed, 'Who are the significant moral entrepreneurs?'; and later still 'What solutions are advocated and by whom?' By applying these questions and others in his analysis of recent news coverage of AIDS, rave/ecstasy use, child abuse and paedophilia, Critcher is able to 'get behind' moral panics and properly interrogate both their ideological underpinnings and the way in which they can be invoked to drive through (often regressive) social change.

Further reading

Cohen, S. (1973) *Folk Devils and Moral Panics: The Creation of the Mods and Rockers.* St Albans: Paladin.
Critcher, C. (2003) *Moral Panics and the Media.* Maidenhead: Open University Press.

JER

Multiculturalism

The vast majority of societies are, and arguably have always been, composed of a number of communities, religions and cultures, each characterized by (usually overlapping) values, beliefs and practices. In its most general sense, multiculturalism recognizes this plurality of culture and community as a positive feature of contemporary societies and aims at counteracting the decades of Western governmental practices that were directed at assimilating Black communities into mainstream White culture. Multiculturalism can therefore be considered as a theory of racialized identity which informs institutional practices. While there are many different approaches to multiculturalism (see Parekh, 1997), it is perhaps most fruitful to concentrate on the theory and practice of *pluralist* multiculturalism, given its influence and rise to an almost normative status within governmental and media policy.

Up until the end of the 1970s, 'social equality' was interpreted (at least in the mainstream) as Black people's right to be 'White like Us'. Consequently, the very notion of social equality was brought into question, because it appeared tainted by a value system which viewed White culture as the 'normal' and most desirable culture. In response, pluralist multiculturalists suggested that to argue for equality ignores differences within society, and instead we should celebrate *cultural diversity* and 'the right to be different'. Kenan Malik (1996: 217) offers four core ideas that underpin this multiculturalism:

> first, that social groups define themselves by their history and identity; second, that the particular history and identity of each group sets them apart from other social groups; third, that it is important to recognise this plurality of differences as a positive aspect of society today; and finally, that the struggle for racial equality takes the form of a struggle for group identity.

Malik is particularly antagonistic towards this approach to multiculturalism, arguing that all pluralists want is for 'their particular history, their particular culture, their particular story to be acknowledged. Pluralism is about accepting the common framework of society but arguing that we want to be included too' (1996: 263). Pluralist multiculturalism focuses on symbolically recognizing – and just as importantly *celebrating* – racial and **ethnic** difference without requiring policy-makers to contest **racism** and racial inequalities. It therefore encourages White university lecturers to teach courses on the contributions of Black British communities, but doesn't address the embarrassingly low number of Black University lecturers; pluralist multiculturalism encourages journalists to write about Black communities in complimentary ways but does not require newspapers to employ more Black journalists, and certainly not at an editorial level.

Too often 'multi-cultural reporting practices' have adopted a 'superficial and seemingly static understanding of cultural difference' (Cottle, 2000: 217; see also Richardson, 2001b), emphasizing the 'exotic', the 'colourful' and the 'different' (Cottle, 1993). Somewhat ironically therefore, this 'saris, samosas and steel-bands' approach to multiculturalism maintains the power of White mainstream culture, since

154

'White-ness' remains the normative culture against which the 'exotic difference' of Black communities is judged.

Further reading

Cottle, S. (ed.) (2000b) *Ethnic Minorities and the Media*. Buckingham: Open University Press.

Malik, K. (1996) *The Meaning of Race: Race, History and Culture in Western Society*. Basingstoke: Macmillan.

JER

Multimedia

The **reporter** of the future may be equipped with more than just a pen and notebook or microphone; add a digital camera (still and motion pictures) and the truly multimedia **journalist** will be born. Multimedia has assumed many identities and been given countless definitions over the years, depending on the context within which it is mentioned (Feldman, 1997; Wise, 2000; De Wolk, 2001). The most practically applicable, particularly in relation to the **Internet**, would appear to be that put forward by Feldman who describes it as the 'seamless integration of data, text, sound and images of all kinds within a single, digital information environment . . . a new content experience on the Web' (1997: 24, 155). Deuze says multimedia **journalism** can be defined in two ways: As the presentation of a **news** story package on a **website** using two or more **media** formats; or as the integrated presentation of a news package through different media but not necessarily simultaneously (2004: 140).

The development of multimedia from slide shows with sound (Wise, 2000: 1) to the age of digital video (Feldman, 1997: 25) has been influenced by many factors, including economic, cultural and technological; it has meant different things in different eras. The key concept and technology behind modern-day multimedia is **digitization** (Wise, 2000: 2).

One of the major strengths of **online journalism** is that the **world wide web** can facilitate multimedia better than any other medium – a single journalist can be responsible for gathering all this material, demanding that journalists learn new multimedia skills, making them more versatile and breaking down the once-rigid barriers between different mediums (Reddick and King, 2001: 242–3) and, in some cases, leading to role **convergence** (De Wolk, 2001: 111).

Multimedia is having a profound effect on the style of journalism being produced on the world wide web: 'New media technology is enabling the emergence of a new form of news perhaps best described as **contextualized journalism** . . . [which] incorporates not only the multimedia capabilities of digital platforms but also the interactive, **hypermedia**, fluid qualities of online communications and the customizable features of addressable media' (Pavlik, 2001: 217). **Hypertext** naturally supports multimedia interfaces as it is based on the interlinking of nodes that can contain different media (Nielsen, 1995: 6). Multimedia can provide multiple textures to journalism – even more so with the eventual convergence of **television** and the world wide web (Ward, 2002: 22). The *BBC* and *CNN* offer their content effectively online and video in particular will grow in importance for major broadcasters like them as the quality and speed of delivery improves (ibid.: 135). The advantages of multimedia for web users include range and flexibility of access, plus the availability of archives varied and rich in content (ibid.: 137–138).

Multimedia online news can also offer specific features such as webcasting, can provide maps and diagrams, and polls, in addition to nurturing partnerships and resulting in mergers between different media companies, for example, with NBC and MSNBC who can deliver news on television, cable and the world wide web (Hall, J. 2001: 42–3). De Wolk says multimedia will distinguish the news and information of the future (2001: 13–15), with **reporters** taught to 'think visually for every **story** they produce and to abandon words when graphics or video or stills works better' (Stevens, in De Wolk, 2001: 106).

One disadvantage of offering multimedia on the world wide web is that those without broadband technology, which allows users to download (large) files and access websites faster due to far greater **bandwidth**, cannot view good quality video footage (BBCi, 2003). 'The most exciting part of online journalism is the future. The technical bogeyman is the bandwidth' (De Wolk, 2001: 119). This situation is likely to improve, however, as broadband becomes more common on home PCs.

See *Interactivity*

Further reading

Deuze, M. (2004) 'What is Multimedia Journalism?' *Journalism Studies*, 5(2): 139–52.
De Wolk, R. (2001) *Introduction to Online Journalism*. Boston: Allyn and Bacon.
Feldman, T. (1997) *An Introduction to Digital Media*. London: Routledge.
Hall, J. (2001) *Online Journalism: A Critical Primer*. London: Pluto Press.
Nielsen, J. (1995) *Multimedia and Hypertext: The Internet and Beyond*. London: Academic Press.
Pavlik, J.V. (2001) *Journalism and New Media*. Columbia, NY: University Press.

156

Reddick, R. and King, E. (2001) *The Online Journalist: Using the Internet and Other Electronic Resources*, 3rd edn. Orlando, FL: Harcourt Brace and Company.

Stevens, J. (2001) 'Where Are the New Storytellers?', in De Wolk, R. *Introduction to Online Journalism*. Boston: Allyn and Bacon.

Ward, M. (2002) *Journalism Online* Oxford: Focal Press.

Wise, R. (2000) *Multimedia: A Critical Introduction*. London: Routledge.

MGH

Myth

Imagine for a moment the visual rhetoric which a broadcast news item about 'juvenile delinquency' may use. The journalist could establish the setting by using a montage of shots: graffiti; a broken window; a derelict house; a burnt out car; all presented over a hip-hop soundtrack. These images, and the marriage of sound and vision, invoke a myth of crime and youth crime in particular: that it is urban and 'inner city' specifically; that it is correlated with deprivation; that it is working class; that it is Black. Despite the fact that as much crime is committed by white middle-class juveniles (particularly drug crime), a piece on youth crime will only usually open with shots of leafy suburbia if the journalist is creating an explicit juxtaposition between a story and 'what we expect'. This is the basis of a myth. Developed by Roland Barthes ([1957]2000), a myth is a sign which takes on the (often ideological) values of wider society and makes them seem natural. In the terms of semiotic theory (see **sign**), myths 'are connotations that appear to be denotations' (Lacey, 1998: 68). We 'automatically' associate red roses and romance; we 'automatically' associate masculinity with strength and athleticism (well, my thesaurus does anyway); we 'automatically' associate good looks with success. But these are myths: social constructions (re)produced in and by **discourse**.

Further reading

Barthes, R. ([1957]2000) *Mythologies*. London: Vintage.

JER

Narrative

In essence, narrative is 'the **story**'. 'Journalists', Bell argues 'are professional story tellers of our age. The fairy tale starts: "Once upon a time." The news story begins: "Fifteen people were injured today when a bus plunged . . ." The journalist's work is focused on the getting and writing of stories' (1991: 147) and 'good stories' are always at the centre of good journalism.

When considering narratives, we first need to distinguish between the narrative *content* and the narrative *form* (Montgomery et al., 2000). Narrative content is the actual sequence of events in the story: in essence, the plot, or the structure of actions. The basic narrative structure, first discussed by Aristotle in his *Poetics* (1962), develops along the following trajectory: introduction of characters and setting, rising action, introduction of complication, climax in which the complication is overcome, and the final resolution. However, news narratives are very rarely this complete because of their focus on ever-unfolding social events. Instead the news is structured around a simpler plot which 'contains three inter-related events, of which the first and third state a certain situation, while the second is active. The third event depicts a change in the state of affairs as compared to the first event' (Prince, 1973, cited in Alasuutari, 1995: 71). In other words, news narrative is constituted by a three-part structure of *setting, complication* and *outcome*, lacking a final resolution. This plot is not only a sequence of events but an order of *meaning*. We need to apply knowledge in order to establish a coherent link between the situation and the action, or the relationship between events in a plot.

Narrative *form* is the sequence in which events are presented to us. A narrative may be fragmented, episodic, chronological or employ non-sequential devices such as 'flash-backs'. Hard news narratives are organized in relation to the **inverted pyramid**, with more significant elements located at the top of a story, and hence rarely take a chronological form. In terms of the three-part plot structure suggested above, news narrative usually takes the form: *complication* (the actual reported 'event'), the *outcome* and then the *setting* or background to the story. The significance of this narrative form, particularly to the way in which news is read and understood, has been studied most fruitfully by Bell (1991).

However, if the discussion ended here, then we would omit the true significance of narrative. As Foss (1996: 399) suggests, 'narratives help us impose order on the flow of experience so that we can make sense of events and actions in our lives'. Further, 'stories usually concern noteworthy [newsworthy?] events' (ibid.: 192). And, because 'stories recount events that depart from the ordinary, they also serve to articulate and sustain common understandings of what the culture deems ordinary' (Ochs, 1997: 193). Thus, narratives are a reflection and a product of nothing less than our 'general cultural assumptions and values – what we consider important, trivial, fortunate, tragic, good, evil, and what impels movement from one to another' (Martin, 1986: 87). As such, news narratives illustrate and propagate social values, providing us with a means of organizing and therefore comprehending the events of the world around us.

Further reading

Bell, A. (1991) *The Language of News Media*. Oxford: Blackwell.
Montgomery, M., et al. (2000) *Ways of Reading: Advanced Reading Skills for Students of English Literature*. London: Routledge.
Ochs, E. (1997) 'Narrative', in van Dijk, T.A. (ed.) *Discourse as Structure and Process*. London: Sage, pp. 185–207.

JER

Narrowcasting/niche broadcasting

A term of the moment in the early to mid-1990s. As the number of broadcast outlets expanded exponentially and technological advance made production cheaper, so the fight for audiences became tougher. At the same time, broadcasters became more sharply aware of who they were **broadcasting** to – the **target audience**. They redoubled efforts to find gaps in the market and develop new types of programming that would attract viewers.

With the advent of cable and satellite television it became possible to assume that only a limited number of people, or a particular group of people, would be interested in a particular programme, a notion exploited successfully in subjects like music and sport by MTV and Sky.

The idea is more entrenched in American and Australian broadcasting. The Australian Broadcasting Authority (2002) goes so far as to formally define narrowcasting services as those which either target special interest groups, are intended for limited locations like arenas, last for a limited period or provide programmes of limited appeal.

Further reading

Australian Broadcasting Authority (2002) *Narrowcasting for Radio: Guidelines and Information about Open Subscription Narrowcasting Radio Services*, available at www.aba.gov.au/radio.

MK

159

National press

For geographical reasons (including the pattern of its road and rail network) and because of a long historical continuity in its newspaper industry, Britain has more truly 'national' newspapers than most large democracies. There are five upmarket daily papers (*The Times, Daily Telegraph, Independent*, the *Guardian, The Financial Times*), two mid-market (*Daily Mail, Daily Express*) and three downmarket (the *Sun, Daily Mirror, Daily Star*) and their Sunday stablemates, all based in London (Tunstall, 1996: 7). British readership habits run comparatively deep. The total circulation of these daily papers, jostling in this fiercely competitive market, remains around 12 million copies, a figure higher than the combined total of the circulations of the French, German, and Spanish national press (Sanders, 2003: 4–5). 'Because they are so competitive, these [British] newspapers have none of those inhibitions which semi-monopoly generates elsewhere. The London newspapers are less restrained than the leading newspapers of most other countries' (Tunstall, 1996: 3). This energy, and the fact that London is an extremely dominant, national political arena, bestow on these papers, rather than television or radio, a significant **agenda setting** function. Consequently the political positions (historically, predominantly right-wing) adopted by editors of Britain's national newspapers, or by their corporate owners, are regarded as particularly influential, compared to the influence of national press in other European states. Cost-cutting reductions in the number of the national newspaper journalists based in other British cities and regions (ibid.: 73–5) means this agenda is now even more London-centric, perhaps making editors slower to recognize social change and trends.

The febrile rivalry for exclusive and investigative stories in this market is possibly one reason why British journalists are more likely to approve the use of some news-gathering methods (e.g. **chequebook journalism**, subterfuge) which American journalists tend to disapprove of (Henningham and Delano, 1998: 157).

MNH

New media

This is a broad **communication** concept which can refer to any of the following related terms: emerging digital technologies and platforms;

online journalism; and electronic and **multimedia** publishing (particularly on the **Internet** and **world wide web**).

MGH

New technology

The **media** have undergone a series of technological revolutions since Johann Gutenberg's first printing press in the 1400s effectively paved the way for the emergence of the press nearly 200 years later (De La Mare, 1997).

All have been dramatic in their impact on the industry, including the advent of **radio, television** and the **Internet**, but none have been bloodier or more controversial than the computer-based print technology imposed on the **national press** between 1986 and 1989 which 'marked a decisive watershed for British newspapers' (Franklin, 1997: 101).

The first significant print technological innovation of the twentieth century took place at the *Wolverhampton Star* series which went over to web offset in the 1960s, abandoning the century-old hot-metal process. Other local newspaper groups followed, some introducing colour printing, but this trend did not spread into the national press in the UK until later (Franklin and Murphy, 1998b: 14).

The second phase, 'more radical and more significant', followed the introduction two decades later of new industrial relations legislation by Margaret Thatcher's government which effectively outlawed secondary strike action and intimidatory pickets (ibid.: 15). It meant that **free newspaper** publisher Eddie Shah won his battle with the National Graphical Association (NGA) over the imposition of new technology in the North West of England (Franklin, 1997: 101).

Until then, skilled printers, operating the linotype machines used in the hot-metal method, and their unions had been successful in resisting the computer-based technology which enabled **journalists** and **advertising** staff to input their work directly, reducing the need for many of the printing jobs and therefore cutting costs, but Shah's victory precipitated the climate of change on a national scale.

Media mogul Rupert Murdoch led the national revolution by moving production of his UK newspapers, previously based on **Fleet Street**, to a new, non-union plant at Wapping in East London, a fact he managed to keep secret from the unions until the last minute. Murdoch set up an alternative distribution system and took on an alternative production

161

workforce to operate the new technology. Predictably, the unions did not agree to Murdoch's new terms and his Fleet Street workers were involved in a year-long cycle of mass picketing and violence outside 'Fortress Wapping', which was protected by '12-foot-high spiked steel railings topped by coils of razor wire and monitored by closed-circuit TV cameras' (Greenslade, 2003). The ensuing trouble resulted in some workers being jailed and their unions fined. Murdoch's rival press groups subsequently introduced new technology, leading to a wave of redundancies in the industry (Curran and Seaton, 1997: 102–3), with Wapping marking the 'beginning of the end of Fleet Street' (Greenslade, 2003). Former *Sunday Times* editor Harold Evans described it as the 'emancipation of journalism from the decadent print unions' (Evans, 1994: xvii).

The new technology gave management more control over the production process, while providing more opportunity for editions to be updated with late **stories**. Colour printing was introduced and facsimile transmission adopted, allowing the simultaneous printing of newspapers to take place at different sites (Franklin, 1997: 101).

New technology has continued to have a major effect on the industry in general, and on **journalists** in particular, with the arrival of the Internet as a **source** of information and news, and the introduction of high-powered laptop computers, portable telephones and digital cameras making it possible for stories and images to be filed within seconds in an age of around-the-clock news. The trend has meant in many cases the isolation of journalists from the **newsroom**, an increase in **freelance** work and the need for multi-skilling (ibid.: 102).

162

Many thought new print technology would produce an age of press plurality to challenge the dominance and power enjoyed by established publishers, but in reality the launching of new national titles still required major resources, 'downsizing' the production force did not alter the economics of publishing (Curran and Seaton, 1997: 103), and technological change has simply strengthened the hand of the powerful newspaper monopolies (Franklin, 1997: 102–3). In this way, it also failed to produce a corresponding editorial revolution, except for the addition of two national titles and the arrival of fatter newspapers (Curran and Seaton, 1997: 105).

Further reading

Curran, J. and Seaton, J. (1997) *Power without Responsibility*, 5th edn. London: Routledge.
Evans, H. (1994) *Good Times, Bad Times*, 3rd edn. London: Phoenix.
Franklin, B. (1997) *Newszak and News Media*. London: Arnold.

Franklin, B. and Murphy, D. (1998a) 'Changing Times: Local Newspapers, Technology and Markets', in Franklin, B. and Murphy, D. (eds) *Making the Local News: Local Journalism in Context.* London: Routledge, pp. 7–23.

Greenslade, R. (2003) 'The Night I Gave Murdoch a Bollocking', *Media Guardian*, 29 September, p. 6.

MGH

News

George Bernard Shaw famously said: 'Newspapers are unable, seemingly, to discriminate between a bicycle accident and the collapse of civilization' (cited in Randall, 2000). Implicit in that remark is the notion that one may be considerably more 'newsworthy' than the other (except perhaps to the victim of the bicycle accident). And if that's the case, then on what are **journalists** basing their judgement when they decide something either is or isn't news and worthy of inclusion in a newspaper or bulletin?

When asked to define news, most people would say it's something that's happened, something new, something they didn't know before, something that affects their life, or something they're interested in (Harcup, 2004). News is also about the unusual – you don't find bulletins and newspapers filled with items about how the traffic ran smoothly and there were no multiple pile-ups. Therefore news is selective in two ways: what is it about a **story** that makes it news, and, of all the newsy stories that happen, why do some make headlines and others not see the light of day?

Writers who've exhaustively analyzed the content of newspapers and **broadcast** bulletins have tried to define **news values**. Norwegian academics John Galtung and Mari Ruge (1965b) devised an influential list of 12 factors: frequency, threshold, unambiguity, meaningfulness, consonance, unexpectedness, continuity, composition, reference to elite nations, reference to elite people, reference to persons and reference to something negative. This has been built on by others including Bell (1991), who adds competition, predictability, co-option, and prefabrication and Harcup and O'Neill (2001) who redefine and refine some of the original list. Journalist David Randall is more pragmatic and devises a 'sliding scale for stories' (Randall, 2000: 28) topped by the degree to which people are permanently affected by a story. McQuail (2000) suggests that these lists do not provide a complete explanation and Hartley (1982: 80) says they can 'disguise the more ideological determinants of a story'.

163

It is widely acknowledged that **journalism** does not function in a vacuum. Journalists are people, with their own opinions and foibles. This 'gatekeeper' view of news is based on a 1950 study in America by David Manning White which examined how a wire editor selected stories and concluded that the choices were subjective and based on the editor's own 'set of experiences, attitudes and expectations' (in Harcup, 2004). It was developed further by Pamela Shoemaker (1991b) to take in other factors, including that journalists are partly influenced by society. Other writers have argued that news is a 'construct', that events and facts are turned into news when viewed through a 'cultural prism' (Watson, 1998: 107). Boorstin (1963) suggested that many news items aren't events at all but 'pseudo-events', activities designed to attract media coverage.

There are also professional mores like **objectivity, impartiality, balance, fairness** (Tuchman, 1972; Rock, 1973). Media sociologists have argued that journalism is 'fundamentally interpretative' (McNair, 2001: 51). News becomes news because the owners of the news producing organization say it is (Curran, 1990), therefore the concentration of media ownership is important. Or because media owners have political affiliations. Technological developments, such as the advent of satellite link-ups and desktop editing, are also a factor (MacGregor, 1997).

These approaches tend to concentrate on the constraints journalists operate under, but a view which seeks to integrate them has been developed by Hall et al. (1978) and Schlesinger (1991) among others. At its heart is the power relationship between the media and society's elite forces such as the government and industry.

For rookie reporters trying to find their feet in busy **newsrooms**, the speed at which news judgements are made is dizzying and the reasons not altogether transparent, at least at first. And in these cases, news is what the news editor says it is.

Further reading

Bell, A. (1991) *The Language of News Media*. Oxford: Blackwell.

Boorstin, D. (1963) *The Image: Or What Happened to the American Dream*. Harmondsworth: Pelican.

Curran, J. (1990) 'The New Revisionism in Mass Communication Research: A Reappraisal', *European Journal of Communication*, 5: 135–64.

Galtung, J. and Ruge, M. (1965a) 'The Structure of Foreign News: The Presentation of the Congo, Cuba and Cyprus Crises in Four Norwegian Newspapers', *Journal of International Peace Research*, 1: 64–91.

Hall, S. et al. (1978) *Policing the Crisis*. London: Macmillan.

Harcup, T. (2004) *Journalism: Principles and Practice*. London: Sage.

Harcup, T. and O'Neill, D. (2001) 'What Is News? Galtung and Ruge Revisited', *Journalism Studies*, 2(2): 261–80.

Hartley, J. (1982) *Understanding News*. London: Methuen.

MacGregor, B. (1997) *Live, Direct and Biased: Making Television News in the Satellite Age*. London: Arnold.

McNair, B. (2001) *News and Journalism in the UK*. New York: Routledge.

McQuail, D. (2000) *Mass Communication Theory*. London: Sage.

Randall, D. (2000) *The Universal Journalist*. London: Pluto.

Rock, P. (1973) 'News as an Eternal Recurrence', in Cohen, S. and Young, J. (eds) *The Manufacture of News*. London: Constable.

Schlesinger, P. (1991) *Media, State and Nation*. London: Sage.

Shoemaker, P.J. (1991b).'Gatekeeping', in Tumber, H. (1999) (ed.) *News: A Reader*. Oxford: Oxford University Press.

Tuchman, G. (1972) 'Objectivity as a Strategic Ritual: An Examination of Newsmen's Notions of Objectivity', *American Journal of Sociology*, 77(4): 660–70.

Watson, J. (1998) *Media Communication: An Introduction to Theory and Process*. Basingstoke, Macmillan.

MK

News agency

Organizations that gather and distribute **news** to a range of **media** (and sometimes non-media) clients on a local, regional, national or international scale are known as news agencies. Some are government-owned or state-backed. The major agencies, also known as wire services, sell news and other types of information to media companies (newspapers, broadcasters and online suppliers) and other outlets, including governments, business and finance institutions, and private individuals (Boyd-Barrett, 1998a: 19). Many news agencies employ **freelance journalists** (Van den Bergh, 1998: 196–7) but most will also have permanent staff.

165

The original 'Big Four' major western news agencies included the US-based United Press International (UPI) (Boyd-Barrett, 1980: 14), but that has had financial difficulties leading to a restructuring (Herbert, 2001: 39–40). The leading contemporary agencies are generally acknowledged to be AFP (Agence France-Presse), AP (Associated Press) and *Reuters* (Boyd-Barrett, 1998c: 15). Reuters and AP also provide **television** services (Paterson, 1998: 79). While these three distribute information globally, they also have a close affinity with particular countries, AFP with France, AP is American-based and Reuters with the United Kingdom (Boyd-Barrett, 1998a: 19). Agencies like these have 'historically, been one of the most formative influences in the development of the very concept "news" in the western world, aiming to satisfy the appetite of many daily retail media, regardless of political persuasion, so they put forward the concept of "impartiality" as a valued journalistic objective'. Thus the news agencies have played an '**agenda-setting**' role (Boyd-Barrett, 1980: 19) and their growth throughout the world has had an effect on news **globalization** (Herbert, 2001: 42). News agencies could also be said to be crucial to the **public sphere** ideal originated by Jürgen Habermas whose view was that the news media could help citizens to learn about society and, through rational discussion based on that information, make informed decisions about the world (Habermas, 1989).

There are many well-known national agencies, including the *Press Association*, the national news agency of the UK and Ireland (The Press Association, 2003), the Information Telegraph Agency of Russia (ITAR-TASS) – the successor to the former Soviet TASS news agency – and Deutsche Presse-Agentur (DPA) (Boyd-Barrett 1998c: 4). In addition, there are agencies which are 'alternative' to the mainstream media, like the Inter Press Service, the radical developing world co-operative (ibid.: 12).

While print and online publications rely on the news agencies for much of their daily news, **television** receives most of its pictures, with or without narration, from television news agencies, including Worldwide Television News (WTN), and co-operative news exchanges like the Geneva-based Eurovision. 'Too often, the footage that comes into a **newsroom** from a global news agency is the footage that viewers eventually see' (Herbert, 2001: 40–2). Many new commercial stations were designed to rely heavily on agencies in this way (Paterson, 1998: 79). Major **public service** broadcasters also exchange television news as an 'important alternative to the practices of commercial television news agencies' (Boyd-Barrett, 1998c: 12).

News agencies are sometimes presented as among the least interesting or glamorous of the different media forms in that their news tends to be considered as wholesale resource material which needs to be reconfigured for a specific **audience**. Early theorization of agencies sees them as hidden but powerful, while they have also been services of **propaganda** in wartime (ibid.: 6–7).

See *Impartiality*

Further reading

Boyd-Barrett, O. (1980) *The International News Agencies*. Thousand Oaks, CA: Sage.
Paterson, C. (1998) 'Global Battlefields', in Boyd-Barrett, O. and Rantanen, T. (eds), *The Globalization of News*. London: Sage.

MGH

166

News angle

The perspective from which a **story** is reported is the news angle (also known as news peg or news hook). The particular slant a **news** item takes can depend on a variety of things, including the strength of the content (whether it contains important, interesting, unusual, different, hard-hitting, responsive or predominantly descriptive information), and the type of **media** organization (local, national or otherwise) publishing or **broadcasting** the story. It also relies on editorial judgement (see **news values**) as news is a '*selective* view of what happens in the world' (Harcup, 2004: 30, italics in original). Hicks says a distinction should be made between a '**reporter**'s interpretation of events' and news presented for **propaganda** purposes (Hicks et al., 1999: 13).

The first paragraph of a story – known as the intro in the UK and the lead in the USA (Evans, 2000: 91) – is based on the news angle and usually sets the tone for the rest of the article. News angles are sometimes predicated on recycled stories and the peg that the article hangs on is not always a particularly strong one; for example, the *Guardian* front-page splash reporting a killing from a year earlier and the resulting court case (Harcup, 2004: 30–1).

Further reading

Evans, H. (2000) *Essential English for Journalists, Editors and Writers*. London: Pimlico.
Harcup, T. (2004) *Journalism: Principles and Practice*. London: Sage.
Hicks, W., Adams, S. and Gilbert, H. (1999) *Writing for Journalists*. London: Routledge.

MGH

News bunny

The news bunny was one of the many bizarre creations of Trinity Mirror's cable tabloid television station *Live TV*, during the leadership and creative direction of ex-*Sun* editor Kelvin MacKenzie (1995–97). During the station's news bulletins, the news bunny – a journalist dressed in a giant grey and pink rabbit suit, wearing a two-piece suit and bow tie – signalled his approval or disapproval of particular news reports by gesturing, in the Roman manner, thumbs up or thumbs down. Each rabbit outfit cost £1,200 (Horrie and Nathan, 1999: 374). McKenzie became obsessed with the bunny and would shout at journalists in the newsroom 'Don't you realize that this station *is* newsy bunny?' But even MacKenzie judged the bunny inappropriate on certain occasions: bunny was banned during news reporting of the death of Leah Betts, the young woman who died after taking ecstasy. The news bunny became involved in a succession of publicity stunts, including attending the state opening of Parliament in 1996 and – in the same year – gaining an exclusive interview with Tony Blair: the news bunny even stood in the Tamworth by-election representing the News Bunny Party (ibid.: 377).

Live TV's self-consciously and shamelessly tacky approach also featured topless darts, bouncing dwarfs, a weather forecast read in Norwegian, and Tiffany, who removed items of clothing as she read the financial news to reveal 'Tiffany's Big City Tips'. But the news bunny proved to be the station's most popular asset, attracting a peak audience of 200,000 viewers. The demise of the news bunny, however, accompanied the closure of *Live TV* and its sale to NTL cable for £20 million in October 1999. But it seems you can't keep a good rabbit down. In May 2003, *Live TV*'s former managing director and head of programming announced they were planning to relaunch the station on *BSkyB* in July 2003 (Cozens, 2003).

See *BSkyB, Dumbing down, Newszak, Tabloid.*

Further reading
Cozens, C. (2003) 'News Bunny Back Say Live TV Lads', *Guardian*, 16 May, p. 21.
Horrie, C. and Nathan, A. (1999) *Live TV: Telly Brats and Topless Darts.* London: Simon and Schuster.

BF

News editor

The **journalist** in day-to-day charge of a **newsroom** is usually the news (or wire) editor whose duties include selecting **stories** for inclusion, a role in line with the concept of a **gatekeeper** (Harcup, 2004: 33). News editors, who are usually directly answerable to the **editor**, also allocate tasks to the **news** team and instruct **reporters** on which **news angles** should be pursued when chasing stories.

Boyd uses a warlike analogy for broadcast news editors, describing them as 'generals . . . [who] set the objectives, weigh the resources and draw up the plan of campaign. Under their command are the officers and troops on the ground' (2001: 46). He adds that when a good story breaks, the news editor must – like the general – be ready to 'switch forces rapidly from one front to another to meet the new challenge' (ibid.: 47). **Website** news editors have the additional gatekeeping decision of which **hyperlinks** to use in **stories** and which to omit (Dimitrova et al., 2003: 402).

Further reading

Boyd, A. (2001) *Broadcast Journalism: Techniques of Radio and Television News*, 5th edn. Oxford: Focal Press.

Dimitrova, D.V., Connolly-Ahern, C., Williams, A.P., Kaid, L.L. and Reid, A. (2003) 'Hyperlinking as Gatekeeping: Online Newspaper Coverage of the Execution of an American Terrorist', *Journalism Studies*, 4(3): 401–14.

Harcup, T. (2004) *Journalism: Principles and Practice*. London: Sage.

MGH

Newsgathering

The apparently 'undisciplined and chaotic' (Harrison, 2000) process of collecting information, opinion and facts that are likely **news** material is co-ordinated within a **newsroom**, but happens both inside and outside the office.

It involves **reporters**, correspondents, producers, **news editors**, and planners. They use sources such as people, documents, **news releases** and the **Internet** – and other media outlets. They use equipment from a pen and notebook to audio recorders and cameras.

It's been described as a machine (Yorke, 2000) and is perceived as something distinct from news processing, which is turning a selection of stories into newspapers and programmes. In large organizations, and **television** in particular, the complex practical logistics of newsgathering involve a team of people working to a particular programme deciding the allocation of technical resources and **journalists**, reacting to information and making judgements about what's worth covering or following up.

At the sharp end of print, broadcast and online newsrooms, are reporters and correspondents filing material, discussing the shape of **stories** with those in the middle, the news editors and producers.

This highly organizational aspect of newsgathering, including the necessity of dealing with the unexpected, (Tuchman, 1973) has been often analyzed. It produces 'routines' (Ettema et al., 1987) and news selection itself takes place 'within a shared journalistic culture' (Harrison, 2000).

Then there is the process of finding news itself. McManus (1994b) identifies three methods: minimally active discovery, for example, press releases and wire services; moderately active discovery, for example, follow-ups or suggesting an idea; and highly active discovery, for example, attending meetings or investigating.

Further reading

Ettema, J. et al. (1987) 'Professional Mass Communication', in Berkowitz, D. (ed.) (1997) *Social Meanings of News: A Text Reader*. Thousand Oaks, CA: Sage.

Harrison, J. (2000) *Terrestrial TV News in Britain: The Culture of Production*. Manchester, Manchester University Press.

McManus, J. (1994b) 'The First Stage of News Production: Learning What's Happening', in Berkowitz, D. (ed.) (1997), *Social Meanings of News*. London: Sage.

Yorke, I. (2000) *Television News*, Oxford: Focal Press.

MK

News management

The phrase news management is largely self-explanatory and refers to the various techniques which organizations and individuals deploy in their efforts to 'manage' the news and influence media coverage of their activities. Consequently, news management has a close affinity with discussions of **agenda setting**, agenda building and **framing**.

Since the mid-1990s, news management has become almost synonymous with spin as political actors and agencies in political parties, pressure groups, parliament and government, increasingly vie to win highly contested access to space in news media in order to promote favourable images and reports of their major policies and leading politicians: a process described as the 'packaging' of politics (Franklin, 2004a).

Governments have unique access to a number of institutional mechanisms which offer them possibilities for news managing. These range from censorship to D Notices and include the Prime Minister's Press Secretary's daily briefings of the lobby. Since Labour's election victory in 1997, the government has established a centralized and expanded press office and a *Strategic Communications Unit* at Number 10, the *Media Monitoring Unit* in the Cabinet Office and has recruited an unprecedented number of special advisers to enhance its capacity for news management.

The Labour Government has become so enthusiastic about the possibilities for managing news media discussions of its affairs that some **journalists** believe it has, on occasion, become bullying and disdainful in its attitude towards **lobby** journalists (Oborne 1999: 181) with one senior

170

journalist describing the government and its Director of Communications as 'control freaks' (Jones, 2002).

Alastair Campbell's criticisms of the BBC's coverage of the war with Iraq, as well as his specific criticism of journalist Andrew Gilligan's use of a single anonymous source for his allegation concerning the 'sexing up' of a (dodgy) dossier, were widely interpreted by journalists as an attempt by Campbell to manage the news and divert media criticism away from the Prime Minister (Preston, 2003b: 13). Such robust attacks on a news organization might also trigger journalists to engage in **self-censorship** for fear of government flak: significantly, the strategies of news managers do not always go to plan. The subsequent **Hutton Inquiry** supported Campbell's criticisms of the *BBC* and prompted the resignation of Director General Greg Dyke and Chair of the *BBC Board of Governors* Gavin Davies: the findings of the Butler inquiry, however, were highly critical of Campbell and the government's news management activities.

Further reading

Franklin, B. (2003) 'A Good Day to Bury Bad News? Journalists, Sources and the Packaging of Politics', in Cottle, S. (ed.) *News, Public Relations and Power*. London: Sage.

Jones, N. (2002) *The Control Freaks: How New Labour Gets its Own Way*. London: Politicos.

Oborne, P. (1999) *Alastair Campbell, New Labour and the Rise of the Media Class*. London: Aurum Press.

Preston, P. (2003b) 'It's a Charade and We All Know It', *Guardian*, 7 July, p. 13.

BF

News release

They arrive in their thousands, day after day, are scrutinised for as long as three seconds, and most end up in the newsroom bin. But the humble news release, or press release, can be the basis of many a good **story** either followed up by a diligent reporter, or, in the case of less well resourced or less picky newsrooms, printed as it stands.

Media savvy organizations see news releases as an important way of getting out information. Organizations from charities, through lobby groups to governments, employ armies of press officers to write them. They can be straightforward – 'Schoolkids knit record-breaking scarf' – but also an illustration of the ever continuing tension between the journalist and the press officer and refined by the development of the **video news release**. Scholars such as Oscar Gandy have argued, however, that news releases constitute significant **information subsidies** which support under-resourced news organization and consequently may prove influential in shaping news agendas. Certainly this is the view of some government **spin doctors**.

On 11 September 2001, with the eyes of the world's journalists on the collapse of the twin towers in New York, government press officer Jo Moore sent her now notorious email suggesting it was a good day to get out anything they wanted to bury. 'Councillor's expenses', for example? (Harcup, 2004). In a news release dated 12 September her department issued press release number 0388, 'Consultation begins on council allowances' (DTLR, 2001). It was a good story, but didn't exactly make headlines.

News releases have been categorized as 'pseudo-events' (Boorstin, 1963) in that they aren't a way of reporting the news, but of making the news. And Allan Bell (1991) points out that their 'prefabrication' increases the likelihood of the subject matter making the **news** because they can be processed quickly.

Reading news releases backwards is recommended practice in many **newsrooms** – the most interesting bit is often right at the end.

Further reading

Bell, A. (1991) *The Language of News Media*. Oxford: Blackwell.
Boorstin, D. (1963) *The Image: Or What Happened to the American Dream*. Harmondsworth: Pelican.
Harcup, T. (2004) *Journalism: Principles and Practice*. London: Sage.

MK

Newsroom

Full of people with a phone strapped to one ear, fingers flying over keyboards. There are screens flickering and deadlines looming, piles of paper everywhere and half empty coffee cups in the bin. This stereotype still exists to an extent, although there's no cigarette smoke nowadays and it's not quite as noisy. But the newsroom is still the focal point of any **newsgathering** operation whether print, broadcast or online.

It's a place where **editors** can talk to **news editors**, news editors to **reporters**. It's a window on the world with wire services, **press releases,** telephone calls coming in. The day's output can be planned and executed.

But according to Nerone and Barnhurst (2003), the development of the newsroom, and its role in news production, are linked closely to changes in technology and working practices, particularly the separation of what they call the mechanical, the business practices and the editorial. Newsrooms didn't exist as a place to write and discuss news until the mid-nineteenth century (Hoyer, 2003) while newspapers have been around since the seventeeth century. The increasing **convergence** of print, broadcast and online so far hasn't led to the demise of the newsroom, but they do look more than ever like any other office.

The only person who shouldn't be in a newsroom is a reporter, who should be out, reporting.

Further reading

Hoyer, S. (2003) 'Newspapers Without Journalists', *Journalism Studies*, 4(4): 451.
Nerone, J. and Barnhurst, K.G. (2003) 'US Newspaper Types, the Newsroom and the Division of Labor, 1750–2000', *Journalism Studies*, 4(4): 435.

MK

News values

These are the (somewhat mythical) set of criteria employed by journalists to measure and therefore to judge the 'newsworthiness' of events. The news, whether produced by a newspaper or a broadcaster, needs to be interesting, or otherwise appealing, to the **target audience**. News values, and the notion of newsworthiness that they are derived from, are meant to be the crystallized reflection of, or 'ground rules' for deciding, what an identified audience is interested in reading or watching. These 'ground rules may not be written down or codified by news organizations, but they exist in daily practice and in knowledge gained on the job' (Harcup and O'Neill, 2001: 261).

The study of news values takes two broad forms: first, journalists and ex-journalists have provided lists of the kinds of qualities which, in their experience and estimation, a story should possess. For example, Alistair Hetherington (1985), a former editor of the *Guardian*, has suggested: significance; drama; surprise; personalities; sex, scandal and crime; numbers (magnitude of the story); and proximity. Second, in the chosen approach of academics, lists are derived via summarizing the themes of a sample of news reports and, working backwards, suggesting criteria which events need to show evidence of in order to qualify as 'the news'. The most influential list of this kind was offered by Galtung and Ruge (1965a), based on their study of three international crises (Congo, 1960; Cuba, 1960; and Cyprus, 1964). Galtung and Ruge offer 12 news values which, they suggest, are employed in gauging newsworthiness: frequency (events being favoured over processes); intensity (labelled 'threshold'); unambiguity; cultural proximity (labelled 'meaningfulness');

173

predictability (labelled 'consonance'); unexpectedness; continuity (follow-up stories); composition (a balance of stories); references to elite peoples; references to elite nations; personification; and negativity. Galtung and Ruge predict that the more an event satisfies these criteria, the more likely it is of being reported as news.

In a recent study of three British national daily newspapers, Harcup and O'Neill (2001) re-tested these news values and found that they were inadequate in certain respects. They suggest, in agreement with Tunstall (1971), that 'by focusing on coverage of three major international crises, Galtung and Ruge ignored day-to-day coverage of lesser, domestic and bread-and-butter news' (Harcup and O'Neill, 2001: 276). Second, they argue that some of Galtung and Ruge's news values are a product not of the selection of events but of the way in which events have been written about, or *constructed*, by journalists. Take the news value 'unambiguity', for example: 'most journalists are trained to write unambiguous angles to stories that may be ambiguous, complex or unclear' (ibid., 2001: 277). Other news values, while 'still resonant today' would better reflect the selection criteria of newspaper coverage if they were either worded in a slightly different way ('composition', for example, is part of newspaper agenda) or else combined (references to elite peoples and elite nations become a single value) (ibid.).

On the basis of this appraisal, Harcup and O'Neill suggest an updated list of ten news values which events must satisfy in order to be selected as 'news': reference to the power elite (individuals, organizations and nations); reference to celebrity; entertainment (e.g. sex, human interest, drama); surprise; good news (e.g. rescues, personal triumph); bad news (e.g. tragedy, accident); magnitude; relevance (cultural proximity, political importance); follow-up stories; and the newspaper's agenda (both politically and relating to the structure of the genre).

While this list may better summarize the content of contemporary newspapers, it still doesn't deal with the **ideological** reasons behind their use. Illustrating that ephemeral issues are newsworthy, for example, does little to explain *why* this is the case, nor to interrogate whether it is in the **public interest** to pander persistently to 'what interests the public'.

Further reading

Galtung, J. and Ruge, M. (1965a) 'The Structure of Foreign News: The Presentation of the Congo, Cuba and Cyprus Crises in Four Norwegian Newspapers', *Journal of International Peace Research*, 1: 64–91.

Harcup, T. and O'Neill, D. (2001) 'What Is News? Galtung and Ruge Revisited', *Journalism Studies*, 2(2): 261–80.

Hetherington, A. (1985) *News, Newspapers and Television*. London: Macmillan.

JER

174

Newszak

A conscious neologism of journalist Malcolm Muggeridge, the term newszak was intended to reflect changing **news values** and news formats evident in print and broadcast **journalism** across the 1980s and 1990s (Franklin, 1997: 4). The implication was that these changes were for the worse and the resonance with the term muzak is clear.

Newszak allegedly marked: (1) a retreat from investigative journalism and 'hard' news to the preferred terrain of 'softer' consumer or life style stories; (2) a focus on entertainment rather than information resulting in '**infotainment**'; (3) journalists' preferences for human interest above the **public interest**; (4) **news** reports characterized by sensationalism rather than measured judgement; (5) the triumph of the trivial above the weighty which guaranteed that gossip about celebrities from soaps, sport and the royal family, assumed greater news salience than significant events of public consequence; and (6) the neglect of international affairs and the foregrounding of a domestic agenda typically dominated by crime stories. In summary, newszak reflects journalists' preference for 'stories which interest the public above stories which are in the public interest' (Franklin, 1997: 4). Newszak is what McNair calls 'bonk journalism' (1994; 145), what Andrew Marr describes as 'bite-sized McNugget journalism' and what Harold Evans warns against as signalling 'the drift from substantive news to celebrity hunting, from news to entertainment' (Evans, 1996: 1).

The 'usual suspects' are held responsible for the proliferation of newszak: the increasingly competitive market place in which news **media** operate; recent government policy which favours deregulation of media markets and regulation of content with a 'lighter touch'; new technologies for print and broadcast media which have prompted de-skilling, multi-skilling, casualization and job cuts along with an explosion of new **radio** and **television** stations on cable, satellite and digital platforms, and, finally, the growth in **freelance** journalism and public relations which, for the first time since the earliest days of journalism, have placed a large part of news production outside news media organizations and specifically the **newsroom**.

The debate about newszak engages both those who 'lament' the alleged decline in traditional journalism (Engel, 1996; Sampson, 1996) as well as those enthusiasts, typically cultural theorists, who wish to celebrate the emergence of more popular cultural forms (Langer, 1998). For Simon Jenkins (ex-editor of *The Times*), Newszak's critique of contemporary

175

journalism represents little more than a romantic fallacy which recalls a 'golden age' of journalism, a heyday which 'was always when the person discussing the subject came into newspapers' (cited in Engel, 1996).

See *Broadloid, Dumbing down, Tabloid.*

Further reading

Djerf-Pierre, M. (2000) 'Squaring the Circle: Public Service and Commercial News on Swedish Television 1956–99', *Journalism Studies*, 1(2): 239–60.
Franklin, B. (1997) *Newszak and News Media.* London: Arnold.
Langer, J. (1998) *Tabloid Television: Popular Journalism and the 'Other News'.* London Routledge.
Winston, B. (2001) 'Towards Tabloidisation? Glasgow Revisited 1975–2001', *Journalism Studies*, 3(1): 5–20.

BF

Obituary

An obituary is an article published after a person's death, summarizing his/her life, its achievements and possibly any notable failures. A well-read part of upmarket newspapers, in which they usually command a special page, obituaries are written in a more literary style than news articles (Starck, 2004a, 2004b).

Max Hastings, former editor of the Daily Telegraph, credited his obituaries editor Hugh Montgomery-Massingberd with transforming its obituary column 'from a murky backwater of the paper into the most brilliant feature of its kind in the business' (2002: 94–5).

If a subject is particularly famous or prominent, and especially if very old, long obituaries are prepared while the subject lives, to guard against the deadline pressures caused by sudden death.

Obituaries can provide an opportunity for journalists to revisit bygone incidents of notoriety, because the dead can't sue for libel.

MNH

Objectivity

If the notion of **impartiality** is the professional lodestar of modern **journalism**, particularly in UK broadcast newsrooms, then where does this leave the idea that **journalists** either are, can be or should be objective?

176

The two ideas are often taken to be much the same thing and used interchangeably (Harcup, 2004). But although there is some relationship, they rest on rather different world views. Whereas impartiality, as expressed in press and broadcasting codes of practice, is taken to include notions of **fairness**, even-handedness, and **accuracy**, objectivity is philosophically a tougher nut. It's predicated on the notion that there are observable things external to the mind; that there are independently verifiable 'facts' that can be separated from subjective values (Schudson, 1978 in Tumber, 1999).

This concept arose in the late nineteenth and early twentieth century with the pursuit of scientific knowledge and philosophical discussion about the nature of absolute truth, or whether there could even be such a thing. The arguments became more subtle later on with discoveries by Einstein, Heisenberg and others that the physical world could change with the position of the observer, and the very act of observation influences the thing being observed. The act of putting a thermometer into hot water to measure the temperature will change the temperature.

McNair (1998: 68) defines three characteristics of objective journalism: the separation of facts and opinion, a balanced account of a debate and the validation of journalistic statements by reference to authoritative others. It could be argued that these apply to impartiality as well.

Journalism is often seen as a way of helping others understand the world around them, or getting at the truth. If you subscribe to the view that there is no single absolute truth, as cultural relativists do, then it follows that journalists can't lay claim to some special status or ability that helps them find it. McNair (1998: 73) suggests that this view would lead to the kind of reporting that doesn't deny that an alternative reading of events may be available.

The idea of objectivity was also subverted by the 'new journalism' or **gonzo journalism** of the 1960s exemplified by Tom Wolfe and Hunter Thompson which embraced subjectivity. As Thompson put it, 'The only thing I ever saw that came close to Objective Journalism was a closed circuit TV setup that watched shoplifters in the General Store at Woody Creek, Colorado' (in McNair, 1998: 75).

So when journalists claim to be objective, or hold objectivity up as the professional holy grail, the extent to which it is achievable or desirable is at least questionable. Sanders (2003: 45) says it may be true that the term is a relic of scientism and should be discarded, 'but while it continues to denote the struggle for fairness and impartiality in reporting, it's probably worth hanging on to'.

177

key concepts

Further reading

McNair, B. (1998) *The Sociology of Journalism*. London: Arnold.
Sanders, K. (2003) *Ethics and Journalism*. London: Sage.
Tumber, H. (ed.) (1999) *News: A Reader*. Oxford: Oxford University Press.

MK

Off the record

The phrase has several related but distinct meanings. People who choose to be confidential **sources** for journalists should firmly and quickly establish what meaning applies, when offering information.

The source may, in insisting that his/her contact with the journalist remains a secret:

1 be content for the information provided to be published, provided there is no attribution to identify the source (i.e. the information can be used but is non-attributable); or

2 be content for the information provided to be published, provided there is no attribution to identify him/her as the source, *and* provided the journalist is able to get *someone else* to confirm the information and to be the attributable source (i.e. the original source is providing a tip-off); or

3 not want the information to be published at all (especially if it will be obvious who might have provided it) but be content for it to be used to guide the journalist's inquiries, or to influence the news angle and/or to help the journalist avoid publishing other, erroneous information.

178

There are also related terms with gradations of meaning, e.g. 'background' and 'deep background'. See Newslab's Interviewing Glossary http://www.newslab.org/resources/intvgloss.htm. Middleton (1993: 44) reserves the term 'off the record' for (3) above.

BBC reporters Andrew Gilligan and Susan Watts were asked, in their evidence to the **Hutton Inquiry**, what they felt 'off the record' meant. See http://www.the-hutton-inquiry.org.uk/content/hearing_trans.htm.

In **investigative journalism**, sources who want to remain off the record have limited use, in that witnesses willing to testify *on* the record will be needed to defend any subsequent libel action.

Some commentators feel that journalists, particular those reporting politics, now rely too much on off-the-record sources, leaving the media and therefore the public vulnerable to **spin** distorting the truth, because such sources, as they are not identifiable, cannot be held accountable by the public for what they say. The source may use the off-the-record relationship to float speculative stories to test public reaction, or to serve a hidden agenda.

Further reading
Middleton, D. (1993) *Pocketbook of Newspaper Terms.* Edinburgh: Merchiston Publishing.

MNH

Official Secrets Act

The UK's official secrets legislation is primarily devised to punish foreign spies and traitors, but has also been used – controversially – against British civil servants leaking information for reasons of conscience, and against journalists investigating the state apparatus and government policy.

The 1911 Official Secrets Act, passed after spy scares in pre-war tension between Britain and Germany, created in its Section 2 a wide-ranging 'catch all' power, making it illegal for anyone to knowingly receive and to further disclose, without proper authority, information classified as officially secret, whatever the actual nature of the information.

In 1970 Jonathan Aitken, then a journalist, and Brian Roberts, editor of the *Sunday Telegraph*, were prosecuted under Section 2 after the paper published an article about the Nigerian civil war, in which Britain supported the Nigerian government. It drew on a 'confidential' British diplomatic report, critical of corruption in Nigeria. At the trial the judge was scathing about aspects of the prosecution, and the jury acquitted the defendants (Hooper, 1988: 112–32).

In 1977 the government secured Section 2 convictions in the 'ABC trial' in which two investigative journalists Crispin Aubrey and Duncan Campbell, and a former Army signals officer were prosecuted after Aubrey and Campbell's research into defence communications, including the secret base GCHQ. But the judge did not jail them, and the Government endured criticism for a prosecution seen as oppressive, bearing in mind Parliament's ignorance of the scale of GCHQ's monitoring of telephone calls worldwide (Hooper, 1988: 133–56; Robertson and Nicol, 2002: 557–8).

In 1984 a jury – apparently ignoring a judge's ruling that, under the 1911 Act, there could be no **public interest** other than 'the interests of the

179

state' – acquitted Clive Ponting, a senior civil servant in the Ministry of Defence, prosecuted after he anonymously sent correspondence to a Labour MP about the controversial sinking of the Argentinian battleship the Belgrano by a British submarine during the Falklands War (Ponting, 1985).

In 1985 the government chose to use the common law of confidence in its – ultimately unsuccessful – legal battle with the press to prevent coverage of the memoirs of Peter Wright, a former scientific officer with MI5 (Hooper, 1988: 310–43; Welsh and Greenwood, 2003: 307).

In 1989 the government passed another Official Secrets Act which replaced Section 2. It has much tighter definitions of what type of information should be protected as secret. But the government refused to include any public interest defence in it, and its use – 'more than any other piece of legislation' – is circumscribed by political considerations (Robertson and Nicol, 2002: 556). No journalist has yet been prosecuted to trial under this Act, though the media has been involved in legal skirmishes with the government over publication of information from former intelligence officers.

See *D notice, Human Rights Act.*

Further reading

Fielding, N. and Hollingsworth, M. (1999) *Defending the Realm, MI5 and the David Shayler Affair.* London: André Deutsch.

Fielding, N. and Tomlinson, R. (2001) *The Big Breach.* Edinburgh: Cutting Edge Press.

Franks, Lord (Chairman) (1972) *Report and Evidence of the Committee on Section 2 of the Official Secrets Act 1911.* Cmnd 5104. London: HMSO.

Home Office (1978) *Reform of Section 2 of the Official Secrets Act 1911.* London: HMSO.

Ponting, C. (1990) *Secrecy in Britain.* Oxford: Basil Blackwell.

Robertson, K.G. (1982) *Public Secrets: A Study of the Development of Government Secrecy* London: Macmillan.

Turnbull, M. (1988) *The Spy Catcher Trial.* London: Heinemann.

Vincent, D. (1998) *The Culture of Secrecy: Britain 1832–1998.* Oxford: Oxford University Press.

MNH

Online advertising

The **world wide web** was slow to take off as an advertising medium in its early years (Clapperton, 2003) and many companies stopped advertising in the online **media** by 1999, instead using traditional media to draw customers to their **websites** (J. Hall, 2001: 167). However, there have been signs that online advertising has started to recover in line with improved general economic conditions (Clapperton, 2003).

Internet users have not responded favourably to online advertising formats such as banner ads, usually situated above the name of the online publication at the top of a web page and which links to the advertiser's website (ibid.). Banner ads were first introduced by Hotwired and are used widely on the web (Whittaker, 2000: 139).

Other, even less successful, forms of online advertising include pop-ups, which appear in their own windows on top of the web page content, and interstitials that appear as browsers move to other pages. Ad-bots are more inventive in that they can be triggered by commercially linked words or phrases in discussion and other interactive environments on the web (J. Hall, 2001: 168).

Providing free content on the web has clearly been seen by some as a way of attracting readers, but plans by some **news** sites to start charging for certain services saw falls in the amount of traffic and advertisers seeking reduced rates (ibid.: 170). In addition, the distinction between editorial and advertising has not always been as clear and distinct online as it has in traditional media (which describes a combination of the two as **advertorials**), marketing material sometimes masquerading as **news stories** or editorial content (ibid.: 172).

Advertisers were initially suspicious of **audience** figure claims made by **websites** until the establishment of international auditing bodies such as the Audit Bureau of Circulation and Nielsen//NetRatings who agreed international standards for measuring web traffic (ibid.: 167). Newspapers like the *Wall Street Journal* (WSJ) have been able to include online subscriptions with their print **circulation** (Thompson, 2003).

Payments for online advertisements have operated in several ways, one being a set price per thousand page impressions (i.e. when a page containing the advert is accessed by the user). Another is the click-through rates method whereby a (higher) fee is charged when a consumer uses the link on the advert to go to the advertiser's website (Whittaker, 2000: 139–40).

Cookies, 'ubiquitous on news sites', are small text files sent by web servers (content provider or advertiser) to browsers to get and store information about an online consumer's Internet habits and movements, although the programme can be disabled (J. Hall, 2001: 168–9, 248).

Paid-for or sponsored listings in search engines such as *Google* are starting to pay off; Danny Meadows-Klue, president of the Internet Advertising Bureau (IAB), says: 'Sponsored listings mean you get the person clicking through right at the point when they're most inclined to buy your product' (Clapperton, 2003). Google – widely acknowledged to handle more queries than any other search engine – has also started to place paid listings on web pages rather than putting them into search results. This is known as contextual advertising in which advertisements are displayed, automatically or semi-automatically, based on a page's content; the ad reflects the context or subject matter of that particular web page (Sullivan, 2003).

See *Advertising*

Further reading

Clapperton, G. (2003) 'Back on Stream', *The Guardian New Media*, 20 October, p. 42.
Hall, J. (2001) *Online Journalism: A Critical Primer*. London: Pluto Press.
Sullivan, D. (2003) 'Google Throws Hat into the Contextual Advertising Ring', 4 March. http://searchenginewatch.com/jereport/print.php/34721_2183531.
Whittaker, J. (2000) *Producing for the Web*. London: Routledge.

MGH

Online journalism

In the physical sense, anyone connected to the **Internet** through their computer can be deemed to be online. The term can also have a conceptual value (Ward, 2002) in that it refers to a new form of **journalism**, which has become a **mass communication** medium in its own right in an age of **globalization**; for example, the **world wide web** version of a newspaper is said to be the online or web edition. Online journalism can be described as 'quality **news** and information posted on the internet (particularly the world wide web)' (De Wolk, 2001). **New media** technology means content can be presented in a far richer way than possible in the traditional mediums of print and broadcast, leading to the 'emergence of a new form of news perhaps best described as **contextualized journalism**' which facilitates the use and application of **multimedia, interactivity, hypertext** and customization (Pavlik, 2001: 217) and the rise of the multimedia **journalist** (Reddick and King, 2001: 243), although the basic skills remain the foundation (Hall, J. 2001: 87).

There are other ways in which the electronic medium has affected the role of the journalist who has faster access to far more information (both old and new) than previously, enhancing both the researching and reporting process (Ward, 2002: 19, 23). Due to the 'ubiquitous nature of news and information in today's online environment', the journalist has to become a far more skilful story-teller, which includes guiding the reader through the 'myriad of **websites** and other forms of online content . . . and establish which forms are reliable'. Speed, accuracy and truth could also be affected on the Internet as technology and marketing could take precedence over journalism (Herbert, 2001: 9).

Further reading

De Wolk, R. (2001) *Introduction to Online Journalism*. Boston: Allyn and Bacon.
Hall, J. (2001) *Online Journalism: A Critical Primer*. London: Pluto Press.
Herbert, J. (2001) *Practising Global Journalism*. Oxford: Focal Press.
Pavlik, J.V. (2001) *Journalism and New Media*. Columbia, NY: University Press.
Reddick, R. and King, E. (2001) *The Online Journalist: Using the Internet and Other Electronic Resources*, 3rd edn. Orlando, FL: Harcourt Brace and Company.
Ward, M. (2002) *Journalism Online*. Oxford: Focal Press.

MGH

Orientalism

The accumulative body of ('Western') knowledge, institutions and political/economic policies which simultaneously assume and construct 'the Orient' as different, separate and 'Other'. In some of the 'stronger' texts this develops to the point that the Orient is assumed to be the antithesis of the Occident, or 'the West', wherein *They* are represented as the negation of *Us*. Thus,

> The perceived Arab tendency towards verbosity and antagonistic dispute is the opposite of the self-ascribed European norms of negotiation, consensus and rational dialogue. The more and more frequently emphasized Islamic inclination towards fundamentalism is supposed in contrast with Christian tolerance and democratic pluralism. (Blommaert and Verschueren, 1998: 19)

In the most widely referenced critique (also see Sardar, 1999; Tibawi, 1964), Edward Said (1978) examines Orientalism via Foucault's notion of **discourse**. In doing so, Said attempts to illustrate how power operates through discourse, how power produces knowledge and therefore how knowledge about 'the Orient' is itself an index of social power relations. In the words of Foucault (1979: 27), 'There is no power relation without

183

the correlative constitution of a field of knowledge, nor any knowledge that does not presuppose and constitute at the same time power relations'.

Said's critique of Orientalism therefore develops along two mutually supporting lines in accordance with this knowledge/power nexus. First, Orientalism should be considered a 'style of thought based upon an ontological and epistemological distinction between "the Orient" and (most of the time) "the Occident" (Said, 1978: 2). In short, when people think about 'the East' they embark with an already fixed idea that 'the Orient' is different; that *They* are different from *Us*. This contrasting discourse may, of course, take many forms but they are largely reducible to two, gender-specific, types: the xenophobic, which fixate on threatening or repellent characteristics; and the xenophilic, which fixate on attractive elements of the Other. Xenophobic Orientalist representations (e.g. despotic leaders, fundamentalism, terrorism) demean, degrade and, ultimately, demonize (predominantly) Eastern men; the xenophilic varieties (e.g. the harem, veiling, the geisha) sensualize, passivize and exoticize Eastern women. Both modes of Orientalist representational discourse objectify, essentialize and **stereotype** the vast diversity of social life in countries and societies geographically east of the Mediterranean Sea.

Second, Orientalism takes the form of a 'corporate institution for dealing with the Orient – dealing with it by making statements about it, authorizing views of it, describing it, teaching it, settling it, ruling over it' (Said, 1978: 3). The news **media** represent an increasingly important part of this 'corporate institution'. It is predominantly through the mass media that Western non-Muslims 'learn about' Islam and, more specifically, what makes *Them* different from *Us*. Unfortunately, Muslims are not given the column space or airtime to represent themselves and instead the news media foreground non-Muslim 'experts' and their often prejudicial or inaccurate opinions about Islam (Richardson, 2001b, 2004). When a Muslim is quoted, he (and it usually *is* a he) is included to provide the 'Muslim opinion' to balance a report. This sourcing routine 'reduce[s] the rich variety of life to a simplified limited framework informed by "Occidental cultural legacies"' (Poole, 2002: 252), drives a wedge between *Them* and *Us* and contributes to the Orientalist construction of *an* Orient, a single Muslim 'Middle East' and a single 'Muslim opinion'. And given journalism's preoccupation with the repellent or sensational (exemplified in the fascination with 'Muslim terrorism'), this construction in turn reinforces the belief that they are 'dangerously different'.

184

Further reading

Poole, E. (2002) *Reporting Islam: Media Representations of British Muslims*. London: I.B. Tauris.

Richardson, J.E. (2004) *(Mis)Representing Islam: The Racism and Rhetoric of British Broadsheet Newspapers*. Amsterdam: John Benjamins.

Said, E.W. (1978) *Orientalism*. London: Penguin Books.

Sardar, Z. (1999) *Orientalism*. Buckingham: Open University Press.

JER

Othering

The process by which people are made to seem mildly or radically different. Through othering strategies, people are positioned as an out-group – as 'an Other'. However, given that the word '*Other* is an elliptical pronoun . . . that can refer to practically anything, depending on the context or situation' (Riggins, 1997: 4), the term requires further definition.

Self-identity is the result of a dialogue between self and other: I define what I am in contrast to what I am not; equally, we define others in terms which reflect their difference from us. However, personal identity is a fluid rather than a stable state in which the self draws on multiple identities – for example, son, husband, graduate, Socialist, Englishman, European, etc. – any of which may be emphasized at a given point at the expense of others. On this point, Hall (1994: 392) has argued that identity should be thought of 'as a "production" which is never complete, always in process, and always constituted within, not outside representation'. This process of identity places the self within different in-groups at different times. Logically therefore, people considered, and *represented*, as part of the in-group – as part of 'We' – in certain contexts can be considered and represented as different, *as Other*, in other contexts. This is Othering: the process by which individuals or groups, who in certain contexts or viewed from certain (political, ideological) perspectives are, or *could* be, positioned as part of the group 'We', are rhetorically distanced from Us and (re)presented as 'Other'.

Implicit in Othering is a hierarchy in which They are thought, and represented, as being subordinate and/or inferior. While it may not be entirely accurate to conclude that Othering *necessarily* 'dehumanises and diminishes groups, making it easier for victimisers to seize land, exploit labour and exert control' (Riggins, 1997: 9), hierarchies are organizing **metaphors** from which discourse can easily slip into discrimination and domination along sexist, anti-Semitic, **racist** or otherwise ethnicist lines.

Further reading

Hall, S. (1994) 'Cultural Identity and Diaspora', in Williams, P. and Chrisman, L. (eds), *Colonial Discourse and Post-Colonial Theory: A Reader*. New York: Columbia University Press, pp. 392–403.

Riggins, S.H. (ed.) (1997b) *The Language and Politics of Exclusion: Others in Discourse*. Thousand Oaks, CA: Sage.

JER

Ownership

The question of media ownership has proved highly contentious in the British setting and poses a continuing problem for government media policy (Doyle, 2002: 83–138; Franklin, 2001: 146–160; Department of National Heritage, 1995). More specifically, policy debate has focused on the growing trends towards (1) the concentration of media ownership among a small (and decreasing) number of corporations and individual owners; and (2) cross-media ownership. Rupert Murdoch's News Corporation illustrates both trends by its ownership of a number of national newspapers along with the *Sky* satellite television channel: similarly, Richard Desmond owns the *Daily Express*, the *Sunday Express*, a portfolio of magazine titles (including *Asian Babes*) and a number of interactive 'pay-to-view' pornographic websites.

The objection of groups such as the *Campaign for Press and Broadcasting Freedom (CPBF)* to this concentration of media ownership in cross-media conglomerates is that this *economic* circumstance has implications for the *cultural* and *political* realm by narrowing choice, diversity and range of programming, but also by limiting the bounds of public debate about political and other matters (CPBF, 1996; Doyle, 2002: 9–43). The role of **proprietorial influence** on editorial matters in newspapers, for example, is well documented in a series of editors' autobiographies (Evans, 1984; Neil, 1996).

The evidence documenting the concentration of media ownership in the UK is unequivocal. In the **national press**, for example, News International owns 35.8 per cent of the newspaper market by circulation, while the Mirror Group owns 19.6 per cent, Associated Newspapers 17.6 per cent, Richard Desmond 12.5 per cent and the Barclay Brothers 6.9 per cent. In aggregate, the five largest newspaper groups control 92.4 per cent of the market by circulation (based on ABC figures, April 2004). The ownership of **local newspapers** is similarly characterized by concentration. The 200 companies publishing local newspapers in 1992 reduced to 137

key concepts

186

by 1998 and 96 in 2003. But while 47 of these companies own a single newspaper, the largest 20 groups own 85 per cent of regional titles and control 96 per cent of weekly circulation: the five largest groups own 76 per cent of newspapers by circulation (www.newspapersoc.org). In television, the entire *ITV* network is owned by a single company following the merger between Granada and Carlton in 2003.

Statutory regulation has done little to apply a brake on these accelerating trends towards concentration of media ownership, with successive governments pursuing policies specifically designed to **deregulate** media markets, thereby removing existing restrictions on ownership (Goodwin, 1998: Freedman, 2003).

Further reading

Doyle, G. (2002) *Media Ownership*. London: Sage.
Evans, H. (1984) *Good Times, Bad Times*. London: Coronet.
Freedman, D. (2003) *Television and the Labour Party, 1951–2001*. London: Cass.
Goodwin, P. (1998) *Television under the Tories: Broadcasting Policy 1979–97*. London: BFI.

BF

Oxygen of publicity

This phrase was coined by Prime Minister Margaret Thatcher in 1985 when Leon Brittan, then Home Secretary, persuaded the *BBC* Governors to postpone and then re-edit the documentary *Real Lives* which featured Irish Republican politician Martin McGuinness and DUP Councillor Gregory Campbell. Thatcher wanted to ban the programme before she had seen it on the grounds that it would provide terrorists with the 'oxygen of publicity'. BBC journalists voted in support of industrial action to protest at what they judged to be the governors' supine response to Government pressure (Franklin, 2004a: 77).

The *Real Lives* affair occurred during an extremely low point in relations between government and journalists, especially BBC journalists. In 1982, the Conservative Government expressed its dissatisfaction with the BBC coverage of the Falklands War and, in 1985, with a particular *Panorama* programme which showed armed members of the IRA policing a road checkpoint at Carrickmore (Bolton, 1990: 64). But while the phrase arose in a specific context, it signalled a more general meaning which included elements of **censorship** and **news management**. The government did not directly censor the *Real Lives* programme, but its public objections to the programme, including the Prime Minister's own forcefully expressed criticisms, placed considerable pressure on the BBC which resulted in the postponement and re-editing of the programme and the removal of those sections to which the government objected.

The logic of Thatcher's argument concerning the oxygen of publicity, moreover, revealed at least some degree of commitment to the view that television messages may influence their audiences. Expressed broadly, Thatcher seemed to be offering a reworked version of the maxim that there is no such thing as bad publicity. In this particular case, that a terrorist group might benefit from a news organization such as the BBC reporting its activities: without the oxygen of publicity, the offending political group might suffocate and die.

Further reading

Bolton, R. (1990) *Death on the Rock and Other Stories*. London: W.H. Allen.

BF

Photojournalism

A teenage stowaway falling to his death from a DC-8 jet at Sydney . . . a naked little girl running away screaming from a napalm bomb attack in Vietnam . . . the execution of a Vietcong prisoner shot in the head at point-blank range by a Saigon police chief: these are just a few of the many still photographs, moments frozen in time, which have made photojournalism such an important and dramatic part of newspaper (and magazine) history. Harold Evans talks of the 'unbeatable power of the **news** photograph . . . the capacity of the single image to lodge itself permanently in the memory' (1979: 6). He describes photography's 'uniqueness as a contribution to understanding the world we cannot see for ourselves', adding that words are not enough to convey 'our invisible environment' (ibid.: Introduction). Catching that **story**-telling moment requires, among other things, technique and luck: 'The writer has a second chance, the photographer rarely' (ibid.: 20–1).

Ironically, newspapers were unexcited about photographs when they first became available for use in the press more than 150 years ago and they avoided printing pictures of the Boer War and the Klondike gold rush; these appeared in albums and exhibitions (ibid.: 1). Older readers of *The Times* opposed the idea of photos when they were first introduced (Lister, 2004: 9).

However, photojournalism has clearly had a crucial role to play in the print press, with flash and high-speed photography introducing a new immediacy to news reporting, while pictures are a much-used element among the **multimedia** available on the **Internet** (Reddick and King, 2001: 241). Descriptive photographs can be used to tell a story (Evans, 1979: 17), while some newspapers have attempted to establish themselves as **sources** of reliable evidence and photographs have been used as ways of anchoring eyewitness written reports (Taylor, 2000: 131). Photojournalism is also symbolic, an economical and effective example of this being the 'mug-shot' – a facial image – although this introduces the danger of **propaganda** as it can impose a fixed character on the subject (Evans, 1979: 11). However, while there has been a revolution in the use of photojournalism in newspapers, most leading news **websites** have gone backwards in their use of pictures, according to Ken Kobré, Professor of Photojournalism at San Francisco State University. He explains that photos are rarely used to create drama or excitement and instead are utilized merely to break up a long, grey column (Meek, 2004).

Evans says it is fashionable to believe – wrongly – that the still news photograph has been rendered obsolete by the arrival of **television** (1979: 1), while there are other perceived problems relating to photojournalism, including the trivializing of news in the contemporary press, which uses pictures for entertainment rather than for **documentary** reasons. It is also argued that 'shocking photographs are a measure of the press's contribution to debate in a civilized society', although the imagery used tends to be restrained, with some notable exceptions (Taylor, 2000: 129). The view that newspapers which print black-and-white pictures are weak by comparison with their colourful counterparts or colour television is misguided as there are occasions when the former is preferable (Evans, 1979: 13).

Things may not always be what they seem in a photograph: 'The camera cannot lie; but it can be an accessory to untruth'. There are many possible stages in the process: a photographer may stage-manage a situation; there is likely to be selective influence from the picture editor; and there are the captions (not normally written by the photographer) which accompany – and could change the meaning of – the images (ibid.: Introduction). Chemical photography has become an 'antique form' in the age of **digitization**, which means a documentary image can be fabricated (Taylor, 2000: 132); digital image manipulation has three basic forms – addition, subtraction and modification (Pavlik, 2001: 87). The publishing of fake photographs purporting to show British soldiers abusing an Iraqi prisoner led to an apology from the *Daily Mirror* newspaper and the departure of **editor** Piers Morgan (Williams and Kerr, 2004: 5). **New technology** has also meant that images can now be transferred directly from a camera to the pages of a newspaper in minutes, *The Times* being the first in the UK to use this technique. It is a far cry from when the process could take weeks or even months (Lister, 2004: 9).

The alleged **dumbing down** of the media has resulted in the saturation photographing of celebrities, the most famous – and tragic – case being that of the death of Princess Diana and her friend Dodi Al Fayed, who both died in a road accident in Paris in 1997 while the car they were in was being pursued by the paparazzi. The episode refocused attention on issues of **privacy,** press intrusion and harassment by photographers and **journalists,** as well as on the editorial values of newspapers that were being guided by market considerations (Bromley and Stephenson, 1998: 9).

Despite photojournalism's chequered history, most editors would insist that, for provoking the reader, there remains enormous power in a single still photograph (Evans, 1979: Introduction); even a mediocre picture attracts an **audience** (ibid.: 1) and many do not need to portray a sensational event to justify themselves (ibid.: 9). As to any doubts regarding the importance of photojournalism: 'It is more than a coincidence that the Vietnam war was at once the most unpopular in American history and the most photographed' (ibid.: Introduction).

Further reading

Bromley, M. and Stephenson, H. (eds) (1998) *Sex, Lies and Democracy: The Press and the Public.* New York: Longman.
Evans, H. (1979) *Pictures on a Page: Photo-journalism, Graphics and Picture Editing.* London: Book Club Associates.
Lister, S. (2004) 'Times Is First for a Perfect Picture Service', *The Times*, 28 June, p. 9.
Meek, C. (2004) 'Photo Opportunities Wasted', 1 July, *dotJournalism.*
Pavlik, J.V. (2001) *Journalism and New Media.* Columbia, NY: University Press.
Reddick, R. and King, E. (2001) *The Online Journalist: Using the Internet and Other Electronic Resources*, 3rd edn. Orlando, FL: Harcourt Brace and Company.
Taylor, J. (2000) 'Problems in Photojournalism: Realism, the Nature of News and the Humanitarian Narrative', *Journalism Studies*, 1(1): 129–43.
Williams, A. and Kerr, J. (2004) 'Editor Steps Down', *Daily Mirror*, 15 May, p. 5.

MGH

190

Plurality test

The incorporation of a 'plurality test' into the **Communication Act 2003** reflected a substantial lobbying campaign by Lord Puttnam who was concerned that the highly concentrated ownership of the UK media, combined with the further **deregulation** of ownership envisaged by the Act, might result in a deterioration of the quality and range of broadcast programming available to audiences.

The Enterprise Act 2002 empowers the Secretary of State to issue an 'intervention notice' in a media merger, to allow time for consideration of the implications of any takeover/merger on viewer choice and quality of programme provision. *Ofcom* is required to conduct an inquiry into possible outcomes of any merger and report back findings. The final decision will rest with the Secretary of State which signals the sensitivity of this issue for politicians and their desire to retain control in such matters. The Act creates the prospect of a number of scenarios where the plurality test may be operationalized: a national newspaper with 20 per cent or more of the market wishing to buy *Channel 5*.

The Act states that in carrying out its duties Ofcom is 'required to achieve . . . the maintenance of a sufficient plurality of providers of different radio and television services' and must also have regard to 'the desirability of promoting the fulfilment of the purposes of public service broadcasting in the United Kingdom' (Communication Act 2003, Part 1 Section 3 (2 (d) and Section 4 (a)).

See *Competition, Regulation*

Further reading
The Communications Act 2003 (2003) available at www.legislation.hmso.gov.uk/acts/acts2003.

BF

Portal

Originally described as a service that simply provided access to the **Internet** (Tata Institute of Fundamental Research, 2003), the term portal has evolved (and is still evolving) to assume many different, and contradictory, definitions, some considering it to be another way of saying a search engine or a new name for a **website** (Sochats and Robins, 2002). The term is probably best applied to any homepage or website, personal or corporate, which acts as a gateway, via **hypertext** links, to a variety of services on the Internet (J. Hall, 2001: 23; Whittaker, 2000: 33). These services generally include features like search engines, web-based **email**, directories of people and businesses, and shopping guides (Reddick and King, 2001: 27). For this reason, portals tend to be (automatically or intentionally) the page that the user first views when calling up a browser to access the Internet.

Many general interest portals allow the user to customize a homepage with just the information they want (Reddick and King, 2001: 27), with personalized pages offering a range of regularly used links and, possibly, elements from other sites such as a **news** ticker. Portals may also appear as simple indexes, as in the case of news aggregators, or be more complex, offering a wide range of services such as Yahoo! (Hall, 2001: 23).

There are also horizontal (covering a broad range of general interest topics) and vertical (focusing on one subject and usually aimed at a specific community of users) portals (Tata Institute of Fundamental Research, 2003).

Further reading

Hall, S. (2001) 'Conjoined Twin Flies Home After Deal', the *Guardian*, 18 June.
Reddick, R. and King, E. (2001) *The Online Journalist: Using the Internet and Other Electronic Resources*, 3rd edn. Orlando, FL: Harcourt Brace and Company.
Whittaker, J. (2000) *Producing for the Web*. London: Routledge.

MGH

Prejudice

In the law of **contempt of court**, prejudice is the term used to describe, inter alia, the influence which media coverage may have on the outcome of a pending or ongoing criminal or civil trial, or other type of judicial hearing. It is generally accepted in Britain that judges are sufficiently intellectual and experienced not to be swayed by media coverage of or comment on court cases. But most witnesses, juries and, to an extent, magistrates are considered vulnerable to prejudicial influence. British journalists are trained to know that the Contempt of Court Act 1981 prohibits publication of anything which would create a substantial risk of serious prejudice to an 'active' court case.

See *First Amendment.*

Further reading

Robertson, G. and Nicol, A. (2002) *Media Law*. 4th edn. London: Penguin.
Welsh, T. and Greenwood, W. (2003) *McNae's Essential Law for Journalists*, 17th edn. London: LexisNexis.

MNH

Press baron

National newspapers have traditionally been owned by powerful and rich businessmen known as press barons, although these proprietors are now often referred to as **media moguls**, largely as a result of cross-media **ownership**.

Seymour-Ure says barons 'were often supreme egotists: flamboyant, assertive, idiosyncratic, ostentatious, ruthless – yet inspiring great loyalty and affection. A newspaper suits such behaviour . . . it is a natural tool for the autocrat.' Despite great wealth, they were not out to maximize profits. Some press owners were self-made businessmen, while others inherited newspapers, as in the case of Rupert Murdoch, whose father built an empire in Australia which his son has since done on a world scale. Other heirs were not as successful; Beaverbrook's Express group did not prosper under his son, Max Aitken (Seymour-Ure, 1991: 34–5).

Press barons need to have huge fortunes to be able to afford to own and run newspapers, which is an expensive business: 'Lord Beaverbrook, one of history's great press barons, insisted on people re-using envelopes to save money. In the end, Robert Maxwell's pockets weren't deep enough, which is why he dipped his hand into those of his pensioners' (BBC Online, 2003).

Traditionally, press barons also have a hunger for power and influence. Stanley Baldwin, British prime minister three times in the 1920s and 1930s, offered this view of the role of press barons such as Lord Rothermere and Lord Beaverbrook: 'What proprietorship of these papers is aiming at is power, and power without responsibility – the prerogative of the harlot throughout the ages' (Curran and Seaton, 1997: 42). The majority of barons saw their newspapers as a means to an end, usually in advance of a political cause or party and, particularly before 1945, the pursuit of their own career, public or political (Seymour-Ure, 1991: 35).

Alfred Harmsworth (later Lord Northcliffe) is generally recognized as being the 'progenitor of truly popular **journalism** and mass-circulation newspapers', assisted by his brother Harold, later to become Lord Rothermere (Franklin, 1997: 80).

See *Proprietorialism*

Further reading

BBC Online (2003) 'Want to Be a Press Baron? Read this first', 21 November, available at: http://news.bbc.co.uk/1/hi/magazine/3225990.stm.

Curran, J. and Seaton, J. (1997) *Power without Responsibility*, 5th edn. London: Routledge.

Franklin, B. (1997) *Newszak and News Media*. London: Arnold.
Seymour-Ure, C. (1991) *The British Press and Broadcasting since 1945*. Oxford: Basil Blackwell.

MGH

Press freedom

The freedom of the press is a bulwark of democracy, a protection against state and/or oligarchical repression. Historically it is a freedom hard-won in past centuries, by political activists, writers and journalists who, to nurture it, risked jail or execution. In totalitarian countries that struggle continues. In many democracies press freedom is guaranteed in their constitutions.

Press freedom is an essential part of the broader human right of freedom of speech/freedom of expression – the liberty to express and exchange opinions and information, and to seek self-fulfilment as individuals in self-expression and in the holding of chosen beliefs.

> Political philosophers sometimes regard the liberty as a *natural right* of individuals as against the state, which must be recognised whether or not, either in general or particular cases, it is for the benefit of society as a whole. The right is on some versions of this approach regarded as internally connected with fundamental concepts of human dignity and the right of each person to equal respect and concern. Other arguments for the free speech principle are more obviously utilitarian in spirit. (Barendt, 1985: 5)

The nineteenth century liberal John Stuart Mill is the UK philosopher most associated with general utilitarian arguments – that freedom of speech permits societies, through open debate, to establish what is true, thereby helping all types of knowledge to develop. The protection of such freedom in modern constitutions is probably more closely connected with one particular utilitarian theme – 'the desirability of an informed electorate' (Barendt, 1985: 4). Press freedom can be interpreted, in some contexts, as being distinct (wider or narrower) from any general freedom of speech (ibid.: 67–77).

Press freedom means that anyone can, if they have the means, launch a newspaper, magazine or website to publish their views. But this freedom is not absolute. There are competing human rights, e.g. the protection of reputation against **defamation**, to preservation of public order. These and national security considerations cause societies to limit press freedom to varying degrees. A characteristic of a free society is that the courts or government, to avoid censorship, will only use 'prior restraint' – i.e. legal force to stop the media publishing certain matter – in narrowly, clearly defined circumstances. But though normally publishers will not be constrained *before* they publish, they may subsequently face legal action, e.g. libel or criminal proceedings, if matter published breaches the rights of other people.

The UK has no formal constitution. Its common law (i.e. case law made by judges) gradually evolved to offer some recognition of freedom of speech as a fundamental principle to be upheld, though there was generally no presumption made in its favour when weighing it against other rights (Robertson and Nicol, 2002: ix). In 2000 the **Human Rights Act** took effect to incorporate the European Convention of Human Rights into UK domestic law. The Convention's Article 10 sets out a specific right to freedom of expression. This will oblige UK judges, in their rulings, to begin developing general principles of press freedom (Nicol et al., 2001: 8).

See *First Amendment, Regulation.*

Further reading

Curran, J. and Seaton, J. (1997) *Power without Responsibility*, 5th edn. London: Routledge.
Humphreys, P.J. (1996) *Mass Media and Media Policy in Western Europe*. Manchester: Manchester University Press.
Sanders, K. (2003) *Ethics and Journalism*. London: Sage.

MNH

Presupposition

A presupposition is a taken-for-granted, implicit claim embedded within the explicit meaning of a text or utterance. Presuppositions are marked in a variety of ways in texts, Reah (2002: 106) lists three linguistic structures common to presupposed meaning. First, certain words, such as change of state verbs (stop, begin, continue) or implicative verbs (manage, forget) invoke presupposed meaning in their very use: 'stop' presupposes movement; 'forget' presupposes a great deal, including an attempt to remember. Second, the definite article ('the _') and possessive articles ('his/her _') trigger presuppositions. For example: 'the challenge facing the modern world' not only presupposes *a* challenge exists but also that *a* modern world does too (see also Fairclough, 2000: 27; 163). Third, presuppositions are present in 'wh- questions', such as 'why', 'when', 'who', etc. So, a politician being asked 'who is responsible for the poor state of the National Health Service?' is actually being asked two questions: the explicit request to name someone; and the presupposed question 'Is someone responsible for the poor state of the National Health Service?' which remains implicit.

Fourth, Reah omits to mention that presuppositions can also be embedded within noun phrases themselves. Sometimes this embedding is largely uncontentious; on other occasions, usually because the noun refers to social or political subjects, the presupposed meaning is more questionable. Take the following question and answer:

Q: What's the future if uneconomic pits continue to be around . . .?
A: Well – as you know Miss Chalmers . . . for the last 40 minutes I've been explaining to you that the NCB in Britain is the most efficient and technologically advanced industry in the world. (from Harris, 1991: 85)

In a similar way to the 'wh- question' above, here the interviewer (intentionally or otherwise) embeds a presupposition that 'uneconomic pits exist' in a question ostensibly about the future of coal mining in the UK. The respondent resists the presupposition by challenging the question itself.

Further reading

Fairclough, N. (2000) *New Labour, New Language?* London: Routledge.
Reah, D. (2002) *The Language of Newspapers.* London: Routledge.

JER

196

Primary definition

The process by which powerful **sources** succeed in influencing the news **agenda** setting in accordance with their own version of events. Coined by Hall et al. (1978), primary definition predicts that 'those in powerful or in high status positions who offer opinions about controversial topics will have their definitions accepted, because such spokesmen are understood to have access to more accurate or specialized information on particular topics than the majority of the population'. The inclusion of sources is based on a 'hierarchy of credibility' in which the opinions of establishment institutions – the government, leaders and key members of mainstream political parties, the judiciary, the police and other agencies of law and security – are given primacy, while the opinions of the politically or socially marginal are relegated to a minor role. This occurs, not through any conspiracy between journalists and these elite sources, but as a consequence of the pressure to write to deadlines combined with the professional requirement of **objectivity** (and the need for 'authoritative sources' in particular), which push journalists towards the time-saving **information subsidies** of elites and their well-resourced **public relations** departments.

Primary definition has been the subject of intense debate, with criticisms taking four broad forms. First, from a methodological point of view, primary definition 'fails to focus upon the source–media relation from the standpoint of the sources themselves' (Schlesinger, 1989: 284). In doing so, Hall et al. ignore the questions of how sources anticipate media criteria of inclusion, tailor their news releases according to news outlet and develop **news management** strategies (including choreographed media events, **spin** and outright manipulation) in order to gain favourable news coverage (Franklin, 1998).

Second, there are sometimes significant difficulties in distinguishing between who Hall et al. suggest should be regarded as primary sources. Assuming that 'the government' are a primary source, does this include all government MPs or just those who form part of the executive?

Third, there is Schlesinger's (1990) related criticism that Hall et al. assume too much unity within primary definers. While this is a common criticism of any research which claims that social elites exert dominance over the news media to the detriment of other social groups (see **lapdog theory**), Hall et al. are particularly susceptible due to the implied binary of the organizing metaphor: primary sources supply the dominant message and marginal sources supply the dissenting message.

Fourth, for Schlesinger (1990), primary definition fails to acknowledge or account for the way in which source–media relations can change over periods of time. The capacity to define the news agenda can shift, with some organizations only holding primacy for a limited period. This is best illustrated by Hall et al.'s inclusion of trades unions as primary definers – a level of status and credibility which, Manning (1998) illustrates, the news media no longer grant to organized labour.

Further reading

Hall, S. et al. (1978) *Policing the Crisis*. London: Macmillan.
Manning, P. (2001) *News and News Sources: A Critical Introduction*. London: Sage.

Schlesinger, P. (1990) 'Rethinking the Sociology of Journalism: Source Strategies and the Limits of Media Centrism', in Ferguson, M. (ed.) *Public Communication: The New Imperatives*. Thousand Oaks, CA: Sage.

JER

Prime Minister's Press Secretary (PMPS)

Bernard Ingham, press secretary to Margaret Thatcher from November 1979 to 1990 described the role of the PMPS as 'a bridge . . . between media and government' (Ingham, 1991: 164). Ingham orchestrated a two-way flow of political communications informing the Prime Minister about media reporting of her government but also advising her about what information to release to the media: and with what **spin**! In brief, the role of the PMPS is to handle all aspects of the Prime Minister's press relations.

George Steward, an official from the Foreign Office News Department, was the first Press Secretary appointed in 1931 by Ramsey MacDonald, who wanted professional advice on how to handle the Conservative-dominated press (Cockerell et al., 1984: 37). A central brief for the post has always been the management of news media to guarantee that Number 10's spin on political events secures prime coverage in press reports (Harris, 1990: 74). Bernard Ingham achieved a certain notoriety for the post by centralizing government communications at Number 10, amid allegations that Thatcher was using her PMPS to brief the **Lobby** against her opponents in the Cabinet. The power of the office increased substantively during Ingham's tenure: one journalist dubbed Ingham the 'Minister of Information' (ibid.: 170) while another described him as 'the real deputy Prime Minister' (Lawson, 1990: 32).

From 1997 to 2003, Alastair Campbell, Blair's press secretary, built on Ingham's legacy to establish an even more centralized system of government communications (Franklin, 2004a). In 1998, Campbell established the *Media Monitoring Unit*, the *Strategic Communications Unit* and worked with an expansive corp of special advisers in the No 10 Press Office in an unprecedented effort to manage news coverage of the new Labour Government (Franklin, 1998; Blick, 2004). His abrasive and confrontational approach to journalists during the twice-daily lobby briefings prompted some journalists to describe Campbell and other

198

senior Labour politicians as 'control freaks' (Jones, 2002). In 2000 Campbell became Director of Communications, delegating his previous PMPS role of briefing the lobby to his deputies Godric Smith and Tom Kelly, the Prime Minister's Official Spokespersons (PMOS). Campbell resigned on 29 July 2003 following a very public row with the BBC about the Corporation's reporting of the Iraq war, the death of scientist Dr David Kelly and the establishment of the **Hutton Inquiry**. Many observers suggested that Campbell's reliance on spin and his own growing public profile were inimical to his continuation in the post of PMPS, which traditionally stressed the anonymity of the postholder (Jones, 2003; Oborne and Walters, 2004). Campbell's successor is David Hill, a public relations specialist and previously Director of Communications for the Labour Party.

Further reading

Blick, A. (2004) *People Who Live in the Dark: The History of the Special Adviser in British Politics*. London: Politicos.
Cockerell, M. et al. (1984) *Sources Close to the Prime Minister: Inside the Hidden World of the News Manipulators*. London: Macmillan.
Franklin, B. (2004a) *Packaging Politics: Political Communications in Britain's Media Democracy*. London: Arnold.
Ingham, B. (1991) *Kill the Messenger*. London: HarperCollins.
Jones, N. (2002) *The Control Freaks: How New Labour Gets its Own Way*. London: Politicos.
Oborne, P. and Walters, S. (2004) *Alastair Campbell*. London: Aurum.

BF

Privacy

199

Most of the UK controversies about, and official inquiries into, journalistic ethics have been triggered by concern about privacy. Journalistic intrusions into an individual's privacy fall into two basic categories:

- invasion of physical and personal space to gather information about or images of you – which could include journalists laying siege in a **media scrum** to your home, persistently knocking on your door or ringing you, following you, filming who you meet, listening to/recording your conversations, pestering your friends for information;
- the publication of (true) private facts, e.g. about relationships, sexual orientation, sexual habits, finances, health.

Perhaps a third category of intrusion is the publication of speculation about an individual's private thoughts or feelings, which, while neither true nor libellous, could hinder their actual or potential relationships, for instance speculation, while Prince William remains unmarried, about who his girlfriend may be.

Concern about the intrusive nature of the emerging modern press led to Samuel Warren and Louis Brandeis publishing their seminal article 'The Right to Privacy' in the *Harvard Law Review* in 1890, in which they wrote:

> The press is overstepping in every direction the obvious bounds of propriety and of decency. Gossip is no longer the resource of the idle and of the vicious, but has become a trade, which is pursued with industry as well as effrontery. To satisfy a prurient taste the details of sexual relations are spread broadcast in the columns of the daily papers. (Warren and Brandeis, 1890)

They correctly forecast that the common law could develop to protect privacy, but such development was very limited in the UK during the twentieth century because judges – wary of restricting **press freedom** – held back from creating a distinct civil tort of privacy, and Parliament held back from creating one by statute.

In 1991 the British press, responding to the **Calcutt** Committee's report into privacy, improved its ethical **self-regulation** by launching the *Press Complaints Commission*, and later increased protection of privacy by amending its code of practice after the death in 1997 of Princess Diana, initially perceived as being caused by press photographers pursuing her, rather than – as was the case – by a chauffeur under the influence of alcohol (Press Complaints Commission, 1997). Britain's adoption of the European Convention of Human Rights into domestic law in October 2000 means that UK judges must now – in cases concerning alleged intrusion – consider both its Article 8, protecting privacy, and Article 10, protecting press freedom. Supermodel Naomi Campbell's 2004 House of Lords victory over the *Daily Mirror*, after it revealed details of her treatment for drug addiction, suggests the Convention's adoption will push the common law of confidence further towards a privacy tort [Campbell V. MGN Ltd [2004] UKHL 22]. The tabloid press fear the courts will consistently view the PCC's concept of privacy as too limited. The UK media also fear development of data protection law along European lines will create new 'image' rights (Tench, 2004). But few people can afford to use the civil courts. Any privacy tort will mainly benefit the rich.

See *Ethics, Human Rights Act, Public interest.*

Further reading

Culture, Media and Sport Select Committee (2003) *Fifth Report: Privacy and Media Intrusion.* London: HC.

Department for Media, Culture and Sport (2003) Response to the Fifth Report of the Culture, Media and Sport Select Committee on 'Privacy and Media Intrusion', at http://www.parliament.uk/parliamentary_committees/culture__media_and_sport/ cm_5985.cfm.

Frost, C. (2000) *Media Ethics and Self-regulation.* London: Longman.

Keeble, R. (2001) *Ethics for Journalists.* London: Routledge.

Robertson, G. and Nicol, A. (2002) *Media Law.* 4th edn. London: Penguin.

Rozenberg, J. (2004) *Privacy and the Press.* Oxford: Oxford University Press.

Sanders, K. (2003) *Ethics and Journalism.* London: Sage.

Shannon, R. (2001) *A Press Free and Responsible.* London: John Murray.

MNH

Producer choice

As the broadcasting environment of the late 1980s became more competitive, the *BBC* was once again under attack for being bureaucratic, inefficient and costly. The Broadcasting Act of 1990 paved the legislative way for an expansion in **radio** and **television** and in an effort to introduce competition and free up the market it stipulated that the BBC should take 25 per cent of its programmes from **independent producers**. John Birt – now Sir John – had taken over as Director General of the BBC in 1992 and producer choice was seen as a way of introducing an internal market within the BBC. For the first time, programme-makers could go outside the Corporation to buy services such as design, graphics or studio space if it were cheaper than staying in-house.

Introduced in April 1993, Birt argued that producer choice would deliver 'greater freedom for programme-makers, more value on the screen, greater efficiencies, less bureaucracy and a devolution of power' (*Guardian*, 30 October 1991, in Franklin, 1997: 186). There was much protest. It was feared the BBC could become an organization that commissions programmes rather than makes them *and* broadcasts them. There was the spectacle of producers haggling with colleagues in service departments over contracts. Programme-makers had to account for all their expenditure. And there were anomalies, for example, CDs cost more to borrow from the BBC library than to buy in a shop (BBC, 2003).

Reflecting upon the experience of producer choice, Jane Mote, one-time executive editor of BBC London, recalled that 'the price of doing anything within your own department rocketed. Suddenly real animosity grew' (Sennitt, 2002).

There is some evidence that the BBC under former Director General Greg Dyke began to move away from some aspects of the internal market. For example, producers no longer had to pay directly for many library services (BECTU, 2000), there's a one-off annual cash transfer from programme departments instead.

Further reading

Franklin, B. (1997) *Newszak and News Media*. London: Arnold.
Sennitt, A. (2002) 'This Is LDN'. available at: http://www.rnw.nl/realradio/features/html/bbcldn020301.html.

MK

Producers' guidelines

A publicly available code of ethics expressing the values and standards the *BBC* expects of its journalists and programme-makers. It brings together aspects of legal **regulation** and codes of practice.

In the introduction to the fourth edition, the former BBC Director General Greg Dyke described the 358 pages as 'a working document for programme teams to enable them to think their way through some of the more difficult dilemmas they may face' (BBC, 2003). For BBC employees, including **freelances** and **independent producers**, the Guidelines are 'more than a moral responsibility . . . also a contractual obligation' (ibid.).

First published in 1993, the Guidelines summarize 'the BBC's fundamental editorial values such as **impartiality**, **accuracy**, **fairness**, editorial independence and commitment to appropriate standards of taste and decency'.

The controversial **Hutton Inquiry**, which seriously criticized the BBC's journalism in the wake of the death of government scientist Dr David Kelly, led to something of a restatement of these 'guiding principles' in the Neil Report of June 2004.

Further reading

BBC (2004) *The BBC's Journalism after Hutton: The Report of the Neil Review Team*, at http://www.bbc.co.uk/info/policies/neil report/.

Hutton (2004) *Report of the Inquiry into the Circumstances Surrounding the Death of Dr David Kelly*, CMG. London: The Stationery Office. Neil Report (2004) http://www.bbc.w.uk/info/policies/neil_report.

MK

Production format roles

These are a tool for analyzing authorship of texts (Goffman, 1981). Authorship of a **text** can be a collective enterprise, with a number of individuals responsible for the meanings and arguments which a text communicates – both in terms of specific claims and the overall position a text takes on an issue – aside from the person speaking or the person whose name is at the top of the story. In short, the person (or people) responsible for a message may not be the person who actually speaks it. The production format roles are a way of dissecting 'the author' in order to better understand these processes.

Goffman suggests that 'the author' can be broken down into three functional roles: the author, the animator and the principal. Taking each in turn: the author is the person who has selected the words and put them together; the animator is the 'body engaged in acoustic activity', or the person who is actually speaking or disseminating these words; and the principal is the person 'whose position is established by the words that are spoken, someone whose beliefs have been told, someone who is committed to what the words say' (ibid.: 144). In the simplest cases, all three functional roles are played by the same person: if I engaged you in conversation, I would select words I considered right for the job, I would speak them and they would (to a varying degree of success) communicate my opinion. However, consider TV advertising: here the animator would usually be an actor, but the author and principal roles are taken by individuals within the advertising agency. Similarly, a newspaper report may be authored by a journalist and animated by sub- and copy-editors, but the principal of the article may be a politician, or a corporation, or the proprietor of the newspaper, whose position on an issue is being supported.

Further reading

Goffman, E. (1981) *Forms of Talk*. Philadelphia, PA: University of Pennsylvania Press.

JER

203

Promise of performance

In order to be awarded a full licence to launch a **commercial radio** station, applicants have to tell the regulatory body *Ofcom* (which superseded the *Radio Authority*), among other things, the shape of their programming. This covers everything from how much music, what sort of music, how much speech, what sort of speech, how much news, how much of it local. It bears some comparison to the efforts in the early 1990s to introduce a '**quality threshold**' into **television** licensing but without applicants having to reach a particular standard.

This publicly available 'promise of performance' is a formal undertaking on the part of the applicant. It can be modified or clarified during the application process but will determine the station's character and style and play a part in the licensing decision.

After six months on air, the promise of performance becomes a mutually agreed programming 'format', which is meant to give the service flexibility to evolve without changing its fundamental character. Licence holders can only modify it with the agreement of Ofcom, and if the changes do not 'substantially alter' the character of the service, or narrow listening choice (Ofcom, 2004b).

Further reading

Ofcom (2004b) 'Ofcom Guidance for the Public Interest Test for Media Mergers'. http://www.ofcom.org.uk/codes_guidelines/broadcasting/media_mergers/.

MK

Propaganda

The systematic propagation of political beliefs. The first recorded use of the word propaganda has been traced to the seventeenth century, 'when Pope Gregory XV named in 1622 the [*Sacra*] *Congregatio de Propaganda Fide* (Congregation for the Propagation of the Faith), a missionary organisation set up by the Vatican to counteract the rival ideas of the Protestant reformation' (Clark, 1997: 7). The original meaning of 'propaganda' was therefore clearly not laden with the pejorative overtones it currently has, since this department of papal propagandists proudly performed 'the task of reviving Catholicism in Reformation Europe and strengthening it in the New World' (Taylor, 1995: 111).

The negative connotations associated with propaganda stem mainly from government campaigns during the First World War – particularly those of the British Government, who 'set the standard in modern propaganda or others to follow' (Taylor, 1995: 3). During the First World War, '[f]acts were deployed selectively yet rationally, while falsehoods were eschewed in the belief that they would ultimately be exposed and thereby jeopardise the credibility of those facts that had been released' (ibid.). As this quote perhaps demonstrates, propaganda usually operates by utilizing established facts, building on conventional (but often **mythic**) beliefs and, in particular, playing on the fears or desires of the **target audience**. Indeed, 'Propaganda is as much about confirming as about converting public opinion' (Welch, 1993: 9), and authors have adopted a variety of metaphors (e.g. 'fertile ground') to describe propaganda's ability to utilize existing beliefs. Take the opinion of Aldous Huxley (1936), for example:

> Propaganda gives force and direction to the successive movements of popular feeling and desire; but it does not do much to create these movements. The propagandist is a man who canalises an already existing stream. In a land where there is no water, he digs in vain. (cited in Welch, 1993: 9)

Alternatively, Doherty (2000: xvi) prefers to suggest that 'propaganda operates like a gas introduced deliberately into a particular environment. But it is a gas which depends for its potency upon the presence of suitably reactive elements in the atmosphere . . . Otherwise, it is harmless and inert.'

The German Nazi Party were highly successful in applying the lessons learnt during the First World War, with Dr Joseph Goebbels (working simultaneously as the Reich Propaganda Minister, the President of the Reich Chamber of Culture and the Director of the Reich Propaganda Central Office) standing as the master of its craft. Supporting the 'fertile ground' theory suggested above, Welch (1993: 15) shows that the principal aims of Nazi propaganda were to respond to 'the growing sense of crisis', the 'mobilization of disaffection' and 'to appeal to both the interests and the ideals of the *Mittelstand* [middle classes]'. Indeed, there is now 'considerable evidence to suggest that Nazi policies and propaganda reflected (many of) the aspirations of large sections of the population' (ibid.: 9), rather than the populace being duped or 'brainwashed' by Nazi propaganda, as is often assumed.

Of course, it is simply not the case that propaganda is something solely used by 'the Enemy'. Such a perception may have arisen due to the fact that 'Our propaganda' is usually given a euphemistic (or propagandistic!) label in order to make it appear more palatable. For example, John W. Rendon of The Rendon Group – the PR company hired by the CIA to promote globally the idea of invading Iraq and deposing Saddam Hussein – claimed in 1998 that he is 'a person who uses communication to meet public policy or corporate policy objectives. In fact, I am an information warrior and a perception manager' (Miller et al., 2004: 42) – a propagandist by any other name.

'Our propaganda' is given a variety of names: '**public relations**', when political beliefs are propagated in domestic audiences; 'public diplomacy', when beliefs are propagated in foreign audiences (see Snow, 2004); or 'psychological operations' (PsyOps), when beliefs are propagated in 'Enemy audiences' (see Taylor, 2003). Contrary to popular assumptions, it is amongst *democracies* and not dictatorships that propaganda continues to be most frequently used – emanating from the powerful in order to sediment their **hegemony**. As Taylor (1995: 4) explains, 'In pluralistic democracies, which purport to exist on the basis of consensus rather than coercion, persuasion . . . becomes an integral part of the political process.' More critically, political discourse in Western democracies demonstrates that '[t]he less the state is able to employ violence in defence of the interests of elite groups that effectively dominate it, the more it becomes necessary to devise techniques of "manufacture of consent"' (Chomsky, 1986: 19) to help propagate expedient public opinion.

Further reading

Miller, L., Stauber, J. and Rampton, S. (2004) 'War is Sell', in Miller, D. (ed.), *Tell Me Lies: Propaganda and Media Distortion in the Attack on Iraq*. London: Pluto Press, pp. 41–51.

Taylor, P.M. (2003) '"We Know Where You Are": Psychological Operations Media during Enduring Freedom', in Thussu, D.K. and Freedman, D. (eds) *War and the Media: Reporting Conflict 24/7*. London: Sage, pp. 101–13.

Welch, D. (1993) *The Third Reich: Politics and Propaganda*. London and New York: Routledge.

JER

Propaganda model

Perhaps the most systematic and theoretically rigorous **lapdog theory of journalism**, the **propaganda** model of Herman and Chomsky ([1988]2002) was developed in order to (first) prove and (second) explain the persistently uncritical reliance of the news media on corporate and otherwise elite sources. Herman and Chomsky ([1988]2002) illustrate that the news media serve political and/or economic elites, promoting their agenda(s) and protecting their interests to the exclusion of democratic views and the welfare of the majority more generally. In the words of Klaehn (2003: 363), the model 'is concerned with the question of how the interrelations of state, corporate capitalism and corporate media can be seen to influence media content'.

Contrary to certain criticisms the model does not suggest any 'conspiracy', either between journalists or between the news media and (other) elite forces. Herman and Chomsky explicitly reject 'intent' and 'motivation' in favour of concentrating on what journalists actually *do*, which they show can be explained in terms of structural factors and other elements of the model (for example, 'flak' and elite ideology). Indeed, the propaganda model is perhaps best described as 'a model of media behaviour and performance, not of media effects' (Herman, 2000: 103) in which the structural and financial characteristics of the news media are subject to precise and meticulous analysis.

The central premise of the propaganda model is that '[m]oney and power will penetrate the media by direct control or indirect influence and will filter out the news thought unfit for most of us to consider' (Herman, 1995: 81–2). More specifically, Herman and Chomsky ([1988]2002) propose five 'filters' on the production of news, each influencing the emphasis, tone and fullness of treatment which the media grants to different individuals, social groups and ideological perspectives. These five filters are, in turn:

- the size, **ownership** and profit orientation of the mass media;
- **advertising** as the primary source of media income;
- journalists' reliance on government, corporate and military **sources**;
- 'flak' as a method of controlling media dissidence;
- anti-communism as a control **ideology**, framing media representation.

'In aggregate', Franklin suggests, 'these five filters select and structure the news in ways which mobilise ideological support among the public for the "national interest" – a euphemism for the interests of the powerful among corporate, military and political elites' (1997: 44). As a direct result of the influence and interaction of the five news filters, Herman and Chomsky predict that a large-scale dichotomization of reporting will occur in the news media. 'Worthy victims' of nations unfriendly or unaccommodating to the interests of corporate elites will be treated in a manner wholly

207

different to the 'unworthy victims' of regimes who are accommodating to these interests. Such dichotomization will occur all the way down the production process, and will be visible in both macro analyzes (choices of subject matter; bounding of the debate; editorial support for dominant interests) and micro analyzes (tone of the article; emphasis; framing of issues; fullness of treatment) of media output. The outcome of 'filtering' is therefore that 'undesirable content' is excluded and the news media are enabled to mobilize 'support for the special interests that dominate the state and private activity' (2002: xi).

Given the mounting concentration of media ownership into the hands of fewer and fewer companies, the acceleration towards a deregulated and overwhelmingly commercial global media system (shifting from a non-commercial, public service model, particularly in Europe and Asia) and the triumph of global capitalism more generally, the applicability of the propaganda model has arguably increased over recent years.

Further reading

Herman, E. and Chomsky, N. ([1988] 1994) *Manufacturing Consent: The Political Economy of the Mass Media*. New York: Pantheon.

Herman, E.S. (1995) *Beyond Hypocrisy: Decoding the News in an Age of Propaganda*. Boston: South End Press.

Klaehn, J. (2003) 'Behind the Invisible Curtain of Scholarly Criticism: Revisiting the Propaganda Model', *Journalism Studies*, 4(3): 359–69.

JER

Proprietorialism

The **ownership** of a **media** business provides the opportunity to dictate the style of **journalism** and influence company policy (Harcup, 2004: 13). Lord Beaverbrook told the Royal Commission on the Press in 1949 that he ran the *Daily Express* 'merely for the purpose of making **propaganda**', while Robert Maxwell intimated that the *Daily Mirror* was his personal megaphone (Curran and Seaton, 1997: 48, 76). Paul Foot, the ex-*Mirror* **journalist**, says such influence on journalism is 'absolutely insufferable' (Harcup, 2004: 14).

The exploits of Northcliffe, Rothermere and Beaverbrook were perfect examples of interventionist proprietors. For instance, Northcliffe's newspapers tried to dictate government policy relating to a defeated Germany in 1918 (Franklin, 1997: 99–100). Stanley Baldwin, British prime minister three times in the 1920s and 1930s, offered this view of the role of **press barons** such as Lord Rothermere and Lord Beaverbrook: 'What proprietorship of these papers is aiming at is power, and power without responsibility – the prerogative of the harlot throughout the ages' (Curran and Seaton, 1997: 42).

The interventionist tradition of proprietorship waned during the 1960s, but did not completely disappear (ibid.: 73). And it is still apparent, with even shareholders in media companies also getting in on the act: investors in *Trinity Mirror* demanded to know whether the controversy over the *Daily Mirror*'s faked pictures of Iraqi prisoner abuse would damage **advertising** or profits – within 24 hours **editor** Piers Morgan had been sacked (Burt and Kirchgaessner, 2004: 8). Andrew Neil, editor of *The Sunday Times* from 1983–84, recalls that Rupert Murdoch had a subtle control over his newspapers, which included appointing editors on the same wavelength as him (1997: 202).

Harold Evans, former editor of *The Times* and *The Sunday Times*, offers this summary of proprietorialism: 'Ultimately, all stands or falls on the values and judgement of the proprietor' (Evans, 1994: 460). He says a proprietor of commercial and political leaning who interferes in the running of a quality newspaper will erode its standards and cites the detrimental impact which Rupert Murdoch's decision to publish the Hitler diaries **stories** had on *The Times* and *The Sunday Times*: 'The credibility of both quality papers was seriously damaged' (ibid.: 463).

Most journalists probably encounter very little proprietorial influence, although a survey in the United States discovered that nearly a third of local journalists admitted they softened the tone of a story in line with their employer's interests (Pew Research Center 2000, in Harcup, 2004: 14).

Not all media enterprises are privately owned; the *BBC* is funded by the **television licence fee** levied by the British government, while the *Scott Trust* owns the *Guardian*, separating editorial and financial matters (Harcup, 2004: 15).

Herman and Chomsky put forward a **propaganda model** of how the US media operate, with concentrated ownership, wealth and profit orientation being the first of five filters through which **news** choices are affected ([1988]2002: 1–14).

Further reading

Burt, T. and Kirchgaessner, S. (2004) 'Raised Voices and Lower Reputations', *Financial Times Creative Business*, May 25, p. 8.

Curran, J. and Seaton, J. (1997) *Power without Responsibility*, 5th edn. London: Routledge.

Evans, H. (1994) *Good Times, Bad Times*, 3rd edn. London: Phoenix.

Franklin, B. (1997) *Newszak and News Media*. London: Arnold.

Harcup, T. (2004) *Journalism: Principles and Practice*. London: Sage.
Herman, E. and Chomsky, N. ([1988]1994) *Manufacturing Consent: The Political Economy of the Mass Media*. New York: Pantheon.
Neil, A. (1997) *Full Disclosure*. London: Pan Books.

MGH

Public access broadcasting

While readers' letters to the editor have always guaranteed citizens' mediated participation in political debate and the **public sphere**, the development of radio and television generated new and specific programme formats designed to provide an impartial and balanced forum in which listeners and viewers can participate with other members of the public and/or politicians to discuss matters concerning politics and governance.

These programmes, which have proliferated since the pioneer programme *Any Questions* first aired in 1948, typically assume one of three formats. Studio debates involve audiences posing questions to a panel of politicians (*Question Time*), while phone-in debates (usually a radio format) require the public to pose questions to politicians via the telephone or Internet (*Nicky Campbell* or the inflammatory US 'Shock Jocks' such as Morton Downey Jnr.). Finally, there are single-issue debates in which the public (the audience) listens to expert presentation for and against a particular issue and then decides matters with a vote (*The Nation Decides*, which assessed the merits of the royal family).

Public access broadcasting has three broad ambitions: first, representation (of citizens in the public sphere); second, increased accountability (by interrogating political elites); third, mobilization (of the public to participation in the political process). McNair et al. (2002) identify public access broadcasting as part of the process of 'deliberative democracy' helping to sustain 'a healthy public sphere', while others are more sceptical, suggesting that political involvement via media does not constitute genuine participation (Putnam, 2000). Livingstone and Lunt (1994) confirm the democratic potential of what they describe as 'talk show democracy', for yet others public access broadcasting risks offering an illustrative exemplar of the **dumbing down** of political reporting 'descending at times to mediated mob rule'. Despite the controversy concerning its contribution to mediated democracy, public access broadcasting is flourishing. More than 10 million people regularly watch or listen to the eight programmes included in McNair et al.'s study (2002: 409).

Further reading

Livingstone, S. and Lunt, P. (1994) *Talk on Television*. London: Routledge.

McNair, B. et al. (2002) 'Public Access Broadcasting and Democratic Participation in the Age of Mediated Democracy', *Journalism Studies*, 3(3): 407–22.

Putnam, R. (2000) *Bowling Alone: The Collapse and Revival of American Community*. New York: Simon and Schuster.

BF

Public interest

This term is used specifically in legal contexts, and in a wider sense in media contexts of **ethics**, communications policy and social responsibility. It can denote specific criteria by which the usual legal rights of an individual or organization, e.g. to defend their reputation, or protect confidential matters, **privacy** or copyright, are justifiably over-ridden by the need for information to be published to benefit society, e.g. to help it understand events or scrutinize people in the public eye.

Similarly, journalists' ethical codes of conduct (e.g. those used by *Press Complaints Commission* and *Ofcom*, and the BBC **Producers' Guidelines**) recognize that in some circumstances, because of the actual or potential social importance of the matter being probed, there must be public interest exceptions to ethical norms of news-gathering and of what should be published, e.g. it is justifiable for journalists' to use subterfuge and hidden microphones to investigate criminals.

There are various definitions of public interest in UK statute and common law. In consideration of what is legal and/or ethically proper, there is not necessarily a straightforward choice of what is in the public interest and what isn't, but of which public interest should prevail. For example, there is a general public interest that medical records should remain confidential. But the media, in exceptional circumstances, may argue there is an over-riding public interest in publishing an individual's health records, without his/her consent.

With monotonous regularity, judges and politicians remind journalists that 'the public interest' does not equate with what most interests the public's prurient curiosity.

In another context, UK **competition** law requires media **regulation** agencies, when they decide whether to grant broadcast licences or permit media mergers or takeovers, to consider 'the public interest' as regards **accuracy** in news coverage, scope for freedom of expression, **plurality** of ownership and – in the broadcast sector – **impartiality** and programme quality. In this way, the usual rights of property owners to buy shares or entire companies without needing state approval may be over-ridden in media sectors.

See *Public interest test*

Further reading

Blumler, J.G. (1992) *Television and the Public Interest: Vulnerable Values in West European Broadcasting*. London: Sage.

Feintuck, M. (1999) *Media Regulation, Public Interest and the Law*. Edinburgh: Edinburgh University Press.

Gibbons, T. (1998) *Regulating the Media*, 2nd edn. London: Sweet and Maxwell.

Humphreys, P.J. (1996) *Mass Media and Media Policy in Western Europe*. Manchester: Manchester University Press.

Negrine, R. (1998) *Parliament and the Media: A Study of Britain, Germany and France*. London: Pinter.

McQuail, D. (1992) *Media Performance, Mass Communication and the Public Interest*. London: Sage.

Shannon, R. (2001) *A Press Free and Responsible: Self-regulation and the Press Complaints Commission 1991–2001*. London: John Murray.

MNH

Public interest broadcasting

A phrase coined by Richard Eyre, when head of the ITV Network Centre, to describe a new approach to broadcasting which he believed would supersede **public service broadcasting**. In his 1999 MacTaggart lecture, Eyre announced that the public service tradition 'will soon be dead. It's a gonner'. A number of reasons explain this imminent demise and transition in broadcasting philosophy and organization.

First, public service broadcasting relies on a system with active broadcaster and passive viewers in which 'viewers could be reasonably expected to eat what they were given because we the broadcasters knew it was good for them'. But in a competitive, market broadcasting system 'free school milk doesn't work when the kids can go and buy coke because its available and they prefer it and they can afford it'. Second, the public service tradition relies on regulators who will not be able to cope with a multi-channel system in which 'the vast number of sources of broadcast information will be impossible to monitor'. By contrast 'public interest broadcasting doesn't need regulators to sustain it', and regulation 'as a sort of conscience by rule book won't exist', but will be replaced by broadcasters and 'the viewers'. Third, public service lacks any precise definition. Eyre characterizes a member of the *ITC* who admitted, 'We keep trying to get our heads around it, but we don't get very far' as the 'unsustainable in pursuit of the undefinable'. Public interest broadcasting is destined to become the 'economic mainstay of mass television' because it acknowledges the importance of market forces and consumers' programming preferences, but combines these with the requirement for responsible broadcasters operating in the **public interest**.

See *Public access broadcasting.*

Further reading

Eyre, R. (1999) 'Public Interest Broadcasting', MacTaggart Memorial Lecture, Edinburgh International Television and Film Festival, 27 August. Reproduced and edited in Franklin, B. (2001) *British Television Policy: A Reader.* London: Routledge, pp. 43–6.

BF

Public interest test

One of two significant amendments to the **Communication Act 2003**, following sustained lobbying by Lord Puttnam, the *Voice of the Listener and Viewer* (VLV) and other groups, places an obligation on the new regulatory body *Ofcom* to address viewers as citizens as well as consumers and to further their interests as both citizens and consumers. Putnam's intention in proposing the public interest amendment was to buttress the tradition of **public service broadcasting** against the consequences of growing competitive and market trends in the broadcasting system. The amendment triggered a major shift in emphasis for Ofcom which was conceived initially as essentially an *economic* regulator for telecommunications and broadcasting.

The Act expresses this distinction in Part 1, Section 3(1(a) (b)). 'It shall be the principal duty of *Ofcom*, in carrying out their function', the Act declares, '(a) to further the interests of citizens in relation to communication matters; and (b) to further the interests of consumers in relevant markets where appropriate by promoting competition'. The public/citizen interest requirement means, for example, that any proposal to reduce the licence fee which might promote the interests of consumers by reducing the costs for television services, might potentially clash with their interest as citizens since licence fee cuts might reduce the quality and range of programming on BBC services.

Puttnam's amendment championing citizens was opposed by Lord Currie who chairs Ofcom. Currie argued that in any media takeover or merger it would be unclear whether the priority lay with protecting the consumer or the citizen and this would trigger judicial reviews and protracted legal battle between media groups.

See *Regulation*

Further reading

Communication Act 2003 (2003), DTI and DCMS (2000) *A New Future for Communications.* London: The Stationery Office.

BF

Public journalism/ Civic journalism

Public or civic **journalism** emerged in America following the 1988 Presidential elections which, for many journalists (Davis Merritt, *Wichita Eagle*, Cole Campbell, *St. Louis Post-Dispatch* and Jack Swift of the *Columbus Ledger-Enquirer*) and journalism scholars (notably New York University professor Jay Rosen), marked a nadir in political campaigning and political reporting, which illustrated the need for a new style of journalism which might reverse the growing trend towards citizens' disengagement from the democratic process. Subsequently, public journalism has become highly contested both as a theory and a practice informing news gathering and reporting in American newsrooms (Campbell, 2000; Davis, 2000; Glasser, 2000; Rosen, 2000).

Public journalism argues that journalists have a responsibility to promote civic commitment and citizen participation in democratic processes; journalism should promote, as well as help to improve, the quality of public or civic life. A central argument is that public journalists should report stories and issues from the perspective of ordinary citizens rather than articulating the viewpoints of senior political figures or local elites. Contra mainstream journalists, public journalism should provide a public forum or **public sphere** where ordinary citizens can be helped to identify and resolve public problems

(Charity, 1995; Merritt, 1998). In Jay Rosen's words, public journalism involves

> seeing people as citizens rather than spectators . . . making it easier for people to become engaged in, as well as informed about public life, local culture and politics. Seeing discussion and debate as democratic arts that journalists have a clear interest in strengthening . . . learning to frame the news in a way that invites people into civic activity and political conversation . . . reducing the personal and professional costs of an unearned or reflexive cynicism that is strongly rooted in newsroom culture. Finally, reclaiming for trained professionals a stronger civic identity, so that journalists can be better citizens and better journalists for fellow citizens. (2000: 680)

But Rosen's suggestion that the perspectives of ordinary citizens should guide news coverage has prompted critics to allege that public journalism challenges journalists' central professional commitment to **objectivity**. Davis claims objectivity has been 'declared a sham or at least old fashioned' (2000: 687). Others have been similarly critical. Journalism scholar Theodore Glasser, for example, claims that conceptually public journalism remains 'conspicuously underdeveloped' and needs to 'establish a sturdy foundation of concepts and principles' (2000: 684). For others, public journalism represented little more than 'a **market-driven** gimmick to boost circulation' (Shepard, 1994: 30): even radical journalism scholars who are broadly supportive of public journalism acknowledge that newspaper companies have promoted the idea to boost declining profits (Hardt, 1999). For their part, not all journalists have been persuaded to the cause. A study cites a journalist complaining 'about the "mumbo jumbo management crap"' while 'another worried that the pressure to "insert a quote from some average Joe" into every news story leads to tokenism' (Stepp, 2000, p 28). Finally, some journalists have argued that public journalism's concern to involve readers in the news making process involves journalists 'handing over' their professional responsibilities to readers and sources, 'whether they are asking them what questions to ask the candidates, what stories should be written this week, what good neighbours should be celebrated or what "good causes" the paper should get behind' (Davis, 2000: 687). The strength of feeling generated by discussion of public journalism is evident by Davis' conclusion that 'public journalism has been proselytised by people who do not understand it in ways that do not make sense' (ibid.: 687).

Further reading

Davis, S. (2000) 'Public Journalism: The Case Against', *Journalism Studies*, 1(4): 686–8.

Glasser, T. (2000) 'The Politics of Public Journalism', *Journalism Studies*, 1(4): 683–5.
Merritt, D. (1998) *Public Journalism and Public Life: Why Telling the News is Not Enough*, Mahwah, NJ: Lawrence Erlbaum Associates.
Rosen, J. (2000) 'Questions and Answers About Public Journalism', *Journalism Studies*, (1)4:: 679–82.
Stepp, C. (2000) 'Reader Friendly', *American Journalism Review*, July/August: 23–35.

BF

Public relations

It has been defined as 'the practice of presenting the public face of an organisation (be it a company, educational institution, hospital, or government) or individual, the articulation of its aims and objectives and the official organisational view on issues of relevance to it'. Consequently, public relations is understood to fulfil a largely representational role with the overall ambition of encouraging 'target publics to engage sympathetically at emotional and intellectual levels with the organisation in order to encourage publics to take on board the organisation's point of view' (L'Etaing, 2004: 2).

Public relations has expanded rapidly in the UK since 1945 in terms of its numbers of practitioners (Miller and Dinan, 2000; Davis, 2002: 173), the university provision for their education and training, and their professional organization in bodies such as the Institute of Public Relations (IPR) (Fedorcio et al., 1991; Michie, 1998: 17). But L'Etaing identifies a paradox: this substantive growth in PR has not been matched by a corresponding *professionalization* of the field. This paradox is explained, she argues, by the failure of the IPR to establish control over public relations practice.

Journalists typically dislike public relations practitioners (L'Etaing, 2004, Chapter 5) because allegedly they lack the objectivity which journalism demands. But the antipathy may reflect news media's growing reliance on PR copy which is replacing stories generated by journalists. The Editor of *PR Week* estimated that a minimum 50 per cent of broadsheets' copy and 'more for tabloids' is now provided by 'PRs' who now 'do a lot of journalists' thinking for them' (*Guardian*, 13 May 1996: 10). As **sources** become increasingly influential in shaping newspaper content, the tail begins to wag the dog (Tunstall, 1983; Franklin, 1997, Davis, 2002): the **fifth estate** of PR practitioners is taking over. Habermas has even suggested that, 'public relations . . . techniques have come to dominate the public sphere' (1989: 193).

Public, as well as academic, discourses have similarly been critical and increasingly associated public relations with **propaganda, spin** and **spin doctors**. Franklin (1988, 2004, Chapter 5), for example, has illustrated the effectiveness of PR practitioners, especially in local government, in **agenda setting** key areas of democratic debate, while Gandy's (1982) concept of **information subsidies** illustrates how structural inequalities are reinforced by public relations practice. McNair (1996), Schlesinger (1990) and Miller (1998) have explored media–source relations and criticized the implications of public relations for citizen access to the public sphere.

Further reading

Davis, A. (2002) *Public Relations Democracy: Public Relations, Politics and the Mass Media in Britain.* London: Sage.

Franklin, B. (1997) *Newszak and News Media.* London: Arnold.

Franklin, B. (2004a) *Packaging Politics: Political Communications in Britain's Media Democracy.* London: Arnold.

L'Etaing, J. (2004) *Public Relations in Britain: A History of Professional Practice in the Twentieth Century* Mahwah, NJ: Lawrence Erlbaum.

BF

Public service broadcasting

The idea that broadcasting should be organized as a public service, rather than a market-driven activity, has influenced the development of journalism decisively throughout the twentieth century.

Public service broadcasting (PSB) is closely associated with John Reith, the first Director General of the *BBC*, who argued that the fundamental purposes of broadcasting were to 'educate, inform and entertain'. For Reith this implied that broadcasting should be protected from commercial pressures and the profit motive; should provide radio and television programmes with universal audience appeal and reach; should be organized as a monopoly to ensure 'unified control', and should be closely regulated to guarantee high quality programming. Broadcasting's 'responsibility' was to 'improve the audience', to 'carry into the greatest number of homes everything that is best in every department of human knowledge, endeavour and achievement' (Reith, 1924: 34): a responsibility which frequently triggered the criticism that PSB was inherently paternalistic.

In 1985, the Broadcasting Research Unit (BRU) identified eight 'main principles' of PSB. (1) Geographic universality – programmes should be available to everyone; (2) universality of Appeal – programmes should cater for all tastes; (3) minorities (ethnic or cultural) should enjoy particular programming provision; (4) broadcasters should nurture a sense of national identity and community; (5) broadcasting should be protected from vested interests, whether economic and political, to ensure impartiality and balance; (6) costs should be shared equally by everyone who receives the service – the **licence fee**; (7) broadcasting should be structured to encourage **competition** between broadcasters resulting in higher quality programming not increased audience size or **dumbing down**; (8) public guidelines for broadcasting should liberate not restrict programme-makers (BRU, 1985: 25–32). These principles of public service broadcasting have provided not merely an aspirational ideal type, but an account of the particular organizational form which broadcasting has assumed in both the public and private sectors of British broadcasting.

During the early 1980s the Thatcher Government's commitment to free market economics and broadcasting **deregulation**, combined with the development of cable and satellite broadcasting technologies, signalled the emergence of a multichannel system which challenged fundamental tenets of public service broadcasting. At the same time, a series of editorials in *The Times* attacked the licence fee and urged the government 'to begin a process of redefining public service broadcasting' (12 January 1985). Later that year, the *Peacock Committee* was commissioned to investigate the prospect of replacing the licence fee with advertising revenues as the source of BBC finances. Peacock eventually rejected the proposal but, in 1988, a government White Paper announced the ambition to create 'a more competitive and open broadcasting market' which would place 'the viewer and listener at the centre of broadcasting policy' in order to reduce the paternalism of PSB and give audiences 'a greater choice and a greater say' (*Broadcasting in the '90s*, 1988, para 1.2).

The idea that PSB represented little more than the outmoded, paternalistic, ideology of a self-serving broadcasting elite, which denied viewers freedom of choice in programming and led to economic inefficiency, gained currency throughout the 1980s. Rupert Murdoch used the platform of the 1989 MacTaggart lecture to denounce the 'propagandists' and challenge the 'consensus among established broadcasters . . . that a properly free and competitive television system will mean the end of "quality" television and that multi-channel choice equals multi-channel drivel'.

The emergence of an expansive, market-driven, multi-channel broadcasting ecology, with programmes funded by **subscription**, sponsorship, **advertising** and pay-to-view, has undoubtedly undermined public service principles. Even at the BBC, funded by the licence fee, **competition** for **audience** share guarantees broadcasters' preoccupation with ratings: a preoccupation which has prompted allegations of a move downmarket to attract viewers (Barnett and Seymour, 1999: 2). But PSB has proved resilient. Its history is characterized by change reflecting broader political, technological and broadcasting developments. The most recent government White Paper on broadcasting suggests that PSB will play 'a key role' in television's digital future: PSB's significance is threefold. First, 'it ensures that the interests of all viewers are taken into account'. Second, it provides 'a counter-balance to fears about concentration of ownership and the absence of diversity of views'. Finally, 'there are strong cultural justifications for public service broadcasting . . . it allows our community to talk to itself' (DTI and DCMS 2000, paras 5.3.9–5.3.12).

But policy change continues. In autumn 2003, Ofcom launched a three-phase review of public service broadcasting which was completed in late 2004. The second phase report (30 September 2004) made three key recommendations. First, a new public service broadcaster should be established, with an annual budget of £300 million, to ensure 'plurality' in public service broadcasting. The new channel would be a publisher/commissioner of programmes rather than a programme-maker. The channel's budget would be derived from direct taxation, a tax on existing broadcasters' turnover or a supplement (£15) to the licence fee. Second, the BBC would remain fully funded by the licence fee for the duration of the next charter period (beginning 2007) but would subsequently be partially funded by subscription. Finally, Ofcom accepted the market logic of the positions of Channels 3 and 5 in the new digital age and recommended reducing their commitments to public service broadcasting, especially the provision of regional and children's programming (www.ofcom.org.uk/codes_guidelines/broadcasting/tv/psb_review/reports).

Further reading

DTI and DCMS (2000) *A New Future for Communications*. London: Stationery Office.
Franklin, B. (2001) *British Television Policy: A Reader*. London: Routledge.
Reith, J. (1924) *Broadcast Over Britain* London: Hodder and Stoughton.
Stevenson, W. (2000) 'The BBC in the Future', in *e-britannia*. Luton: University of Luton Press.
Tracey, M. (1998) *The Decline and Fall of Public Service Broadcasting*. Oxford: Oxford University Press.

BF

Public sphere

A concept proposed and developed by the neo-Marxist Jürgen Habermas (1989), which describes a space for the free exchange of ideas through rational **communication**. Habermas argues that this space – 'conceived as the sphere of private people come together as a public' (1989: 27) – emerged as capitalist markets and institutions replaced the feudal centrality of the Church in defining social life. An increasingly powerful class (predominantly middle-class men), grounded in the philosophy and culture of the Enlightenment, created, for the first time, an opportunity and a channel to criticize the authority of the state (Harrison, 2000: 19). Thus, the public sphere is simultaneously an intellectual space, a deliberative democratic space as well as an institutional space, centred on coffee houses, theatres, debating societies, libraries and other fora, which stand between the 'system' and private activities of members of a society (the 'lifeworld').

Within the public sphere, 'arguments could be weighed according to evidence and logic, the same universalistic criteria being applied to all communication, irrespective of the social position of those engaged in such exchanges' (Manning, 2001: 5). This procedure relates to what Habermas terms the 'ideal speech situation', characterized, in turn, by three levels of communicative rationality:

At the logical level, argumentation is evaluated as a 'product' by applying logical and semantic rules:

> speakers may not, for example, contradict themselves ... At the dialectical level, argumentation is evaluated as a 'procedure' aimed at achieving consensus ... for example speakers should be sincere ... At the rhetorical level, argumentation is evaluated as a communicative 'process' ... for example, that free participation in the discussion is not limited by external factors. (van Eemeren et al., 1996: 342)

Habermas argues that these three levels of interaction can serve as a critical standard for assessing everyday discussion and debate.

The concept of the public sphere therefore provides a useful critique of public communication in late capitalism. For Habermas, it was precisely the same 'capitalist markets that stimulated the growth of the institutions and meeting places' of the public sphere 'that by the nineteenth century were already weakening and contaminating it, through a process he terms re-feudalisation' (Manning, 2001: 5). Habermas claims that, contrary to the ideal democratic communication between rational participants, 'money and power, imperatives of the so-called system, have infected communication in the lifeworld' (Harrison, 2000: 19). Hence, the power of money and class to skew and dominate debate, thereby hindering open and rational discussion, have replaced the obstacles previously posed by the autocratic dominance of Church and State.

Of course, the concept has not been without its critics. First, that his theory 'rests upon an idealised account of [the public sphere's] conditions in the eighteenth century and on an over-pessimistic reading of its decline in the twentieth century' (Manning, 2001: 8). Second, even if the public sphere is open to all, it is doubtful that the 'ideal speech situation' could ever have been achieved 'given that power relations permeate all human intercourse and all processes through which knowledge or communication is generated' (Simon, 1995: 114, cited in Manning, 2001: 6). Even the ideals of rationality and universality do not entail any *substantive* equality, given that 'in an arena operating in the principle of procedural equality, some individuals are automatically excluded because they lack the "cultural capital" necessary to participate' (Wahl-Jorgensen, 2001: 307).

Further reading

Habermas, J. (1989) *The Structural Transformation of the Public Sphere*. Cambridge: Polity Press.

JER

Quality threshold

A phrase used to describe the minimum standard or quality of programming provision necessary to pass the first stage of the **franchise auction** procedure for the allocation of a licence to broadcast in one of the 15 regions of the Channel 3 commercial television network. The Broadcasting Act 1990 (Part 1, Chapter 2, Section 16 (1) and (2)) detailed closely the rigorous programming requirements necessary to clear the quality threshold and charged the *Independent Television Commission* with the responsibility to ensure that potential licence holders would be able to meet them. This demanding regulatory regime constituted what the then Home Secretary described as a 'veritable Beechers Brook' for the television companies to hurdle.

To 'leap' this quality threshold and meet statutory requirements, programming must include: high quality national and international news broadcast in peak time (Section 16 (2) (a)); other high quality

221

programmes ((2) (b)); regional programmes ((2) (d)); religious programmes and programming for children ((2) (e)); programmes which are 'calculated to appeal to a wide variety of tastes and interests' ((2) (f)); programmes originating from Europe ((2) (g)); and, finally 25 per cent of programmes broadcast across each 12-month period of the licence must originate from the independent sector of broadcasting ((2) (h)) (Franklin, 2001: 137–8).

Further reading

The Broadcasting Act 1990 (1990) London: HMSO.
Franklin, B. (2001) *British Television Policy: A Reader.* London: Routledge.
Goodwin, P. (1998) *Television under the Tories: Broadcasting Policy 1979–97.* London: BFI.

BF

Racism

Racism consists of prejudicial **ideological** beliefs about the innate inferiority of an other 'race' or 'races', and the discriminatory behaviour, practices and policies which originate, and draw strength from such beliefs. By the old adage, 'racism = prejudicial beliefs + power'. Taking these two components of racism in turn: first, all forms of racism are underpinned by a belief in 'a natural relation between an essence attributed to a human population, whether biological or cultural, and social outcomes that do, will or should flow from this' (Anthias, 1995: 288). Thus, racists believe that human potential is forever controlled by our 'racial essence': this 'racial essence' is assumed to wield a *positive* or progressive influence over whites and a *negative* or regressive influence over non-whites (by whatever way 'non-white' is defined at any particular point in time).

Second, racism should not be conceptualized as merely the belief that there are different 'races', or even the belief that certain 'races' are better than others. Racism denotes *structures* and *practices*, and any examination of racism should demonstrate the way(s) that racist beliefs encourage both behavioural manifestations of 'street racism' (such as verbal rejection, avoidance, discrimination, physical attack and extermination) and support and maintain inequitable systems of social power. It is at this level that the role of journalism becomes significant: what role has journalism played and plays in relation to racist behaviour and racist social structures? Does it help reinforce racism, both in the minds of people and in social institutions, or does it oppose and resist them?

Unfortunately, across the years and seemingly as a matter of routine, the news **media** have predominantly depicted Black and Asian people in terms of difference, deviance, threat or otherwise as a problem to white society (Braham, 1982; Campbell, 1995; Cottle, 2000a; Ferguson, 1998; Hartmann and Husband, 1974; Richardson, 2004; van Dijk, 1991, 2000). Some causes of media **stereotyping** and misrepresentation are associated with institutional, rather than personal traits. Prejudicial portrayals are often generated in an unintentional way, through organizational understandings of **news values**, through emphasizing conflict and impact, writing for 'the middle ground of white opinion and interests' (Cottle, 1999: 196) and the favouring of elite (white) **sources**. Such misrepresentation often occurs despite the explicit desire of many journalists to *avoid* prejudice. This phenomenon – in which the administrative characteristics of an organization can 'bring about systematic discriminations that [are] unintended at the level of the individual action of the institution's members' (Reisigl and Wodak, 2001: 9) – is termed institutional racism. Widely debated during and immediately after the Stephen Lawrence Inquiry (1999), institutional racism was defined by the Inquiry as:

> The collective failure of an organisation to provide an appropriate and professional service to people because of their culture, colour or **ethnic** origin. It can be seen or detected in processes, attitudes and behaviour which amount to discrimination through unwitting prejudice, ignorance, thoughtlessness, and racist stereotyping which disadvantage minority ethnic people. (1999: paragraph 6.34)

This definition of 'institutional racism' has not gone uncriticized. The political right have suggested it unfairly implies that everyone working in a particular institution is racist; the political left, somewhat paradoxically, have attacked the term because it unhelpfully shifts criticism away from workers who act in a racist manner by incorrectly imagining institutional practices devoid of human agency (Essed, 1991). On this point, Krausneker (1999, in Reisigl and Wodak, 2001) has suggested 'structural racism' as a replacement for the term. He claims 'structural racism' may be preferable, since it retains the organized nature of contemporary racism while avoiding the 'de-personalising, abstract . . . perspective' of *institutional* racism, which risks 'making anonymous the responsible actors who perform the discriminatory practices in the name of an institution or as its representatives' (Reisigl and Wodak, 2001: 9).

223

Further reading

Cottle, S, (1999) 'Ethnic Minorities in the British News Media: Explaining (Mis)Representation', in Stokes, J. and Reading, A. (eds) *The Media in Britain: Current Debates and Developments.* Houndsmills: Macmillan.

Cottle, S. (2000a) 'Media Research and Ethnic Minorities: Mapping the Field', in Cottle, S. (ed.), *Ethnic Minorities and the Media: Changing Cultural Boundaries* pp. 1–30 Buckingham: Open University Press.

Reisigl, M. and Wodak, R. (2001) *Discourse and Discrimination: Rhetorics of Racism and Anti-Semitism.* London: Routledge.

Dijk, T.A. van (1991) *Racism and the Press.* London: Routledge.

JER

Radio

Britain, America, Australia, South Africa and the Netherlands were all early pioneers in developing radio and establishing broadcasting stations. The equipment manufacturers were the driving force – Marconi in Britain, Westinghouse Corporation in America, Philips in the Netherlands.

In February 1920 the Post Office gave permission to the Marconi Company to broadcast to wireless enthusiasts. But it wasn't until May 1922 that the first licensed broadcast was made by the Marconi-owned, London-based station 2LO.

Also in 1920, in America a Pittsburgh station owned by the Westinghouse Corporation made the first scheduled broadcast – the results of the presidential election, although a station in San Jose, California, had been **broadcasting** as early as 1909. Sydney Broadcasters Ltd aired a musical recital in 1922. Three stations in South Africa went on air in July 1924. In the Netherlands the Philips Company began short wave transmissions to what is now Indonesia in 1927 (Crook, 1998).

All the early broadcasters were commercial. The British Broadcasting Company of 1922 was a consortium of manufacturers and only became the British Broadcasting Corporation set up by Royal Charter in 1927. It was at this point that the UK and American approach to the new medium diverged sharply, with much of American radio putting the market in the driving seat, while Britain went down the **public service broadcasting** route. Broadcasters in both countries pointed to the disadvantages of each 'highly coloured declarations about the other system became central props of each group's self-defence' (Hilmes, 2003). She goes on to doubt the usefulness of such dualisms, given the similar social functions of each.

There is much debate over the characteristics of radio. It is often seen as a medium enjoyed while doing something else – the ironing, driving. There is much complaint that radio is still an 'invisible medium', neglected in public perceptions of the impact of the media (Garner, 2003).

Radio has moved far in the century of its existence. The development of digital technology has made space for an almost infinite number of stations; programmes can be accessed on the Internet, breaking down national boundaries. But according to Wilby and Conroy (1999), radio is a 'living medium' whose essence is 'that moment of one-to-one live communication between two human beings. Its material is the human imagination. Its venue is the mind.'

The doomsayers have long predicted that television will kill radio, much as newspapers feared radio in its early days. Radio is now more ubiquitous than ever. In the UK more than 90 per cent of the population listen to the radio for at least five minutes every week.

Further reading

Crook, T. (1998) *International Radio Journalism, History, Theory and Practice*. London: Routledge.

Hilmes, M. (2003) 'British Quality, American Chaos', *The Radio Journal*, 1(1): 13.

Garner, K. (2003) 'On Defining the Field', *The Radio Journal*, 1(1): 7.

Wilby, P. and Conroy, A. (1999) *The Radio Handbook*. London and New York: Routledge.

MK

Reach/share

Nothing sets the blood of **radio** bosses pounding more than the imminent release of the quarterly listening figures. Who's up, who's down and whose jobs may be on the line.

Audience measurement of UK radio is presently based on a diary system, where a sample of the population notes down its listening over a given survey period. It is administered by *RAJAR*, Radio Joint Audience Research, and covers *BBC* **local radio**, network radio, and **commercial radio**, both local and national.

Each of the UK's 300-plus stations has a defined geographical Total Survey Area (TSA) in which there is a population aged 15 or over. A station's reach is the number of people in that area who listen to a particular station for more than five minutes in a week, then expressed as a percentage of the number of people who could listen to it.

But not only do stations care passionately about their reach, they also care about their share of listening. This is rather different. RAJAR adds up the total number of hours broadcast in every TSA, then works out what percentage of those hours is obtained by any given station.

MK

Readers' Editor (Ombudsman)

Stephen Pritchard introduced himself as Readers' Editor at the *Observer* in 2001 with a dictionary definition of 'mistake' and the blunt assertion that newspapers make them. His job is to 'respond to readers' concerns and complaints, compile corrections each Sunday and write a monthly column based on your preoccupations and suggestions'.

Pritchard is one of only a handful of readers' editors in the UK. The first, Ian Mayes at the *Guardian*, was appointed in 1997 at the instigation of editor Alan Rusbridger who had been inspired by the 'seriousness with which the larger American daily papers approach the task of getting things right' (Preston, 2002). The *Independent*, the *Independent on Sunday*, the *Daily Mirror* and the *Sun* have also made appointments.

The Organisation of News Ombudsmen lists 46 members around the world, in newspapers, **radio** and **television**. They're in high profile companies like National Public Radio and the *New York Times* in America as well as regional papers. They do not all operate in quite the same way but at their heart is the idea that **news** organizations should be more open and accountable and seen to be so (Mayes, 2004). Crucially, readers' editors are independent of their organization.

The UK was relatively late to the game. The concept stretches back to 1922 when the Japanese paper *Asahi Shimbun* established a committee to receive and investigate reader complaints. In 1938 another big Japanese paper, *Yomiuri Shimbun*, set up a staff committee to monitor the paper's quality. The first American appointment was in 1967 at the *Courier-Journal* and the *Louisville Times* in Kentucky.

Journalistic conduct in Britain's newspapers and magazines is regulated by the much criticized *Press Complaints Commission*, but it seems where readers' editors have been appointed they have been popular and increase trust in a paper and its **journalists** (Mayes, 2004; Preston, 2002).

Further reading
Pritchard, S. (2001) 'I'm Here for the Readers: Introducing Your Man at the *Observer*', The *Observer*.

226

Mayes, I. (2004) 'Trust Me – I'm an Ombudsman', *British Journalism Review*, 15(2): 65–70.

Preston, P. (2002) 'Readers' Editors Do a Great Job, But the Real Work is the PCC's', The *Observer*.

MK

Readers' letters

Newspapers print a wide range of correspondence from their readers, from advice pages, question and answer pages (for example, the *Guardian's Notes and Queries* column) and the problem pages of **agony aunts**. These pages serve as fora for dialogue and debate between newspaper and readership, allowing certain readers 'to express their opinions, their fears, their hopes – and, just as important, air their grievances' (Jackson, 1971: 152).

'Letters to the editor' represent the model genre of readers' letters. Argumentative in tone and written about more politically 'weighty' topics than other readers' letters, research on letters to the editor has recently grown substantially (Morrison and Love, 1996; Richardson, 2001a; Richardson and Franklin, 2003, 2004; Wahl-Jorgensen, 2001, 2002; Lynn and Lea, 2003; Wober, 2004). Historically, letters to the editor 'played a role in establishing the distinctive sphere of journalism . . . and were constitutive of an increase in the amount of space devoted to politics by the press' (Bromley, 1999: 148). They remain dominated by criticism, debate and the airing of political grievances.

Through letters to the editor, newspapers represent *their view* of the everyday talk of their readership, as expressed in their daily postbag. **Local newspaper** editors claim their letters' pages are 'an open platform for protest and debate' (Jackson, 1971: 154), while letters to **tabloid** editors tend to share the immediate and often sensational style of reporting throughout the rest of the paper (Cudlipp, 1953; Tunstall, 1977; Bromley, 1998a). Equally, in keeping with their **style guides**, most letters to the editor published in **broadsheet** newspapers are more formal, written in emotionally controlled language and 'could still be categorised under the heading of "debate"' (Bromley, 1998a: 152).

Wahl-Jorgensen argues that, contrary to these ostensible differences between newspapers, letters editors use four rules to 'determine what kind of debate occurs on the letters pages' (2002: 70). First, the rule of relevance, which privileges letters which fit with the newspaper's current news agenda; second, the rule of brevity, which privileges short, punchy

227

letters; third, the rule of entertainment, judged in relation to reader preferences; and fourth the rule of authority, which excludes ungrammatical writing and privileges writers with 'argumentative clout' (either arguing from personal experience or expertise). In sum, these four rules prevent 'a large proportion of letter writers from getting their opinions published' (ibid.: 77). In the same way as research on **news values**, the validity of these criteria may form the focus of future research.

Further reading

Bromley, M. (1998a) "Watching the Watchdogs?' in Calling the Press to Account', in Bromley, M. and Stephenson, H. (eds), *Sex, Lies and Democracy.* London: Longman.
Richardson, J.E. and Franklin, B. (2003) '"Dear Editor": Race, Readers' Letters and the Local Press', *Political Quarterly,* 74(2): 184–92.
Richardson, J.E. and Franklin, B. (2004) 'Letters of Intent: Election Campaigning and Orchestrated Public Debate in Local Newspapers' Letters to the Editor', *Political Communication,* 21(4): 459–78.
Wahl-Jorgensen, K. (2001) 'Letters to the Editor as a Forum for Public Deliberation', *Critical Studies in Mass Communications,* 18(3): 303–20.
Wahl-Jorgensen, K. (2002) 'Understanding the Conditions for Public Discourse', *Journalism Studies,* 3(1): 69–81.

JER

Readership

228

In newspaper terms, a reader is someone who spends at least two minutes reading or looking at a publication, while readership represents the total number of individuals within a target **audience** reading a particular publication (although active reader purchases do not necessarily reflect a newspaper's **circulation** figures). Readership figures are calculated using respondents within the target audience who have seen the publication within the appropriate period. Nearly 85 per cent of British people read a **local** (regional) **newspaper**, an increase of 883,000 since 2000, while the readership of local weekly paid-for titles has risen by almost 15 per cent in the past decade. This is in contrast to national newspapers which are read by 70.5 per cent of the adult population, a fall of nearly one-and-half million readers since 2000 (*The Newspaper Society*, 2004). MORI, the National Readership Survey (NRS) and the Joint Industry Committee for Regional Press Research (JICREG) all produce studies based on newspaper readership.

Newspaper readers are divided into grades relating to social class and based on the occupation (or previous occupation if retired) of the chief income earner of a particular household. The grades range from A, which is upper middle-class, to E, which might include a casual or lowest grade worker. Grade D is working-class people usually doing skilled manual work (*The Newspaper Society*, 2004). 'Hardly anything so divides the British by class as does their newspaper reading habits (Worcester, 1998: 41). Statistics suggest there is a direct correlation between **tabloid** and **broadsheet** designs and values, and the age and social class of readership, but this relationship is not fixed or determined solely by the market (Bromley and Stephenson, 1998: 3).

The content of the popular tabloids has been adjusted to meet the needs of their newspaper readerships which evidently prefer human interest stories to hard **news**, in which they are only marginally interested, as well as being obsessed with show business (particularly celebrities) and the royal family (Stephenson, 1998: 20). However, while the public still buys tabloid newspapers by the millions, there is evidence to show it does not support press intrusion into the royal family (Worcester, 1998: 39). Despite a boost in tabloid newspaper sales following **media** revelations about footballer David Beckham's personal life, a *Guardian*/ICM opinion poll showed overwhelming public support for the introduction of a **privacy** law (Travis, 2004).

Further reading

Bromley, M. and Stephenson, H. (eds) (1998) *Sex, Lies and Democracy: The Press and the Public*. New York: Longman.

The Joint Industry Committee for Regional Press Research (JICREG), http://www.jicreg.co.uk (accessed 21 April 2004).

MORI, http://www.mori.com/ (accessed 21 April 2004).

National Readership Survey, http://www.newspapersoc.org.uk/home.html (accessed 21 April 2004).

Worcester, R. (1998) 'Demographics and Values: What the British Public Reads and What It Thinks about its Newspapers', in Bromley, M. and Stephenson, H. (eds) *Sex, Lies and Democracy*. London: Longman, pp. 39–48.

MGH

Reconstruction

In December 1998 shockwaves reverberated through the broadcast industry when the *Independent Television Commission* fined Carlton plc subsidiary Central Television £2 million for 'grave breaches' of its **programme code**. It was the largest financial penalty of its type and, said the ITC, reflected an 'unprecedented breach of compliance'.

Two years previously, Carlton had made a **documentary**, *The Connection*, which was transmitted on the ITV network in October 1996. The programme claimed to demonstrate the existence of a major new route for drug-running into the UK, but, said the ITC, 'much of what was offered as evidence used to substantiate this was fake'.

A lot of what was filmed was not what it seemed. While the ITC accepted that Carlton hadn't reconstructed a raid on a cartel leader's house, in ten other areas, the company was found to have deceived viewers. For instance, what was described as a 'secret location' turned out to be the producer's hotel bedroom; drug runners shown were acting the parts and the heroin shown was sweets; a drug runner seen apparently boarding a plane in Columbia on its way to London never left Colombia.

But a year later, *Channel 4* was caught out in a reconstruction and was fined £150,000 by the ITC. The documentary *Too Much Too Young: Chickens*, shown in September 1997, told the story of two Glasgow rent boys. In three sequences, the boys were apparently approached by punters. In fact, the sequences were reconstructions, with members of the production crew or their friends acting as the punters. The ITC acknowledged that the extent of viewer deception was not comparable with *The Connection*.

Reconstructions can be used to good effect. They're a staple on programmes like *Crimewatch UK* (BBC) and satisfy viewers who've become used to seeing events that are being talked about unfold in front of them. But Section 3.7 of the ITC (now *Ofcom*) programme code requires that any reconstruction must be captioned as such on screen, as does the BBC **Producers' Guidelines**. The BBC also stipulates that **news** programmes should not normally stage reconstructions of current events.

Further reading

BBC (2002) *Producers' Guidelines*, Ch. 2, Pt. 2: 'Accuracy'. London: BBC.
ITC (1998) 'ITC Imposes £2m Financial Penalty for *The Connection*', press release 118/98, 18 December.
ITC (1999) 'ITC Imposes Financial Penalty on Channel Four for *Too Much Too Young: Chickens*', press release 10/99, 26 February.
Ofcom (2003) *Programme Code*, Section 3.7. London: Ofcom.

MK

Referential strategies

Referential strategies are approaches to naming individuals or groups of people, through which social memberships – for example, in-groups, out-groups, self and other – are constructed and represented. The manner in which social actors are named identifies not only the group(s) which they are associated with (or at least the groups which the speaker/writer *wants* them to be associated with), it can also signal the group which the speaker/writer is a member of and the relationships between the namer and the named.

We all simultaneously possess a multitude of identities, roles and characteristics which can be drawn upon to represent us equally accurately. You, the reader, may, for example, be female, as well as being a mother, as well as being a student, as well as being British, as well as being a Christian, as well as being Black, and so on, adding many other categories. As Reisigl and Wodak (2001: 47) illustrate, the manner in which journalism necessarily has to name social actors, and thus exclude them from or include them within different categories, 'can serve many different psychological, social or political purposes or interests on the side of the speakers or writers'. For example, a social actor may be individualized ('Paul Edwards went...') in order to emphasize his ordinariness or 'every man' qualities; or else collectivized under a broad range of groupings, each with different explicit and implicit meanings (see van Leeuwen, 1996). Thus, we can, with a little effort, imagine an individual who could as accurately be labelled as a father (*somatization*), or a 'local man' (*spatialization*), or a Kurd (*ethnification*), or a drunk (*negative anthroponym*), or an asylum seeker (*problematization* and increasingly *racialization*), or as a foreigner (*de-spatialization*), or a Communist (*politicization*), or a range of other collectivized terms. There are significant and clearly apparent differences between the explicit and implicit meanings of these terms and the referential strategies they invoke.

Further reading

Reisigl, M. and Wodak, R. (2001) *Discourse and Discrimination*, London: Routledge.

JER

Regulation

Regulation is law specific to a particular occupation, industry or potentially harmful activity, additional to the general, criminal law and civil tort. The extent of such regulation of the media varies between democracies. It can be structural regulation (to ensure plurality), or content regulation (e.g. to uphold journalistic **ethics** and quality television programming).

In most democracies, as in Britain, the broadcast media is subject to regulation to a far greater extent than the press. The British press, though subject to special provision in merger and **competition** law, is (within general law) free to publish what it wants and be partisan in politics and public affairs, in accordance with the philosophical doctrine of **press freedom**. No government permission is needed to launch a newspaper, magazine or website. As regards ethics, the UK press has a system of **self-regulation** (the *Press Complaints Commission*), with no financial sanction for any ethical transgressions.

But the commercial sectors of British radio and television are statutorily regulated, in terms of ownership, competition, access to the airwaves, programming content, journalistic **accuracy, impartiality** and ethics. Laws define the **public interest** tests in this regulation. *Ofcom*, the regulator which in 2003 replaced various predecessor agencies, has, as they did, the power to impose fines or even, in the last resort, revoke a broadcaster's operating licence if Ofcom requirements or codes are breached. Originally, a major rationale for such regulation was that because available transmission frequencies were scarce, not everyone could enjoy access to the airwaves, therefore licensed broadcasters must share it with other representative members of the public, e.g. by providing diverse, balanced programming. But the arrival of multi-channel technology (satellite, cable and digital) has weakened this rationale. Other arguments for broadcast regulation are that:

1 Television and radio are more influential on public opinion than the press, and more difficult to control as regards offensive material, e.g. it is hard, without regulation, to prevent children being exposed to unsuitable broadcasts.
2 Society is entitled to remedy the deficiencies of an unregulated press with a regulated broadcast sector, and this is preferable to regulating both sectors (Barendt 1995: 3–10).

Though the UK political trend in recent years has been towards market-friendly 'lighter' regulation, the amount of power exercised by media moguls means it remains reasonable their businesses should continue to be regulated (Feintuck, 1999: 5). The BBC is subject to increased regulation under the new Ofcom system.

See *Plurality test, Public Interest Test*

232

Regulation

Further reading

Blumler, J.G. (1992) *Television and the Public Interest*. London: Sage.

Curran, J. and Seaton, J. (2003) *Power without Responsibility*, 6th edn. London: Routledge.

Freedman, D. (2003) *Television and the Labour Party, 1951–2001*. London: Cass.

Gibbons, T. (1998) *Regulating the Media*, 2nd edn. London: Sweet and Maxwell.

Humphreys, P.J. (1996) *Mass Media and Media Policy in Western Europe*. Manchester: Manchester University Press.

McQuail, D. (1992) *Media Performance, Mass Communication and the Public Interest*. London: Sage.

Negrine, R.M. (1994) *Politics and the Mass Media in Britain*, 2nd edn. London: Routledge.

O'Malley, T. (1994) *Closedown: The BBC and Government Broadcasting Policy 1979–92*. London: Pluto Press.

Robertson, G. and Nicol, A. (2002) *Media Law*, 4th edn. London: Penguin.

MNH

Reporter

A journalist who gathers material to be published as a news report, i.e. a **story**, or a feature.

The earliest usage recorded by the *Oxford English Dictionary* to denote people working for newspapers is from 1798, in the USA. This usage evolved from the British medieval use of the word to describe a recounter or narrator.

A general news reporter is usually low-ranking in a media organization, though he/she may progress to be a specialist reporter with particular expertise. e.g. a crime reporter, medical reporter, showbiz reporter, diplomatic correspondent.

MNH

Representation

The process through which words and images stand in for ideas, individuals, social groups and other categories. In the words of Pickering (2001: xiii), representations have the power to select, arrange and prioritize certain assumptions and ideas about different kinds of people, bringing some to the fore, dramatizing and idealizing or demonizing them, while casting others into the social margins, so that they have little active public presence or only a narrow and negative public image.

A great deal of academic ink has been spilt attempting to pin down the relationship between representation and reality and, specifically, the extent to which words or images either accurately characterize or twist 'reality'. In describing this process of media (mis)representation, analysts have utilized a range of metaphors including gates, distorting lens and selective filters.

Many now argue that, since all representations are to a greater or lesser degree *selective*, all representations are, somewhat ironically, *mis*representative of the true breadth and complexity of modern societies. Such an argument reached its zenith in post-modern approaches to media outputs, perhaps exemplified in Baudrillard's work on simulacrum and his claim that the Gulf War (1990) did not take place. What we were offered, he alleged, 'was not a representation of the reality of the Gulf War, nor even an approximate construction of its characteristics, but a set of signs that bore no relation whatsoever to the reality of the war' (Macdonald, 2003: 15). Less excessively, there are significant **ethical** factors to bear in mind when deliberating the degree of fit between reporting and reality. Consider the reporting of '**race**', for example: 'should representations portray the "negative" realities of "raced" lives [e.g. unemployment, poor educational attainment] and therefore seemingly endorse wider cultural typifications, or portray a more "positive" imagery but then be accused of distorting reality?' (Cottle, 2000a: 12).

Perhaps instead of talking about representation – the degree of correspondence between **text** and reality – it may be more fitting to speak of construction, and the manner in which the news media help discursively *construct* (versions of) 'reality'. As Macdonald (2003: 14) has argued, this would allow us to move both journalism and analysis beyond debating 'the possibility of attaining proximity to "the real" and onto a more productive discussion about the "interaction between the media's role in forming the "frames of understanding" we construct in our heads about the material world, and the actuality of our behaviour and attitudes'.

Further reading

MacDonald, M. (2003) *Exploring Media Discourse*. London: Arnold.
Pickering, M. (2001) *Stereotyping: The Politics of Representation*. Houndsmills: Palgrave.
The Pilkington Report (1962) London: HMSO.

JER

Right of reply

In some European countries, but not in the UK, **regulation** imposes a specific legal duty on media organizations to grant to any person or organization a right of reply, e.g. page space or airtime, to correct factual inaccuracies published about them. In some nations, this statutory right of reply includes opportunity to respond to published criticism, or unfair portrayal (Paraschos, 1998: 78–83). Irrespective of law, journalistic codes of **ethics** recognize, to varying extents, that parties subject to inaccuracy or attack should be granted a right of a reply (i.e. irrespective of any legal right).

In the UK, the 'reply' opportunity cast in the *Press Complaints Commission*'s voluntary code is limited to opportunity to reply to inaccuracies. Usually, this is interpreted by the press as publication of correspondence on the letters page. The last Royal Commission on the Press (McGregor, 1977: 204) and the **Calcutt** Committee (Calcutt, 1990: 42–5) rejected the idea of a statutory right of reply. The latter proposed that the PCC code should include a right of proportionate opportunity to reply to published criticisms (i.e. as well as to inaccuracies) (Calcutt, 1993: 18). But the press rejected the proposal. It feels a wide right of reply would be open to abuse (e.g. should a racist politician be permitted to reply to editorial criticism of his/her racism?).

Some critics of the UK press have, denouncing its **self-regulation** as ineffective against its political bias and inaccuracies, lobbied for Parliament to create a statutory right for replies to be published with 'due prominence'. But successive UK Governments, reluctant to be seen as interfering with the **press freedom**, have declined to make such law, despite it being proposed in several Private Members' Bills (O'Malley and Soley, 2000: 78-93, 128–31).

Further reading

Barendt, E. (1995) *Broadcasting Law: A Comparative Study*. London: Clarendon.
Gibbons, T. (1998) *Regulating the Media*, 2nd edn. London: Sweet and Maxwell.
Humphreys, P.J. (1996) *Mass Media and Media Policy in Western Europe*. Manchester: Manchester University Press.
Robertson, G. (1983) *An Inquiry into the Press Council*. London: Penguin.

MNH

235

Rolling news

From the moment the *New York Times* splashed a front-page photograph of US President George Bush Snr watching the progress of the first Gulf War on **television**, news reporting has never been the same (Tracy, 1995). The station so dominating his attention was *CNN*, the 24-hour news channel launched 11 years earlier by Ted Turner in 1980.

Originally dubbed Chicken Noodle News by sceptical American television networks (MacGregor, 1997), the brash new kid on the block was a genuine innovation. It used the latest technologies, had flexible working practices, relied on live links rather than polished packages and didn't worry about using pictures from other sources. It could produce round-the-clock **news** coverage for a third of the budget needed by the conventional network programmes.

Criticism was instant. 'Let CNN send out the kids to gather the news – vacuum it all up and disgorge it without any picking and choosing, and then let the networks explain what it's all about,' said one anonymous network correspondent (Kimball, 1994, in MacGregor, 1997). And the service haemorrhaged money, losing $77 million in the first five years.

Its philosophy was straightforward. Get to where the action is, film it and get the pictures out. When President Reagan was shot less than a year after CNN went on air, it beat the networks to the story by four minutes and stayed with it for 29 hours. It was the only channel to broadcast live the *Challenger* space shuttle disaster in 1986. It brought in the ratings (Barker, 1997).

While this approach was new to television, and only possible because of new satellite and cable technology, radio in America had been doing a form of rolling news for years. It was a common format for speech output stations and arrived in Britain with the launch of the **commercial radio** station LBC in London in 1974.

In 1989 Sky News picked up the CNN baton, rapidly establishing for itself a serious reputation. The *BBC* was later in on the act. During the first Gulf War, it had experimented with separate output on Radio 4 long wave devoted to war coverage. Nicknamed 'Scud FM', it was a hit and led eventually to the creation of BBC Radio Five Live. In television, BBC News 24 and the *ITV* News Channel joined the band of rolling news providers.

But the criticisms haven't changed since the early days of CNN. Rolling news services can respond quickly to big events, but images can be broadcast without context or explanation (Doward, 2003). And on a slow newsday, there are repeats of items run previously, and hapless **reporters** standing outside buildings with nothing much to say. On **radio** it can lead to endless speculation rather than analysis and reporting. Harrison (2000) argues that the development of these varying formats can reduce the amount of information transmitted and make it more difficult for the audience to absorb it.

Further reading

Barker, C. (1997*) Global Television: An Introduction*. Oxford: Blackwell.

Doward, J. (2003*) '*Sky Wins Battle for Rolling News Audience', *Observer*, April 6.

George, M. (2003) 'Bell Attacks Iraq Rolling News Coverage', BBC News Online, 23 May, at www.bbc.co.uk.

Harrison, J. (2000) *Terrestrial TV News in Britain: The Culture of Production*. Manchester, Manchester University Press.

MacGregor, B. (1997) *Live, Direct and Biased: Making Television News in the Satellite Age*. London: Arnold.

Tracy, M. (1995) 'Non-Fiction Television', in Smith, A. (ed.) *Television: An International History*. Oxford: Oxford University Press.

MK

Royal Commissions on the Press

The Royal Commission is a mechanism by which the British government can oversee the press and has been used three times since 1945 (Tulloch, 1998: 71). The three post-war Royal Commissions on the Press (1947–49, 1961–62 and 1974–77) coincided with the growing concern within the government, and among political parties and other groups within society, relating to the role, responsibility and accountability of the print **media** in the twentieth century (O'Malley, 1998: 84). All three commissions concentrated on the role of the press within the democratic system (i.e. its public affairs coverage) rather than the human interest, sport and entertainment content which forms the bulk of material in national newspapers (Curran and Seaton, 1997: 327).

The establishing of the first Royal Commission resulted from a House of Commons debate on the performance of the press in which it was argued that 'existing forms of control, management and **ownership** were prejudicial to the free expression of opinion and the accurate presentation of **news**' (Smith, 1974: 32). The demand for an inquiry came from the Labour movement, particularly the *National Union of Journalists*

237

(O'Malley, 1998: 87). However, the commission was to prove embarrassing to the Labour Government as the report warned against the 'excessive development of the official information machine' while also recommending the press be overseen by a voluntary general council, although the industry did not do anything until forced to set up its own *Press Council* in 1953 (Tulloch, 1998: 71–2).

The second Royal Commission criticized the council, calling for it to comply with the 1949 recommendations by having a lay chairman and 20 per cent lay membership which was subsequently done (Tulloch, 1998: 72). The commission, under Lord Shawcross, also looked into the economic factors affecting the press in view of the fact that 17 daily and Sunday newspapers had ceased publication since the previous Commission's report. The council's terms of reference were subsequently widened through the creation of a special Press Amalgamations Court which would scrutinize transactions relating to newspaper ownership (Smith, 1974: 50–3).

A combination of long-term worries over the economic structure of the press, and the subsequent effects on standards, independence and choice, were behind the decision to set up the third commission which told the revamped *Press Council* it had failed to show it could deal satisfactorily with complaints against newspapers, prompting more structural changes (Tulloch, 1998: 72).

All three commissions had called for strengthening **self-regulation** of the press, advocating a continuing minimum amount of interference from the State in newspaper ownership and management. In the process, they have failed to turn the growing concerns about the press into workable policies (O'Malley, 1998: 93–4).

238

See *National press*

Further reading

Curran, J. and Seaton, J. (1997) *Power without Responsibility*, 5th edn. London: Routledge.

McNair, B. (1999) *News and Journalism in the UK*, 3rd edn. London: Routledge.

O'Malley, T. (1998) 'Demanding Accountability' in M. Bromley and H. Stephenson (eds), *Sex, Lies and Democracy: The Press and the Public*. New York: Longman.

Tulloch, J. (1998) 'Managing the Press in a Medium-sized European Power', in M. Bromley, and H. Stephenson (eds) *Sex, Lies and Democracy: The Press and the Public*. New York: Longman.

MGH

Scripts

A portion of knowledge, often shared unconsciously 'within a group of people and drawn upon in making sense of the world' (Fowler, 1991: 43). Scripts provide knowledge about stereotypical social relations such as 'the family', conventional or ritualized socio-cultural events such as 'a wedding', institutionalized interactions, such as 'a press conference', and an infinite range of other social encounters. A script will usually contain knowledge about a setting, 'a sequence of events and actions, and the typical or optional actors that participate in them' (van Dijk, 1998: 58) thereby providing a blueprint of how to act in such situations. Scripts therefore act as an 'interface between **ideologies** and other social representations, on the one hand, and everyday experiences and practices, and especially **discourse**, on the other hand' (ibid.: 133).

JER

Self-censorship

The term encompasses the thought process which prompts journalists, in deference to the news and/or political values adopted and propagated by their line managers and/or employers, to ignore or minimize certain angles or viewpoints when they research and produce journalism. Such self-censorship tends, therefore, to marginalize or ignore in the news agenda the experiences and views of some social groups, and of political activists perceived as radical, and instead to pander to dominant views within the corporation's hierarchy of what its audience should, or want to, see or hear.

Self-censorship is insidious because a journalist who wants his/her work published, to maintain job security and career advancement, will realize that he/she should not delve into certain political issues, or else should only produce work which conforms to his/her newsroom's dominant values. Self-censorship can become a self-serving, instinctive reflex, spawning a shallow or partisan approach, far-removed from concepts of **objectivity** and **fairness**.

Self-censorship also occurs at a more general, occupational level. The 'chilling effect' of UK **defamation** law may cause journalists to avoid tackling stories which have a high risk of provoking an expensive libel action. In nations where oppressive governments curb **press freedom**, self-censorship will be essential if a journalist is to avoid punishment inflicted by the state, and therefore eases the task of any official censors.

Self-censorship also occurs when journalists who are granted access to public figures, e.g. politicians or celebrities, or to the military in war zones, tone down criticism in their questions or reports, in case such access should be withdrawn. Patriotism during war can also lead to self-censorship among journalists.

See *D notice, Manufacturing consent.*

Further reading
Herman, E.S. and Chomsky, N. (1994) *Manufacturing Consent: The Political Economy of the Mass Media.* London: Vintage.
Pew Research Center (2000) 'Self Censorship: How Often and Why: Journalists Avoiding the News', 30 April http://people-press.org/reports/display.php3?ReportID=39.

MNH

Self-regulation

The media, and journalists collectively or individually, self-regulate their work when they acknowledge **ethics** should govern it, and therefore follow ethical rules and procedures.

In the UK, the doctrine of **press freedom** has made governments reluctant to impose any statutory **regulation** of ethics – e.g. financial penalty for unethical conduct, or punitive restraint on publication – on the newspaper and magazine sectors. These fund their own organization to adjudicate on complaints about their journalism. From 1953 it was the *Press Council*. Since 1991 it has been the *Press Complaints Commission*. This system, despite much controversy, has endured, modified itself and is now securely established.

Among the advantages of such a self-regulatory system, in addition to the inherent protection from state interference in the press, are that it costs virtually nothing for the public to complain to it (whereas, for example, a libel action in the UK courts would be beyond the pockets of most people); that it can flexibly adapt ethical rules to meet new circumstances; and that because these rules are drawn up by industry 'insiders' (in the case of the PCC, by the code committee of editors), they are more likely to be respected by journalists than rules devised by any statutory regulators imposed by the state (Wakeham, 1998).

The disadvantage of this system of self-regulation is that those running the adjudication body are accountable to the press industry, whose co-operation permits it to function, as much or more than they are to the public. The PCC, despite some elements of independence, is self-regulation by grace of press corporate proprietors, who fund it, set its parameters and – because they will not permit it to impose financial sanctions on their publications – keep it relatively toothless. Robertson and Nicol (2002: 676) state that the PCC is 'something of a confidence trick', unable to set the press's house in ethical order, and primarily designed to ward off the prospect of statutory regulation. Press co-operation with the PCC is controlled by high-ranking corporate executives and editors, not by the rank-and-file journalists themselves – one reason why journalists cannot be considered as 'professionals'. As individuals they do not exercise control of their own self-regulatory organization. All journalists can, though, self-regulate themselves by conscience.

For historical and other reasons, UK broadcasters are subject to statutory regulation of ethics.

See *Calcutt.*

Further reading

Feintuck, M. (1999) *Media Regulation, Public Interest and the Law.* Edinburgh: Edinburgh University Press.
Frost, C. (2000) *Media Ethics and Self-regulation.* London: Longman.
Gibbons, T. (1998) *Regulating the Media,* 2nd edn. London: Sweet and Maxwell.
Jempson, M. and Cookson, R. (eds) (2004) *Satisfaction Guaranteed? Press Complaints Systems Under Scrutiny.* Bristol: Mediawise.
Keeble, R. (2001) *Ethics for Journalists.* London: Routledge.
O'Malley, T. and Soley, C. (2000) *Regulating the Press.* London: Pluto Press.
Robertson, G. and Nicol, A. (2002) *Media Law,* 4th edn. London: Penguin.
Sanders, K. (2003) *Ethics and Journalism.* London: Sage.
Shannon, R. (2001) *A Press Free and Responsible.* London: John Murray.

MNH

241

Sensationalism

Claims of sensationalism, which is the use and presentation of content designed to cause interest or excitement, have been levelled at **journalists** since at least the 1880s during which decade W.T. Stead distinguished it from untrue or exaggerated **journalism** and described it as 'justifiable up to the point that it is necessary to arrest the eye of the public and compel them to admit the necessity of action' (Stead, cited in Bromley, 1998b: 29–30).

Closely linked to the **dumbing down** debate, sensationalism has increasingly been associated almost exclusively with the **tabloid** press (Bromley, 1998b: 84) and the creed of the *Daily Mirror*, printed as a front-page manifesto by Silvester Bolam, **editor** from 1948 to 1953, might apply to all tabloids:

> The *Mirror* is a sensational newspaper. We make no apology for that. We believe in the sensational presentation of **news** and views, especially important news and views, as a necessary and valuable public service in these days of mass **readership** and democratic responsibility . . . sensationalism does not mean distorting the truth. It means vivid and dramatic presentation of events so as to give them a forceful impact on the mind of the reader. It means big headlines, vigorous writing, simplification into familiar everyday language, and the wide use of illustration by cartoon and photograph . . . no doubt we make mistakes, but we are at least alive. (Waterhouse, 1993: 36–7)

The title of Matthew Engel's book about the British popular press is taken from an anonymous nineteenth-century verse about journalism: 'Tickle the public, make 'em grin, The more you tickle, the more you'll win; Teach the public, you'll never get rich, You'll live like a beggar and die in a ditch'. (Engel, quoted in Stephenson, 1998: 17).

Stephenson argues that all newspapers, particularly the tabloids, are now run as businesses and no longer adhere to any public service values such as those expected of **broadcasting** organizations (1998: 19), although Franklin describes how a **television** news report can contain an 'insensitive conjoining of the sentimental and the sensational' (1997: 3).

National newspapers came under sustained criticism during the 1980s and 1990s for various things, including its sensationalism, such as the press's treatment – which resulted in an apology by News International (Chippindale and Horrie, 1990: 338) – of the Hillsborough football stadium tragedy. It showed how this type of coverage can alienate sections of the public and prompt investigations like **Calcutt** into press intrusions into **privacy** (Tulloch, 1998: 73–4, 84).

See *National press*

Further reading
Bromley, M. and Stephenson, H. (eds) (1998) *Sex, Lies and Democracy: The Press and the Public*. New York: Longman.
Chippindale, P. and Horrie, C. (1990) *Stick It Up Your Punter*. London: Mandarin Paperbacks.
Franklin, B. (1997) *Newszak and News Media*. London: Arnold.

242

Tulloch, J. (1998) 'Managing the Press in a Medium-sized European Power', in M. Bromley, and H. Stephenson (eds) *Sex, Lies and Democracy*. New York: Longman.

Waterhouse, K. (1993) *Waterhouse on Newspaper Style*. London: Penguin.

MGH

Share

See *Reach.*

Shovelware

Perceived by some as a disparaging term, it is used to describe content moved wholesale from one communication medium to another with little or no alteration or adaptation for style, appearance or **usability** purposes. An example would be moving stories from print to the **world wide web** without taking advantage of the interactive and **hypertext** benefits of the online medium. 'Long stories should not be shoveled in but broken up, layered and surrounded by a hypertext presentation that makes them truly interactive' (Pryor, 1999).

However, shovelware might not always be a bad thing, particularly for those who want to read an exact copy of the print edition of a newspaper (many now offer electronic editions which are replicas of the print version) which they cannot otherwise access, for example, for geographical reasons (Ward, 2002: 125).

The early development of online **news** followed two paths, one of which was taken by the traditional print and broadcast **media**, which attempted to apply old models of the market to the world wide web. The previous day's print news was placed online, leading to 'stale and often pinched content, the result of a completely inadequate repurposing process' as much of it was separated from the graphically pleasing elements such as headlines and photos. This resulted in it being given the deprecatory description of shovelware and in users mainly ignoring it except possibly as a useful archive. Most news providers quickly abandoned the practice of shovelware (J. Hall, 2001: 28-9).

Early **television** drama could be considered to have been 'shovelled' from the stage (ibid.: 252), while shovelware is also jargon for software put onto a CD-ROM or tape to fill up remaining space or a software compilation placed, without any attention to organization or usability, onto a CD-ROM (The Jargon Dictionary, 2003).

Further reading

Hall, J. (2001) *Online Journalism: A Critical Primer*. London: Pluto Press.
Ward, M. (2002) *Journalism Online* Oxford: Focal Press.

MGH

Sign/Signification

Derived from Ferdinand de Saussure's (1974) structuralist linguistics, signification is a useful concept in the study of language and culture, offering a theory of how meanings are produced and distributed and a method of analysing them. Saussure divides a sign into two component parts: the signifier and the signified. The signifier is the actual word – for example, the word 'dog' – and the signified is the concept or idea that this word refers to – in this case, a (usually) four-legged (usually) domesticated canine animal. The relation between the signifier and the signified is arbitrary (though this is not the case with **icons**), and together they make up the sign. Meaning is produced through a process of selection and combination, where signs are selected from the wealth of options and combined to make an utterance. Thus, the noun phrase 'my / red / chair' is meaningful because of the accumulated meaning of its constituent signs and the systematic relations between these signs. This meaning can be developed through introducing additional signs, thus 'my / beautiful / new / red / chair'; or altered by substituting signs, thus 'your / blue / chair'.

Barthes ([1957]2000) developed de Saussure's approach and applied it to French popular culture. Language, he argued, is more than just reference (i.e. a system in which terms are conventionally taken to refer to certain objects or concepts). Take the word 'dog', for example, which de Saussure suggests is the signifier for a four-legged domesticated canine. How do we explain that the word is also used as a term of abuse, to signify an unattractive (usually female) person? Barthes explains this by adding a second level of signification which he called *connotation*. He describes this formally in the following way: 'the first system [denotation] becomes the plane of expression or signifier of the second system [connotation . . .] The signifiers of connotation . . . are made up of signs (signifiers and signifieds united) of the denoted system' (Barthes, 1967: 89–91). Less formally, signs have two levels of meaning: their denoted meaning and the connoted meaning; the connoted meaning is the combination of the denoted sign and the values we project onto it, or our socio-cultural and political evaluation of it. Thus, in this case, the negative connotations of the sign 'dog' (dirty, ugly, hairy) are retained and projected onto the unfortunate person being insulted.

Barthes' most famous examination of connoted meaning focuses on a 1955 cover of the magazine *Paris Match*. At the first (denotative) level of signification, this cover shows a young black boy saluting the French tricolour flag; at the second (connotative) level, this cover signifies a positive image of French colonial rule. As Barthes ([1957]2000: 119) explains:

> I see very well what it signifies to me: that France is a great empire, that all her sons, without colour discrimination, faithfully serve under her flag, and that there is no better answer to the detractors of an alleged colonialism than the zeal shown by this Negro in serving his so-called oppressors.

Even if we do not 'buy into' the connoted meaning of the photo – in other words, we do not see it signifying 'that France is a great empire [etc.]' – it nevertheless states the fact of French imperiality. As Storey (1993: 81) suggests, the photo of 'the black soldier saluting the flag can be seen as *naturally* conjuring up the concept of French imperiality', in other words conjuring the idea that France had/has an Empire. This is achieved through the **myths** that the denoted meaning of the photo summon in the consumer/reader.

Further reading

Barthes, R. ([1957] 2000) *Mythologies*. London: Vintage.
Saussure de, F. (1974) *Course in General Linguistics*. London: Collins.

JER

245

Silly season

The summer month of August is traditionally viewed as **journalism**'s silly season, in which there is very little serious **news**, allowing senior editorial staff in particular to take holidays. Politicians are in the middle of their long break from Parliamentary duty and government offices are short-staffed, suggesting nothing of major importance is likely to happen and resulting in the **media** turning to the reporting of more trivial matters (Williams, 2002).

However, history shows that in fact the 'silliest August **story** of all is the idea that it's quiet . . . the news keeps on breaking'. The start of the Vietnam War (1964), the erection of the Berlin Wall (1961), the IRA's assassination of Lord Louis Mountbatten (1979), Iraq's invasion of Kuwait (1990) and the death of Princess Diana (1997) were among the major August events of the past 50 years. Furthermore, the most famous **investigative journalism** scoop of all began on 1 August 1972 with the *Washington Post*'s first report on **Watergate** which ultimately forced the resignation of President Richard Nixon – also in the month of August – two years later (Williams, 2002).

Additionally, the silly season can refer to holiday periods like Christmas and Easter as they are also times when major news **sources** like Parliament, local councils and the courts all take breaks (Gage, 1999: 50).

So what is the reality of the silly season? 'It's just a futile, short-staffed hope that nothing will happen' (Williams, 2002).

Further reading

Gage, L. (1999) *A Guide to Commercial Radio Journalism*. Oxford: Focal Press.
Williams, H. (2002) 'Beware the Silly Season', *Guardian Unlimited* (31 July) http://www.guardian.co.uk/silly/story/0,10821,766668,00.html (accessed 31 March 2004).

MGH

Sketch writers

These, according to Matthew Parris, one of the most accomplished practitioners of the art, are 'a strange breed' that are 'something of an anachronism' (Parris, 2003: 367). But they complement the factual parliamentary coverage of **gallery reporters** and the authoritative political news delivered by **lobby** correspondents: albeit that the latter is replete with government spin. The survival of sketch writers reflects the insatiable public curiosity about Parliament. 'As long as accounts of the Commons have been written,' Parris claims 'people have been curious to know more than what was said: how it was said, what the atmosphere in the chamber was like. They wanted to know about moods, behaviour, appearance, eccentricity, comedy, even dress' (ibid.: 267–8).

Contemporary sketch writers like Quentin Letts, Simon Hoggart and Frank Johnson form part of a substantive tradition within the history of parliamentary journalism (Letts, 2003). Charles Dickens, for example, worked as a political journalist at the *Morning Chronicle* between 1834 and 1836 and published some of the columns which he wrote as *Sketches by Boz* (Parris, 2003: 367). But the journalist typically associated with modern sketch writing is Henry Lucy who wrote 'The Diary of Toby MP' in *Punch* from 1881 to 1886. Lucy's diary masqueraded as an MP's diary account of the week in Westminster, but readers knew that Toby was Mr Punch's dog who was featured on the front cover of the magazine with his owner every week (Sparrow, 2003: 61).

Perhaps unsurprisingly given their concern to publish 'cheap jokes, unfair barbs and a slanted version of the day's events' (Hoggart, 2002: pii), sketch writers have found less favour with politicians than reporters in the gallery. Hoggart acknowledges, 'some MPs hate it. Tony Benn . . . curled his lip with contempt when he told me he never read what I wrote' (Hoggart, 2002: ii). But the public concern to know 'more than what was said', the increased focus on MPs' personal lives in parliamentary coverage (Franklin, 1997: 236), and the decline of gallery reporters since the 1990s, signal a growing significance for sketch writers: as Simon Hoggart of the *Guardian* observed, 'now they have just us' (2003: 1).

Further reading

Hoggart, S. (2002) *Playing to the Gallery: Parliamentary Sketches from Blair Year Zero*. London: Atlantic Books.
Parris, M. (2002) *Chance Witness: An Outsider's Life in Politics*. London: Viking.
Sparrow, A. (2003) *Obscure Scribblers*. London: Politicos.

BF

Soft news

Father saves son's life by donating a kidney, David Beckham wears a skirt, record numbers gather at Stonehenge to mark the summer solstice, conjoined twins die during surgery. These sorts of **stories** aren't going to have a direct impact upon people's lives in the way that a tax increase or a change of government will, but they do provoke a reaction in the audience. This is news that makes you go 'Aah!' or 'Wow'. It's about the first, the last, the fastest, the slowest, the biggest, the most expensive.

But as with all attempts to categorize **news**, the edges are blurred. Tuchman (1973) noted over a two-year study that one American television station presented some stories as soft, feature material that its competitor presented as **hard news**. Soft news can be seen as something 'interesting because it deals with the life of human beings' (Mott, 1952, in Berkowitz, 1997: 176) or it concerns human foibles. Boyd says for a story to be 'of human interest it should upset, anger, amuse, intrigue or appal (the audience) or be about people who have a similar effect' (2001: 139).

See *Dumbing down.*

Further reading
Boyd, A. (2001) *Broadcast Journalism,* 5th edn. Oxford: Focal Press.
Tuchman, G. (1973) 'Making News by Doing Work', in Berkowitz, D. (ed.) (1997) *Social Meanings of News: A Text-Reader.* London: Sage.

MK

Sources

The people, places and organizations that supply **journalists** with ideas and general information (and often quotes) for potential **news stories** and features are known as sources, some of which may be routine points of contact, while others may be one-offs. The names and contact details of sources, examples of which might be the emergency services and council departments, are kept in a contacts book, paper or electronic versions (Harcup, 2004: 44–6). Cuttings, archival material, broadcast recordings and a variety of documents and **websites** found on the **Internet** can also be useful sources of information. On occasions, journalists pay sources for information, a process known as **chequebook journalism** though the practice is potentially corrupting (Sanders, 2003: 115–17), raising issues of **ethics**.

A **reporter** needs to build up trust with sources (Randall, 2000: 33) of information which could be a substantial supply of ready-made content from government departments, businesses and other powerful institutions, or from 'voices' which are poorer in resources but often still as relevant and significant (McQuail, 1992: 83). The journalist–source relationship has been explored at length by academics and it has been argued that organizations such as the police act as **primary definers** in that they supply the **media** with many of the crime news stories, giving them influence in how stories are reported and debated (Harcup, 2004: 49). Journalists may sometimes receive information 'off the record', meaning it is not for public release, although sources sometimes use the phrase when they intend it to be non-attributable (used without a named source), a common ploy in political reporting such as the **lobby** system. A story can be given to the media under an **embargo**, which is giving it to them in advance of the publication time or date so features can be prepared (Sanders, 2003: 112–13). Greenslade reports that British national newspapers daily quote a sizeable number of anonymous sources (2004a: 6–7).

It can be a sensitive and tricky relationship between the media and governments whose informational purposes might be beyond the objective needs of those it is supplying (McQuail, 1992: 83–4), a form of **propaganda** which has become known as **spin**. Well-written press releases or **public relations** hand-outs could also influence the publishing process. When selecting which information and news to use, the media should neither be influenced by the convenience or power of sources nor should they ignore marginal or minority groups and causes (ibid.: 84, 128).

The independence of journalism can be compromised by an over-reliance on a limited number of news sources (such as **news agencies**), although some dependence is recognized for organizations who do not originate many of their own stories (ibid.: 128).

One of the great principles and traditions of journalism is that journalists must protect the identity of their news sources, and it particularly applies to controversial or **investigative journalism** stories such as the famous **Watergate** scandal in the early 1970s in which Richard Nixon was eventually forced to resign as US president; 'Deep Throat', whose true identity has never been revealed, was the alias for the source who tipped off journalists Bob Woodward and Carl Bernstein (Todorovich, 1997). More recently, *BBC* correspondent Andrew Gilligan refused to name his source for the explosive story that an Iraqi weapons dossier was 'sexed up' by the British government to justify the US-led war on Iraq in 2003. The whole episode led to the suicide of weapons expert Dr David Kelly who had been identified by the Labour Government as being the main source of the story, a claim denied by Dr Kelly and questioned by the *BBC*. It also led to a call from the Foreign Affairs Committee that reporters should be forced to name their sources when making allegations under Parliamentary Privilege which provides protection against libel in both Houses and its committees (BBC News Online, 2003).

The best stories can come from 'whistleblowers', who are often people well placed in an organization passing on documents or tip-offs to the media, although journalists should always question the motive (Randall, 2000: 53) as sources have their own agenda (Sanders, 2003: 107). In the light of the controversy surrounding the Iraqi weapons dossier, Jeremy Dear, General Secretary of the *National Union of Journalists* (NUJ), insisted 'whistleblowers' should be protected, as it might deter them in future, arguing that one of the main roles of journalists was to expose wrong-doing and bad practice. **Freelance** journalist Robin Ackroyd won an appeal but faced an ongoing legal battle over his stance not to name the source of medical information given to him about Moors murderer Ian Brady, while BBC reporter Peter Taylor refused to reveal several sources at the Bloody Sunday inquiry. Sarah Tisdall was sent to prison for four months in 1983 after the *Guardian* was forced to name her as the source of its story about the arrival of Cruise missiles in the UK (Walker, 2003).

Further reading

BBC News Online (2003) 'Journalists "Should Name Sources"' (18 July) http://news.bbc.co.uk/1/hi/uk_politics/3076337.stm (accessed 5 November 2003).

Greenslade, R. (2004a) 'So Just Who's Who?', *Media Guardian*, 23 February, pp. 6–7.

Harcup, T. (2004) *Journalism: Principles and Practice*. London: Sage.

McQuail, D. (1992) *Media Performance, Mass Communication and the Public Interest*. London: Sage.

Randall, D. (2000) *The Universal Journalist*. London: Pluto.

Sanders, K. (2003) *Ethics and Journalism*. London: Sage.

Tdorovich, L. (1997) 'Deep Throat Suspects' (June 13) http://www.washingtonpost.com/wp-srv/national/longterm/watergate/deept.htm.

Walker, D. (2003) 'Journalists "Most Protect Whistleblowers"' (19 July) http://news.bbc.co.uk/1/hi/uk_politics/3076813.stm.

MGH

Spin

This has become increasingly common in public **discourses** about politics since the 1990s. 'Spin' has come to imply the particular angle, meaning or interpretation assigned to a political event by a **spin doctor**. Romola Christopherson, a government information officer, described New Labour's spin strategy as 'Labour's three 'Rs".

> First, rhetoric – getting the message and encapsulating the message in a marketing slogan – New Labour, New Britain, People's Princess – all those soundbites, getting that rhetoric absolutely clear and right and accessible. That's the first 'R'. Second 'R' is repetition, repetition, repetition, repetition. When you're bored with repeating it, it probably means that people are beginning to pick it up. The final 'R' is rebuttal, which is don't let any attack on you go without walloping back at it. (cited in *Control Freaks*, Channel 5, 28 September 2002)

Academic and broadcaster Ivor Gaber distinguishes between 'above' and 'below the line' spin. 'Above the line' spin includes those activities that 'would have caused an "old fashioned" press officer no great difficulty': activities such as drafting government/party announcements, reacting to or rebutting such announcements, publicizing speeches or announcements, reacting to breaking news/events and keeping all players 'on message' (Barnett and Gaber, 2001: 102–6; Gaber, 2001: 507–18).

'Below the line' spin is typically more covert, associated with the spin doctor rather than the press/information officer and has less to do with imparting information than strategies and tactics for the manipulation of information (Barnett and Gaber, 2001: 106–13). Below the line spin involves setting and driving the **news** agenda, but also 'firebreaking' (deliberately constructing a story to divert journalists away from an embarrassing story, e.g., Campbell's leak to the *Sunday Times* that MI6 was investigating Chris Patten when the story of Robin Cook's affair broke), or 'stoking the fire' (the precise opposite of firebreaking by gathering and providing information to sustain a story which an opponent is finding embarrassing, e.g. Labour spin doctors' efforts to fuel the story of rifts between John Major and the anti-Europeans in the Conservative Party) or 'undermining a personality' (e.g. the off-the-record description of Gordon Brown as 'psychologically flawed', Harriet Harman as 'incapable of joined-up thinking', while a 'senior government aide' suggested that Mo Mowlam's illness had left her 'without the intellectual rigour for her job' with another anonymous 'adviser' claiming to be 'dismayed at her erratic behaviour' (Franklin 2004a).

For their part, the most accomplished spin doctors try to deny the significance of spin, arguing that it is **journalists** who are the real spin doctors and claiming that the age of spin is at an end. Consequently Alastair Campbell identified a 'growing gap between the real agenda and the media-land agenda . . . and yes, we have to be honest enough to think about our own role in how this situation developed. 'Spin' never was as important as people imagine and it's even less important now' (Campbell, 1999). But on 29 August 2003, when Campbell resigned as Director of Communication, it was widely believed that his close association with spin (at least in the public mind) and the extent to which spin had become politically unacceptable offered some explanation for his action. His resignation also triggered predictable, if erroneous announcements of the 'End of Spin' in many national newspapers (e.g. 'Exit the Spinmeister', The *Independent*; 'The End of Labour's Spin Cycle?' *The Times*; and 'Time for Labour to Jump off Spin Roundabout?' the *Guardian*).

Further reading

Barnett, S. and Gaber, I. (2001) *Westminster Tales: The Twenty-first Century Crisis in Political Journalism*. London: Continuum.

Campbell, A. (1999) *Beyond Spin: Government and the Media*. London: Fabian Special Pamphlet no 42.

Gaber, I. (2001) 'Government by Spin: An Analysis of the Process', *Media, Culture and Society*, 22(4): 507–18.

BF

Spin doctor

The phrase spin doctor entered British political vocabulary during the late 1980s and its meaning is captured broadly by the entry in *Chambers 21st Century Dictionary* as 'someone, especially in politics who tries to influence public opinion by putting a favourable bias on information presented to the public or to the media'. The term has a strongly pejorative implication suggesting that the **spin** placed on information is misleading and may be consciously intended to be so: spin doctors manipulate rather than merely manage news agendas (Gaber, 2001; Jones, 1995). Consequently, Clare Short, while a minister in the Labour Government, denounced the 'black arts' of the spin doctors in her own party, designating them 'the people who live in the dark shadows' (Blick, 2004).

The first printed appearance of the phrase spin doctor was on 21 October 1984 in a *New York Times* editorial previewing a presidential debate. 'Tonight at about 9.30, seconds after the Reagan–Mondale debate ends', the editorial claimed,

> a bazaar will suddenly materialize in the press room. A dozen men in good suits and women in silk dresses will circulate smoothly among reporters, spouting confident opinions. They won't be just press agents trying to import a favorable spin to a routine release. They'll be spin doctors, senior advisers to the candidates. (Safire, 1993: 740–1)

The phrase conjoins the words 'spin' – signalling the interpretation or particular meaning placed on an event – and 'doctor' implying not the medical sense of the word, but rather to 'falsify' (as in doctoring the evidence) (Esser et al., 2000: 213).

In the UK setting, the phrase spin doctor is particularly associated with the growing body of special advisers, who are hired by government (especially New Labour) to manage and advise about press relations (Blick, 2004). One such adviser/spin doctor, Jo Moore, triggered widespread opprobrium among journalists, politicians and the public when she emailed her colleagues in the press office at the Department of Transport on 11 September 2001, the day of the attack on the World Trade Center, claiming that today was 'a good day to bury bad news'.

Further reading

Esser, F., Reinemann, C. and Fan, D. (2000) 'Spin Doctoring in British and German Election Campaigns', *European Journal of Communication*, 15(2): 209–41.
Gaber, I. (2001) 'Government by Spin: An Analysis of the Process', *Media, Culture and Society*, 22(4): 507–18.
Jones, N. (1995) *Soundbites and Spin Doctors*. London: Cassell.

BF

Spoiler

A story published by one media organization to 'spoil' the impact of another's exclusive. The spoiler will not match the rival's exclusive in terms of the quality of new information, access to key sources or pictures. But, to save face and sales, it will brazenly present another angle, either new or rehashed, on the same subject matter, e.g. revelations about a celebrity. The 'spoiler' practice is most evident in the tabloid and magazine press, where intense market competition means that a publication which knows it has been scooped by a rival will do its best to obscure this from readers. So, side by side on the newstands will be the real **scoop** and – often put together at short notice – the spoiler. The casual buyer may be confused enough to choose the latter. In **chequebook journalism**, the 'spoiler' may be based on the cheaper testimony of lesser players in the story, if the main character has been bought up by a rival.

MNH

253

Stereotype

Originally, a stereotype was an object used in printing, where it referred to 'text cast in rigid form for the purposes of repetitive use' (Pickering, 2001: 9). An aspect of this original meaning is retained in its contemporary usage, defined by Allport (1954: 191) as 'an exaggerated belief associated with a category. Its function is to justify (rationalise) our conduct in relation to that category.' A number of theoretically important features of stereotypes are mentioned in this influential definition. First, stereotypes are exaggerated beliefs, involving either an inflation of a characteristic (e.g. the fetishization of Black physicality) and/or an over-generalization from part (*a* Black male *criminal*) to whole (Black male *criminality*). Second, the idea that stereotypes are an exaggeration implies that they contain a kernel of truth. For example, Prager and Telushkin (2003) argue that Jews *do* consider themselves to be a Chosen People (God chose to give them His Torah) and *do* show high levels of social solidarity, but anti-Semitic stereotypes misrepresent and exaggerate these characteristics in order to portray Jews as self-interested and clannish, respectively.

Of course, this is the power of stereotypes: they resonate with what we (and others) *think to be true*; if their falsity were self-evident, then they would be rejected out of hand. Therefore, 'insofar as they often have a grain of truth', are stereotypes just ill-fitting categories that we use as 'moderately useful guides for predicting behaviour' (Cashmore, 1988: 295)? Quite simply, no, they are not. As Allport suggests, a third feature of stereotypes is that they function to rationalize our conduct and justify our actions. In the case of negative stereotypes, they act as an expression of prejudice and function as a tool to justify discrimination (see **racism**). Thus, stereotypes are not simply defectively defined social categories; they underpin and give meaning to social action.

Stereotypes are present in, and affect, news coverage in many ways. Fowler (1991: 17) goes as far as to argue that the formation of news events is 'a reciprocal, dialectical process in which stereotypes are the currency of exchange'. Developing this argument, Fowler suggests that stereotypes are an expression of the **news value** of 'meaningfulness', as proposed by Galtung and Ruge (1965a):

> 'Meaningfulness', with its subsections 'cultural proximity' and 'relevance', is founded on an **ideology** of ethnocentrism, or . . . more inclusively, homocentrism: a preoccupation with countries, societies and individuals perceived to be like oneself; . . . and with defining groups felt to be unlike oneself. (Fowler, 1991: 16)

In this way, the stereotypical representation of 'Others' may be one (negative) feature of news discourse facilitated and maintained through the very values upon which news is constructed.

Further reading

Pickering, M. (2001) *Stereotyping: The Politics of Representation*. Houndsmills: Macmillan.

JER

Story

A news article, or news item, published by the media as a factual account, or the material or events being researched to produce this. The *Oxford English Dictionary* records such media usage of the word as American in origin, with the earliest example being from 1892, but also records the word's use, dating in England from the thirteenth century, to describe a true or presumed-true narrative or historical account.

Its continuing newsroom usage acknowledges that **narrative** technique is needed to hold the **audience**'s attention to the story's end.

MNH

Style

This describes the variations or patterns in texts which result from choices, made by the speaker or writer, between alternatives which express more or less the same meaning. Jucker, in one of the few studies of linguistic style in newspapers, defines style as 'a comparative concept in that it describes some relevant differences between a **text** or a **discourse** and some other texts or discourses' (1992: 1). Thus, we may speak of formal and informal styles, of specialized and lay styles, of elite and colloquial styles, and so on, which are open for newspapers to adopt.

It is important, however, not to over-emphasize the issue of 'choice' when discussing style, since 'self-conscious linguistic choice is a relatively marginal aspect of the social processes of text production and interpretation' (Fairclough, 1995b: 18). Rather, Jucker (1992: 8) argues that stylistic differences should 'be seen as a correlate of the addressee(s)', with newspaper styles differing according to papers 'adapting to different **audiences**'. In doing so, a certain mode of address is perceived to be more acceptable to the audience and hence is adopted in favour of less attractive alternatives. The style which a **journalist** uses therefore tells you a great deal about the identities of both the journalist and the audience, and also something about the assumed relationship between them.

Further, it should be remembered that media institutions typically have 'explicit policies on at least some aspects of language use. Rules about usage are commonly codified in a "style guide" or "style book" whose prescriptions journalists are expected to observe and editors to enforce' (Cameron, 1996: 315). Cameron illustrates that while these **style guides**

255

are framed as purely functional or aesthetic judgements . . . it turns out that these stylistic values are not timeless and neutral, but have a history and a politics. They play a role in constructing a relationship with a specific imagined audience, and also in sustaining a particular **ideology** of news reporting.

Further reading

Cameron, D. (1996) 'Style Policy and Style Politics', *Media, Culture and Society*, 18(3): 315–33.

Tucker, A.H. (1992) *Social Stylistics: Syntactic Variation in British Newspapers*. Berlin: Mouton de Gruyter.

JER

Style guide

Nothing arouses more ire and irritation among sections of the population than bad use of the English language. **Journalists** who write for a living upset these people at their peril. They must also run the gauntlet of grouchy sub-editors in **newsrooms** across the country capable of apoplexy at a misplaced apostrophe. As Lynne Truss puts it: 'it's tough being a stickler for punctuation these days' (2003: 2).

All **news** organizations have a concept of a distinctive house style which is the language in which **stories** should be written. Many newsrooms have their own style books (print, electronic and **world wide web**-based versions) which contain rules, reminders, and points of clarification and correct use of English, although style evolves and changes over time. In 2003 *BBC* Training and Development issued a new 90-page version of its News Styleguide to student journalists as well as its own staff. Local newsrooms will have proper spellings of local places and in broadcast will ensure that their **reporters** know the correct pronunciation of, for example, Furneux Pelham or Barnoldswick. The *Guardian*'s online style guide (www.guardian.co.uk/styleguide) begins with a quote from singer Meat Loaf: 'When I see my name spelt with one word I want to slap and choke people. If you do that, you got to be a moron. It's on every poster, every album, every ticket as two words. If you spell it as one, you're an idiot. Bottom line.'

The underlying ethos of such guides is the 'plain, terse style of writing' recommended by George Orwell (Harcup, 2004: 128). Orwell also laid down six elementary rules relating to writing style; these included the use of active rather than passive prose and never use a long word when a short word will do (Orwell, 1946: 156). 'By keeping a consistent style in matters of detail a publication encourages readers to concentrate on *what* its writers are saying' (Hicks and Holmes, 2002: 19, emphasis in original). It provides a unified approach to areas in which there are permissible variants, but it does not mean imposing an identical writing style on all journalists; this would not work well with, for example, **columnists** (McNay, 2004).

Style guides, an example of which is given in Tony Harcup's *Journalism: Principles and Practice* (Harcup, 2004: 130–9), are usually in alphabetical order and will explain how various words and phrases should be used (or whether they should be used) and presented; for example, if and when clichés should be used in copy. Keith Waterhouse's book on newspaper style is widely recognized as a classic guide to the proper use of English in the popular press in the UK (Waterhouse, 1993).

But it has been argued that style guides are not neutral – they also have an ideological effect in that they construct a relationship with an **audience** (Cameron, 1996, in Harcup, 2004).

As Cyril Connolly, former literary **editor** of the *Observer* and *The Sunday Times* book reviewer, put it in 1938: 'Literature is the art of writing something that will be read twice; journalism what will be grasped at once.'

Further reading

Connolly, C. (1938) 'Enemies of Promise', in Allen, J. (2003) *The BBC News Styleguide*. London: BBC.
Harcup, T. (2004) *Journalism: Principles and Practice*. London: Sage.
Hicks, W. and Holmes, T. (2002) *Subediting for Journalists*. London: Routledge.
Waterhouse, K. (1993) *Waterhouse on Newspaper Style*. London: Penguin.

MGH and MK

Subscription

This is one method of financing the production and broadcasting of radio and television programmes: alternatives include the **licence fee**, **advertising** and sponsorship. Typically, subscribers pay an agreed monthly fee to receive a particular television channel or bundle of channels: or viewers can subscribe to a particular programme (a chosen film or special sporting event) although this is called pay-per-view.

The *Peacock Committee*, which was established in 1985 to explore the possibility of replacing the BBC licence fee with paid advertising, concluded that the UK should move in three identified phases to 'a fully fledged broadcasting market' in which 'subscription should replace the licence fee' as a funding mechanism for the *BBC* (Peacock, 1986, paras 671–700). Peacock believed subscription offered the best mechanism for viewers (consumers) to express their programming preferences in a broadcasting market. The move to subscription was, to some degree, technology dependent since broadcasters required the ability to encrypt, transmit and decode programming in individual homes, but 'the trigger for the changeover to subscription' is 'a political decision' (Peacock, 1986, para 674). Since 2000, the widespread availability of television programming delivered by cable and satellite, especially Sky Television, has triggered a substantial increase in the provision of television services funded by subscription. In 2004, for the first time, revenues from subscription (£3.3bn) outstripped advertising (£3.24 bn) and the proportion of the licence fee allocated to programme production (£2.3bn), signalling a significant shift in the financial structures of broadcasting (Ofcom, 2004c).

Critics of subscription (Blumler, 1992) argue that it undermines a number of elements central to public service broadcasting identified by the *Broadcasting Research Unit* (BRU) (1985): significantly (1) universality of availability – that all programmes should be available to the whole population; and (2) universality of payment – that one main instrument of broadcasting should be directly funded by all viewers (BRU, 1985: 25–32).

Further reading

Broadcasting Research Unit (1985) *The Public Service Idea in British Broadcasting: Main Principles*. Luton: John Libbey.
Ofcom (2004c) 'The Communications Market 2004' 9 August.http://www.ofcom.org.uk/research/industry_market_research/mi_index/cm/cmpdf/?a=87101.
Peacock, A. (1986) *Report of the Committee on Financing the BBC*. London: HMSO.

BF

Tabloid

A term registered in the late 1800s as a trademark applied to chemical substances, tabloid has for a long time been identified as what politicians like to call 'certain sections of the press', the red masthead tabloids (or 'red tops') described sometimes as the 'gutter press' (Waterhouse, 1993: 30–1) with its 'concentration on sex and celebrity' (Stephenson and Bromley, 1998: 2). Thus, the term is used more often as a concept than in physical reference to the more compact size of a tabloid newspaper.

Tabloid **journalism** describes the changing journalistic mood which has seen the **news media** become part of the entertainment industry rather than being a forum for informed debate about important issues of public concern; **stories** to interest the public instead of stories in the public interest (Franklin, 1997: 4).

It is apparent that the tabloid style has now infiltrated all newspapers, tabloid or **broadsheet**, to some extent (Waterhouse, 1993: 32). Tabloid journalism conjoins the sentimental and the sensational, and the prurient and the populist, often exploiting personal tragedy for public spectacle with scandal and **sensationalism**, often masquerading as 'human interest' (Franklin, 1997: 3).

The relationship of the tabloid newspapers to the quality press is, for some at least, encapsulated by the *Sun*'s **advertising** campaign parodying that of the *Financial Times* ('No *FT*, no comment') 'No *Sun*, no fun' (Stephenson and Bromley, 1998b: 1). The confusion of broadsheet and tabloid subjects has led to fears that broadsheet journalism and tabloid journalism will become indistinguishable, resulting in the '**dumbing-down** effect' (Bromley, 1998: 25) also referred to as tabloidization (McNair, 1999: 44).

Waterhouse says the contribution of tabloids to journalism is 'considerable . . . with professional detachment, one can judge their technical achievements without necessarily endorsing their philosophy'. He backs this up by citing GOTCHA! as the most memorable headline of the Falklands Campaign in the 1980s. He adds: 'The tabloids are vulgar, of course. But then if they were not vulgar then they would not be the tabloids.' Waterhouse says tabloid style can have both a positive and negative effect on the language structure of newspapers. It can be excitable and exuberant, always vigorous, sometimes vitriolic but heavy-handed and meaningless at its worst (Waterhouse, 1993: 35–6).

Tabloid style takes its references from a wide range of **sources**, including **television**, advertising slogans, song lyrics and catch phrases, plus a repository of popular quotations, the result being a mix of puns, allusions and word play (ibid.: 38–9).

All the mass **circulation** newspapers are now tabloid in size, with the broadsheets also starting to produce compact editions. The *Independent* published a twin format for a while until becoming a fully-fledged tabloid on 17 May 2004. *The Times* followed The *Independent*'s lead in producing two versions, though early studies revealed substantial differences between the two editions, with the editorial content of the broadsheet being far superior to its smaller counterpart (Greenslade, 2004c: 6). Both newspapers have gained readers since launching a tabloid edition (Cozens, 2004).

See *National Press*

Further reading

Bromley, M. (1998b) 'The "Tabloiding" of Britain', in Bromley, M. and Stephenson, H. (eds), *Sex, Lies and Democracy*. New York: Longman.
Cozens, C. (2004) 'Guardian Agrees £50m for Relaunch', *Guardian Unlimited*, 29 June.
Curran, J. and Seaton, J. (1997) *Power without Responsibility*, 5th edn. London: Routledge.
Greenslade, R. (2004c) 'Little Echo', *MediaGuardian*, 19 January, p. 6.
Neil, A. (1997) *Full Disclosure*. London: Pan Books.

MGH

Target audience

The individual(s) whom a speaker intends or desires to address with a **text**. It is important to recognize that the individuals *receiving* (reading or watching) texts are not always the target audience, or the group for whom they are intended. Bell (1991: 91) breaks 'the audience' down into four sub-groups, 'according to whether the persons are known, ratified and/or addressed by the speaker'. These groups are determined by the communicators' expectations and intent: 'the target audience who is addressed, the auditors who are expected but not targeted, the over-hearers who are not expected to be in the audience and the eavesdroppers who are expected to be absent' (ibid.: 92).

Communicators can easily misjudge the composition of their audience. This can offend over-hearers whose sensitivities were not considered, or upset eavesdroppers, such as children, who were expected to be absent from the audience. **Moral panics** have developed when a communication genre (e.g. 'slasher movies') or a particular product (e.g. '*Child's Play 3*') apparently become available to children – a segment expected to be absent from the audience.

Advertising provides the clearest example of targeted communication, with most people understanding that its form, content and placement are 'comprehensively adjusted to appeal to an identified audience' (Atkin and Richardson, 2003: 39). In fact, *all* **discourse** is addressed to a target audience, whether it is a newspaper or the book you are currently reading

(Burke, 1950). In the tradition of political rhetoric (see **propaganda**), the target audience are always the group(s) of individuals who 'have the capacity to act as "mediators of change"' (Jasinski, 2001: 68). During the war against Yugoslavia in 1999 for example, 'the MoD identified four target audiences, according to the Defence Committee: the British public, Milošević and his supporters, NATO allies and Kosovo Albanians' (Curtis, 2003: 21). The Defence Committee concluded that the 'campaign directed against home audiences was fairly successful' and 'if anything, the UK's contribution to *the war of perceptions* was of more significance than its strictly military contribution' (cited in Curtis, 2003: 22, emphasis added).

On occasion, the target audience is different from the audience directly addressed by the speaker or text. Consider, for example, George W. Bush's 2000 address to the convention of the National Association for the Advancement of Colored People (NAACP). The audience attending the convention was less important than the indirect target audience reached via the broadcast of the speech. Through addressing a Black American convention, Bush 'conveyed a message to the indirect [target] audience through the act of addressing the direct audience' (Jasinski, 2001: 69).

JER

Taxes on knowledge

This was the phrase used by critics to describe the various duties imposed by governments on nineteenth-century **newspapers**. The effect of these 'taxes' was to inflate the cover price of newspapers, thereby reducing their public availability. Abolition of these 'taxes on knowledge', along with developments in postal services, expansion of markets and **advertising** revenues, improvements in printing technology and the spread of working-class literacy, was a precondition for the emergence of modern mass circulation newspapers (Black, 2002: 171–200).

The advertising duty which taxed all newspaper advertisements was abolished in 1853, the newspaper stamp duty which imposed a fixed levy on the sale of each copy of a newspaper was withdrawn in 1855, while the paper duties which taxed the paper on which the news was printed was repealed in 1861 (Weiner, 1969: xi). The stamp duty had been highly effective in stemming the growth of the radical press. The government increased the duty by 266 per cent between 1789 and 1815 and

261

prosecuted 1130 cases of selling unstamped newspapers in London alone between 1830 and 1836 (Curran and Seaton, 1997: 11). The removal of these 'taxes' created the circumstances for the 'establishment of a free press but also a cheap one' (Lee, 1978: 117).

Not all journalists and editors favoured the prospect of cheap newspapers, with *The Times* declaring its self-interested opposition by claiming that it was desirable to 'confine the newspaper press . . . in the hands of a few persons with large capitals' while the Provincial Newspaper Society argued that cheap newspapers would reduce both journalistic standards and the 'gentlemanly status' of proprietors (ibid.: 118).

Further reading

Black, J. (2001) *The English Press 1621–1861*. Gloucestershire: Sutton Press.
Curran, J. and Seaton, J. (1997) *Power without Responsibility*, 5th edn. London: Routledge.
Weiner, J.H. (1969) *The War of the Unstamped: The Movement to Repeal the British Newspaper Tax 1830–6*. Ithaca, NY: Cornell University Press.

BF

Television

The concept behind the ubiquitous box in the corner of the room dates back 120 years. In 1884, Russian-born Paul Nipkow invented a scanning system which dissected a scene into a pattern of pixels, or 'picture dots' which could then be transmitted and reproduced as a visual image. The world's first public demonstration came in 1925 when John Logie Baird showed his television system in Selfridge's department store, London. Three years later he sent the first 'intelligible' TV signal across the Atlantic and the BBC began experimenting with television transmissions in 1929 (Crisell, 2002). Baird's system ultimately lost out to a more sophisticated one developed by EMI but the *BBC* claimed the credit for the first high definition service transmitted from Alexandra Palace in north London to about 400 households which began in November 1936.

Television – literally 'seeing at a distance' – was not the instant success of **radio**. It was seen as relatively unreliable, frivolous, expensive and a toy for the rich. 'The programmes the viewers wanted were dominated by the concept of the West End show.' (Hood, 1980: 60). The first outside broadcast, the coronation of George VI in May 1937, was a huge success, but early television was brought to an abrupt halt by the outbreak of the Second World War and resumed only in 1946.

Then the service began to grow rapidly, thanks to backing in the

Hankey Report of 1945 which declared 'Television is here to stay' (Briggs, 1979: 187) and that the BBC should lead it. The coronation of Queen Elizabeth II in 1953, watched by over half the UK population, showed that television was indeed here to stay. But there was ambivalence within the BBC and elsewhere over what television was for – light entertainment or something more. Wartime Prime Minister Winston Churchill dismissed television as 'that tuppenny Punch and Judy show' (in Crisell, 2002: 84). Television news and current affairs pioneer Grace Wyndham Goldie (1977) says the broadcasters were used to words, not pictures and, she suggests, distrusted the visual.

By 1955 viewing began to exceed listening for the first time and by 1958 nine million people had paid the combined radio and television **licence** fee (Crisell, 2002). The birth of commercial television in 1955 came after a battle which ranged the pro-monopoly forces against a growing post-war view that in a democracy **broadcasting** should carry as few restrictions as possible. It didn't stop the BBC's first director general Lord Reith comparing the effect of commercial television upon civilization to that of dog-racing, smallpox and bubonic plague (in Crisell, 2002: 86). In the event it was set up as an extension of the public service concept: **public service broadcasting**.

The 1980s saw the next great leap forward in the provision of television services. The Broadcasting Act of 1982 paved the way for *Channel 4*, set up to provide the kind of programming that was not offered by the BBC and *ITV*, innovative programming to minority audiences.

It took more than 40 years to create four television channels, but less than another 20 for hundreds to become available, thanks to satellite, cable and digital technologies – and **deregulation** within Britain and Europe. Rupert Murdoch's Sky Television went on air in 1989 and its rival British Satellite Broadcasting a year later. The two companies merged in 1990 to form *BSkyB*. By 1995 the then Independent Television Commission had licensed 170 satellite and cable services.

The latest addition to the line-up of terrestrial channels was *Channel 5* which launched in March 1997.

Further reading

Briggs, A. (1965) *The History of Broadcasting in the United Kingdom*, vol. II: *The Golden Age of Wireless*. Oxford: Oxford University Press.
Crisell, A. (2002) *An Introductory History of British Broadcasting*. London: Routledge.
Goldie, G. (1977) *Facing the Nation: Television and Politics, 1936–1976*. London: Bodley Head.
Hood, S. (1980) *On Television*. London: Pluto Press.
Lindley, R. (2002) *Panorama*. London: Politicos.

MK

263

The record of a communicative event. Therefore, texts need to display two characteristics: first, they need to be recorded or recordable, as, for example, a newspaper report, a billboard advertisement, a film, a television programme, etc. A text must have a sense of stability and durability so different individuals may read, enjoy or otherwise respond to its message(s). Thus, interpersonal **communication**, such as a facial expression, a conversation or even a speech do not constitute 'texts' unless they are recorded. At this first level, the text is conceptualized as a *product*.

Second, texts must communicate – in other words, they must generate and exchange meanings. At this second level the text can be conceptualised as a *process* – that is, as a process of meaning-making from the production through to the reception and decoding of the text. The meaning of a text is 'open-ended' and may be understood to 'mean' different things when decoded in different contexts. Thus, a text may hold different meanings to me rather than you; or hold different meanings when read or decoded now rather than in 100 years time.

Further characteristics of texts also need to be mentioned. First, texts are multi-functional, performing simultaneous tasks. The theory of Systemic Functional Linguistics, developed by Halliday and Hasan (Halliday, 1994; Halliday and Hasan, 1989), assumes that texts simultaneously fulfil 'ideational', 'inter-personal' and 'textual' functions. In other words, texts 'simultaneously represent aspects of the world (the physical world, the social world, the mental world); enact social relations between participants in social events and the attitudes, desires and values of the participants; and coherently and cohesively connect parts of texts together' as a united whole (Fairclough, 2003: 27). Finally, texts are very often multi-vocal and **intertextual**, in that they contain many voices, opinions and meanings vying for dominance. This is of particular interest for journalism – a genre of communication which, due to the requirement of **objectivity**, is necessarily multi-vocal.

Further reading

Fairclough, N. (2003) *Analysing Discourse*. London: Routledge.
Halliday, M.A.K. (1994) *An Introduction to Functional Grammar*, 2nd edn. London: Arnold.

JER

264

Trade press

Magazines, journals and websites aimed at niche business/commercial **audiences**, rather than at the general public. This specialist media sector is known as B2B (business to business). In 2004, some 700 companies published around 5,000 B2B titles in the UK, according to the Periodical Publishers Association.

Further reading
Periodical Publishers Association website: http://www.ppa.co.uk/.

MNH

Transitivity

Transitivity describes the relationships between participants and the roles they play in the processes described in reporting, basically, the 'who (or what) does what to whom (or what)'. These relations between participants depend upon the process represented by the principal verb of a sentence. In English there are four principal types of verbs, and therefore four different types of process which a sentence can use. First, *verbal* processes, such as speaking, shouting or singing. Second, verbs can be *mental* processes such as thinking, dreaming and deciding. Third, *relational* processes of being, such as have, seem and be (or is), which involve an agent and an attribute. And fourth, *material* processes, which can be further divided into: *transitive* action involving two or more participants – the agent and the afflicted (or object) of the action (for example, 'W kicked X', 'Y pushed Z'); and, *intransitive* action with only one participant (for example, 'X ran', 'Y wrote', 'Z flew', etc.).

While this may seem very fixed, with neatly demarcated types of verb processes, in fact transitivity allows us to describe the same event using different processes. For example, we may choose to represent an event as an action process rather than as a relationship, or vice versa; as an active transitive process (for example, '100 union members barricaded the factory gates) or as a passive transitive process (for example, 'the factory gates were barricaded'). Transitivity therefore forms the *very foundation* of **representation**: it provides choices in the way in which an event is represented and choices in the way we represent an event's participants. Successive studies of journalism have shown that there is often social or ideological significance between these choices. They not only illustrate

265

journalists' points of view, they also construct and reconstruct *social* points of view.

Further reading

Fairclough, N. (2000) *New Labour, New Language?* London: Routledge.
Fowler, R. (1991) *Language in the News*. London: Routledge and Kegan Paul.
Montgomery, M. et al. (2000) *Ways of Reading*. London: Routledge.

JER

Two-step flow

The two-step flow model of **media effects** has its origins in Lazarsfeld, Berelson and Gaudet's study *The People's Choice* (1944), which attempted to assess the impact of media election coverage on voting behaviour in American presidential elections. The conclusions of the study proved contentious and challenged the findings of previous studies by suggesting that the influence of media on **audiences** was more modest and complex than previously realized (Klapper, 1960: 32).

Contra the hypodermic model of media effects, Lazarsfeld argued that: (1) voters' electoral choices were highly resistant to media influence; (2) media coverage tended to reinforce rather than change people's existing opinions (Lazarsfeld et al., 1944: 88–9); (3) the small minority of voters who were undecided were the least likely to listen and watch election coverage; and (4) interpersonal **communication** – discussions with friends, family, workmates, but especially 'opinion leaders' – was more influential in shaping political views than media election coverage (ibid.: 150). These opinion leaders were respected members of social groups who were better informed about politics, more likely to consume information provided by media and served as conduits for media messages to members of their social groups: they formed a barrier against any direct influence of media on individuals, selecting and interpreting media messages and creating a two step flow of communications. Opinion leaders performed 'a key communications role' (ibid.: 152). Consequently, the two-step flow model argued for **audiences'** ability to select and interpret media messages and conceptualized viewers/listeners as members of social groups which structured their access to news media and shaped the impact on media upon them.

The emergence of rival accounts of media effects has triggered criticisms of the two-step flow model: (1) for underestimating the influence of media; (2) for focusing on media influence in the short term (across the four weeks of an election period) rather than assessing the longer-term influence of television on attitudes (Lewis, 1991: 157); (3) for confusing respondents' claims that they had *not changed their minds* with the different conclusion that they had *not been influenced* (Hall, 1982: 59); and (4) for identifying a two-step flow of communication rather than a more complex multi-step flow model (Howitt, 1982: 21) which additionally might involve interchangeable roles with the same individual being 'opinion leader' or 'follower' depending on the particular topic (McQuail, 1987: 272). But the two-step flow model of communication effects offered a salutary caution against the contemporary assumption of media as an all powerful Leviathan: it also reasserted the importance of interpersonal communication in an age when communications were becoming increasingly mediated.

See *Uses and gratifications.*

Further reading

Lewis, J. (1991) *The Ideological Octopus: An Exploration of Television and Its Audience.* London: Routledge.

BF

Two-way

When Andrew Gilligan went on the *Today* programme on BBC Radio 4 at 6.07 a.m. on 29 May 2003 and precipitated the row which led to the explosive **Hutton Inquiry** (2004), he was using one of the most common devices in **news** broadcasting: the semi scripted, live conversation with the programme presenter. And as the Hutton inquiry unfolded, broadcast **journalists** around the country shifted uncomfortably and thought 'There but for the grace of God . . .'.

In the mid-1980s, two-ways were relatively rare. Interviewing your own journalists about a story was seen by programme producers as a last resort, to be used if no authoritative sources could be found, or maybe to give context and analysis by specialist correspondents who knew the **story** and the subject inside out.

But as news output expanded exponentially, so did the use of this handy little technique. As part of the imperative to get information on air as quickly as possible, **rolling news** channels on radio and television go straight to reporters at the scene of the story, often regardless of how little there may be to say. Pre-recorded packages are followed up with the

267

ubiquitous question and answer session with the **reporter** who filed it. Two-ways are seen as a way of making the story accessible, lending immediacy and getting across information in a more natural way (UKPG, 2004). They're cheap and quick, with no need to spend hours in edit suites preparing material. But Harrison (2000) queries just how much they help viewers and listeners understand the story.

Sensible and experienced reporters and correspondents have always taken care to prepare their words, and to discuss beforehand with the presenter or producer what is to be said. Many will write at least the gist of their points on paper. This common-sense approach has been endorsed by the BBC's internal Neil Report (2004) which looked at lessons that could be learned from the criticisms contained in the Hutton Inquiry Report.

But there is always the risk of the slip of the tongue, the injudicious turn of phrase, even minor factual inaccuracy. They come with a serious health warning.

Further reading

Hutton (2004) *Report of the Inquiry into the Circumstances Surrounding the Death of Dr David Kelly*, available on: http://www.the-hutton-inquiry.org.uk.

MK

Usability

Ever got hopelessly lost on a **website** or not been able to perform what appeared to be a simple function? The survival of a website depends on the quality of its usability, which assesses how easy an interface is to use and whether it satisfies the needs of visitors: 'If a website is difficult to use, people leave' (Nielsen, 25 August 2003). The importance of usability in web design is underlined by Nielsen who says: 'Usability rules the Web' (Nielsen, 2000: 9). Web usability possesses the following five quality components relating to users: learnability, efficiency, memorability, errors and satisfaction, although there are others, too (Nielsen, 25 August 2003). Findability, through browsing, searching and asking, is critically important for overall usability (Rosenfeld and Morville, 2002: 5).

More importance has been attached to usability in the **Internet** economy than in traditional physical product development where customers usually pay for the product before experiencing how useful it is; with a website, users experience the usability before deciding whether to proceed further into the site or spend any money (Nielsen, 2000: 10).

Nielsen, widely regarded as the world's leading expert in web usability, recommends designers carry out user testing – ideally before the website is published – although this need not be a complex or costly process (Nielsen, 19 March 2003). There are also plenty of usability guidelines for websites, **intranet** sites and **email** newsletters available for designers to follow (Nielsen Norman Group, 2003) such as making site maps easier to use to help navigation. Usability is closely connected with **accessibility** and **information architecture** in that all of these concepts relate to web customer satisfaction.

Further reading

Nielsen, J. (2000) *Designing Web Usability*. Indianapolis: New Riders Publishing.

Rosenfeld, L. and Morville, P. ([1998]2002) *Information Architecture for the World Wide Web*, 2nd edn. Sebastopol, CA: O'Reilly and Associates.

MGH

Uses and gratifications

This approach to the analysis of media impacts on **audiences** was pioneered by Blumler and Katz (1974, and Katz, 1959) and reversed the traditional research agenda by asking why people used the media rather than inquiring into what effects, if any, the media might have on audiences. In Katz's own words, the research question was 'not "what do the media do to people?" but "what do people do with the media?"' (Katz, 1959: 2).

Blumler and Katz argued that an active audience, constituted by discriminating individuals, consciously and strategically use the **media** to gratify certain needs. They identified four such needs: (1) *diversion* – television provides an escape from everyday life; (2) *personal relationships* – **television** offers companionship and conversation, especially for people who live alone; (3) *personal identity* – television provides personality role models against which viewers can compare their own liifestyles; and (4) surveillance – television provides information about many aspects of the viewer's environment. The same programme may gratify different needs for different viewers. Consequently, some people may watch *EastEnders* for companionship, others for entertainment, others for escapism and still others to confirm their prejudices about Londoners!

The uses and gratifications approach offered a corrective to earlier assertions of the ability of media to influence audiences, but itself became

269

subject to critical review on four grounds (Lewis, 1991). First, it engaged in tautological and circular reasoning: namely, the uses of media by particular audiences provide the only evidence that the needs, which the media are supposed to satisfy, actually exist in the first place (Hart, 1991: 43). Second, there is little agreement about the basic needs which are allegedly met by media: McQuail, for example, offers a distinctive typology of needs which embraces information, personal identity, integration and social interaction and entertainment (1987: 73). Third, the assumption that individuals purposefully select programmes to view is seriously undermined by studies which report the extent of unplanned viewing: some viewers may watch a programme simply because it is on and they have nothing better to do. Finally, Morley and others regret the retreat from the sociological character of the **two-step flow** analysis which conceptualized relations between media and audiences in a social setting rather than the individual and psychologistic approach of uses and gratifications (Morley, 1980: 13).

Further reading

Blumler, J.G. and Katz, E. (1974) *The Uses of Mass Communications*. London: Sage.
Lewis, J. (1991) *The Ideological Octopus*. London: Routledge.

BF

Video journalist (VJ)

The advent of low-cost, high-quality, lightweight digital equipment set television accountants all of a dither – no need any longer to use a camera operator, sound operator and reporter to cover a story. A one-person crew to do the lot would be just fine. And cheap.

The video journalist first made an appearance in 1994 at the now defunct London cable news station Channel One. It aimed to make high quality news cheaply by breaking down the barriers between jobs and encouraging multi-skilling. The idea came from cable television in America (Boyd, 2001) and while the Channel One experiment resulted in some distinctly wobbly pictures at times, there were advantages other than just the cost. Other television companies, particularly in the regions, found themselves following suit. As the VJs themselves discovered new ways of doing the job – and its limitations – the quality improved.

Initially, the big news broadcasters like the *BBC* and *ITN* were sceptical. If you're worrying about framing interviewees, the quality of the sound *and* getting the pictures, how can you do the journalism properly?

And much specialist visual expertise risked being lost. Many VJs are also trained editors, which raises a further question about checks and balances on the technical and journalistic quality of a news item. If only one person has seen the story through from start to finish, something may have been missed and potential improvements, or problems, gone unrecognized.

Apart from cost, one real advantage of using one person crews in some circumstances was spotted quickly – larger crews can be intrusive whereas one person can get closer to the subject.

But ten years on, all the large news broadcasters have incorporated VJs into their newsgathering systems. By 2006, the BBC expect to have trained a third of its newsroom staff in videojournalism techniques (Stevens, 2002). The flexibility and increasing professionalism of those at the new front line has given hungry newsrooms more than just food for thought and the tools to tell stories in different ways.

Further reading

Boyd, A. (2001) *Broadcast Journalism: Techniques of Radio and Television News*, 5th edn. Oxford: Focal Press.
Stevens, M. (2002) 'Small Camera, Big Vision', *UK Press Gazette*, 9 September.

MK

Video news release (VNR)

This refinement of the ubiquitous **news release** has been around since the late 1950s, but gained currency and sophistication during the 1980s. They originated as straightforward **news** releases with moving pictures added, made by companies, lobby groups, government agencies using professional filming and editing techniques as just another way of getting across a message (Boyd, 2001). But while some are harmless fillers, some are scarcely disguised **propaganda**.

The dilemma for the **journalist** comes when the pictures are good, and not available from another source. According to Yorke, some journalists fear that some organizations would prefer to compile their own VNRs, over which they exercise complete control, rather than allow **television** news teams access to shoot their own material (Yorke, 2000: 25).

During the first Gulf War, **newsrooms** received material shot from inside occupied Kuwait showing resistance fighters dropping molotov cocktails onto an Iraqi military vehicle (MacGregor, 1997). It was shot on domestic VHS, looked authentic and was used. Only after the war did it emerge that the Kuwaiti government had paid over a million dollars to an

271

American PR firm to produce 24 VNRs sent to news organizations around the world.

And they are used. A study in America (Harmon and White, 2001) tracked 14 VNRs and logged 4,245 airings across the USA. They discovered that smaller stations were more likely to use longer segments and that the most common use was as a voice-over story in an early evening bulletin. VNRs to do with children and their safety or health got the most usage.

Further reading

Boyd, A. (2001) *Broadcast Journalism: Techniques of Radio and Television News*, 5th edn. Oxford: Focal Press.
MacGregor, B. (1997) *Live, Direct and Biased: Making Television News in the Satellite Age.* London: Arnold.
Yorke, I. (2000) *Television News*, Oxford: Focal Press.

MK

Virtual community

Howard Rheingold used this term for the title of a book about the collections of people who commingle on the **Internet** in a wide variety of computer-mediated social groups usually based on mutual interest and irrespective of geographical proximity. Online activities within these communities can range from intellectual discussions and exchanging information to flirting and playing games. 'People in virtual communities do just about everything people do in real life, but we leave our bodies behind . . . the richness and vitality of computer-linked cultures is attractive, even addictive' (Rheingold, 1994: 3).

Virtual communities, which became popular in the 1980s when millions of students gained Internet access, can take many forms: two common ones are Usenet – a global network of discussion groups (Hall, J., 2001: 253) – and MUDs (Multi-User Dungeons), imaginary computer worlds where people use words and programming languages to engage in a variety of online activities, including solving puzzles and power games (Rheingold, 1994: 69, 145). Like the newsgroups found in Usenet, Instant Relay Chat (IRC) services, bulletin boards and mailing lists, the most popular of which are ListServs, can also be community-forming, in addition to providing **journalists** with useful **news** and information on events, one example being 9/11 (Allan, 2002: 121, 129).

Feldman says that the notion of a virtual community created by the communications power of network and bound together by common interest, aspiration or belief 'is becoming the key to building a thriving new wired world' (1997: 96). His vision is of a worldwide community sharing equally in a 'rich future of **media**, information and global communications' (ibid: 166). Assuming the issues of equal global access can be successfully addressed, online communities can offer a democracy in which the **world wide web** becomes the primary arena for discussion: 'in such an electronic **public sphere** a **journalism** capable of mapping those discourses is a necessity' (Hall, J., 2001: 213).

Online community news sites have been run in partnership with traditional media, while the web community publishing model enables local individuals and organizations to self-publish on the world wide web (ibid.: 21).

Being able to define a particular community online assists potential advertisers in targeting a specific group of people (De Wolk, 2001: 56). Any community organized around commodified forms such as football, gardening or sex should be profitable for the media (Hall, J., 2001: 211).

Further reading

Allan, S. (2002) 'Reweaving the Internet', in Zelizer, B. and Allan, S. (eds) *Journalism after September 11*. London: Routledge.
De Wolk, R. (2001) *Introduction to Online Journalism*. Boston: Allyn and Bacon.
Hall, J. (2001) *Online Journalism: A Critical Primer*. London: Pluto Press.
Rheingold, H. (1994) *The Virtual Community*. London: Minerva.

MGH

Watchdog journalism

273

The characterization of journalism as a social 'watchdog' springs from a classical liberal conception of the power relationship between government and society within a democratic state. The watchdog theory of journalism is based on a pluralistic view of social power and can be seen as 'a simple extension to the (newspaper) press of the fundamental individual rights to freedom of opinion, speech, religion and assembly' (McQuail, 1994: 128). The watchdog metaphor imbues the press with the role of being a forum for discussion, investigators of impropriety, an adversary to monopoly over power and knowledge and the defenders of truth, freedom and democracy. This is embodied in the traditional idea of a 'fourth estate', historically accredited to Edmund Burke: 'There are three estates in Parliament, but in the reporter's gallery yonder sits a fourth estate more important than they all' (Carlyle, 1841, cited in Donohue et al., 1995: 118).

More specifically, the theory of a watchdog press can be summarized as adhering to the following three assumptions. First, the news media are essentially autonomous; second, journalism acts in the public interest, looking after the welfare of the general public rather than that of society's dominant groups; and third, that the power of the news media is such that they are able to influence dominant social groups to the benefit of the public.

This perspective has been criticized on a number of grounds: first, the public interest is a particularly slippery concept to attempt to define, let alone serve, given that there is more usually a configuration of organized interests rather than a single public interest. This, combined with the journalists' preoccupation with the cultural and symbolic power of the 'expert **source**', results in a state of affairs whereby only the more powerful pressure groups gain access to the forum of media debate (Fowler, 1991; Manning, 2001). Second, due to the nature and need for **objectivity** in news reporting, whether that is ritualized, regulated or legislated, journalists do not have the capacity to endlessly sermonize in news articles, but must necessarily adopt objective rules of engagement. Hence, 'what seems to be sharp questioning of high government officials by reporters' are predominantly questions 'posed previously by contending [elite] powers' (Donohue et al., 1995: 118).

Third, the news media are simply *not* autonomous. The vast majority of news producers are either corporations, with often diverse financial interests in other areas of the entertainment business (for example, Disney, AOL Time Warner, News Corporation) or else are owned by large corporations with financial interests in other sectors (e.g. General Electric, which owns NBC). Printed and broadcast journalism often betrays a loyalty towards these parent companies, vested interests and the pursuit of profit rather than the protection or championing of the public. Studies of outputs and media performance (see: **propaganda model**) show that it is highly unlikely that institutions so firmly embedded in the corporate world (through ownership, licensing, advertising and the sourcing of information) would take a consistently anti-establishment line.

Further reading

Donohue, G.A. et al. (1995) 'A Guard Dog Perspective on the Role of the Media', *Journal of Communication*, 45(2): 115–32.

JER

274

Watergate

The Watergate scandal, exposed by *Washington Post* reporters Bob Woodward and Carl Bernstein, and other American journalists, concerned improper practices by Republican aides of President Richard Nixon to spy on, and besmirch the reputation of, his Democrat opponents. The scandal, therefore, arose from abuse of power to pollute the electoral process. Woodward and Bernstein began to unravel it after investigating a 1972 burglary at an office block in Washington, where the Democrats had a base. The building's name, Watergate, became that of the scandal which went far wider, and higher, than the burglary plot. Journalists gradually identified the aides and government officials involved in 'dirty tricks' against the Democrats, and in raising money to fund them. Woodward and Bernstein were helped by an anonymous source, 'Deep Throat', whose identity still remains a secret. Ultimately, in a seismic shock to the American political system, Nixon resigned from the Presidency rather than face impeachment over his role in an attempted cover-up of the scandal.

Woodward and Bernstein described their Watergate work in a book, *All the President's Men*. An Oscar-winning film of the same title projected their achievement to an international audience, while accurately portraying some of the routine drudgery, setbacks and ethical dilemmas such work involves.

The Watergate story remains, to many, the epitome of **investigative journalism** as a bulwark of democracy. The suffix 'gate' is now used to denote any scandal. It is a sobering thought that Britain's **defamation** laws – far harsher than those of the USA – would probably do much to suppress any similar investigation in the UK. See also http://www.bbc.co.uk/crime/caseclosed/watergate.shtml

See *Adversarial journalism.*

Further reading

Bernstein, C. and Woodward, B. (1974) *All the President's Men*. New York: Simon and Schuster.
Schudson, M. (1992) 'Watergate: A Study in Mythology', *Columbia Journalism Review*, May/June 1992, available at:. http://archives.cjr.org/year/92/3/watergate.asp.

MNH

Weblog

A popular type of **website** presented in the style of an online diary or journal by the author who is known as a 'blogger', it usually includes personalized commentary and analysis on any topic or **news** event, while also using **hypertext** links to other, related, sites. These weblogs (or 'blogs' as they are also known) have developed a 'blogging' community of their own, sometimes described as the 'blogosphere'. The postings in weblogs are usually in reverse chronological order and can contain any type of content ranging from basic text to various forms of **multimedia** (Perrone, 2004; Raynsford, 2003). They often include a facility for visitors to give their comments on each entry (McIntosh, 2003).

Some **media** organizations, including *Guardian Unlimited* and the *BBC*, have joined the trend by compiling their own weblogs (Raynsford, 2003), although some are not keen on the idea of their own **journalists** keeping weblogs during the course of their work. For example, *CNN* ordered correspondent Kevin Sites, who posted audio reports, photographs and accounts of his experiences during the 2003 war on Iraq, to end his personal log of the conflict (Croad, 2003).

The launch of http://www.blogger.com/ in 1999 (subsequently bought by Google) made it easy for non-technical people to create their own weblog without any web expertise, leading to an explosion of these types of sites (Naughton, 2003). There are various competing software packages, which are usually either free or cost little to individual users. The pioneering Blogger, which is the most famous and popular, is now owned by the *Google* search engine (McIntosh, 2003). However, as many weblogs tend to be anonymous, some doubt their authenticity and legitimacy while others welcome the opportunity to have their opinions published on a global scale (Croad, 2003). It can be seen as providing 'reportage in a raw and exciting form' (Raynsford, 2003), but has also led to 'journalistic unease . . . further reinforced by the way the blogging community refuses to accept the news "agenda" as determined by mainstream media' (Naughton, 2003). Some **new media** experts have doubted whether a new form of **journalism** has emerged, questioning the trustworthiness of the content in addition to the fact that it is unprocessed (Raynsford, 2003).

The US-led war on Iraq in 2003 bred a new type of weblog called 'warblog', some of which provided first-hand accounts of the conflict, the most famous being the one at http://www.dear_raed.blogspot.com purportedly written by the Baghdad-based Salam Pax, although he was accused by some of being a propagandist (Croad, 2003).

Further reading

Croad, E. (2003) 'Blogs Bring Personal View of War', 27 March, *dotJournalism*, available at: http://www.journalism.co.uk/news/story607.html.

McIntosh, N. (2003) 'Start here: Setting up a Website', *Guardian Unlimited*, 25 September, available at: http://www.guardian.co.uk/online/story/0,,1048698,00.html.

Pax, S. (2003) 'Where Is Raed?'. http://www.dear_raed.blogsplot.com.

Raynsford, J. (2003) 'Blogging: the New Journalism?', 25 March, *dot.Journalism*, available at: http://www.journalism.co.uk/features/story604.html.

MGH

Website

A set of information-laden pages grouped together and usually situated on the **world wide web** constitute a website of which there are millions of varying types in existence, making it almost impossible to categorize them. Sex, politics, sport, philately – you name it, every subject known to humankind is almost certainly covered on a website somewhere. An individual or organization, official or otherwise, can set up a website (Ward, 2002: 12–13), which can contain any number of pages in addition to the homepage, the 'starting point for the visitor' (Whittaker, 2000: 33).

A coded language called Hypertext Markup Language (HTML) is commonly used to create a web page and format the content in a standardized way so it can be viewed in a browser on different computer operating systems (ibid.: 14). **Hypertext** links are used to connect the pages together in addition to pointing at other websites and documents elsewhere on the web. HTML can be coded by hand, but this can be time-consuming; web-authoring software like Macromedia Dreamweaver (Pavlik, 2001: 199) makes the process of designing and producing the pages far easier and quicker.

Every (published) website is identifiable by a unique domain name which is assigned by authorized registrars worldwide under the overall auspices of the non-profit making *Internet Corporation for Assigned Names and Numbers (ICANN)*. The domain name is the address – also known as the Uniform Resource Locator (URL) – that users type into the browser to call up a website or page (Whittaker, 2000: 31). Using http://www.bbc.co.uk as an example, bbc identifies the *BBC* as the organization and the co.uk is a top level domain name which recognizes it as a UK-based company. An information storage area usually provided by an *Internet Service Provider (ISP)* is needed for a site to be published on the web (Ward, 2002: 12).

277

One of the great benefits of online publishing and **broadcasting**, 'one of the most dramatic adoptions of **new media** technology in history', is that websites and the relaying of (**multimedia**) information cost relatively little to produce and promote, particularly when compared with the print medium, while also reaching a much wider audience (Reddick and King, 2001: 162–5).

Further reading

Pavlik, J.V. (2001) *Journalism and New Media*. Columbia, NY: University Press.
Reddick, R. and King, E. (2001) *The Online Journalist: Using the Internet and Other Electronic Resources*, 3rd edn. Orlando, FL: Harcourt Brace and Company.
Ward, M. (2002) *Journalism Online*. Oxford: Focal Press.
Whittaker, J. (2000) *Producing for the Web*. London: Routledge.

MGH

World Wide Web

The invention of English-born scientist Tim Berners-Lee, the world wide web is the public and popular face of the **Internet** and a **mass communication** medium. Also known as WWW or the web, it is the interface which allows computer users to view and exchange data (Ward, 2002: 10) through a browser which commonly uses Hypertext Markup Language (HTML) to present content in **multimedia** formats.

The web is home to millions of **websites** and documents which are linked by a common protocol, Hypertext Transfer Protocol (HTTP), enabling different operating systems to share the same data. One of the web's great strengths is the way in which **hypertext** links are used to facilitate public information-sharing on a global scale (Whittaker, 2000: 14; Reddick and King, 2001: 23). The seemingly infinite amount of data stored on the web makes it a valuable **source** of information, although it also means users – and particularly **journalists** – have to be selective (Ward, 2002: 12).

The origins of the web can be traced back to 1989 when Berners-Lee submitted the first proposals while working at *Conseil Européen pour la Recherche Nucléaire (CERN)*, the nuclear physics laboratory (CERN, 2003; The Living Internet, 2003). The web was born with the creation of the first text web browser in 1990, although the major impetus was provided three years later by the National Center for Supercomputing Applications at the University of Illinois with the development of Mosaic, a graphical browser capable of displaying images in addition to text

(Whittaker, 2000: 9–10). Internet Explorer and Netscape Navigator have since become the two most used web browsers. In a decision that helped the web to grow substantially, Berners-Lee and *CERN* officially declared that the web technology and program code was in the public domain; hence anyone could use and improve it (The Living Internet, 2003).

In 1994, Berners-Lee founded the *World Wide Web Consortium (W3C)* in collaboration with *CERN* to promote the web's evolution and ensure its interoperability by developing common protocols (World Wide Web Consortium, 2003).

Further reading

Reddick, R. and King, E. (2001) *The Online Journalist: Using the Internet and Other Electronic Resources*, 3rd edn. Orlando, FL: Harcourt Brace and Company.
Whittaker, J. (2000) *Producing for the Web*. London: Routledge.

MGH

Yellow journalism

This developed in America during the 1880s but had its roots in the new penny papers exemplified by the *New York Sun*, published by Benjamin Day in 1833 and targeted at a newly literate American working-class readership. Yellow journalism, characterized by its sensational and emotive content, contrasted starkly with the rational and sober emphasis of the existing newspapers and is typically seen as the precursor of modern **tabloid** journalism (Bessie, 1938).

The *New York Sun* eschewed the traditional editorial mix of politics and commerce preferring 'scandalous tales of sin' and 'the immoral antics of the upper class' (Ornebring and Jonsson, 2004) combined with extensive reporting of crime and police news (Emery and Emery, 1978: 120). The *Sun* became an immediate commercial success but was criticized for its alleged sensationalism and vulgarity (Schudson 1978: 23). But the *Sun* did not offer a **'dumbed down'** version of the respectable 6 cents newspapers like Benjamin's *New York Signal*, so much as a radically different conception of what constituted news.

Despite its critics, the penny press expanded with James Gordon Bennett launching the *New York Herald* in 1835 and Horace Greeley founding the *New York Tribune* in 1841. Bennett added sports news, readers' letters, more crime news and special editions while Greeley developed Day's *Sun* by conducting and publishing a campaigning and crusading style of journalism with routine tirades against alcohol and tobacco, which would find its UK counterpart in W.T. Stead's investigative journalism which denounced child prostitution and led eventually to his imprisonment. Bennett argued that 'the newspaper's function is not to instruct but to startle'; publishers should 'Raise hell and sell newspapers' (Bessie, 1938: 40).

The 1880s and 1890s marked the period of yellow journalism. It began with Joseph Pulitzer's purchase of the *New York World* from Jay Gould for $346,000 in 1883. The paper's immense commercial success reflected Day's tried and tested formula which focused on sensation and crime, combined with Greeley's campaigning journalism and Pulitzer's own commitment to aggressive marketing and promotion (Conboy, 2002: 56). Pulitzer, like his predecessors, was criticized for the surfeit of sensational stories in the paper which allegedly corroded the professional values of serious journalism, but Pulitzer's crusading journalism was committed to social change as well as profit. In July 1883 when 700 garment workers died during a heat wave, Pulitzer's *New York World* published banner headlines denouncing the use of immigrant child labourers in the garment industry sweat shops. Pulitzer used sensationalism because he believed it was the only way to reach the people on whose behalf he was struggling editorially. 'I want to talk to a nation' he said, 'not a select committee' (Bessie, 1938: 42).

Sensationalism gave way to drama with the outbreak of the yellow wars in 1895 when William Randolph Hearst took over the *New York Journal* and committed the paper to even more vigorous campaigning journalism than Pulitzer. The paper promptly began publishing under the masthead 'While others talk, the *Journal* acts'. Ornebring and Jönsson (2004) argue that while yellow journalism 'epitomised everything that good journalism should be', it also articulated a 'grassroots-based populist critique against established corporate and governmental elites' and could be described as 'an alternative public sphere'.

Further reading

Bessie, S. (1938) *Jazz Journalism*. New York: Dutton.

Conboy, M. (2002) *The Press and Popular Culture*. London: Sage.

Emery, E. and Emery, M. (1978) *The Press and America: An Interpretative History of the Mass Media*. Upper Saddle River, NJ: Prentice Hall.

Ornebring, H. and Jönsson, A.M. (2004) 'Tabloid Journalism and the Public Sphere: A Historical Perspective on Tabloid Journalism', *Journalism Studies*, 5(3): 283–97.

Schudson, M. (1978) *Discovering the News: A Social History of the American Newspaper*. New York: Banc Books.

BF

PART II

Institutions

Association of British Editors A senior occupational group that, in April 1999, merged with the Guild of Editors to form the Society of Editors.

Association for Journalism Education (AJE) Founded in 1997, the AJE is a forum for staff from higher education institutions in the UK and Ireland which run degree courses which include practical training in journalism. It aims to uphold high standards in such teaching and to promote and support research into **journalism education**. See http://www.ajeuk.org

(UK) Association of Online Publishers (AOP) The UK AOP is an industry body formed in July 2002 to present a unified voice to industry and government in addressing the issues and concerns relating to all aspects of **Internet** publishing. *BBC, BSkyB*, Guardian Unlimited, FT.com and News International are among the AOP membership. See http://www.ukaop.org.uk/

Audit Bureau of Circulations (ABC) The non-profit organization, founded in 1931 and governed by advertisers, advertising agencies and media owners, which provides independent verification of the circulations of United Kingdom newspaper and magazines. The ABC data helps determine the value of a publication's advertising space (e.g. how many consumers will see it). Other countries have similar organisations. See http://www.abc.org.uk

BBC Board of Governors Twelve people appointed by the Queen on advice from ministers to regulate the *BBC* on behalf of its viewers and listeners. They act as trustees of the **public interest**, safeguard the BBC's independence, set objectives and monitor performance. They are accountable to the **licence fee** payers and Parliament. The role of the governors and their relationship to **regulation** is under review after the **Hutton Inquiry** and the BBC's own internal investigation of its practices. In March 2005, the Government's Green Paper on broadcasting recommended that the regulatory role of the Government be conducted by a Board of Trustees after 2007. See http://www.bbccharterreview.org.uk.

BBC Online With a vast and impressive collection of more than 2 million web pages, the BBC almost certainly has the largest online presence of any single media organization in the world. However, the sheer size and overall success of its **Internet** operation have provoked controversy since its beginnings in 1996. An independent review commissioned by the *DCMS* and carried out by former *Trinity Mirror* chief executive Philip Graf said when the findings were released in May 2004 that the BBC's online remit had been too widely drawn and broadly interpreted, and that it should prioritize **news**, current affairs and education. The Graf Report insisted it was impossible to prove whether the BBC's online operation had forced commercial competitors out of the market, though it might have deterred investment by its rivals. It added some sites were difficult to justify in terms of the corporation's **public service** remit and that communication with industry had been poor. As a result of the report, the BBC announced the closure of five **websites** and promised it would draw up a tighter remit. See http://www.bbc.co.uk/

British Broadcasting Company (BBC) Forerunner of the *British Broadcasting Corporation*. It was set up in 1922 by a consortium of **radio** equipment manufacturers including Marconi, Western Electric and Metropolitan Vickers who'd begun broadcasting to London, Birmingham and Manchester in May of that year. The company's first general manager was a dour Scottish engineer, 34-year-old John Reith, whose strong belief in the principles of **public service** shaped the development of all **broadcasting** in Britain. While the company was set up to make money for wireless manufacturers, it was never driven by the need for profitability thanks to a government-approved licensing system for the receiving equipment, the **licence fee**.

British Broadcasting Corporation Created by Royal Charter on 1 January 1927 from the *British Broadcasting Company,* the BBC is a **public service** broadcaster paid for by the public through the **licence fee**. It operates ten **radio** networks, eight **television** channels and interactive TV, more than 50 **local radio** and television services and one of the world's biggest and most popular **websites**. The BBC *World Service* is not paid for by the licence fee and the BBC also has a commercial arm operating ten television channels whose profits help fund BBC public services. See http://www.bbc.co.uk

British Internet Publishers' Alliance (BIPA) Formed in December 1998, BIPA's main purpose is to 'promote the growth and development of new

Internet services in a manner which permits a wide diversity of entrants to the market, on a free and fair competitive basis'. Its membership includes major newspaper groups, magazine publishers, **radio** and **television** broadcasters, and Internet businesses. See http://www.bipa.co.uk/

British Journalism Review A valuable asset for British journalism, both academically and professionally. Published quarterly by Sage, *BJR* is one of the few periodicals (along with *Columbia Journalism Review* and *Rhodes Journalism Review*) to contain debate, analysis and scrutiny of journalism from both professionals and academics.

British Satellite Broadcasting BSB went on air in 1990 as Britain's second satellite broadcaster. This short-lived and disastrous venture was licensed in the mid-1980s by the then Independent Broadcasting Authority to take Britain into the age of satellite **television**. From the start it faced fierce competition from Rupert Murdoch's fledgling Sky Channel and never overcame serious financial and technical difficulties. Less than nine months after its official launch it merged with Sky to become *BSkyB*. It was best known for the 'squarial', an object of 1980s absurdity on a par with the ill-fated Sinclair C5.

Broadcast Journalism Training Council (BJTC) This accredits broadcast **journalism** courses in colleges and higher education. It is a partnership made up of the major **broadcast** employers including the *BBC, ITN/IRN, BSkyB*, Carlton TV, the *Commercial Radio Companies Association* and Skillset and representatives of accredited courses. The BJTC lays down broad guidelines for curriculum, staffing and resources, advises on and inspects course structures and, if they meet the required standard, accredits them.

Broadcasters' Audience Research Board (BARB) provides estimates of how many people are watching **television** at any given time and gives a minute-by-minute breakdown of the stations picked up in the UK at national and regional level. The figures are obtained from panels of households owning televisions representative of viewing behaviour. The panel itself is chosen through a continuous establishment survey involving about 52,000 interviews a year. Once on the panel, all the television sets

285

and video cassette recorders are electronically monitored via a set top box which records information about what's being watched. Viewers register their presence in the room by clicking a personalized button. The information is downloaded overnight and sent to broadcasters.

Broadcasting Complaints Commission (BCC) Created in 1981, the Commission had, under statute, regulatory jurisdiction to investigate complaints about unfair or unjust treatment in TV and radio programmes, and about unwarranted infringement of privacy. Following the Broadcasting Act 1996, it was replaced in 1997 by the *Broadcasting Standards Commission*. See **regulation**.

Broadcasting Entertainment Cinematograph and Theatre Union (BECTU) This has over 25,000 members working in film, **radio, television** and other associated areas. It was created in 1991 from a merger between the Association of Cinematograph Television and Allied Technicians (ACTT) and the Broadcasting and Entertainment Trades Alliance (BETA). The union can trace its history back to the 1890s and the establishment of the National Association of Theatrical Television and Kine Employees (NATTKE), which first represented theatre and music hall staff. In 1989 NATTKE merged with the Association of Broadcasting Staff (ABS), which had been set up in the 1940s as an internal organisation to represent BBC staff, to create BETA.

Broadcasting Research Unit (BRU) Established in 1980, this was an independent body which conducted independent research into broadcasting policy until it closed in the early 1990s. See **Public Service Broadcasting**.

Broadcasting Standards Commission (BSC) Established by the Broadcasting Act 1996, the Commission was from 1997 the statutory regulator for standards of taste, decency, fairness, and for the protection of privacy, in all television and radio broadcast in the UK. It replaced and merged the roles of its predecessor bodies, the *Broadcasting Complaints Commission* and the *Broadcasting Standards Council*. It produced codes of conduct and adjudicated on complaints. In 2003 it was replaced by *Ofcom*. See **regulation**.

Broadcasting Standards Council (BSC) The Council, launched in 1988, originally as a 'watchdog' body to monitor levels of sex and violence in television programmes, was given statutory powers in 1990. By law, UK broadcasters had to include, in their own codes, the Council code's standards on taste and decency. It adjudicated on complaints against broadcasters that its code had been breached. Confusingly, some of its functions overlapped with the *Independent Television Commission*. In 1997 the Council was replaced by the *Broadcasting Standards Commission*. See **regulation**.

BSkyB Created in 1990 through a merger of Rupert Murdoch's Sky Television and the rival UK satellite broadcaster *British Satellite Broadcasting*. From small beginnings in the late 1970s, Sky TV was a little watched and relatively unknown service operating in Europe. But in 1983 it was bought by one of the world's **media moguls**, looking to expand his involvement in the UK market where News International already owned two national newspapers. From losses of £14 million a week in 1990, BSkyB is now the UK's leading and most profitable pay **television** company offering over 40 satellite and digital channels, including Britain's first **rolling news** channel, *Sky News*.

Cable Authority (CA) Established in 1984 to license and be the statutory regulator for cable television in the UK, its duties included upholding standards of taste and decency, and ensuring due accuracy and impartiality in UK cable news programmes. Under the 1990 Broadcasting Act, it was replaced by the *Independent Television Commission*. See **regulation**.

Cable News Network (CNN) Currently owned by Time Warner, this was founded in 1980 by American **media mogul** Ted Turner and is generally credited for introducing the concept of 24-hour **news**. Its worldwide reputation was fully established in 1991 with its global coverage of the first Gulf War. In addition to providing a **television** network both at home and overseas (through CNN International), Atlanta-based CNN also has a large **news website** (http://www.cnn.com/) which was created in 1995. As a fledgling organization, it was derogatorily known as Chicken Noodle News (or Network).

Campaign for Press and Broadcasting Freedom (CPBF) A non-profit making organization that works 'to promote policies for a diverse, democratic and accountable media'. Based in the UK – and now Canada – the CPBF has initiated a number of campaigns on the concentration of media ownership, censorship, the future of the local press, broadcasting deregulation and other significant issues. It has also conducted research on journalism and publishes *Britain's Media: How They Are Related*, which analyzes the impact of media concentration.

Campaign for Quality Television This group has been active periodically to promote the concept of public service television, to help ensure choice and quality for UK viewers. It seeks to influence legislators. The Campaign was originally set up in 1988 to express the concerns of programme-makers about pending broadcast legislation, and was re-launched in 1995. It has produced research reports. See **public service broadcasting**.

Ceefax An electronic **news** and general information service produced by the *BBC* and first broadcast live on **television** in September 1974, Ceefax was the world's first teletext system. It was followed closely by the *ITV*-run Oracle now known as *Teletext*. The Ceefax service, originally named internally as Teledata, is now available on both analogue and digital platforms with the use of the appropriate equipment. Following a staff merger within the BBC in 2004, the same stories are transmitted for both analogue and digital television transmissions, as well as for the corporation's **websites** and mobile phone services.

Central Office of Information This rather Orwellian-sounding department provides an in-house publicity and promotions service for public sector clients. The COI refers to itself as the 'government's communication expert', and works 'in partnership with client departments and agencies to provide effective communications solutions' (www.coi.gov.uk). Recent advertising campaigns include a recruitment drive for the RAF, a national awareness campaign to highlight a national firearms amnesty and a national campaign against benefit fraud (running from June 2003 to March 2004), which aimed 'to create a climate of unease towards benefit fraud and to undermine its social acceptability' (ibid.).

Channel 4 Created by the Broadcasting Act of 1982, Channel 4 has a brief to **broadcast** radical and innovatory programming that appeals to a culturally diverse **audience** and is not provided by either the BBC or ITV. It is a publisher/broadcaster in that it does not make its own programmes but commissions them from **independent producers**. Channel 4 broadcasts to the whole UK apart from some parts of Wales which are served by *S4C*. The Channel 4 Group also operates pay **television** channels including E4, E4+1 and three film channels. Channel 4's one hour evening **news** programme is provided by *ITN*.

Channel 5 The newest commercial terrestrial **television** channel launched in March 1997 with a programme philosophy described by its Chief Executive as 'modern mainstream' and aimed at a younger audience than other commercial channels. Channel 5 went some way to breaking the mould of television **news** by allowing its presenters to stand in the studio, or lean against a desk rather than sit behind it, innovations copied by other broadcasters. Channel 5's news service is provided by *ITN*.

The Commercial Radio Companies Association (CRCA) is the trade body for commercial radio in the UK. It is a voluntary non-profit-making body funded by the subscriptions of its member companies and exists to promote the interests of commercial **radio** to the government and the regulator *Ofcom* among others. It is managed by a board of 12 directors and is the joint owner, with the *BBC* of *RAJAR*, the body that researches radio **audiences** nationally and locally.

289

Davies Review In 1998 the Secretary of State for Culture, Media and Sport established the Davies Independent Review to consider the future funding of the *BBC*. Chaired by Gavyn Davies, the committee's report in 1999 recommended retention of the **licence fee** and the establishment of a digital licence supplement to help the BBC launch digital TV. See **digitization**.

Demos This is an independent think-tank for hire, which works with government, corporations, NGOs, schools and professional bodies. Recent independent work has included research on: British competitiveness for the Department of Trade and Industry; the 'digital divide' for the information technology corporation EDS UK; and on a 'policy framework that promotes competition and innovation, while safeguarding the public interest' for the telecommunications corporation Cable & Wireless. See www.demos.co.uk

Department of Culture, Media and Sport (DCMS) This is responsible for, among other things, UK Government policy on **broadcasting**, film, the music industry, and **press freedom** and **regulation**. The DCMS was jointly responsible with the *DTI* for the **Communication Act 2003**, which introduced one regulatory body, *Ofcom*, for the broadcasting **media** (in place of the five that previously existed) and reformed the rules on media **ownership**. See http://www.culture.gov.uk

Department of Trade and Industry (DTI) The UK government body in charge of promoting enterprise, innovation and creativity in business. The DTI was jointly responsible with the DCMS for the **Communication Act 2003**. See http://www.dti.gov.uk/

European Journalism Training Association (EJTA) The Association, established in Brussels in 1990, aims to stimulate European co-operation in **journalism education**. More than 50 universities and institutes are members. They exchange views on the best practice in such teaching. See http://www.ejta.nl/

Fairness and Accuracy in Reporting (FAIR) A US news media watch group who, since 1986, have been providing constructive critiques of news output and, where applicable, commending good journalistic practice. FAIR 'work to invigorate the First Amendment by advocating for greater diversity in the press, and by scrutinizing media practices that marginalize public interest, minority and dissenting viewpoints' (www.fair.org). FAIR publishes an award-winning magazine of media criticism – Extra! (www.fair.org/extra/index.html) – and produces the weekly radio programme *CounterSpin*, 'the show that brings you the news *behind* the headlines' (www.fair.org/counterspin/index.html).

Google It started as a college research project in the mid-1990s and turned into what has become widely recognized as the world's largest and most-used search engine, capable of returning results to keyword entries in a fraction of a second and in many different languages. Google says its mission is to make the world's information universally accessible and useful. That information includes maps, **news** headlines, images and Usenet messages dating back to 1981. Its founders, Larry Page and Sergey Brin, were Stanford University PhD students when they began the work that was to produce a hugely successful global company. Google Inc. opened its door in Menlo Park, California, on 7 September 1998, and is now based at the Googleplex, Google's current headquarters in Mountain View, California. The **Internet** company made a successful debut on the Nasdaq stock market in August 2004. For the record, Google is a play on 'Googol' which is the mathematical term for a one followed by 100 zeros. See http://www.google.co.uk and http://www.google.com/

Government Information and Communication Service (GICS) Set up following the recommendations of the Mountfield Report (November 1997), the GICS is the public relations arm of the British government. The overall aim of GICS is 'to ensure that clear messages are conveyed to the whole target audience in the most cost-effective way' (www.gics.gov.uk/handbook/context/0200.htm). More specifically, the GICS has four strategic objectives: 'to explain the working policies and actions of Ministers and their departments, including their executive agencies; to create awareness of the rights, benefits and obligations of individual citizens and groups of citizens; to persuade groups of citizens to act in accordance with agreed policies in defined circumstances; and to ensure and demonstrate the proper use of taxpayers' money' (www.gics.gov.uk/handbook/context/0100.htm). The GICS operates through its four central units – the GICS Development Centre, the central *Media Monitoring Unit*, the GICS Operations Unit and the *Government News Network* – and reflects the great emphasis the Blair Government places on the role of presentation in achieving policy objectives.

Government News Network (GNN) Part of *GICS*, which aims to act as 'adviser to all government departments and agencies on regional communication issues' (www.gics.gov.uk/thegicstoday/gics-centre.htm). Previously part of the *Central Office of Information* (COI) where it was known as the COI Regional Network, the GNN became part of GICS on April 1 2002. The GNN is also responsible for the government News

291

Distribution Service (NDS) – the chosen delivery mechanism for nearly all Whitehall press notices (ibid.).

Independent Broadcasting Authority (IBA) See *Independent Television Authority* (ITA).

Independent Radio News (IRN) Provider of a 24-hour service of national and international **news** to most of the UK's **commercial radio** stations since independent **radio** began in Britain in October 1973. The service is distributed by satellite and the **Internet** and paid for by a unique advertising scheme which gives client stations an annual loyalty bonus. IRN is now owned by *ITN* and operates from adjacent studios.

Independent Television Authority (ITA) The ITA was the statutory body established in 1954 to license and regulate commercial television, launched in the UK in 1955. ITA duties included upholding balance in political coverage and ensuring programmes did not breach good taste. It owned transmitters used by ITV, so it could vet controversial output. In 1972 the ITA was renamed the *Independent Broadcasting Authority*, with duties extended to licensing and regulating commercial (independent) radio. It published guidelines to uphold **accuracy**, **impartiality** and **ethics** in these sectors' journalism. Under the 1990 Broadcasting Act, the IBA was replaced by the *Independent Television Commission* and the *Radio Authority*. See **public service broadcasting**, **regulation**.

Independent Television Commission (ITC) The Broadcasting Act 1990 created the ITC as the statutory body licensing and regulating commercial TV in the UK, replacing the *Independent Broadcasting Authority* and the *Cable Authority*. In 1996 further law gave it such power over digital terrestrial TV. Unlike the IBA, the ITC was not involved in prior approval of programmes, or in transmission. But it had wider powers than the IBA to enforce licence conditions and codes, including requirements for journalistic **accuracy** and **impartiality**. It operated in a regulatory framework which relaxed **competition** restrictions on cross-media ownership. See http://www.Ofcom.org.uk/static/archive/itc/itc_publications/itc_notes/index.asp.html. In 2003 the ITC was replaced by *Ofcom*. See **commercial radio, digitization, public service broadcasting, regulation, television**.

Independent Television News (ITN) One of the world's largest **news** organisations producing news and factual programmes for British and overseas broadcasters, including *ITV, Channel 4, Channel 5*. Through its subsidiary ITN Radio, it is contracted by *IRN* to provide news for commercial radio. ITN began at the birth of independent **television** in 1955 when it was founded as an independent organization owned by the original 15 regional television companies. Now it is jointly owned by ITV plc, the *Daily Mail* and General Trust, United Business Media and Reuters. ITN also has three business units, ITN Archive, ITN Factual and ITN International.

ITV/Channel 3 Independent Television is the commercially funded, regionally based **television** network previously known as the ITV Network and made up of regional broadcasters including Carlton/Granada and the breakfast contractor GMTV. ITV traces its history back to the creation of commercial television in Britain in 1955. Now operated by ITV plc, it also owns the free to air digital channel, ITV2, operates a **rolling news** channel, ITV news and a children's channel, CiTV. ITV provides national and regional **news** programmes on its terrestrial services with national and international news provided by *ITN*.

International Federation of Journalists (IFJ) The world's largest organization of journalists, representing around 500,000 members in more than 100 countries, which aims to 'defend press freedom and social justice through strong, free and independent trade unions of journalists'. The IFJ steers clear of adopting an explicitly political view, but promotes freedom of political and cultural expression, defends basic human rights, is opposed to discrimination of all kinds and condemns the use of media to propagandize or to promote intolerance and conflict (www.ifj.org/default.asp?Issue=IFJ&Language=EN). In 2001, the IFJ launched a quality campaign, 'aimed at defending ethical rights of journalists, promoting independent journalism, and campaigning for public service values in broadcasting and limits to media concentration' (www.ifj.org/default.asp?Issue=QUALITY&Language=EN).

293

Internet Architecture Board (IAB) This is an *IETF* committee and advisory body of the *ISOC*, which oversees the technical functioning of the **Internet** in relation to communication protocols, procedures and standards. The IAB was the Internet Advisory Board when originally set up in 1983 before being renamed the Internet Activities Board two years later, assuming its present title in the early 1990s. See http://www.iab.org/

Internet Assigned Numbers Authority (IANA) IANA was created in 1972 by the US Defense Information Systems Agency to oversee Internet Protocol address allocation and the management of the global Domain Name System (DNS), although these services are now performed by *ICANN*. Under ICANN, IANA continues to oversee the operation of the DNS. See http://www.iana.org/

Internet Corporation for Assigned Names and Numbers (ICANN) Formed in 1998, ICANN is an international, non-profit-making governing body which manages the global Domain Name System (DNS) and has responsibility for Internet Protocol address space allocation; these functions were originally performed by *IANA* and other entities. It also maintains the authoritative Whois database for various top-level domains. Previously, only one entity offered domain registration services, but ICANN has accredited a large number of companies worldwide to add to the domain name database, known as the Shared Registration System. *Nominet UK* is the central registry for .uk **Internet** names. See http://www.icann.org/

Internet Engineering Task Force (IETF) Formed in 1986, the IETF is a large, open, non-profit-making international community of network designers, operators, vendors and researchers concerned with the smooth operation of the **Internet**. See http://www.ietf.org/

Internet Service Providers (ISPs) Also known as IAPs (Internet Access Providers), ISPs offer varying levels of **Internet** access – and services such as **email** and web hosting – to individuals, organizations and companies, while many of them also have **websites** which act as **portals** to the **world wide web**. Domain names are usually registered though an ISP which will submit the application to *Nominet UK* or another international registry. ISPs are connected to each other through Network Access Points (NAPs). AOL (America Online) is one of the best-known ISPs, of which there are thousands globally.

Internet Society (ISOC) A professional body with membership of more than 150 organizations and 16,000 individuals in over 180 countries, the ISOC has since 1992 provided leadership and global co-ordination in addressing issues relating to the growth and development of the **Internet**. It is the organizational home for groups dealing with network policy issues like the *IAB* and the *IETF*. See http://www.isoc.org/

Internet Watch Foundation (IWF) The UK-based IWF works in partnership with many organizations, including the government, the police and *ISPs*, to minimize the availability of illegal Internet content, particularly child abuse images. It provides an Internet hotline to deal with reports from the public. The IWF, which since its formation in 1996 has operated from offices in Oakington near Cambridge, is governed by a board consisting of an independent chair, six non-industry and three industry representatives. See http://www.iwf.org.uk/

Johnston Press It was founded 1767 in Falkirk as F Johnston & Co Ltd and changed its name to Johnston Press plc in 1988. At time of writing, Johnston Press own 482 newspapers, including the *Daventry Express, East Fife Mail, Leeds Express, Manx Independent, Matlock Mercury & West Derbyshire News, Northumberland Gazette* and *Suffolk Free Press*. In March 2002, Johnston Press acquired Regional Independent Media's 53 regional newspaper titles for a reported £560 million, making Johnston Press the fourth largest regional press group in the UK.

Massachusetts Institute of Technology (MIT) The institute, which admitted its first students in 1865, is an independent educational establishment of international renown. It is organized into five schools which contain 27 academic departments, in addition to laboratories and centres. The MIT Media Lab (http://www.media.mit.edu/research/index.html), the outline of which was formed by Nicholas Negroponte and Jerome Wiesner, opened its doors in 1985 and has a growing focus on how electronic information overlaps with the everyday physical world. See http://web.mit.edu/

Mechanical-Copyright Protection Society (MCPS) This is a not-for-profit organisation founded in 1924 and licences the reproduction of recorded sound. It represents over 17,000 composers, songwriters and music publishers. It presently operates as an alliance with the *Performing Right Society*.

Media Monitoring Unit Part of the *GICS*, the Media Monitoring Unit keeps government departments and agencies informed of news developments 24 hours a day. Funded via subscriptions from government departments (and therefore the tax-payer), the Unit aims to provide: 'a co-ordinated watch for breaking stories; thorough early morning, lunchtime and evening thematic news summaries; tip-offs and intelligent read-outs of running stories; transcripts of selected items; and a media monitoring/cutting service to Ministers on overseas visits' (www.gics.gov.uk/thegicstoday/gics-centre.htm).

MediaWise The PressWise Trust, an independent charity set up in the UK in 1993 by 'victims of media abuse', is supported by concerned journalists, lawyers and politicians. It provides advice, information, research and training on media **ethics**, and aims to influence public debate on media conduct. Presswise is preparing to transform into a new organization, called MediaWise. See http://www.presswise.org.uk

296

Microsoft Bill Gates is the person most associated with the phenomenal growth and success of Microsoft Corporation – the world's largest company which created the Windows operating system, installed on the vast majority of personal computers, and the popular Internet Explorer browser. However, he actually co-founded the computer software giant with fellow student Paul Allen in 1975 after they created the first programming language for computers. Microsoft was so-named because it supplied microcomputer software. Six years later, their MS-DOS operating system was introduced on IBM's new personal computer and was followed soon by the arrival of the Microsoft Windows graphical user interface before the company was successfully floated as an initial public offering in 1986. Allen stepped out of the limelight, but Gates – who quit as chief executive in 2000 to become chief software architect – has made sure that Microsoft, based in Redmond, Washington, remains the market leader, although it has been embroiled in various legal battles including antitrust investigations. For example, in March 2004 Microsoft was ordered by the European Commission to pay a £331 million fine for abusing its dominant market position and told it must reveal secrets of its Windows software, though the company said it would appeal. See http://www.microsoft.com/

National Council for the Training of Journalists (NCTJ) Founded in 1951, after recommendations made by the first Royal Commission on the Press, the NCTJ administers a journalism training system geared primarily to the UK regional and local newspapers. An educational charity since 1993, it offers qualifications, e.g. in shorthand, media law, public administration and news-writing. It accredits training courses at some universities, further education institutes and at commercial centres. It is governed by representatives from press employers, editors, journalism unions and the education field. See http://www.nctj.com/

National Union of Journalists (NUJ) Founded in 1907 and with a membership totalling 34,000, the National Union of Journalists is the oldest and biggest union looking after the working interests of **journalists** in Great Britain and Ireland. It has its headquarters in London and regional and local branches throughout the UK. Members cover the whole range of editorial work – staff and **freelance**, writers and **reporters**, **editors** and sub-editors, photographers and illustrators, working in **broadcasting**, newspapers, magazines, books, on the **Internet** and in **public relations**. Like many other unions, the NUJ has been fighting attempts by **media** organizations, particularly newspaper groups, to end the system of collective bargaining by introducing individual contracts as part of a move to derecognize unions. See http://www.nuj.org.uk/

Newspaper Society (NS) Founded in 1836, the NS represents the interests of the UK's regional and **local newspaper** employers. The owners of more than 90 per cent of the publications in this sector subscribe to the NS. It is governed by their representatives. It offers services to members, e.g. legal advice, promotes the industry to the public and to advertisers, and lobbies politicians about media policy. When national wage agreements

297

existed in the sector, it represented employers in negotiations with unions. See http://www.newspapersoc.org.uk/

Newsquest (Media Group) Ltd The second largest publisher of local and regional newspapers in the UK (after Trinity Mirror PLC). At time of writing, it owns 430 newspapers (including the *Bradford Telegraph & Argus, Southern Daily Echo, Hampshire Chronicle, Lancashire Evening Telegraph, Brighton Evening Argus, Oxford Mail* and the world's oldest newspaper, *Berrow's Worcester Journal*) along with numerous magazines and supplements, 27 Internet sites, contract print facilities and a leaflet and sample distribution service (www.holdthefrontpage.co.uk/ news/2000/12dec/001209nq.shtml). Newsquest (Media Group) Ltd were acquired by the Gannett Corporation in September 1999 for a reported £904 million.

Nominet UK A not-for-profit company established in 1996, Nominet UK is officially recognized as the central registry for .uk **Internet** names. It replaced a voluntary group called the Naming Committee which originally managed the .uk top level domain. See http:// www.nominet.org.uk/

Ofcom Office of Communications. Since 29 December 2003, Ofcom has been the 'super-regulator' of the UK's communications industries, including television and radio. It merged, and inherited statutory duties of, five predecessor bodies: the *Broadcasting Standards Commission*, the *Independent Television Commission*, the *Radio Authority,* the Office of Telecommunications (Oftel, which regulated the telephone industry), and the Radiocommunications Agency. So, Ofcom has power to issue, and revoke, the licences of commercial broadcasters, and to rebuke or fine them for breach of its codes covering taste and decency/harm and offence, **accuracy, fairness, impartiality**, and **privacy**. Ofcom also has the duty to foster plurality, informed citizenship, and promote cultural diversity. It was created because technological **convergence** rendered the former regulatory framework obsolete.

Though billed as a 'light touch' regulator, Ofcom has, in some respects, greater power than its predecessors, e.g. it can fine the BBC for ethical breaches, though duty to uphold the *BBC*'s **impartiality** remains with the *BBC Board of Governors.*

Institutions

Ofcom can also, if the government requests it under **competition** law, investigate whether media mergers (including those of newspapers) are in the **public interest**. See http://www.Ofcom.org.uk. See **commercial radio, ethics, regulation**.

L'Organisation Européenne pour la Recherche Nucléaire (CERN) Particularly famous as the birthplace of the **world wide web**, the Geneva-based European Organization for Nuclear Research is the world's largest particle physics laboratory. It was formed by 12 founding member states, including the UK, in 1954 and now has 20. The CERN acronym comes from the organization's original French title of Conseil Européen pour la Recherche Nucléaire. See http://public.web.cern.ch/public/

Peacock Committee Commissioned in 1985 by the Thatcher Government to investigate the possibility of revising the financing of the *BBC*. The Committee was specifically invited to investigate the possibility of replacing the **licence fee** with advertising revenue – a proposal Peacock eventually rejected in favour of continuing a licence fee index-linked to inflation.

Performing Right Society (PRS) This was founded in 1914 in the wake of the Copyright Act. It ensures individual composers, lyricists and publishers are paid royalties if their music is performed publicly. It works by issuing a music licence to the user – a **radio** or **television** station – who then return detailed reports of music they play. PRS now licenses all terrestrial, cable and satellite broadcasters as well as the use of music on the Internet. It has a range of 40 different tariffs for venues ranging from concert halls to zoos. Individual programme **producers** list music clips used in news programmes in daily 'PasBs', a written record of any programme's content.

Pew Research Center for the People and the Press The Pew Research Center, based in Washington, DC, is an independent opinion research group studying attitudes toward the press, politics and public policy issues. Best known for producing national surveys which measure public attentiveness to major **news stories**, it serves as a useful information resource for political leaders, **journalists**, scholars and **public interest** organizations.

Formerly the Times Mirror Center for the People and the Press (1990-1995), the Pew Research Center is now sponsored by the Philadelphia-based Pew Charitable Trusts which also created The Pew Center for Civic journalism in 1993 to help stimulate citizen involvement in community issues. See http://people-press.org/

Phonographic Performance Ltd (PPL) This is a body which licenses the broadcast and public performance of music and other recordings. It collects the money on behalf of performers and record companies. Pubs, clubs, **radio** and **television** stations – anyone who plays music in public – must have a PPL licence. Created in 1934 by EMI and Decca it now represents 3,000 record companies and 30,000 performers.

Poynter Institute Founded in 1975 by Nelson Poynter, the former owner and **editor** of the *St Petersburg Times* and Times Publishing Company, The Poynter Institute is a school dedicated to teaching and inspiring **journalists** and **media** leaders. It is a financially-independent, non-profit-making organization based in Florida. See http://www.poynter.org/

The Press Association The Press Association, or PA as it is better known throughout the **media**, is the national **news agency** of the UK and Ireland, supplying a wide range of **news** and sports information services to every national and regional daily newspaper, major broadcasters, online publishers, and government and commercial organizations. Its main bases are in Howden (East Yorkshire) and London, while it also has regional offices through the UK and Ireland, including the Glasgow-based Scottish Press Association. It was founded in 1868 by a group of provincial daily newspaper proprietors to provide a more accurate and reliable news information service alternative to the monopoly held by the telegraph companies. PA is a private company with 27 shareholders, most of whom are national and regional newspaper publishers, the biggest being *Trinity Mirror*, United Business Media, Daily Mail and General Trust and News International. In addition to news and sport, its services include weather reporting, audio and video services, **Television** and event listings guides, and response and fulfilment services. See http://www.pa.press.net

Press Complaints Commission (PCC) The self-regulatory body launched in 1991 by the UK's newspaper and magazine employers. Using an **ethics** code drawn up by editors, the PCC adjudicates on complaints about journalistic conduct in these sectors.

It has many critics (e.g. *MediaWise*) but commands more respect than its predecessor, the *Press Council*. It is more streamlined, quicker to issue adjudications, and has successfully negotiated changes tightening the code, including some to minimize press intrusion into people's **privacy**. So far it has helped ward off any prospect of legislation to create new privacy law. PCC duties include upholding **press freedom.** See http://www.pcc.org.uk. See **Calcutt, self-regulation.**

Press Council Established by the UK's newspaper and magazine industries in 1953, after recommendations made by the first Royal Commission on the Press, the Press Council was a self-regulatory body which adjudicated on complaints against journalists and editors in these sectors. It was also charged with upholding **press freedom.** Despite reforms, which included permitting lay people (i.e. unconnected with journalism) to serve on the Council, it was criticized as slow, bureaucratic, and too closely allied to press interests.

It failed to exert sufficient authority after increased competition among tabloid newspapers led to ethical breaches. Discredited, it was closed down in 1990, and was replaced by the *Press Complaints Commission.* See **Calcutt, ethics, self-regulation.**

Press Gazette Trade paper for the British newspaper and magazine industries. Published weekly by Quantum Business Media, the *Press Gazette* discusses the issues, the developments and the personalities of our ever-changing industry, as well as reflecting on journalistic output and best practice. PG also hosts the annual British Press Awards, as voted by the paper's readers.

PressWise See *MediaWise.*

The Producers Alliance for Cinema and Television (PACT) This was founded in 1991 as the UK trade association that represents and promotes the commercial interests of independent companies in film, **television,**

animation and interactive media. With more than a thousand members throughout the UK, it negotiates terms of trade with public service broadcasters and provides services to its members including training, events, business advice and subsidised legal services. See **independent producers**.

Radio Academy Formed in 1983 as the professional body for people working in **radio**, the Radio Academy is organized as a registered charity. Members range from students to *BBC governors*. The Academy is a forum for discussion and development of radio through its organization of conferences, seminars and other events. It hosts the annual prestigious Sony Radio Awards and its Hall of Fame includes radio stars from Alastair Campbell and Richard Dimbleby to Tony Hancock and The Goons.

Radio Authority Now replaced by *Ofcom*, the Radio Authority took over responsibility for the regulation of **commercial radio** from the Independent Broadcasting Authority under the 1990 Broadcasting Act. It operated a licensing system for **radio** stations and short-term broadcasts and devised **codes of practice** for news and programming, sponsorship and advertising and engineering standards. It also administered rules on ownership and could apply sanctions to broadcasters who broke the rules. The Radio Authority codes are being subsumed into Ofcom's new Broadcasting Code.

Radio Joint Audience Research Ltd (RAJAR) Created in 1992 RAJAR operates a single **audience** measurement system for the whole of the UK **radio** industry. In previous years, **commercial radio** collected listening figures for their own audiences, while the *BBC* operated a separate system. It is wholly owned by the *Commercial Radio Companies Association* (CRCA) and the BBC. At present, audiences are measured using a diary reporting system to monitor listening hours but in May 2004 RAJAR began an industry wide consultation process to find ways of enhancing the system, and testing electronic systems of measurement. A new research contract is due to be awarded in September 2005 with electronic measurement likely to start in parallel to diary measurement by April 2006.

Reuters The world's largest international **multimedia news agency**, Reuters is a global information company providing a service for professionals in the financial services, **media** and corporate markets. It was founded in October 1851 by German-born immigrant Paul Julius Reuter who opened a City of London office, transmitting stock market quotations between London and Paris via the new Calais–Dover cable. Reuters, as the agency soon became known, extended its service to the whole British press as well as to other European countries, while also expanding its content to include general and economic **news** from all around the world. It moved to its corporate headquarters in **Fleet Street**, London, in 1939. During both world wars Reuters came under pressure from the British government to serve the country's interests, so it restructured itself as a private company in 1941. The new owners, the British national and provincial press, formed the Reuters Trust to preserve the agency's independence and neutrality. Reuters was floated as a public company in 1984. See http://www.reuters.com/

Royal Television Society (RTS) Formed on 7 September 1927, by a small group of television enthusiasts, the RTS is now a leading forum for discussion and debate on all aspects of the television industry (www.rts.org.uk/). The Society was granted its royal title in 1966 and HRH the Prince of Wales became Patron of the Society in 1997. The RTS provides networking opportunities and promotes professional development through regular meetings, lectures and symposia in 16 regional centres across the UK. It also publishes the magazine *Television*.

S4C Established by the 1980 Broadcasting Act, S4C went on air in 1982. It is a commissioning broadcaster transmitting Welsh language **television** programmes to Wales. It brought together Welsh language programmes which until then had been scattered over output on *BBC* and *ITV*. S4C operates analogue and digital services, with about 32 hours of programming a week in Welsh on the analogue service and 80 hours a week on the digital channel, some of which is provided by the BBC. It also reschedules about 70 per cent of *Channel 4*'s English language programming.

Scott Trust The Scott Trust owns The Guardian Media Group plc, which includes national newspapers the *Guardian*, the *Observer* and the regional

Manchester Evening News, plus the **website** Guardian Unlimited, among its assets. The Trust is a board of ten members chosen from areas of the **media** industry that reflect GMG's business interests. Its main aim is to ensure the commercial success of the London-based GMG and to uphold the Trust's values. Specifically, in 1992 the trustees formally put on record the central objective of the Trust: 'to secure the financial and editorial independence of the *Guardian* in perpetuity: as a quality national newspaper without party affiliation; remaining faithful to liberal tradition; as a profit-seeking enterprise managed in an efficient and cost-effective manner'. The Trust also provides bursaries for student **journalists** in the UK and has recently set up The Newsroom, an archive and visitor centre that 'preserves and promotes the histories and values of the *Guardian*'. The Trust was created in 1936 to maintain the journalistic and commercial principles pursued by C.P. Scott, the *Manchester Guardian*'s long-serving **editor** and proprietor, and also to avoid crippling death duties. The setting up of the Trust resulted in a unique form of press **ownership** and control in Britain. The Trust has a charitable wing called the Guardian Foundation which has a grant-making capacity for use in training and also in the broader area of **press freedom**. See http://www.gmgplc.co.uk/gmgplc/scott/scottintro/

Sky News Launched in February 1989, the News Corporation-owned Sky News, part of Rupert Murdoch's *BSkyB*, was Britain's first (home-produced) round-the-clock **news television** channel, transmitting via satellite. See http://www.sky.com/skynews/home

Strategic Communications Unit Located at 12 Downing Street, the SCU is part of the *GICS* that operates under the jurisdiction of the Prime Minister's Office. Following the recommendations of the Mountfield Report (November 1997), the SCU was launched on 14 January 1998 to co-ordinate longer-term government communication strategy. In the words of the Prime Minister, the SCU is 'responsible for managing strategic communications across all departments and will produce the Government's Annual Report on their performance and achievement of their objectives' (http://www.parliament.the-stationery-office.co.uk/pa/cm199798/cmhansrd/ vo980114/text/80114w06.htm). Originally the Unit comprised six people – two special advisers and four civil servants – but recently this has been increased to eight civil servants and two special advisers, not including the *Prime Minister's Official Spokesperson*, who oversees the Unit. An interim report of the Government Communications Review Group (27 August 2003) recently floated the idea that 'the Strategic Communications Unit should be renamed as the Prime Minister's Communications Support Unit, to avoid confusion with the Strategic Planning and Development function' of a proposed 'Permanent Secretary, Government Communications' (www.number-10.gov.uk/output/Page4405.asp). See *Government Information and Communication Service (GICS)*.

Student Radio Association The national body representing student radio. It offers support and training services, a regular conference and overnight programming for its 80 or so member stations. It is affiliated to the *Radio Academy* and is co-ordinated by an executive of five people helped by nine area representatives and four regional officers. It hosts the annual Student Radio Awards which are watched by the industry for signs of emerging talent.

Teletext A **news** and information **television** service rival to the *BBC*-run *Ceefax*, Teletext was originally named Oracle (Optional Reception of Announcements by Coded Line Electronics) when first produced by *ITV* in the mid-1970s until the licence was taken over at the start of 1993 by a consortium called Teletext UK. Teletext Ltd is currently owned by the Daily Mail and General Trust, and Media Ventures International. In addition to the original analogue services which are available on *ITV*, *Channel 4* and *Channel 5*, Teletext can be accessed on digital television and electronic mobile devices, though its **website** now contains only corporate information rather than any news content. See http://www.teletext.co.uk/

Terrestrial television Terrestrial television **broadcasting** has employed the traditional signal delivery of **radio** waves since the late 1920s, though its analogue method of transmission has come under serious threat from other forms of **communication**, including satellite, cable and community antenna television (CATV), while video and film content can also now be obtained over the **Internet**. In response to this competition, and plans by the British Government to switch off the analogue signal by 2010, multi-channel digital terrestrial television (DTT) has been developed.

Trinity Mirror Born out of the merger of Trinity plc and Mirror Group plc in September 1999, Trinity Mirror is the UK's biggest newspaper publisher, employing around 11,500 staff and producing 250 titles. Its varied **media** portfolio boasts national newspapers including the *Daily Mirror* and regional titles like the *Liverpool Echo* and the *Evening Mail* in Birmingham, in addition to various magazines and **websites**. See http://www.trinitymirror.com/

Voice of the Listener and Viewer (VLV) Founded in 1983, VLV is an independent, non-profit-making association, funded by its members, which represents the citizen and consumer interest in British broadcasting. It lobbies for quality and diversity in radio and television.

Supporting the principles of **public service broadcasting**. See http://www.vlv.org.uk/. See **radio, television.**

Wapping An area of London's Docklands and UK home to News International. On 26 January 1986 Rupert Murdoch moved the *Sun*, *News of the World*, *The Times* and *The Sunday Times* from **Fleet Street** to a custom-built, high-technology 'fortress' at Wapping. The move took place without any consultation with the print unions – the *NUJ*, NGA or SOGAT – whom News International continues to refuse to recognize. Murdoch used the move to introduce computerized printing technologies, revolutionizing the way that newspapers are produced. Previously, typesetters would turn journalists' copy into lines of type, but now journalists themselves were required to input copy directly into a computer system and sub-editors and page editors composed 'newspaper pages' on-screen. These new technologies led directly to the forced redundancy of some 5,000 print workers and indirectly to many more as competing newspapers felt compelled to follow Murdoch's lead.

Web Standards Project (WaSP) Formed in 1998, the Web Standards Project is a grassroots coalition fighting for standards that ensure simple, affordable access to **world wide web** technologies for all. See http://www.webstandards.org/

Women in Journalism (WIJ) WIJ is a networking, campaigning, training and social organization, founded in 1995, for women journalists who work in the UK written media. It grew out of a demand for women to be more effectively represented at senior level in newspapers and magazines. Its aims include campaigning for equal pay and family friendly employment policies, and monitoring the way in which women are portrayed in magazines and newspapers. See http://www.leisurejobs.net/wij/

World International Property Organization (WIPO) The Geneva-based WIPO is an international body with 180 member states dedicated to helping to make sure that the rights of creators and owners of intellectual property are protected worldwide, ensuring they are rewarded and recognized accordingly. WIPO arose out of BIRPI (the better-known French acronym of the United International Bureaux for the Protection of Intellectual Property formed in 1893) and administers 23 international treaties dealing with different aspects of intellectual property protection. See http://www.wipo.int/

The World Service A *BBC* news service funded by the Foreign and Commonwealth Office of the British government to broadcast outside the UK. The World Service report the news in English and 42 other languages, broadcasting on long wave, short wave, local FM frequencies as well as via Digital Cable, Satellite and Astra 1H and, of course, now the Web (www.bbc.co.uk/worldservice/index.shtml). The World Service has an estimated global radio audience of 146 million weekly listeners and registered 279 million page impressions on its website in the 12 months up to March 2004 – 'the highest-ever figure, equating to more than 16 million monthly individual users' (www.bbc.co.uk/worldservice/us/annual_review/2003/director.shtml).

World Wide Web Consortium (W3C) The World Wide Web Consortium was created in October 1994 to lead the **world wide web** to its full potential by developing common protocols that promote its evolution and ensure its inter-operability. W3C, which has local offices in many countries and around 350 member organizations from all over the world, has earned international recognition for its contributions to the growth of the web. See http://www.w3.org/

307

glossary of terms

Acoustic The particular type of sound achievable in a room or space according to the type of surfaces sound is reflected from.

Actuality Sound effects, atmosphere and interviews recorded on location, or recording of a live event.

Ad-lib Unscripted, off-the-cuff remark.

ADSL Asymmetric Digital Subscriber Line. Often referred to as broadband, it provides fast, always-on access to the internet using standard telephone copper lines while also allowing the user to make normal phone calls.

Advertising feature A piece of writing commissioned to be an advert, or to accompany (and therefore to attract) adverts.

AM Amplitude modulation. A term associated with analogue broadcasting on medium wave and a description of how the sound signal gets to the transmitter frequency.

Anchor American term for the person who fronts a high profile news programme.

Archive A store of news stories (or complete newspapers or broadcast bulletins) published previously, and therefore a source of research material for future. Newspaper stories from earlier decades may still be kept as **cuttings** (see below).

Aston A company that makes a system of on screen captioning and industry term in some organizations for the captioning process itself.

Atmos Atmosphere. The addition of natural sound or wild track to add to the authenticity of a piece.

Autocue An electrical device allowing television presenters to read a script while looking at the camera.

Back-announcement When the presenter gives more detail on an item immediately after its transmission, such as a phone number or the name of the reporter.

Back projection When pictures are projected onto a screen behind the presenter.

Back-timing Calculating backwards from the end point of a programme to work out the start time of a particular item.

Bandwidth (see also in concepts) This can refer either to the difference in the range of signal frequencies, measured in hertz, used on a particular transmission channel, or it can indicate the varying amount of digital information carried across a computer network, which is usually calculated in bits per second.

Banner Similar to a newspaper front page masthead, the banner is a section at or across the top of a web page (particularly the homepage) containing content (text and often images) and usually including the name and company logo (if applicable) of the website. The banner, or part of it, could also be an advertisement.

Bed Music backing that runs under news bulletins, station idents or adverts.

Bi-media Covering the same story for both radio and television.

Blurb Those text and graphics in a newspaper or magazine, e.g. on the front page, which enthusiastically tell the reader about articles on other pages, or which will appear in future issues.

Breaking news The earliest reports of any event or journalistic discovery, e.g. of a court verdict, of a plane crash, or a **scoop** (see below) revealing a scandal. To 'break' a story is to publish it before any rivals do.

Brief Notes provided by a researcher or producer summarizing a story and telling a reporter how it will be covered.

Browser A computer program which can display all the content on a web page by deciphering the HTML coding. Only text could originally be viewed until the arrival of graphical browsers. The most common browser is Microsoft's Internet Explorer.

Bulletin News summary in television or radio usually lasting a few minutes at the top of the hour.

Byline A line of type in a news story which tells the reader which journalist wrote it, e.g. 'By Harold Evans'.

Cans Colloquial term for headphones.

Capgen Electronic device for generating captions on television programmes.

Catchline One or two words used to identify a particular story. Also known as slug.

Chapel The British collective name, at workplace level, for members of a media trade union employed there, e.g. the Guardian NUJ Chapel is the term denoting all National Union of Journalist members employed at the *Guardian* newspaper. The term evolved from printers' workshops being called 'chapels'. See also **Father/Mother of the Chapel** (below).

Chapel meeting A meeting of members of a trade union employed at the same media workplace (see **Chapel**, above).

Check calls Calls made by newsrooms several times a day to the emergency services.

Chromakey An electronic way of taking pictures from several sources to make it look as though a television presenter is standing against a particular backdrop. See CSO (below).

Clip Representative section of an interview lasting a few seconds for use in hourly radio news bulletins. Also known as cut or *soundbite* (see below).

CMS Content Management Systems. These are usually used for publishing web pages which can be created and edited using browser-based pre-defined templates without the need for the people inputting the content to know anything about the technology usually involved in producing and updating websites.

Colour piece A journalistic article or broadcast which is primarily descriptive of an event and/or its location, seeking to convey the eye-

311

witness experience and emotions of being there, rather than to clinically narrate the news event.

Commentary Broadcast description of a live event, or, reporter's script read under pictures on a television news item.

Compact The description of a tabloid size newspaper with a broadsheet content. Since 17 May 2004, for example, the *Independent* has been published only in tabloid size, but editor Simon Kellner argues that the serious broadsheet content of the paper means it should be described as a compact rather than tabloid newspaper.

Contact Anyone spoken to by journalists to gain information about a story. See *Source* (in concepts).

Cookies These are small text files sent by web servers when a website is accessed and deposited on a recipient's computer. They can be used to identify users on future visits and also store information about the user's web-surfing habits. This can speed up the web-browsing process, but has led to privacy worries. Browsers can usually be configured to accept or reject cookies.

Copy Copy is a written piece of journalism, ready for any necessary editing.

Copy-taker A copy-taker is employed to key, into a newsroom's computers, stories dictated by phone by journalists at another location. Copy-takers are a breed near extinction, because journalists generally use laptop computers to transmit 'copy' (see above) straight into the newsroom system. Good copy-takers will correct mis-spellings, and take the shine off a reporter's vanity by carping, half-way through the dictation: 'Is there much more of this?'

Copy taster A copy taster is a journalist, usually a sub-editor, who makes an initial selection of what news stories should be considered for publication.

Corpsing The uncontrolled desire to laugh, usually inappropriately, while live on air.

Covert filming Filming without the knowledge or necessarily agreement of the people or places being filmed.

Crossfade Fading in one source of sound while fading out another so that they overlap.

CSO Colour Separation Overlay. See **Chromakey** (see above).

Cue 1: A physical or audible signal to a presenter to begin reading, 2: Written introductory material lasting a few sentences and summarizing a story read by a presenter.

Cutaway Insertion of a picture within a visual sequence used to hide an edit.

Cuttings News stories or features kept in paper form after being cut out, e.g. by scissors, from the page on which they were published. A print journalist applying for a job will usually enclose his/her best work as photocopied cuttings. 'Cuts' is a slang abbreviation of the term. A 'cuttings library' is an old form of **archive** (see above).

Database An electronic facility used for retrieving, storing and classifying information.

Dead air Nothing is being broadcast when it should be. Usually the cue for frantic activity.

Deadline The latest time of day or night, e.g. 5.50 p.m., or the latest date, by which a news story or feature *must* be received by the newsdesk (or by sub-editors or the newsreader) if it is to be included in the next edition of a newspaper, magazine or the next broadcast bulletin.

Delay A device whereby transmission of a live programme can be delayed by a few seconds. Usually used as a precaution against obscenities.

Delayed drop A narrative technique used in print journalism in which the most newsworthy fact of the story is not placed in the introduction, but further down the text, hence 'delayed'. This enables the journalist to use the intro to catch the readers' attention by intriguing them with 'human interest', or by building suspense, e.g: 'When John Doe left his tidy bungalow in Surbiton, bang on 8.07 a.m. as normal, there was no clue that within 20 minutes his life would be changed forever.'.

Digital (see also **Digitization** in concepts). It describes the system by which data is processed in combinations of the digits zero and one, meaning information is transmitted much faster and in a higher quality than previously possible.

Digital multiplex A hierarchical system allowing digital transmission of many different radio stations simultaneously.

Director In a studio, the person in control of the transmission gallery. On location, the person in control of what is to be filmed.

DNS The global Domain Name System (or Server or Service) helps users find their way around the internet by replacing the Internet Protocol (IP) address of a website with a domain name (also known as a web address or URL), making it far easier to remember than a series of numbers. Domain names, an example of which is www.bbc.co.uk, are registered through a registration agent. Information about specific domain names (including whether a particular one is available to register) and IP addresses can be obtained from one of the WHOIS search engines, such as http://www.allwhois.com.

Doorstepping Journalists knocking on doors, and hanging around people's homes and workplaces, when attempting to interview, photograph or film them.

Dreamweaver One of the most popular types of web-authoring software, Macromedia Dreamweaver can be used to create and design web pages. Packages like this are known as WYSIWYG – what you see is what you get.

Drive time Periods of the day such as morning, lunchtime and late afternoon which coincide with peak commuter travel, when more people listen to the radio in their cars.

Dub 1: To make a copy of an item, a programme or an audio source. 2: To add sound to a pre-recorded television item.

Dummy An edition of a newspaper or magazine which is not published, but which is a trial run/test product for a publication due to be launched or one being redesigned.

Duration Exact length in minutes and/or seconds of an item or programme.

Early edition See **First edition** (below).

Ears Adverts which appear on either side of a newspaper's masthead (see below), i.e. in the top corners of its front page.

Editing The process of choosing material from a number of sources to go into a finished item, or choosing items to make up a programme.

Editorial, editorialize Editorial is a word which, confusingly, has several meanings. An 'editorial department' is the physical space within a workplace where journalists work. 'Editorial' material (when the term is used generally) is that part of the content of a publication which is produced by journalists, e.g. news, sport, features but not adverts. But 'an editorial' is a 'leader' (see below), i.e. a comment piece reflecting the publication's viewpoints. 'To editorialize' is to make partisan comment in a journalistic context, and therefore to depart from impartiality.

Effects (FX) Sound recorded on location or taken from an effects library to give an audio illustration that adds to the story, e.g. birdsong, roadworks.

Electronic In the digital age, this often relates to applications and activities involving computers and the internet. It is usually shortened to 'e', for example in email.

Email (see also in concepts) Electronic messages exchanged between internet users on a one-to-one or one-to-many basis. They usually contain text, but can also carry attachments, including multimedia files.

Encryption This involves the coding or scrambling of (usually sensitive or confidential) electronic information so it can be read only by the recipient for whom it is intended, assuming that person has the correct decoding key. One of its major uses is on secure websites.

ENG Electronic newsgathering using portable cameras or camcorders that record pictures and sound to the same source.

ENPS Electronic News Production System. Developed by Associated Press and used by major broadcasters including the BBC and ITN, for radio and television, it manages scripts, wire services, running orders and bulletin clips. Material can be called up by any journalist on demand.

315

Exclusive: a story of significant newsworthiness, initially only present in a single newspaper. Paying a fee to a source often ensures exclusive rights to a story. Other newspapers often attempt to undermine a competitor's exclusive with a spoiler.

Exposé, exposure A piece of investigative journalism which reveals a scandal.

Fade To gradually lower or increase the volume on sound until it becomes audible or inaudible, or to gradually dim pictures to either white or black.

FAQ This stands for 'frequently-asked questions' and is usually a text-based page providing answers for a pre-defined set of questions which a visitor to a website might be expected to ask, such as how to use the site or where to find things. Other uses for FAQs include giving specific information about video games and company information in general.

Feed Supply of a programme or programme items over a remote connection such as ISDN, satellite or mobile links vehicle.

File extension Text and multimedia files (including web pages and documents) all have extensions, a dot followed by two or more letters after the name, which indicates to operating systems and browsers what type it is and the application needed to open it. For example, in Windows all Microsoft Word files end in .doc for document. Other common file extensions include GIF (Graphic Interchange Format), JPG or .JPEG (Joint Photographic Experts Group) and PDF (Portable Document Format). There are also compressed files, which have extensions such as .MPEG (Moving Pictures Experts Group) and .MP3 or MPEG3 (audio files); these can only be opened using decompression software. Most web pages and documents end in .htm or .html.

Filing stories A news story is 'filed' when a reporter has sent it, as complete as possible, to the newsdesk.

Fillers Relatively unimportant items of varying duration used as stand-bys to bring a programme up to the correct length.

First Edition/Early Edition The first version of a newspaper to be produced. Daily newspapers update throughout the night with a final (usually fourth or fifth) edition printed early morning. The edition of the paper is usually indicated on the cover, often by a series of stars. Because newspapers have to be transported, readers living further away from the printing presses are more likely to buy an earlier edition.

Fluff Mistake in newsreading or programme presentation.

FM Frequency modulation. A term associated with analogue broadcasting on VHF and a description of how the sound signal gets to the transmitter frequency.

FoC Father of the Chapel An employee (male) elected by fellow trade union members to lead the **chapel** (see above) at a media workplace, and therefore the person most involved in negotiations with management. If a woman is elected to this role, she is known as the Mother of the Chapel.

Fog index The Gunning Fog index is one of the formulae designed to measure the 'readability' of text in the English language. It was devised by Robert Gunning, a consultant to newspapers and magazines, who was a crusader against jargon. It involves counting, in samples of text, the total of certain types of multi-syllable word, and the number of sentences. Application of the formula gives the number of years in education required to read and understand the text easily. A 1989 survey suggested a reader needed 8.5 years of education to understand the *Sun* newspaper, (i.e. if schooling began when the reader was aged five, the *Sun* required the reading age of a 13-year-old) and around 12 years of education (i.e. the reading age of a 17-year-old) to easily understand *The Times*.

Fold The fold necessarily made in a **broadsheet** paper to transport it easily and display it for sale. The most important stories on a page will be 'above the fold', where most easily seen.

Foldback Means of allowing presenters in the studio to hear programme output in the studio while keeping the microphones live.

Follow up An item based on a story that's already been published or broadcast, but saying something new about it.

Foot in the door A general reference to use of robust, persuasive tactics by journalists **door-stepping** (see above) people reluctant to speak to them, including literally placing a foot against a door's jamb to prevent it being closed in the journalist's face.

317

Format 1: Style and look of a programme. 2: Type of technical material used for recording, e.g. digital video tape, minidisk, BETA, VHS.

Freebie Products (e.g. CDs by pop bands) or services (e.g. a holiday trip) supplied free to journalists or their media employer to encourage them to provide favourable publicity for such goods or services.

Freelance (see also in concepts) A journalist who works on a shift or piecemeal basis for a number of media organizations, rather than full-time for just one. Also known as a 'casual'.

FTP File Transfer Protocol is a tool for sending and retrieving information on the internet; it can also be used for uploading files such as web pages to a server. Formally, it is one of the main sets of rules governing the transfer of information across the internet.

Gallery (Control room) A room adjacent to a studio from where production and technical operations are controlled during transmission of a programme. A gallery will typically contain monitors for studio cameras and outside sources, sound and vision mixing desks and computing equipment linked to the newsroom.

General view (GV) A wide camera shot usually used to establish a location.

GNS General News Service. The BBC's internal service of national and international stories fed to local and regional radio newsrooms.

Graphics Computer-generated captions and treated pictures that explain aspects of television news stories that do not lend themselves to filmed material.

Hack Slightly derogatory, slang term for a hard-nosed male reporter (female hacks are, still more condescendingly, labelled 'hackettes'). Hack can imply that journalists are jaded and venal rather than meticulous and idealistic, but may also be used to denote, in certain contexts, an experienced journalist. Characteristics include being hard-hearted, uninterested in developing friendships or being popular and ruthlessly pursuing the truth. The hack is not just fascinated by war zones, 'he goes there on his holidays'; hacks don't just seek the truth, they're 'obsessed by it' (news.serbianunity.net).

Handout Press release or other publicity material.

Handover 1: Briefing sheet from programme editors or producers going off shift to those coming on. 2: Words used by a presenter to signal the end of their contribution.

Head of Content One of the senior executives among journalists in a media organization. As a job description, its scope varies between organizations, but usually denotes responsibility to oversee the quality of journalistic (news and features) content in the longer term, and to ensure it is geared to the target audience.

Hertz (Hz) Frequency of sound measured in cycles per second. 1000 hertz is a kilohertz (kHz).

Homepage This is usually the main page of a website and the one that a visitor will first see. It often contains introductory material (detailing the aims and purposes of the site) and links to the other main areas of the website.

HTML A universal coded language called Hypertext Markup Language used to create standard web pages and format the content in a way in which it can be viewed in a browser on different computer operating systems. HTML can be coded by hand, but this can be time-consuming and laborious, and the process is quicker and easier using web-authoring software like Macromedia Dreamweaver.

HTTP Hypertext Transfer Protocol defines how information is formatted and transferred from servers to browsers so web pages can be viewed.

Hyperlink (see also **Hypertext** in concepts) Hyperlinks, in the form of short text or graphics, are used to connect web pages and documents within the same website in addition to acting as gateways to other sites and destinations elsewhere on the internet. Email addresses can also be used as links.

Ident See **Jingle** (below).

Intake Term for a newsgathering team contributing to one or more programmes.

Internet (see also in concepts) A huge network of computers and smaller networks linked worldwide which allows people to access information and contact each other.

Interview (see also in concepts) An interview is usually a dialogue between two people, one of whom is questioning the other. In the case of a journalist, this would be in an attempt to find out information from the person being interviewed.

Intro The first paragraph of a report that grabs the audience and gives the main point of the story.

In vision (I/V) Instruction on a television script saying that the presenter should be seen on camera at that point.

In-words (In-cue) First few words of a recorded report written on a cue sheet and useful for checking that the right item is being played.

IP Internet Protocol relates to a unique series of numbers (between 0 and 255) which are assigned to every computer (and website) linking up to the internet. Through the DNS, the IP is translated into the URL and vice versa.

ISDN Integrated Services Digital Network. A way of sending digital audio signals over the telephone system.

ISP (see also in concepts) Internet Service Providers, also known as IAPs (Internet Access Providers), offer varying levels of internet access – and services such as email and web hosting – to individuals, organizations and companies, while many of them also have websites which act as portals to the world wide web. Domain names are usually registered though an ISP which will submit the application to Nominet UK or another international registry. ISPs are connected to one another through Network Access Points (NAPs). AOL (America Online) is one of the best-known ISPs, of which there are thousands globally.

Jingle Short piece of music used to identify a radio or television station, introduce a news bulletin. Also known as ident, sting, or stab.

Jump cut An edit which destroys visual continuity and makes the subject appear to 'jump' from one position in the frame to another.

Junior reporter A reporter who is not yet fully trained.

LAN As suggested by their name, Local Area Networks are much smaller than WANs in that they cover a relatively small geographical area and are typically used in offices and universities with computers connected to a server. LANs exchange data at high speeds and allow users to share information.

Lead The main story on a news page, therefore having the biggest headline.

Leader A comment piece in a newspaper which reflects its viewpoint on events, and any political allegiance it has. It appears in fixed position (in the 'leader column', on the 'leader page') traditionally with the paper's 'masthead' (see below) displayed over it, to add gravitas. Editors hope it helps form readers' opinions. A 'leader writer' is a specialist journalist, deemed informed and witty enough to write leaders, though editors also write their own. Most newspapers usually include two to three leaders, one of which will be shorter and about a lighter subject.

Legs 1: Colloquial term for a camera tripod. 2: Also, in a figurative use, a news story is said to have 'legs' if it proves to be a **running story** (see below), i.e. there are fresh, newsworthy developments, each justifying a further news report, over a long period.

Level The amount of sound registered by a recorder or mixing desk and adjusted to ensure there is no distortion.

Library The place in a media organization where any physical **archive** (see above) of cuttings or photographs or other reference material is kept, to help journalists research their work.

Lift To 'lift' a news story is to publish, without checking for factual accuracy, material already published by another outfit. It is poor journalistic practice, often done under pressure of a **deadline** (see above). There may be libel problems if the original story proves false, and copyright issues if phrases are 'lifted' entire.

Lighting rig/grid Construction of metal bars and cabling suspended from a studio ceiling to hold lights.

321

Link Short section of script read by a presenter connecting one item to another or bridging between interviews.

Links vehicle Mobile production studio used to transmit sound and pictures via microwave to base.

Live Happening now.

Masthead The title-piece of a newspaper, i.e. its name as displayed on its front page, and any artwork or logo used to embellish or project the name, e.g. the lion and unicorn coat of arms used by *The Times*, or the *Daily Express* crusader figure. Also used originally to denote the title and artwork as displayed, inside the paper, above the 'leader column' (see above).

Mic/mike Microphone.

MoC Mother of the Chapel See **FoC Father of the Chapel**, above.

Monitor Screen showing television pictures from one or more sources.

MPEG An abbreviation of the Motion Pictures Expert Group – a collection of some 350 industries and universities charged with the development of video and audio encoding standards. MPEG refers to the standards used for coding audio-visual information (e.g., movies, video, music) in a digital compressed format.

MP3 or MPEG3 An audio coding format. Using MP3, a user can make a data reduction of 1:12, while still maintaining original CD sound quality.

Multimedia (see also in concepts) A combination of different mediums to present content in varying forms. The internet can facilitate multimedia in its fullest sense by being able to accommodate text, audio, still pictures and graphics, animations and video (which can be streamed, meaning it is downloading while being played). However, browsers are not always able to play all files and plug-ins like Macromedia Flash or Apple QuickTime are usually needed to access certain media like music and video clips.

Natural sound Sound recorded at the same time as the pictures.

Newsdesk The desk or desks in a newsroom where the news editor and his/her deputies sit. It is the hub of the news-gathering operation, where reporters are allocated tasks and to which they send their **copy** (see above) to be checked, before any **subbing** (see below).

News flash Interruption of normal programming to bring details of an important breaking story.

Newsgroups Places on the internet where people can make contact with others sharing the same interests or find out about a specific subject. They can be useful sources of news and information for journalists.

NIB News in Brief. Short news stories, usually each of a single paragraph, usually laid out as a column down the edge of a newspaper page.

Noddies Shots of a reporter listening carefully to an interviewee taken after the interview to be intercut later if necessary to hide edits.

Non-linear editing Editing of film or video out of sequence, rather like a word processor cuts and pastes. Pre-digital computerized edit systems could only assemble pieces in order.

OB Outside broadcast.

On message A phrase suggesting that the person speaking and expressing a view is in broad agreement with the ideas of the larger group to which they belong; they are 'on message'. Recently, the phrase has been used to describe the congruence between MPs and parties (especially New Labour) during a period of growing party centralization and party reliance on media-based communication strategies to convey its policies to voters.

OOV Out of vision. An instruction on television scripts that the presenter is reading the script, but not seen on camera.

Op Ed Page The page, or pages, of a newspaper containing the opinion columns and editorials.

Opt-in/opt-out Switching between local and networked programmes. Local programmes opt in to the networked programming and then opt out to their own programmes. Opt-out is also used to designate a point where a pre-recorded item can be ended early.

323

OS Outside source. A programming point remote from the main transmission studio.

Out-cue/out words Final few words of a news report. A 'standard out-cue' is where the reporter signs off with his/her name, organization and location.

Output 1: The team of people preparing a programme for transmission. 2: General programming.

Out-takes Discarded film material. Can show up embarrassingly at Christmas parties.

Overlay/underlay The process of matching a recorded soundtrack with pictures.

Package Pre-recorded radio or television news report or feature lasting between one and three minutes comprising several elements including interviews, commentary, natural sound, effects and, in the case of television, visual sequences.

Packet Data sent over networks like the internet is divided into small packets of information which are reassembled at their destination, a process described as packet-switching.

PasB Programme as broadcast. A written record of the programme content kept to ensure that performers and contributors are paid. Particularly important if snatches of music are used.

Pay off Last paragraph of script in a new item which summarizes the story and points to potential new developments.

Peg A published allusion to a recent news story which, because the allusion can grab audience attention, can be used early in a feature examining the story's wider context, or in any related, human interest piece. Such features are said figuratively to 'hang' on the 'peg', i.e. the allusion justifies their publication that day.

Phone-in Common radio programming format where listeners ring in with points of view.

Picture spread Space in a magazine or newspaper given over primarily to several photographs about a particular event or subject.

Pick up pic A photograph not taken by a media organization photographer but collected from (i.e. 'picked up' from) a member of the public (e.g. from their family album) or another agency (e.g. the police) to illustrate a news story or feature.

Piece to camera Information given by a reporter on location direct to camera, usually used to bridge from one point to another or bring the piece to a conclusion. Also known as stand-upper or stand-up.

Pitch Trying to sell an idea for an item or a programme to a commissioning editor or producer.

Pixel A single dot of visual information. Pixels combine to create the picture.

Plug-ins Computer software which can be downloaded to add extra functionality to browsers so users can receive multimedia information such as animation, audio and video. Examples of plug-ins include Shockwave Player, Real Player and QuickTime.

Prefade Listening to an item through the studio desk immediately before transmission to check that sound levels are correct.

Presenter The person fronting the programme either in vision or behind the microphone. See **anchor** (above).

Press pack A group of journalists, all chasing the same story.

Producer The person in charge of the practicalities involved in a period of programming, a particular programme, or particular item.

Prof button Profanity, or obscenity, button. A device whereby a programme can instantly be taken out of delay to prevent transmission of an obscenity.

Promo On-air promotion of a station or programme. Also known as trail.

Prospects A list of potential news items prepared each day by the forward planning desk. Forms the basis of daily editorial meetings.

Puff Derogative term for text produced by journalists or public relations agencies which praises, without sufficient reason, substance or objectivity, a **contact** (see above) or client, and which therefore has no real journalistic value for the audience.

Q&A A reporter talking live to a presenter about a story they've been covering. See **Two-way**.

Radio car Mobile radio studio used for live or pre-recorded location items.

Reporter A journalist who researches and writes or broadcasts news stories.

Reporting restriction An order made by a court or legal tribunal, or enshrined in statute, which places a legal limitation on what can be published, e.g. the British press cannot normally identify the victims of rape, or children as being in social services' care, or publish comment about any ongoing criminal case.

ROT Record off transmission. Recording made of on-air output.

RSL Restricted Service Licence. A short term broadcast lasting up to 28 days licensed by Ofcom. Used by community groups, student radio, special event teams, football clubs or to test the viability of a radio service in any given area.

Run A run is a continuous batch of production on a printing press, to produce a set number of copies of newspapers, magazines, books, etc.

Running copy Copy (see above) which must be **filed** (see above) by a **reporter** (see above) rapidly in several stages, because of developments in a fast-moving event and because the **deadline** (see above) is so close that the **sub-editors** (see below) must make an immediate start to sub some of it, before the event is over, e.g. a blow-by-blow report of a football match, or the Chancellor's Budget speech.

Running order Written list of the items within a programme, their durations and the exact order they appear.

Running story This term has two distinct meanings. First, a fast-moving news event, or one in which the key facts are not quickly clear, which generates the need for **running copy** (see above) or updates to later editions of the same day's newspaper or to a day's broadcast bulletins, e.g. news 'breaking' about a major disaster. Second, a news event which generates, because of related events, further developments or fresh revelations, media coverage over a period of days, months or even years (e.g. the gradual implosion of Prince Charles's and Princess Diana's marriage).

Rushes Unedited raw material recorded onto camera.

RX Recording.

Scoop, Scooped A scoop is an **exclusive** (see above). A media organization is 'scooped' when a rival publishes a news story first.

Search engine A website which uses software or humans to search documents, files and pages on the internet and then index the data in huge databases, allowing users to look for information usually by keyword or directory (or both). Google, which also has an image search facility, is widely regarded as the most popular search engine in the world.

Senior reporter A reporter who has completed his/her formal training (but who is probably still in his/her early twenties!). See also **Junior reporter** (above).

Server A computer usually connected permanently to the internet and which has huge storage space. It stores files and documents (including web pages), and runs programs, which can all be accessed and used remotely by other (client) computers on the same network. The term server can also refer to the software running on the computer.

Shot list Content and duration details of each section of a package to enable a script to be written accurately.

Signposting In a news story it means emphasizing the central point, amplifying it logically, repeating key points where necessary and summarizing with a pay-off that takes the story forward. May also be used within programmes to trail forward to upcoming items to keep the audience interested.

Slug See **Catchline** (above).

SMS Short Message Service. This facilitates the sending of text messages (for example, news alerts) from one mobile device to another (and also from websites). Multimedia Service (MMS) messages can contain pictures, audio and video though more elaborate mobiles are needed to send them.

Snapper Slang term for a press photographer.

Snatch picture A news photograph taken without the subject's consent and usually, therefore, taken in a brief (i.e. 'snatched') opportunity, e.g. before the subject, realizing what is happening, runs or hides their face.

Soundbite A terse, accessible and memorable way of expressing a more complex idea. Since the mid-1980s, soundbites have been used by politicians to convey complex policy ideas in a simple slogan. Ahead of the 1997 general election, for example, New Labour leader Tony Blair claimed that if elected, the party would be 'Tough on crime and tough on the causes of crime'. The party also claimed that its three policy priorities were 'Education, education, education'. See **Clip** (above).

Spam A form of internet abuse, most commonly referring to unrequested electronic mail often advertising products not usually on general sale like Viagra, while some provide links to non-mainstream websites such as pornographic ones. Spam can also be sent to mobile devices via SMS. The origins of this use of the term spam, which can also refer to junk advertising messages sent to a bulletin board or newsgroup – thereby preventing normal 'conversation' – have been attributed to a Monty Python sketch in which a group of people shouted 'spam' to stop others from talking. Spam, a registered trademark, is a tinned luncheon meat produced by Hormel Foods Corporation.

Spike The place where news stories or features deemed not to merit or be suitable for publication, or which arrive too late, are deposited. A 'spiked' story is therefore a rejected one. In bygone decades, these were literally impaled on metal spikes on the **newsdesk** (see above) or subbing desks. Now 'the spike' is part of the editorial computer system.

Splash The main story on a newspaper's front page.

Spoiler, see concept.

Stand upper See **piece to camera**.

Sting 1: See **Jingle**. 2: 'Sting' is a term used of investigative journalism which, in a denouement involving subterfuge, exposes a rogue or hypocrite. Also, the term 'sting', in a libel case, refers to the most damaging allegation published.

Subbing Re-writing and/or editing news stories and features, while checking them for factual errors or other legal dangers, to make them fit the allocated space in a newspaper, magazine or website, or in broadcast airtime. Also, writing headlines and designing page lay-out, incorporating any photographs.

Sub-editor A journalist who subs. See **Subbing**.

Talent Colloquial and not altogether flattering term for television presenters and reporters.

Talkback Audio link enabling gallery staff to talk to presenters through their ear piece. Open talkback enables presenters to hear everything going on in the gallery and other areas. Closed (switch) talkback means they'll only hear instructions meant for them. May also link different control areas.

Talking head An interviewee. Also used disparagingly with reference to a programme or item that has too much expert opinion at the expense of real people.

TBU Telephone balance unit. A device which enables interviews to be conducted in a studio over the telephone. The interviewer can talk to the interviewee through the desk microphone, balance the sound levels and record the interview into the computer.

Teaser Short headline or sequence of headlines at the start of a programme designed to pique the audience's curiosity and keep them interested.

Throw line A line of script immediately preceding an interview clip that leads into the gist of the interviewee's point without repeating it.

Treatment Detailed written version of a planned programme or item. It

329

will typically include details of interviewees, locations, visual or audio sequences. Usually used for long form programming.

TX Transmission.

URL The Uniform Resource Locator is another name for a web page address (e.g. http://www.bbc.co.uk).

VFD Verified Free Distribution An accepted industry standard for certifying the validity of distribution data for free newspapers which are hand-delivered to individual households in a defined geographical area.

Virus Programs or scripts sent electronically, often to many email addresses at once, usually with the intention of causing loss of information through destruction of files on the recipient computer. They are the most common security threat on the internet, although anti-virus software can be used to combat the problem.

Vision mixer Operator in the gallery who controls fades, dissolves and cuts between different sources during a programme's transmission.

Voice over Commentary recorded over pictures by an unseen reporter.

Voicer, voice piece A way of telling stories in a radio bulletin that uses a named reporter's voice – 'The details from John Smith'. There are usually more details than in a copy story and it allows a change of voice from the newsreader.

Vox pop Literally 'vox populi' or 'voice of the people'. Street interviews conducted as a straw poll of public opinion and edited for transmission.

WAN The internet is the best – and biggest – example of a Wide Area Network which refers to a computer network that spans a large geographical area. They tend to be slower operationally than LANs.

Waveform (wav) Digital display of sound on a computer screen.

Wildtrack Recording of the ambient sound at any location to be used later to add atmosphere to an edited piece.

Wipe 1: An editing device which transitions from one picture to another by making it look as though the second wipes the first off the screen. 2: Erasing material.

Wire A stream of stories flowing into a news organization from a major newsagency, e.g. the Press Association or Reuters. In the age of the telegraphy, these arrived literally by wire, but today are sent and displayed by computer.

Wireless technology The attractive prospect of accessing the internet or sending and processing multimedia information without the need for cables and wires has led to a proliferation in the use of mobile telephone devices – including Portal Digital Assistants (PDAs) – and wireless networking thanks to major advances in technology.

World Wide Web (see also in concepts) The public part of the internet containing millions of websites and documents.

WPB Waste paper bin. Where most of a newsroom's incoming mail ends up.

Wrap A way of telling stories in a radio news bulletin which 'wraps' the reporter's voice either side of a short interview clip.

Yawn factor An informal measure of how boring an item or programme is.

331

Aaronovitch, et al. (2004) *The Hutton Inquiry and its Impact*. London: Politicos.

Alasuutari, P. (1995) *Researching Culture: Qualitative Methods and Cultural Studies*. London: Sage.

Allan, S. (1999) *News Culture*. Buckingham: Open University Press.

Allan, S. (2002) 'Reweaving the Internet', in Zelizer, B. and Allan, S. (eds) *Journalism after September 11*. London: Routledge.

Allport, G.W. (1954) *The Nature of Prejudice*. Cambridge, MA: Addison-Wesley.

Althusser, L. (1971) 'Ideology and Ideological State Apparatuses', in *Lenin and Philosophy and Other Essays*. London: New Left Books.

Anderson, J. (2002) 'Advice Columnist Ann Landers Dead at 83', *Chicago Tribune*, 22 June.

Antaki, C. and Widdicombe, S. (eds) (1998) *Identities in Talk*. London: Sage.

Anthias, F. (1995) 'Cultural Racism or Racist Culture?' *Economy and Society*, 24(2): 279–301.

Applegate, E. (2000) 'Advertising in the United States: Past, Present, Future', *Journalism Studies*, 1(2): 285–303.

Aristotle (1962) *Poetics* (trans. Hutton, J.). New York: W.W. Norton.

Aristotle (1984) *'Sophistical Refutations'* (trans. Pickard-Cambridge, W.A.), in Barnes, J. (ed.), *The Complete Works of Aristotle*. Princeton, NJ: Princeton University Press.

Aristotle (1991) *Aristotle 'On Rhetoric': A Theory of Civic Discourse* (trans. Kennedy, G.A.). Oxford: Oxford University Press.

Article 19 (1989) *No Comment: Censorship, Secrecy and the Irish Troubles*. London: The International Centre on Censorship.

Atkin, A. and Richardson, J.E. (2003) 'Constructing the (Imagined) Antagonist in Advertising Argumentation', in van Eemeren, F.H., Blair, J.A., Willard, C.A. and Snoeck Henkemans, A.F. (eds), *Proceedings of the Fifth Conference of the International Society for the Study of Argumentation*. Amsterdam: ISSA, pp. 39–44.

Atton, C. (2002a) 'News Cultures and New Social Movements: Radical Journalism and the Mainstream Media', *Journalism Studies*, 3(4): 491–505.

Atton, C. (2002b) *Alternative Media*. London: Sage.

Australian Broadcasting Authority (2002) *Narrowcasting for Radio: Guidelines and Information about Open Subscription Narrowcasting Radio Services*, available at www.aba.gov.au/radio.

Bagdikian, B.H. (1987) *The Media Monopoly*. Boston: Beacon Press.

Baistow, T. (1985) *Fourth Rate Estate*. London: Macmillan.

Barendt, E. (1985) *Freedom of Speech*. Oxford: Clarendon Press.

Barendt, E. (1995) *Broadcasting Law: A Comparative Study*. Oxford: Clarendon Press.

Barker, C. (1997) *Global Television: An Introduction*. Oxford: Blackwell.

Barker, M. and Petley, J. (1997) *Ill Effects: The Media/Violence Debate*. London: Routledge.

Barnard, S. (1989) *On the Radio: Music Radio in Britain*. Milton Keynes: Open University Press.

Barnett, S. and Gaber, I. (2001) *Westminster Tales: The Twenty-first Century Crisis in Political Journalism*. London: Continuum.

332

key concepts

Barnett, S. and Seymour, E. (1999) *A Shrinking Iceberg Travelling South: Changing Trends in British Television – A Case Study of Drama and Current Affairs*. London: Campaign for Quality Television.

Barnicoat, T. and Bazalgette, P. (no date) 'Endermol UK: response to the consultation on media ownership rules', available at: www.culture.gov.uk/PDF/media_own_endemol.PDF

Barthes, R. ([1957]2000) *Mythologies*. London: Vintage.

Barthes, R. (1967) *Elements of Semiology*. London: Jonathan Cape.

BBC (1992) *Extending Choice: The BBC's Role in the New Broadcasting Age*. London: BBC.

BBC (1993) *Responding to the Green Paper*. London: BBC.

BBC (1994) *Producer Guidelines*. London: BBC.

BBC (1995) *People and Programmes*. London: BBC.

BBC (2002) *Producers' Guidelines*. London: BBC.

BBC Online (2003) 'Want to Be a Press Baron? Read this first', 21 November, available at: http://news.bbc.co.uk/I/hi/magazine/3225990.stm.

BBC Online (2003) 'Journalists "Should Name Sources"' (18 July) http://news.bbc.co.uk/1/hi/uk_politics/3076337.stm (accessed 5 November 2003).

BBC Online (2004) *The BBC's Journalism after Hutton: The Report of the Neil Review Team*, at http://www.bbc.co.uk/info/policies/neil report/.

Bell, A. (1991) *The Language of News Media*. Oxford: Blackwell.

Bell, M. (1996) 'TV News: How Far Should We Go?' *Critical Studies in Mass Communications*, 13 (3): 7–16.

Bell, M. (1998) 'The Journalism of Attachment', in Kieran, M. *Media Ethics*. London: Routledge. pp. 15–22.

Bell, S. (1999) *Bell's Eye: Twenty Years of Drawing Blood*. London: Methuen.

Belson, W. (1978) *Television Violence and the Adolescent Boy*. Farnborough: Saxon House.

Berelson, B. (1952) 'Content Analysis in Communications Research', in Berelson, B. and Janowitz, M. (eds) (1966), *Reader in Public Opinion and Communication*. New York: Free Press, pp. 260–6.

Berger, G. (2000) 'Grave New World? Democratic Journalism Enters the Global Twenty-first Centry', *Journalism Studies*, 1(1): 81–100.

Berkowitz, D. (1997) *Social Meanings of News: A Reader*. Thousand Oaks, CA: Sage.

Bernstein, C. and Woodward, B. (1974) *All the President's Men*. New York: Simon and Schuster.

Bertrand, C. (2000): *Media Ethics and Accountability Systems*. New Brunswick, NJ: Transaction.

Bertrand, C. (ed.) (2003) *An Arsenal for Democracy: Media Accountability Systems*. Cresskill, NJ: Hampton Press.

Bessie, S. (1938) *Jazz Journalism*. New York: Dutton.

Bird, S.E. and Dardenne, R.W. (1988) 'Myth, Chronicle and Story: Exploring the Narrative Qualities of News', in Berkowitz, D. (ed.) (1997) *Social Meanings of News: A Reader*. Thousand Oaks, CA: Sage, pp. 333–50.

Black, A. (2004) *People Who Live in the Dark: The History of the Special Adviser in British Politics*. London: Politicos.

Black, J. (2001) *The English Press 1621–1861*. Gloucestershire: Sutton Press.

Black, P. (1972) *The Biggest Aspidistra in the World*. London: BBC.

Blick, A. (2004) *People Who Live in the Dark: The History of the Special Adviser in British Politics*. London: Politicos.

Blommaert, J. and Verschueren, J. (1998) *Debating Diversity: Analysing the Discourse of Tolerance*. London: Routledge.

333

Blumler, J.G. (1992) *Television and the Public Interest: Vulnerable Values in West European Broadcasting*. London: Sage.

Blumler, J.G. (1993) 'Public Service Broadcasting in Multi-Channel Conditions: Function and Funding', in Barnett, S. (ed.) *Funding the BBC's Future*. London: British Film Institute, pp. 26–42.

Blumler, J.G., Gurevitch, M. and Nossiter, T. (1989) 'The Earnest Versus the Determined', in Crewe, I. and Harrop, M. (eds) *Political Communications: The General Election Campaign of 1987*. Cambridge: Cambridge University Press, pp. 157–75.

Blumler, J.G. and Katz, E. (1974) *The Uses of Mass Communications*. London: Sage.

Boese, A. (2002) *The Museum of Hoaxes: A Collection of Pranks, Stunts, Deceptions and Other Wonderful Stories Contrived for the Public from the Middle Ages to the New Millennium*. London: E.P. Dutton.

Bolton, R. (1990) *Death on the Rock and Other Stories*. London: W.H. Allen.

Boon, P. (ed.) (2003) *The UK Radio Guide and Directory*. London: Goldcrest.

Boorstin, D. (1963) *The Image: Or What Happened to the American Dream*. Harmondsworth: Pelican.

Boulton, D. (1991) *The Third Age of Broadcasting*. London: Institute for Public Policy Research.

Bourdieu, P. and Wacquant, L. (1999) 'On the Cunning of Imperialist Reason', *Theory, Culture and Society*, 16(1): 41–58.

Boyce, G., Curran, J. and Wingate, P. (eds) (1978) *Newspaper History from the 17th Century to the Present Day*. London: Constable.

Boyd, A. (2001) *Broadcast Journalism: Techniques of Radio and Television News*, 5th edn. Oxford: Focal Press.

Boyd-Barrett, O. (1970) 'Journalism Recruitment and Training: Problems in Professionalization', in Tunstall, J. (ed.), *Media Sociology*. London: Constable.

Boyd-Barrett, O. (1980) *The International News Agencies*. Thousand Oaks, CA: Sage.

Boyd-Barrett, O. (1998a) '"Global" News Agencies', in Boyd-Barrett, O. and Rantanen, T. (eds), *The Globalization of News*. London: Sage.

Boyd-Barrett, O. (1998b) 'The Globalization of News', in Boyd-Barrett, O. and Rantanen, T. (eds), *The Globalization of News*. London: Sage.

Boyd-Barrett, O. (1998c) 'News Agencies as Agents of Globalization', in Boyd-Barrett, O. and Rantanen, T. (eds), *The Globalization of News*. London: Sage.

Braithwaite, N. (ed.) (1996) *The International Libel Handbook*. London: Butterworth-Heinemann Ltd.

Briggs, A. (1965) *The History of Broadcasting in the United Kingdom*, vol. II: *The Golden Age of Wireless*. Oxford: Oxford University Press.

Briggs, A. (1979) *The History of Broadcasting in the United Kingdom*, vol. IV: *Sound and Vision*. Oxford: Oxford University Press.

Braham, P. (1982) 'How the Media Report Race', in Gurevitch, M., Bennett, T., Curran, J. and Woolacott, J. (eds) *Culture, Society and the Media*. London: Routledge, pp. 268–86.

The Broadcasting Act 1990 (1990) London: HMSO.

Broadcasting Research Unit (1985) *The Public Service Idea in British Broadcasting: Main Principles*. Luton: John Libbey.

Bromley, M. (1998a) '"Watching the Watchdogs?" The Role of Readers' Letters in Calling the Press to Account', in Bromley, M. and Stephenson, H. (eds) *Sex, Lies and Democracy*. London: Longman, pp. 147–62.

Bromley, M. (1998b) 'The "Tabloiding" of Britain: Quality Newspapers in the 1990s', in Bromley, M. and Stephenson, H. (eds) *Sex, Lies and Democracy: The Press and the Public*. New York: Longman.

334

Bromley, M. and Stephenson, H. (eds) (1998) *Sex, Lies and Democracy: The Press and the Public*. New York: Longman.

Bromley, M., Tumber, H. and Zelizer, B. (2001) 'Editorial', *Journalism: Theory, Practice and Criticism*, 2(3): 251–4.

Brown, G. and Yule, G. (1983) *Discourse Analysis*. Cambridge: Cambridge University Press.

Brown, M. (2003) 'Now – Can Five Maintain its Momentum?', *Guardian* 14 July, pp. 6–7.

Bryant, M. (2000) *Dictionary of Twentieth Century Cartoonists and Caricaturists*. Aldershot: Ashgate.

Bull, P. (2003) *The Microanalysis of Political Communication: Claptrap and Ambiguity*. London: Routledge.

Burke, K. (1950) *A Rhetoric of Motives*. New York: Prentice Hall.

Burt, T. and Kirchgaessner, S. (2004) 'Raised Voices and Lower Reputations', *Financial Times Creative Business*, May 25, p. 8.

Byrne, C. (2003) 'Sun's Yelland in Shock Departure', *Guardian Unlimited*. http://www.media.guardian.co.uk/presspublishing/stpru/0,7495,873980,00.html.

Calcutt, D. (1990) *Report of the Committee on Privacy and Related Matters*, Cm 1102. London: HMSO.

Calcutt, D. (1993) *Review of Press Self-regulation* Cm 2135. London: HMSO.

Callaghan, K. and Schnell, F. (2001) 'Assessing the Democratic Debate: How the News Media Frame Elite Policy Discourse', *Political Communication*, 18: 183–212.

Cameron, D. (1996) 'Style Policy and Style Politics: A Neglected Aspect of the Language of the News', *Media, Culture and Society*, 18(3): 315–33.

Cameron, D. (2001) *Working with Spoken Discourse*. London: Sage.

Cameron, G., Ju-Pak, K. and Kim, B.H. (1996) 'Advertorials in Magazines, Current Use and Compliance with Industry Guidelines', *Journalism and Mass Communication Quarterly*, 73: 722–33.

Cameron, J. (1967) *Vicky: A Memorial Volume*. London: Allen Lane.

Campaign for Press and Broadcasting Freedom (1996) *Twenty-first Century Media: Shaping the Democratic Vision*. London: CPBF.

Campaign for Quality Television (1998) *The Purposes of Broadcasting*. London: CQT.

Campbell, A. (1999) *Beyond Spin: Government and the Media*. London: Fabian Special Pamphlet no 42.

Campbell, C. (2000) 'Citizens Matter: And That Is Why Public Journalism Matters', *Journalism Studies*, 1(4): 689–95.

Campbell, C.P. (1995) *Race, Myth and the News*. Thousand Oaks, CA: Sage.

Carter, R.E. Jnr (1958) 'Newspaper Gatekeepers and the Sources of News', *Public Opinion Quarterly*, 22: 133–44.

Cashmore, E.E. (1988) *Dictionary of Race and Ethnic Relations*. London: Routledge.

Central Office of Information (2001) *Central Office of Information Annual Report and Accounts*. London: Stationery Office.

Channel 5 Broadcasting (1995) *Application to the Independent Television Commission for the Channel 5 Licence*.

Chantler, P. and Harris, S. (1997) *Local Radio Journalism*. Oxford: Focal Press.

Charity, A. (1995) *Doing Public Journalism*. New York: Guilford Press.

Chippindale, P. and Horrie, C. (1992) *Stick It Up Your Punter: The Rise and Fall of The Sun*. London: Mandarin Paperbacks.

Chomsky, N. (1986) 'Thought Control: The Case of the Middle East', in Chomsky, N. (2002) *Pirates and Emperors, Old and New: International Terrorism in the Real World*. London: Pluto Press pp. 19–37.

Chomsky, N. (1997) *Media Control: The Spectacular Achievements of Propaganda*. New York: Seven Stories Press.

Clapperton, G. (2003) 'Back on Stream', *The Guardian New Media*, 20 October, p. 42.

Clark, T. (1997) *Art and Propaganda in the Twentieth Century: The Political Image in the Age of Mass Culture*. London: Everyman Art Library.

Clarke, N. (2003) *The Shadow of a Nation*. London: Weidenfeld and Nicholson.

Cobb, R. (1989) 'PR Has Radio Taped', *PR Week*, 20 April, pp. 12–13.

Cockerell, M., Hennessey, P. and Walker, D. (1984) *Sources Close to the Prime Minister: Inside the Hidden World of the News Manipulators*. London: Macmillan.

Cohen, S. (1973) *Folk Devils and Moral Panics: The Creation of the Mods and Rockers*. St Albans: Paladin.

Cohen, S. and Young, J. (eds) (1973) *The Manufacture of News: Social Problems, Deviance and the News Media*. London: Constable.

COI (2001) *Annual Reports and Accounts* 2000–1 HC53. London: HMSO.

Cole, P. (1997) 'Do You Care about Tomorrow?', Association of British Editors, speech to journalism training seminar, the Guild of Editors and the Media Society, 30 January.

Cole, P. (2002) 'A New Space Age', in McNay, M. (ed.) *The Guardian Past and Present*. Manchester: Guardian Newspapers, pp. 54–7.

Coleman, S. (1999) *Election Call: A Democratic Public Forum?* London: The Hansard Society.

Coman, M. (2000) 'Developments in Journalism Theory about Media "Transitions" in Central and Eastern Europe', *Journalism Studies*, 1(1): 35–56.

Communications Act 2003 (2003), DTI and DCMS (2000) *A New Future for Communications*. London: The Stationery Office.

Condit, C.M. (1989) 'The Rhetorical Limits of Polysemy', in Lucaites, J.L, Condit, C.M. and Caudill, S. (eds) (1999), *Contemporary Rhetorical Theory: A Reader*. New York: Guilford Press, pp. 494–511.

Conboy, M. (2002) *The Press and Popular Culture*. London: Sage.

Connolly, C. (1938) 'Enemies of Promise', in Allen, J. (2003) *The BBC News Styleguide*. London: BBC.

Corner, J. (1996) *The Art of Record: A Critical Introduction to Documentary*. Manchester: Manchester University Press.

Costera Meijer, I. (2001) 'The Public Quality of Popular Journalism: Developing a Normative Framework', *Journalism Studies*, 2(2): 189–206.

Costera Meijer, I. (2003) 'What is Quality News? A Plea for Extending the Professional Repertoire of Newsmakers', *Journalism Studies*, 4(1): 15–30.

Cottle, S. (1993) '"Race" and Regional Television News: Multiculturalism and the Production of Popular TV', *New Community*, 19(4): 581–92.

Cottle, S, (1999) 'Ethnic Minorities in the British News Media: Explaining (Mis)Representation', in Stokes, J. and Reading, A. (eds) *The Media in Britain: Current Debates and Developments*. Houndsmills: Macmillan, pp. 191–200.

Cottle, S. (2000a) 'Media Research and Ethnic Minorities: Mapping the Field', in Cottle, S. (ed.) *Ethnic Minorities and the Media: Changing Cultural Boundaries*. Buckingham: Open University Press, pp. 1–30.

Cottle, S. (ed.) (2000b) *Ethnic Minorities and the Media*. Buckingham: Open University Press.

Cox, G. (1995) *Pioneering Television News*. London: John Libbey.

Cozens, C. (2003) 'News Bunny Back Say Live TV Lads', *Guardian*, 16 May, p. 21.

Cozens, C. (2004) 'Guardian Agrees £50m for relaunch', *Guardian Unlimited*, 29 June. http://media.guardian.co.uk/site/story/0,14173,1249915,00.html.

Crewe, I. and Harrop, M. (eds) (1989) *Political Communications: The General Election Campaign of 1987*. Cambridge: Cambridge University Press.

Crisell, A. (1994) *Understanding Radio*, 2nd edn. London: Routledge.

Crisell, A. (2002) *An Introductory History of British Broadcasting*. London: Routledge.

Critcher, C. (2003) *Moral Panics and the Media*. Maidenhead: Open University Press.

Croad, E. (2003) 'Blogs Bring Personal View of War', 27 March, *dotJournalism*, available at: http://www.journalism.co.uk/news/story607.html.

Crone, T. (1997) 'Public Are the Losers from this Shameful Travesty', *Press Gazette*, 25 July.

Crone, T. (2002) *Law and the Media*, 4th edn. Oxford: Focal Press.

Cronkite, W. (1997) 'More Bad News', *Guardian*, 27 January, p. 2.

Crook, T. (1998) *International Radio Journalism, History, Theory and Practice*. London: Routledge.

Cudlipp, H. (1953) *Publish and Be Damned: The Astonishing Story of the 'Daily Mirror'*. London: Andrew Dakers.

Culture, Media and Sport Select Committee (2003) *Fifth Report: Privacy and Media Intrusion*, HC 458 – I, ISBN 0 10 501122 8. Oral Evidence and Written Evidence of above report, HC 458 – II, ISBN 0 10 501117 1. Written Evidence of above report, HC 458 – III, ISBN 0 10 501118 X. http://www.publications.parliament.uk/pa/cm/cmcumeds.htm#reports.

Curran, J. (1978) *The British Press: A Manifesto*. London: Macmillan.

Curran, J. (1990) 'The New Revisionism in Mass Communication Research: A Reappraisal', *European Journal of Communication*, 5: 135–64.

Curran, J. and Seaton, J. (1997) *Power without Responsibility*, 5th edn. London: Routledge.

Curran, J. and Seaton, J. (2003) *Power without Responsibility*, 6th edn. London: Routledge.

Curtis, M. (2003) *Web of Deceit: Britain's Real Role in the World*. London: Vintage.

Cutting, J. (2002) *Pragmatics and Discourse: A Resource Book for Students*. London: Routledge.

Daniels, J. (1997) *White Lies: Race, Class, Gender and Sexuality in White Supremacist Discourse*. New York: Routledge.

Davidson, A. (1992) *Under the Hammer: Greed and Glory inside the Television Business*. London: Mandarin Books.

Davis, A. (2002) *Public Relations Democracy: Public Relations, Politics and the Mass Media in Britain*. London: Sage.

Davis, S. (2000) 'Public Journalism: The Case Against', *Journalism Studies*, 1(4): 686–8.

Deacon, D. and Golding, P. (1994) *Taxation and Representation: The Media, Political Communication and the Poll Tax*. London: John Libbey.

Deacon, D., Pickering, M., Golding, P. and Murdock, G. (1999) *Researching Communications: A Practical Guide to Methods in Media and Cultural Analysis*. London: Arnold.

de Burgh, H. (ed.) (2000) *Investigative Journalism: Context and Practice* London: Routledge.

Delano, A. and Henningham, J. (1995) *The News Breed: British Journalists in the 1990s*. London: The London College of Printing and Distributive Trades.

Department for Culture, Media and Sport (2003) *The Government's Response to the Fifth Report of the Culture, Media and Sport Select Committee CM5 985*. London: TSO.

Department of National Heritage (1992) *The Future of the BBC*. London: HMSO.

Department of National Heritage (1995a) *Media Ownership: The Government's Proposals*. Cmnd 2872. London: HMSO.

337

Department of National Heritage (1995b) *Privacy and Media Intrusion: The Government's Response*. CM2918. London: HMSO.

Department of Trade and Industry (2004) *Enterprise Act 2002: Public Interest Intervention in Media Mergers: Guidance on the Operation of the Public Interest Merger Provisions Relating to Newspaper and Other Media Mergers*. http://www.dti.gov.uk/ccp/topics2/guide/ukmediaguide.pdf.

Deuze, M. (2004) 'What is Multimedia Journalism?' *Journalism Studies*, 5(2): 139–52.

De Wolk, R. (2001) *Introduction to Online Journalism*. Boston: Allyn and Bacon.

Diamond, E. (1991) *The Media Show: The Changing Face of the News 1985–1990*. Cambridge, MA: MIT Press.

Dijk, T.A. van (1988a) *News as Discourse*. Hillsdale, NJ: Lawrence Erlbaum Associates.

Dijk, T.A. van (1988b) *News Analysis: Case Studies of International and National News in the Press*. Hillsdale, NJ: Lawrence Erlbaum Associates.

Dijk, T.A. van (1991) *Racism and the Press*. London: Routledge.

Dijk, T.A. van (ed.) (1997) *Discourse as Structure and Process*. London: Sage.

Dijk, T.A. van (1998) *Ideology: A Multidisciplinary Approach*. London: Sage.

Dijk, T.A. van (2000) 'New(s) Racism: A Discourse Analytical Approach', in Cottle, S. (ed.) *Ethnic Minorities and the Media: Changing Cultural Boundaries*. Buckingham: Open University Press, pp. 33–49.

Dimitrova, D.V., Connolly-Ahern, C., Williams, A.P., Kaid, L.L. and Reid, A. (2003) 'Hyperlinking as Gatekeeping: Online Newspaper Coverage of the Execution of an American Terrorist', *Journalism Studies*, 4(3): 401–14.

Djerf-Pierre, M. (2000) 'Squaring the Circle: Public Service and Commercial News on Swedish Television 1956–99', *Journalism Studies*, 1(2): 239–60.

Doherty, M.A. (2000) *Nazi Wireless Propaganda: Lord Haw-Haw and British Public Opinion in the Second World War*. Edinburgh: Edinburgh University Press.

Doig, A. (1992) 'The Retreat of the Investigators', *British Journalism Review*, 3(4): 44–50.

Doig, A. (1997) 'Decline of Investigatory Journalism', in Bromley, M. and O'Malley, T. (eds) *A Journalism Reader*. London: Routledge, pp. 189–213.

Donohue, G.A. Tichenor, P.J. and Olien, C.N. (1995) 'A Guard Dog Perspective on the Role of the Media', *Journal of Communication*, 45(2): 115–32.

Doward, J. (2003*)* 'Sky Wins Battle for Rolling News Audience', *Observer*, 6 April.

Doyle, G. (2002) *Media Ownership*. London: Sage.

DTI and DCMS (2000) *A New Future for Communications*. London: Stationery Office.

DTLR (2001) 'Consultation Begins on Council Allowances', news release, 12 September.

Dyke, G. (2004) *Inside Story*. London: HarperCollins.

ECHR (2003) *European Court of Human Rights: Historical Background, Organisation and Procedure*, September http://www.echr.coe.int/Eng/EDocs/HistoricalBackground.htm.

Eckman, A. and Lindlof, T. (2003) 'Negotiating The Gray Lines: An Ethnographic Case Study of Organisational Conflict Between Advertorials and News', *Journalism Studies*, 4(1): 65–79.

Eemeren, F.H. van, Grootendoorst, R., Snoeck Henkemans, A.F., Blair, J.A., Johnson, R.H., Krabbe, E.C.W., Plantin, C.H., Walton, D.N., Willard, C.A., Woods, J. and Zarefsky, D. (1996) *Fundamentals of Argumentation Theory: A Handbook of Historical Backgrounds and Contemporary Developments*. Mahwah, NJ: Lawrence Erlbaum Associates.

Eggins, S. and Ledema, R. (1997) 'Difference Without Diversity: Semantic Orientation and Ideology in Competing Women's Magazines', in Wodak, R. (ed.) *Gender and Discourse*. London: Sage.

Bibliography

Eldridge, J. (2000) 'The Contribution of the Glasgow Media Group to the Study of Television and Print Journalism', *Journalism Studies*, 1(1): 113–27.

Eliasoph, N. (1988) 'Routines and the Making of Oppositional News', in Berkowitz, D. (ed.) (1997) *Social Meanings of News: A Text Reader*. Thousand Oaks, CA: Sage, pp. 230–53.

Emery, E. and Emery, M. (1978) *The Press and America: An Interpretative History of the Mass Media*. Upper Saddle River, NJ: Prentice Hall.

Engel, M. (1996a) *Tickle the Public: One Hundred Years of the Popular Press*. London: Victor Gollancz.

Engel, M. (1996b) 'Papering over the Cracks', *Guardian*, 3 October, pp. 2–3.

Entman, R. (1993) 'Framing: Toward Clarification of a Fractured Paradigm', *Journal of Communication*, 43 (4): 51–8.

Essed, P.J.M. (1991) *Understanding Everyday Racism: An Interdisciplinary Approach*. Newbury Park, CA: Sage.

Esser, F., Reinemann, C. and Fan, D. (2000) 'Spin Doctoring in British and German Election Campaigns', *European Journal of Communication*, 15(2): 209–41.

Ettema, J. et al. (1987) 'Professional Mass Communication', in Berkowitz, D. (ed.) (1997) *Social Meanings of News: A Text Reader*. Thousand Oaks, CA: Sage.

Ettema, J., Whitney, C. with Wackman, D. (1997) 'Professional Mass Communicators', in Berkowitz, D. (ed.) *Social Meanings of News*. London: Sage.

Evans, H. (1979) *Pictures on a Page: Photo-journalism, Graphics and Picture Editing*. London: Book Club Associates.

Evans, H. (1983) *Good Times, Bad Times*. London: Weidenfeld and Nicolson.

Evans, H. (1984) *Good Times, Bad Times*. London: Coronet.

Evans, H. (1994) *Good Times, Bad Times*, 3rd edn. London: Phoenix.

Evans, H. (1996) Speech to the Guild of Editors, reprinted in *Press Gazette*, 1 November, p. 10.

Evans, H. (2000) *Essential English for Journalists, Editors and Writers*. London: Pimlico.

Evans, H. (2002) 'Attacking the Devil', *British Journal Review*, 13(4): 6–14.

Eyre, R. (1999) 'Public Interest Broadcasting', MacTaggart Memorial Lecture, Edinburgh International Television and Film Festival, 27 August. Reproduced and edited in Franklin, B. (2001) *British Television Policy: A Reader*. London: Routledge, pp. 43–6.

Ezzard, J. (2003) '500 Years of History Ends for Fleet St', the *Guardian*, 24 September.

Fairclough, N. (1993) 'Critical Discourse Analysis and the Marketisation of Public Discourse: The Universities', *Discourse and Society*, 3(2): 193–217.

Fairclough, N. (1995a) *Critical Discourse Analysis*. London: Longman.

Fairclough, N. (1995b) *Media Discourse*. London: Edward Arnold.

Fairclough, N. (2000) *New Labour, New Language?* London: Routledge.

Fairclough, N. (2003) *Analysing Discourse: Textual Analysis for Social Research*. London: Routledge.

Fallows, J. (1997) *Breaking the News: How the Media Undermine American Democracy*. New York: Vintage Books.

Fawcett, L. (2001) *Political Communication and Devolution in Northern Ireland*, End of Award Report to ESRC Award L327253040.

Fedorcio, D., Heaton, P. and Madden, K. (1991) *Public Relations in Local Government*. Harlow: Longman.

Feintuck, M. (1999) *Media Regulation, Public Interest and the Law*. Edinburgh: Edinburgh University Press.

Feldman, T. (1997) *An Introduction to Digital Media*. London: Routledge.

Ferguson, R. (1998) *Representing 'Race': Ideology, Identity and the Media*. London: Edward Arnold.

Fielding, N. and Hollingsworth, M. (1999) *Defending the Realm, MI5 and the David Shayler Affair*. London: André Deutsch.

Fielding, N. and Tomlinson, R. (2001) *The Big Breach*. Edinburgh: Cutting Edge Press.

Fleetwood, B. (1999) 'The Broken Wall: How Newspapers Are Selling Their Credibility to Advertisers', *Washington Monthly*, September http://www.washingtonmonthly.com.

Foss, S.K. (1996) *Rhetorical Criticism: Exploration and Practice*. Prospect Heights, IL: Waveland.

Foucault, M. (1972) *The Archaeology of Knowledge and the Discourse on Language*. New York: Pantheon.

Foucault, M. (1973) *The Order of Things: An Archaeology of the Human Sciences*. New York: Vintage.

Foucault, M. (1979) *Discipline and Punish*. Harmondsworth: Penguin.

Fowler, R. (1991) *Language in the News: Discourse and Ideology in the Press*. London: Routledge and Kegan Paul.

Fowler, R., Hodge, R., Kress, G. and Trew, T. (1979) *Language and Control*. London: Routledge and Kegan Paul.

Fradgley, K.E. and Niebauer Jnr, W.E. (1995) 'London's "Quality" Newspapers: Newspaper Ownership and Reporting Patterns', *Journalism and Mass Communication Quarterly*, 72(4): 902–12.

Franklin, B. (1988) *Public Relations Activities in Local Government*. London: Charles Knight Ltd.

Franklin, B. (1989) 'Local parties, local media and the constituency campaign', in Crewe, I. and Harrop, M. (eds) *Political Communication: The General Election of 1987*. Cambridge: Cambridge University Press, pp. 211–21.

Franklin, B. (1994) *Packaging Politics*. London: Edward Arnold.

Franklin, B. (1996) 'An Obituary for the Press Gallery', *Parliamentary Brief*, 4(4): 13–15.

Franklin, B. (1997) *Newszak and News Media*. London: Arnold.

Franklin, B. (1998a) *Tough on Soundbites, Tough on the Causes of Soundbites: New Labour and News Management* London: Catalyst.

Franklin, B. (1998b) 'No News Isn't Good News: The Development of Local Free Newspapers', in Franklin, B. and Murphy, D. (eds) *Making the Local News: Local Journalism in Context*. London: Routledge.

Franklin, B. (2001) *British Television Policy: A Reader*. London: Routledge.

Franklin, B. (2003) 'A Good Day to Bury Bad News? Journalists, Sources and the Packaging of Politics', in Cottle, S. (ed.) *News, Public Relations and Power*. London: Sage.

Franklin, B. (2004a) *Packaging Politics: Political Communications in Britain's Media Democracy*. London: Arnold.

Franklin, B. (2004b) 'A Damascene Conversion? New Labour and Media Relations', in Ludlam, S. and Smith, M. (eds) *Governing as New Labour: Policy and Politics under Blair*. London: Palgrave, pp. 88–106.

Franklin, B. (2005) 'McJournalism: The McDonaldization Thesis and the UK Local Press', in Allan, S. (ed.) *Contemporary Journalism: Critical Essays*. Milton Keynes: Open University Press.

Franklin, B. and Richardson, J. (2002) 'A Journalist's Duty? Continuity and Change in Local Newspapers' Coverage of Recent UK General Elections', *Journalism Studies*, 3(1): 35–52.

Franklin, B. and Murphy, D. (1998a) 'Changing Times: Local Newspapers, Technology and Markets', in Franklin, B. and Murphy, D. (eds) *Making the Local News: Local Journalism in Context*. London: Routledge, pp. 7–23.

Franklin, B. and Murphy, D. (1998b) 'The Press in the Age of the Conglomerates', in Franklin, B. and Murphy, D. (eds) *Making the Local News*. London: Routledge.

Franklin, B. and VanSlyke Turk, J. (1988) 'Information Subsidies: Agenda Setting Traditions', *Public Relations Review*, Spring: 29–41.

Franks, Lord (Chairman) (1972) *Report and Evidence of the Committee on Section 2 of the Official Secrets Act 1911*. Cmnd 5104. London: HMSO.

Freedman, D. (2003) *Television and the Labour Party, 1951–2001*. London: Cass.

Freedman, L. (2004) 'Misreporting War Has a Long History', in Miller, D. (ed.) *Tell Me Lies: Propaganda and Media Distortion in the Attack on Iraq*. London: Pluto Press, pp. 63–9.

Frost, C. (2000) *Media Ethics and Self-regulation*. London: Longman.

Frost, C. (2004) 'The Press Complaints Commission: A Study of Ten Years of Adjudications on Press Complaints', *Journalism Studies*, 5(1): 101–14.

The Future Funding of the BBC (1999) Report of the Independent Review Panel chaired by Gavyn Davies. London: Department of Culture, Media and Sport.

Gaber, I. (2000) 'Lies, Damn Lies and Political Spin', *British Journalism Review*, 11(1): 60–70.

Gaber, I. (2001) 'Government by Spin: An Analysis of the Process', *Media, Culture and Society*, 22(4): 507–18.

Gage, L. (1999) *A Guide to Commercial Radio Journalism*. Oxford: Focal Press.

Gall, G. (1998) 'Industrial Relations and the Local Press: The Continuing Employers' Offensive', in Franklin, B. and Murphy, D. (eds) *Making the Local News: Local Journalism in Context*. London: Routledge.

Galtung, J. and Ruge, M. (1965a) 'The Structure of Foreign News: The Presentation of the Congo, Cuba and Cyprus Crises in Four Norwegian Newspapers', *Journal of International Peace Research*, 1: 64–91.

Galtung, J. and Ruge, M. (1965b) 'Structuring and Selecting News', in Cohen, S. and Young, J. (eds) (1973) *The Manufacture of News: Social Problems, Deviance and the News Media*. London: Constable, pp. 62–72.

Gamson, W.A. and Modigliani, A. (1987) 'The Changing Culture of Affirmative Action', in Braungart, R.G. and Braubgart, M. (eds) *Research in Political Sociology*. Greenwich, CT: JAI Press, vol. 3, pp. 137–77.

Gandy, O. (1982) *Beyond Agenda Setting: Information Subsidies and Public Policy*. New York: Ablex.

Gandy, O. Jnr (2000) 'Race, Ethnicity and the Segmentation of Media Markets', in Curran, J. and Gurevitch, M. (eds) *Mass Media and Society*. London: Arnold, pp. 44–69.

Gandy, O. Jnr. (2001) 'Reproducing Racism', *Rhodes Journalism Review*, August: 10–11.

Gans, H.J. (1980) *Deciding What's News*. London: Constable.

Gardner, C. (1986) 'How They Buy the Bulletins', the *Guardian*, 17 September.

Garner, K. (2003) 'On Defining the Field', *The Radio Journal*, 1(1): 7.

Gauntlett, D. (1996) *Video Critical: Children, the Environment and Media Power*. London: John Libbey.

Gauntlett, D. (1997) 'Ten Things Wrong With the "Effects" Model', in Dickinson, R., Harindranath, R. and Linne, O. (eds), *Approaches to Audiences*. London: Arnold.

Gee, J.P. (1990) *Social Linguistics and Literacies: Ideology in Discourses*. London: Falmer Press.

Gee, J.P. (1999) *An Introduction to Discourse Analysis: Theory and Method*. London: Routledge.

George, M. (2003) 'Bell Attacks Iraq Rolling News Coverage', BBC News Online, 23 May, at www.bbc.co.uk.

Gerbner, G. (1958) 'On Content Analysis and Critical Research in Mass

341

Communication', in Dexter, L.A. and Manning, D. (eds) (1964) *People, Society and Mass Communications*. New York: Free Press, pp. 476–500.

Gerbner, G. (1967) 'Mass Media and Human Communication Theory', in McQuail, D. (ed.) (1972) *Sociology of Mass Communications*. Harmondsworth: Penguin, pp. 35–58.

Gibbons, T. (1998) *Regulating the Media*, 2nd edn. London: Sweet and Maxwell.

Gieber, W. (1964) 'News is What Newspapermen Make It', in Dexter, L.A. and Manning, D. (eds), *People, Society and Mass Communications*. New York: Free Press, pp. 173–82.

Gillespie, M. (1995) *Television, Ethnicity and Cultural Change*. London: Routledge.

Gillespie, M. (2000) 'Transnational Communications and Diaspora Communities', in Cottle, S. (ed.) *Ethnic Minorities and the Media*. Buckingham: Open University Press, pp. 164–78.

Ginneken, J. van (1998) *Understanding Global News: A Critical Introduction*. London: Sage.

Gitlin, T. (1979) 'Prime-Time Ideology: The Hegemonic Process in Television Entertainment', *Social Problems*, 26: 251–66.

Glasgow Media Group (1976) *Bad News*. London: Routledge and Kegan Paul.

Glasgow Media Group (1980) *More Bad News*. London: Routledge and Kegan Paul.

Glasgow Media Group (1982) *Really Bad News*. London: Writer and Readers.

Glasgow Media Group (1985) *War and Peace News*. Milton Keynes: Open University Press.

Glasser, T. (2000) 'The Politics of Public Journalism', *Journalism Studies*, 1(4): 683–5.

Glencross, D. (1994) 'Superhighways and Supermarkets', a speech to the *Royal Television Society*, 8 March.

Glover, S. (1993) *Paper Dreams*. London: Jonathan Cape.

Goffman, E. (1981) *Forms of Talk*. Philadelphia, PA: University of Pennsylvania Press.

Goldie, G. (1977) *Facing the Nation: Television and Politics, 1936–1976*. London: Bodley Head.

Golding, P. (1989) 'Limits to Leviathan: The Local Press and the Poll Tax', paper presented to the Political Studies Association Annual Conference, University of Warwick, 6 April.

Golding, P. and Murdock, G. (1973) 'For a Political Economy of Mass Media', in Miliband, R. and Saville, J. (eds) *Socialist Register*. London: Merlin, pp. 205–34.

Golding, P. and Murdock, G. (2000) 'Culture, Communications and Political Economy', in Curran, J. and Gurevitch, M. (eds) *Mass Media and Society*. London: Arnold.

Gombrich, E.H. (1978) *Meditation on a Hobby Horse*. Oxford: Phaidon Press.

Goode, E. and Ben-Yahuda, N. (1994) *Moral Panics: The Social Construction of Deviance*. Oxford: Blackwell.

Goodwin, P. (1998) *Television under the Tories: Broadcasting Policy 1979–97*. London: BFI.

Gramsci, A. (1971) *Extracts from the Prison Notebooks*. London: Lawrence and Wishart.

Greatbatch, D. (1998) 'Conversation Analysis: Neutralism in British News Interviews', in Bell, A. and Garrett, P. (eds) *Approaches to Media Discourse*. Oxford: Blackwell, pp. 163–85.

Greenslade, R. (2003) 'The Night I Gave Murdoch a Bollocking', *Media Guardian*, 29 September, p. 6.

Greenslade, R. (2004a) 'So Just Who's Who?', *Media Guardian*, 23 February, pp. 6–7.

Greenslade, R. (2004b) 'Metros on the March', *MediaGuardian*, 19 January, p. 7.

Greenslade, R. (2004c) 'Little Echo', *MediaGuardian*, 19 January, p. 6.

Gunter, B. (2000) *Media Research Methods*. London: Sage.

Habermas, J. (1989) *The Structural Transformation of the Public Sphere.* Cambridge: Polity Press.

Hagerty, B. (2002) 'Editorial', *British Journal Review*, 13(4): 6.

Hall, J. (2001) *Online Journalism: A Critical Primer.* London: Pluto Press.

Hall, S. (1973) 'The Determination of News Photographs', in Cohen, S. and Young, J. (eds) *The Manufacture of News: Social Problems, Deviance and the News Media.* London: Constable, pp. 176–90.

Hall, S. (1980) 'Encoding/Decoding', in Marris, P. and Thornham, S. (eds) *Media Studies: A Reader.* Edinburgh: Edinburgh University Press, pp. 51–61.

Hall, S. (1982) 'The Rediscovery of Ideology: Return of the Repressed in Media Studies', in Gurevitch, M., Bennet, T., Curran, J. and Woollacott, J. (eds), *Culture, Society and the Media.* London: Methuen, pp. 56–90.

Hall, S. (1994) 'Cultural Identity and Diaspora', in Williams, P. and Chrisman, L. (eds), *Colonial Discourse and Post-Colonial Theory: A Reader.* New York: Columbia University Press, pp. 392–403.

Hall, S. (2001) 'Conjoined Twin Flies Home After Deal', the *Guardian*, 18 June. http://media.guardian.co.uk/presspublishing/story/0,7495,508674,00.html.

Hall, S., Critcher, S., Jefferson, T., Clarke, J. and Roberts, B. (1978) *Policing the Crisis.* London: Macmillan.

Haller, B. and Ralph, S. (2001) 'Not Worth Keeping Alive? News Framing of Physician-Assisted Suicide in the United States and Great Britain', *Journalism Studies*, 2(3): 407–21.

Halliday, M.A.K. (1994) *An Introduction to Functional Grammar*, 2nd edn. London: Arnold.

Halliday, M.A.K. and Hasan, R. (1989) *Language, Context and Text: Aspects of Language in a Social Semiotic Perspective.* Oxford: Oxford University Press.

Hammond, J. (1987) 'Ashamed of the Press', *UK Press Gazette*, 23 March, reproduced in Boyd, A. (2001) *Broadcast Journalism, Techniques of Radio and Television News.* Oxford: Focal Press.

Hanna, M. (2000) 'British Investigative Journalism: Protecting the Continuity of Talent through Changing Times', paper presented at the Professional Education section of the International Association for Media and Communication Research, 22nd General Assembly and annual conference, Singapore.

Hanna, M. and Epworth, J. (1998) 'Media Payments to Witnesses: The Press Faces the First Breach of its Post-Calcutt Defences', paper presented to the annual conference of the Association for Journalism Education, London, 15 May.

Hansen, A., Cottle, S., Negrine, R. and Newbold, C. (1998) *Mass Communication Research Methods.*

Hansen, H.V. and Pinto, R.C. (1995) *Fallacies: Classical and Contemporary Readings.* University Park, PA: Penn State University Press.

Harcup, T. (1994) *A Northern Star: Leeds' Other Paper and the Alternative Press, 1974–1994.* Upton: The Campaign for Press and Broadcasting Freedom (North) MNH.

Harcup, T. (1998) 'There Is No Alternative: The Demise of the Alternative Local Newspaper', in Franklin, B. and Murphy, D. (eds) *Making the Local News: Local Journalism in Context.* London: Routledge.

Harcup, T. (2003) 'The Unspoken – Said: The Journalism of Alternative Media', *Journalism: Theory, Practice and Criticism* 4 (3): 356–76.

Harcup, T. (2004) *Journalism: Principles and Practice.* London: Sage.

Harcup, T. and O'Neill, D. (2001) 'What Is News? Galtung and Ruge Revisited', *Journalism Studies*, 2(2): 261–80.

Harding, L., Leigh, D. and Pallister, D. (1997) *The Liar: The Fall of Jonathan Aitken*. London: Penguin.

Hardt, H. (1999) 'Reinventing the Press for the Age of Commercial Appeals: Writings on and about Public Journalism', in Glasser, T. (ed.) *The Idea of Public Journalism*. New York: Guilford Press, pp. 197–209.

Hargreaves, I. (1993) *Sharper Visions: The BBC and the Communications Revolution*. London: Demos.

Hargreaves, I. (2003) *Journalism: Truth or Dare?* Oxford: Oxford University Press.

Hargreaves, I. and Thomas, J. (2002) *New News, Old News*. London: ITC/BSC.

Harmon, M.D. and White, C. (2001) 'How Television News Programmes Use Video News Releases', *Public Relations Review*, 27(2): 213–22.

Harris, P. (1970) *When Pirates Ruled the Waves*. London: Impulse Books.

Harris, R. (1990) *Good and Faithful Servant*. London: Faber and Faber.

Harris, S. (1991) 'Evasive Action: How Politicians Respond to Questions in Political Interviews', in Scannell, P. (ed.) *Broadcast Talk*. London: Sage, pp. 76–99.

Harrison, J. (2000) *Terrestrial TV News in Britain: The Culture of Production*. Manchester, Manchester University Press.

Harrison, M. (1985) *Whose Bias?* Berkshire: Policy Journals.

Harrop, M. (eds) (1989) *Political Communications: The General Election Campaign of 1987*. Cambridge: Cambridge University Press.

Hart, A. (1991) *Understanding the Media: A Practical Guide*. London: Routledge.

Hartley, J. (1982) *Understanding News*. London: Methuen.

Hartmann, P. and Husband, C. (1974) *Racism and the Mass Media: A Study of the Role of the Mass Media in the Formation of White Beliefs and Attitudes in Britain*. London: Davis-Poynter.

Hartmann, P. and Husband, C. (1973) 'The Mass Media and Racial Conflict', in Cohen, S. and Young, J. (eds) *The Manufacture of News: Social Problems, Deviance and the News Media*. London: Constable, pp. 270–83.

Hastings, M. (2002) *Editor* London: Macmillan.

Hattersley, R. (2001) 'The Unholy Alliance: The Relationship between Members of Parliament and the Press', James Cameron Lecture 1996, reprinted in Stephenson, H. (ed.) *Media Voices: The James Cameron Memorial Lectures*, London: Politicos, pp. 227–45. http://www.Number-10.gov.UK.

Hayes, A. (1996) *Family in Print*. Dursley: Bailey Newspaper Group Ltd.

Held, D. and McGrew, A. (2000) *The Global Transformations Reader: An Introduction to the Globalization Debate*. Malden, MA: Polity Press.

Henderson, N. (2003) 'The Henderson Interview', *Radio Magazine*, 25 October.

Henningham, J. and Delano, A. (1998), 'British Journalists', in Weaver, D.H. (ed.) *The Global Journalist: News People Around the World*. Cresskill, NJ: Hampton Press.

Herbert, J. (2001) *Practising Global Journalism*. Oxford: Focal Press.

Heren, L. (1988) *Memories of Times Past*. London: Hamish Hamilton.

Heritage, J. (1985) 'Analysing News Interviews: Aspects of the Production of Talk for Overhearing Audiences', in van Dijk, T.A. (ed.) *Handbook of Discourse Analysis*. London: Academic Press, vol. 3, pp. 95–119.

Heritage, J. (2001) 'Goffman, Garfinkel and Conversation Analysis', in Wetherell, M., Taylor, S. and Yates, S.J. (eds) *Discourse Theory and Practice*. London: Sage.

Herman, E.S. (1995) *Beyond Hypocrisy: Decoding the News in an Age of Propaganda*. Boston: South End Press.

Herman, E.S. (2000) 'The Propaganda Model: A Retrospective', *Journalism Studies*, 1(1): 101–12.

Herman, E. and Chomsky, N. ([1988] 1994) *Manufacturing Consent: The Political*

Economy of the Mass Media. New York: Pantheon.

Herman, E.S. and Chomsky, N. (1994) *Manufacturing Consent: The Political Economy of the Mass Media*. London: Vintage.

Hetherington, A. (1985) *News, Newspapers and Television*. London: Macmillan.

Hicks, W., Adams, S. and Gilbert, H. (1999) *Writing for Journalists*. London: Routledge.

Hicks, W. and Holmes, T. (2002) *Subediting for Journalists*. London: Routledge.

Hilmes, M. (2003) 'British Quality, American Chaos', *The Radio Journal*, 1(1): 13.

Hirst, M. (2003) 'What is Gonzo? The Etymology of an Urban Legend', unpublished paper, School of Journalism, University of Queensland.

Hodgson, F.W. (1996) *Modern Newspaper Practice: A Primer on the Press*. Oxford: Focal Press.

Hodgson, F.W. (1998) *New Subediting*. Oxford: Focal Press.

Hodgson, J. (2001a) 'A Gentlemen's Agreement: Is the D-Notice Committee an Archaic Leftover or Vital to National Security?', *Guardian*, 1 October. http://media.guardian.co.uk/mediaguardian/story/0,7558,560812,00.html.

Hodgson, J. (2001b) 'Francis "Thought False Alibi Was for Archer's Wife"', *Guardian*, 18 June. http://media.guardian.co.uk/presspublishing/story/0,7495,508967,00.html.

Hoggart, R. (1993) *An Imagined Life*. Oxford: Oxford University Press.

Hoggart, S. (2002) *Playing to the Gallery: Parliamentary Sketches from Blair Year Zero*. London: Atlantic Books.

Holtz-Bacha, C. and Frolich, R. (eds) (2003) *Journalism Education in Europe and North America: An International Comparison*. Cresskill, NJ: Hampton Press.

Home Office (1978) *Reform of Section 2 of the Official Secrets Act 1911*. London: HMSO.

Hood, S. (1980) *On Television*. London: Pluto Press.

Hooper, D. (1988) *Official Secrets: The Use and Abuse of the Act*. Sevenoaks: Coronet.

Horgan, J. (2001) '"Government Sources Said Last Night …": The Development of the Parliamentary Press Lobby in Modern Ireland', in Morgan, H. (ed.) *Information, Media and Power through the Ages*. Dublin: University College Dublin Press, pp. 259–71.

Horrie, C. and Nathan, A. (1999) *Live TV: Telly Brats and Topless Darts*. London: Simon and Schuster.

Howitt, D. (1982) *Mass Media and Social Problems*. Oxford: Pergamon Press.

Hoyer, S. (2003) 'Newspapers Without Journalists', *Journalism Studies*, 4(4): 451.

Hume, M. (1997) *Whose War Is It Anyway? The Dangers of the Journalism of Attachment*. London: LM.

Humphreys, P.J. (1996) *Mass Media and Media Policy in Western Europe*. Manchester: Manchester University Press.

Humphrys, J. (1999) *Devil's Advocate*. London: Hutchinson.

Humphrys, J. (2004) 'First Do No Harm', in Franklin, B. (ed.) (2005) *Television Policy: The MacTaggart Lectures*. Edinburgh: Edinburgh University Press.

Hutton, Lord (2004) *Report of the Inquiry into the Circumstances Surrounding the Death of Dr David Kelly*, CMG. London: The Stationery Office. HC247 at http://www.the-hutton-inquiry.org.uk.

Ingham, B. (1991) *Kill the Messenger*. London: HarperCollins.

International Federation of Journalists: www.ifj.org/default.asp?Issue=FREELANCE& Language=EN.

ITC (1998) 'ITC Imposes £2m Financial Penalty for *The Connection*', press release 118/98, 18 December.

ITC (1999) 'ITC Imposes Financial Penalty on Channel Four for *Too Much Too Young: Chickens*', press release 10/99, 26 February.

Iyengar, S. (1991) *Is Anyone Responsible? How Television Frames Political Issues*. Chicago: University of Chicago Press.

345

Jackson, I. (1971) *The Provincial Press and the Community*. Manchester: Manchester University Press.

Jäger, S. (2001) 'Discourse and Knowledge: Theoretical and Methodological Aspects of a Critical Discourse and Dispositive Analysis', in Wodak, R. and Meyer, M. (eds) *Methods of Critical Discourse Analysis*. London: Sage, pp. 32–62.

Jasinski, J. (2001) *Sourcebook on Rhetoric: Key Concepts in Contemporary Rhetorical Studies*. Thousand Oaks, CA: Sage.

Jempson, M. and Cookson, R. (eds) (2004) *Satisfaction Guaranteed? Press Complaints Systems Under Scrutiny*. Bristol: Mediawise.

Johansen, P., Weaver, D.H. and Dornan, C. (2001) 'Journalism Education in the United States and Canada: Not Merely Clones', *Journalism Studies*, 2(4): 469–83.

Jones, N. (1995) *Soundbites and Spin Doctors: How Politicians Manipulate the Media and Vice Versa*. London: Cassell.

Jones, N. (2002) *The Control Freaks: How New Labour Gets its Own Way*. London: Politicos.

Jones, N. (2003) 'A Question of Trust', *The Journalists' Handbook*, 75: pp. 15–28.

Journalist News (2003) 'Pieces in the Jigsaw War', *Journalist*, October/November: 10–11.

Jucker, A.H. (1992) *Social Stylistics: Syntactic Variation in British Newspapers*. Berlin: Mouton de Gruyter.

Katz, E. (1959) 'Mass Communication Research and the Study of Popular Culture', *Studies in Public Communication*, 2: 1–27.

Keeble, R. (2001) *Ethics for Journalists*. London: Routledge.

Kellner, P. (1983) 'The Lobby, Official Secrets and Good Government', *Parliamentary Affairs* 36(3): 275–82.

Kelso, P. (2001) 'We Have Known about This for 15 Years', *Guardian*, 23 July. http://media.guardian.co.uk/mediaguardian/story/0,7558,525816,00.html.

Kennedy, P. (2002), 'People's Champ Leaves NoW in Censorship Row', *Press Gazette online*, 24 January.

Kent, R. (ed.) (1994) *Measuring Media Audiences*. London: Routledge.

Kilborn, R. and Izod, J. (1997) *An Introduction to Television Documentary: Confronting Reality*. Manchester, Manchester University Press.

Kitzinger, J. and Barbour, R. (eds) (1999) *Developing Focus Group Research: Politics, Theory and Practice*. London: Sage.

Klaehn, J. (2003) 'Behind the Invisible Curtain of Scholarly Criticism: Revisiting the Propaganda Model', *Journalism Studies*, 4(3): 359–69.

Klapper, J.T. (1949) *The Effects of Mass Media*. New York: Columbia University Press.

Klapper, J.T. (1960) *The Effects of Mass Communication*. New York: Free Press.

Knightley, P. (1997) *A Hack's Progress*. London: Jonathan Cape.

Kraus, S. and Davis, D. (1976) *The Effects of Mass Behaviour on Political Behaviour*. Philadelphia, PA: Pennsylvania State University Press.

Kress, G. (1983) 'Linguistic and Ideological Transformations in News Reporting', in Davis, H. and Walton, P. (eds) *Language, Image and Media*. Oxford: Basil Blackwell, pp. 120–38.

Kress, G. and Leeuwen, T. van (1996) *Reading Images: The Grammar of Visual Design*. London: Routledge.

Krishnamurthy, R. (1996) 'Ethnic, Racial and Tribal: The Language of Racism?', in Caldas-Coulthard, C.R. and Coulthard, M. (eds) *Texts and Practices: Readings in Critical Discourse Analysis*. London: Routledge, pp. 129–49.

Lacey, N. (1998) *Image and Representation: Key Concepts in Media Studies*. Houndsmills: Macmillan.

Bibliography

Laclau, E. and Mouffe, C. (1985) *Hegemony and Socialist Strategy: Towards a Radical Democratic Politics*. London: Verso.

Langer, J. (1998) *Tabloid Television: Popular Journalism and the 'Other News'*. London Routledge.

Lawson, M. (1990) 'Raising an Eyebrow', *The Independent Magazine*, 24 February, pp. 28–36.

Lazarsfeld, P., Berelson, B. and Gaudet, H. (1944) *The People's Choice*. New York: Duell, Sloan and Pearce.

Leeuwen, T. van (1996) 'The Representation of Social Actors', in Caldas-Coulthard, C.R. and Coulthard, M. (eds) *Texts and Practices: Readings in Critical Discourse Analysis*. London: Routledge, pp. 32–70.

Leigh, D. and Vulliamy, E. (1997) *Sleaze: The Corruption of Parliament*. London: Fourth Estate.

Leitch, V.B. (1983) *Deconstructive Criticism: An Advanced Introduction*. New York: Columbia University Press.

L'Etaing, J. (2004) *Public Relations in Britain: A History of Professional Practice in the Twentieth Century*. Mahwah, NJ: Lawrence Erlbaum.

Letts, Q. (2003) 'Still Thriving, the Daily Sketch', *British Journalism Review*, 1(4): 39–45.

Levinson, P. (1999) *Digital McLuhan*. London: Routledge.

Levy, H.P. (1967) *The Press Council: History, Procedure and Cases*. London: Macmillan.

Lewis, J. (1991) *The Ideological Octopus: An Exploration of Television and Its Audience*. London: Routledge.

Liberty and Article 19 (2000) *Secrets, Spies and Whistleblowers*. London: Liberty and Article 19.

Lindley, R. (2002) *Panorama: Fifty Years of Pride and Paranoia*. London: Politicos.

Linklater, M. (1993) 'An Insight into Insight', *British Journalism Review*, 4(2): 17–20.

Lister, S. (2004) 'Times Is First for a Perfect Picture Service', *The Times*, 28 June, p. 9.

Livingstone, S. and Lunt, P. (1994) *Talk on Television*. London: Routledge.

Lloyd, C. (1999) *Attacking the Devil: 130 Years of The Northern Echo*. Darlington: The Northern Echo.

Lloyd, J. (2004) *What the Media Are Doing to Our Politics*. London: Constable.

Lord Chancellor's Department (1993) *Infringement of Privacy*, consultation paper. London: Lord Chancellor's Department.

Lule, J. (2001) *Daily News, Eternal Stories: The Mythical Role of Journalism*. New York: Guilford Press.

Lynn, N. and Lea, S. (2003) '"A Phantom Menace and the New Apartheid": The Social Construction of Asylum Seekers in the United Kingdom', *Discourse and Society*, 14(4): 425–52.

MacArthur, B. (2004) 'Ego Trips Full of Passion that Set the Tone for Newspapers', *The Times*, 27 February, p. 39.

MacDonald, M. (2003) *Exploring Media Discourse*. London: Arnold.

MacGregor, B. (1997) *Live, Direct and Biased: Making Television News in the Satellite Age*. London: Arnold.

MacGregor, Lord (1977) *Royal Commission on the Press: Final Report*. Cmnd 6810. London: HMSO.

Machin, D. and Thornborrow, J. (2003) 'Branding and Discourse: The Case of Cosmopolitan', *Discourse and Society*, 14(4): 453–71.

Malik, K. (1996) *The Meaning of Race: Race, History and Culture in Western Society*. Basingstoke: Macmillan.

Manning, P. (1998) *Spinning for Labour: Trades Unions and the New Media Environment*. Aldershot: Ashgate.

Manning, P. (2001) *News and News Sources: A Critical Introduction*. London: Sage.

Marks, N. (2000) 'Uncovering the Secrets of "Real" Journalism', *Press Gazette*, 14 January, p. 15.

Marr, A. (2001) 'Is It Possible that No News is Good News?', *The Independent*, 16 March.

Martin, W. (1986) *Recent Theories of Narrative*. Ithaca, NY: Cornell University Press.

Marx, K. ([1848] 1998) 'Manifesto of the Communist Party' (trans. Carver, T.), in Cowling, M. (ed.), *The Communist Manifesto: New Interpretations*. Edinburgh: Edinburgh University Press, pp. 14–37.

Marx, K. and Engels, F. (1974) *The German Ideology* (ed. Arthur, C.J.). London: Lawrence and Wishart.

Mayes, I. (2004) 'Trust Me – I'm an Ombudsman', *British Journalism Review*, 15(2): 65–70.

McCombs, M. and Shaw, D. (1972) 'The Agenda-setting Function of the Mass Media', *Public Opinion Quarterly*, 36: 176–87.

McCombs, M., Shaw, D. and Weaver, D. (1997) *Communication and Democracy: Exploring the Intellectual Frontiers of Agenda-setting Theory*. Mahwah, NJ: Lawrence Erlbaum Associates.

McCormack, S. (2004) 'The Trouble with Two-Ways', *UK Press Gazette*, 6 February.

McIntosh, N. (2003) 'Start here: Setting up a Website', Guardian Unlimited, 25 September, available at: http://www.guardian.co.uk/online/story/0,,1048698,00.html.

McKeen, W. (1991) 'Hunter S. Thompson', in *Twayne's United States Authors* (ed. F. Day). Boston: Twayne.

McKie, D. (1999) *Media Coverage of Parliament*. London: Hansard.

McLaughlin, G. (2002) *The War Correspondent*. London: Pluto.

McManus, J. (1992) 'What Kind of Commodity is News?', *Communications Research*, 19(6): 780–812.

McManus, J. (1994a) *Market Driven Journalism*. London: Sage.

McManus, J. (1994b) 'The First Stage of News Production: Learning What's Happening', in Berkowitz, D. (ed.) (1997), *Social Meanings of News*. London: Sage.

McNair, B. (1996) 'Performance in Politics and the Politics of Performance: Public Relations, the Public Sphere and Democracy', in L'Etaing, J. and Piecka, M. (eds) *Critical Perspectives in Public Relations*. London: International Thompson.

McNair, B. (1998) *The Sociology of Journalism*. London: Arnold.

McNair, B. (1999) *News and Journalism in the UK*, 3rd edn. London: Routledge.

McNair, B. (2000a) *Journalism and Democracy: An Evaluation of the Political Public Sphere*. London: Routledge.

McNair, B. (2000b) 'Journalism and Democracy: A Millennial Audit', *Journalism Studies*, 1(2): 197–211.

McNair, B. (2002) *The Sociology of Journalism*. London: Edward Arnold.

McNair, B. (2001) *News and Journalism in the UK*. New York: Routledge.

McNair, B. (2003) *News and Journalism in the UK*. London: Routledge.

McNair, B., Hibberd, M. and Schlesinger, P. (2002) 'Public Access Broadcasting and Democratic Participation in the Age of Mediated Democracy', *Journalism Studies*, 3(3): 407–22.

McQuail, D. ([1987]2000) *Mass Communication Theory*. London: Sage.

McQuail, D. (1992) *Media Performance, Mass Communication and the Public Interest*. London: Sage.

Media Guardian (2004) 'And Then There Was Murdoch', *Guardian*, 5 January, p. 3.

Meek, C. (2003) 'Internet Is a Boon for Freelancers' (14 October) *dot Journalism*:

www.journalism.co.uk/news/story60.html.

Meek, C. (2004) 'Photo Opportunities Wasted', 1 July, *dotJournalism*.

Melly, G. (2004) 'The Jazzman Cometh', *British Journalism Review*, 15(2): 31–5.

Melvern, L. (1986) *The End of the Street*. London: Methuen.

Melville, R. (1998) 'In Search of the Holy Grail: A Single National Qualification in Journalism across the Whole Industry', paper delivered to the 3rd annual conference of the Association of Media, Cultural and Communication Studies, Sheffield, December.

Merritt, D. (1998) *Public Journalism and Public Life: Why Telling the News is Not Enough*, Mahwah, NJ: Lawrence Erlbaum Associates.

Merton, R.K. (1987) 'The Focused Interview and Focus Groups: Continuities and Discontinuities', *Public Opinion Quarterly*, 51: 550–66.

Meyer, P. (1987) *Ethical Journalism*. Lanham, MD: University Press of America.

Michie, D. (1998) *The Invisible Persuaders*. London: Bantam Press.

Middleton, D. (1993) *Pocketbook of Newspaper Terms*. Edinburgh: Merchiston Publishing.

Miller, D. (1998) 'Public Relations and Journalism: Promotional Strategies and Media Power', in Briggs, A. and Cobley, P. (eds) *The Media: An Introduction*. London: Longman.

Miller, D. (2004) *Tell Me Lies: Propaganda and Media Distortion in the Attack on Iraq*. London: Pluto.

Miller, D. and Dinan, W. (2000) 'The Rise of the PR Industry in Britain, 1979–98', *European Journal of Communication*, 15(1): 5–35.

Miller, L., Stauber, J. and Rampton, S. (2004) 'War is Sell', in Miller, D. (ed.) *Tell Me Lies: Propaganda and Media Distortion in the Attack on Iraq*. London: Pluto Press, pp. 41–51.

Mohammadi, A. (ed.) (1997) *International Communication and Globalisation*. London: Sage.

Molotch, H. and Lester, M. (1974) 'News as Purposive Behaviour: On the Strategic Use of Routine Events, Accidents and Scandals', in Berkowitz, D. (ed.) *Social Meanings of News: A Reader*. Thousand Oaks, CA: Sage, pp. 193–209.

Montgomery, M. (1999) 'Speaking Sincerely: Public Reactions to the Death of Diana', *Language and Literature*, 8(1): 5–33.

Montgomery, M., Durant, A., Fabb, N., Furniss, T. and Mills, S. (2000) *Ways of Reading: Advanced Reading Skills for Students of English Literature*. London: Routledge.

MORI, http://www.mori.com/ (accessed 21 April 2004).

Morley, D. (1980) *The Nationwide Audience: Structure and Decoding*. London: BFI.

Morley, D. and Whitaker, B. (1986) *The Press, Radio and Television: An Introduction to the Media*. London: Commedia.

Morrison, A. and Love, A. (1996) 'A Discourse of Disillusionment: Letters to the Editor in Two Zimbabwean Magazines after Independence', *Discourse and Society*, 7(1): 39–75.

Mosley, D. (1980) *The Nationwide Audience*. London: BFI.

Muntigl, P., Weiss, G. and Wodak, R. (eds) (2000) *European Union Discourses on Unemployment: An Interdisciplinary Approach to Employment Policy-Making and Institutional Change*. Amsterdam: John Benjamins.

Murdock, G. (2000) 'Reconstructing the Ruined Tower: Contemporary Communications and Questions of Class', in Curran, J. and Gurevitch, M. (eds) *Mass Media and Society*. London: Arnold, pp. 7–26.

National Heritage Committee (1993) Fourth Report, *Privacy and Media Intrusion*, Parliamentary Paper 294 of Session 1992–3. London: HMSO.

349

Journalism Studies

National Union of Journalists: www.nuj.org.uk/front/inner.php?docid=SS.

National Readership Survey, http://www.newspapersoc.org.uk/home.html (accessed 21 April 2004).

Negrine, R.M. (1994) *Politics and the Mass Media in Britain*, 2nd edn. London: Routledge.

Negrine, R. (1998) *Parliament and the Media: A Study of Britain, Germany and France*. London: Pinter.

Neil, A. (1997) *Full Disclosure*. London: Pan Books.

Neil, A. (2004) *The Neil Report*. Available at: http://www.bbc.co.uk/info/policies/neil report.

Nerone, J. and Barnhurst, K.G. (2003) 'US Newspaper Types, the Newsroom and the Division of Labor, 1750–2000', *Journalism Studies*, 4(4): 435.

Nicol, A., Millar, G, and Sharland, A. (2001), *Media Law and Human Rights*. London: Blackstone Press.

Nielsen, J. (1995) *Multimedia and Hypertext: The Internet and Beyond*. London: Academic Press.

Nielsen, J. (2000) *Designing Web Usability*. Indianapolis: New Riders Publishing.

Northmore, D. (1996) *Lifting the Lid: A Guide to Investigative Research*. London: Cassell.

NUJ (2003a) 'The Worst-Treated Journalists in Europe', online article in *The Journalist*, 11 September 11 http://www.nuj.org.uk/inner.php?docid=581.

NUJ (2003b) 'Journalists launch biggest pay campaign for a decade', online article in *The Journalist* October 23 http://www.nuj.org.uk/inner.php?docid=591.

O'Malley, T. (1994) *Closedown: The BBC and Government Broadcasting Policy 1979–92*. London: Pluto Press.

O'Malley, T. (1997) 'Labour and the 1947–49 Royal Commission on the Press', in Bromley, M. and O'Malley, T. (eds) *A Journalism Reader*. London: Routledge.

O'Malley, T. (1998) 'Demanding Accountability: The Press, the Royal Commissions and the Pressure for Reform, 1945–77' in M. Bromley and H. Stephenson (eds) *Sex, Lies and Democracy: The Press and the Public*. New York: Longman.

O'Malley, T. and Soley, C. (2000) *Regulating the Press*. London: Pluto Press.

O'Sullivan, T., Dutton, B. and Rayner, P. (1994) *Studying the Media*. London: Arnold.

Oborne, P. (1999) *Alastair Campbell, New Labour and the Rise of the Media Class*. London: Aurum Press.

Oborne, P. and Walters, S. (2004) *Alastair Campbell*. London: Aurum.

Ochs, E. (1997) 'Narrative', in van Dijk, T.A. (ed.) *Discourse as Structure and Process*. London: Sage, pp. 185–207.

Ofcom (2003) *Programme Code*, Section 3.7. London: Ofcom.

Ofcom (2004a) 'Ofcom Publishes Guidance on Media Mergers Public Interest Test', press release, 7 May. http://www.ofcom.org.uk/media_office/latest_news/nr1_20040507.

Ofcom (2004b) 'Ofcom Guidance for the Public Interest Test for Media Mergers'. http://www.ofcom.org.uk/codes_guidelines/broadcasting/media_mergers/.

Ofcom (2004c) 'The Communications Market 2004' 9 August.http://www.ofcom.org.uk/research/industry_market_research/mi_index/cm/cmpdf/?a=87101.

Ornebring, H. and Jönsson, A.M. (2004) 'Tabloid Journalism and the Public Sphere: A Historical Perspective on Tabloid Journalism', *Journalism Studies*, 5(3): 283–97.

Orwell, G. (1946) 'Politics and the English Language', in Orwell, G. (1962) *Inside the Whale and Other Essays*. Harmondsworth, Penguin.

Paraschos, E.E. (1998) *Media Law and Regulation in the European Union: National, Transnational and US Perspectives*. Ames: Iowa State University Press.

Parekh, B. (1997) 'National Culture and Multiculturalism', in Thompson, K. (ed.) *Media and Cultural Regulation*. London: Sage, pp. 163–94.

Parris, M. (2002) *Chance Witness: An Outsider's Life in Politics*. London: Viking.

Pax, S. (2003) 'Where Is Raed?'. http://www.dear_raed.blogsplot.com.

Paterson, C. (1998) 'Global Battlefields', in Boyd-Barrett, O. and Rantanen, T. (eds) *The Globalization of News*. London: Sage.

Pavlik, J.V. (2001) *Journalism and New Media*. Columbia, NY: University Press.

Peacock, A. (1986) *Report of the Committee on Financing the BBC*. London: HMSO.

Peak, S. (ed.) (2002) *Guardian Media Guide 2003*. London: Guardian Books.

Peirce, C.S. (1931–58) *Collected Papers*. Cambridge, MA: Harvard University Press.

Periodical Publishers Association website: http://www.ppa.co.uk/.

Pew Research Center (1999) Striking the Balance: Audience Interests, Business Pressures and Journalists' Values', 30 March http://people-press.org/reports/display.php3? ReportID=67.

Pew Research Center (2000) 'Self Censorship: How Often and Why: Journalists Avoiding the News', 30 April http://people-press.org/reports/display.php3?ReportID=39.

Phillips, A. (2003) 'A Question of Degree', *British Journalism Review*, 14(1): 71–5.

Philo, G. (1990) *Seeing and Believing: The Influence of Television*. London: Routledge.

Philo, G. (2002) 'Television News and Audience Understanding of War, Conflict and Disaster', *Journalism Studies*, 3(2): 173–86.

Philo, G. and Berry, M. (2004) *Bad News from Israel*. London: Pluto Press.

Philo, G. and Miller, D. (1999) 'The Effective Media', in Philo, G. (ed.) *Message Received*. London: Longman, pp. 21–33.

Pickering, M. (2001) *Stereotyping: The Politics of Representation*. Houndsmills: Palgrave.

The Pilkington Report (1962) London: HMSO.

Plumb, S. (2004) 'Politicians as Superheroes: The Subversion of Political Authority Using a Pop Cultural Icon in the Cartoons of Steve Bell', *Media, Culture and Society*, 26(3): 432–9.

Ponting, C. (1985) *The Right to Know: The Inside Story of the Belgrano Affair*. London: Sphere.

Ponting, C. (1988) 'A Fundamentally New Approach to Controlling Information', *UK Press Gazette*, 31 October.

Ponting, C. (1990) *Secrecy in Britain*. Oxford: Basil Blackwell.

Poole, E. (2002) *Reporting Islam: Media Representations of British Muslims*. London: I.B. Tauris.

Porter, C. (2002) 'The Truth about Mags and Ads', *Guardian*, 15 November. http://www.guardian.co.uk/style/story/0,3605,840390,00.html.

Pottker, H. (2003) 'News and its Communicative Quality: The Inverted Pyramid – When and Why Did It Appear?', *Journalism Studies*, 4(4): 501–11.

Poulantzas, N. (1973) *Political Power and Social Classes*. London: New Left Books.

Powers, L. (1995) 'The One Fallacy Theory', *Informal Logic*, 17(2): 303–14.

Prager, D. and Telushkin, J. (2003) *Why the Jews? The Reason for Antisemitism*. New York: Touchstone.

Press Complaints Commission (1997) 'New Code for Press "the Toughest in Europe"', press release, 19 December.

Press Complaints Commission (2003) 'Witness Payments: Important Changes to Editors' Code Announced', press release, 19 March http://www.pcc.org.uk/press/detail.asp?id=93.

Preston, P. (2002) 'Readers' Editors Do a Great Job, But the Real Work is the PCC's', *Observer*, 10 March.

Preston, P. (2003a) 'The Regeneration Game', *Observer*, 14 September.

Preston, P. (2003b) 'It's a Charade and We All Know It', *Guardian*, 7 July, p. 13.

Pritchard, S. (2001) 'I'm Here for the Readers: Introducing Your Man at the *Observer'*, *Observer*, 4 March.

Putnam, R. (2000) *Bowling Alone: The Collapse and Revival of American Community*. New York: Simon and Schuster.

Randall, D. (2000) *The Universal Journalist*. London: Pluto.

Ray, V. (2003) *The Television News Handbook*. London: Macmillan.

Raynsford, J. (2003) 'Blogging: the New Journalism?', 25 March, *dot.Journalism*, available at: http://www.journalism.co.uk/features/story604.html.

Reah, D. (2002) *The Language of Newspapers*. London: Routledge.

Reddick, R. and King, E. (2001) *The Online Journalist: Using the Internet and Other Electronic Resources*, 3rd edn. Orlando, FL: Harcourt Brace and Company.

Reese, S.D. (1990) 'The News Paradigm and the Ideology of Objectivity: A Socialist at the *Wall Street Journal'*, in Berkowitz, D. (ed.) (1997) *Social Meanings of News*. London: Sage, pp. 420–40.

Reese, S.D. (2001) 'Understanding the Global Journalist: A Hierarchy-of-Influences Approach', *Journalism Studies*, 2(2): 173–87.

Reese, S.D. and Cohen, J. (2000) 'Education for Journalism: The Professionalism of Scholarship', *Journalism Studies*, 1(2): 213–27.

Reisigl, M. and Wodak, R. (2001) *Discourse and Discrimination: Rhetorics of Racism and Anti-Semitism*. London: Routledge, pp. 45–54.

Reith, J. (1924) *Broadcast Over Britain* London: Hodder and Stoughton.

Rheingold, H. (1994) *The Virtual Community*. London: Minerva.

Richardson, J.E. (2001a) '"Now Is the Time to Put an End to All This" Argumentative Discourse Theory and Letters to the Editor', *Discourse and Society*, 12(2): 143–68.

Richardson, J.E. (2001b) 'British Muslims in the Broadsheet Press: A Challenge to Cultural Hegemony?', *Journalism Studies*, 2(2): 221–42.

Richardson, J.E. (2004) (*Mis)Representing Islam: The Racism and Rhetoric of British Broadsheet Newspapers*. Amsterdam: John Benjamins.

Richardson, J.E. and Franklin, B. (2003) '"Dear Editor": Race, Readers' Letters and the Local Press', *Political Quarterly*, 74(2): 184–92.

Richardson, J.E. and Franklin, B. (2004) 'Letters of Intent: Election Campaigning and Orchestrated Public Debate in Local Newspapers' Letters to the Editor', *Political Communication*, 21(4): 459–78.

Riddell, P. (1999) 'A Shift of Power and Influence', *British Journalism Review*, 10(3): 26–33.

Riggins, S.H. (1997a) 'The Rhetoric of Othering', in Riggins, S.H. (ed.) *The Language and Politics of Exclusion: Others in Discourse*. Thousand Oaks, CA: Sage, pp. 1–30.

Riggins, S.H. (ed.) (1997b) *The Language and Politics of Exclusion: Others in Discourse*. Thousand Oaks, CA: Sage.

Ritzer, G. (1993) *The McDonaldization of Society*. London: Pine Forge/Sage.

Ritzer, G. (1998) *The McDonaldization Thesis*. London: Sage.

Robertson, G. (1983) *An Inquiry into the Press Council*. London: Quartet Books.

Robertson, G. and Nicol, A. (2002) *Media Law*. 4th edn. London: Penguin.

Robertson, K.G. (1982) *Public Secrets: A Study of the Development of Government Secrecy* London: Macmillan.

Robertson, R. (1992) Globalization: Social Theory and Global Culture. London: Sage.

Rock, P. (1973) 'News as an Eternal Recurrence', in Cohen, S. and Young, J. (eds) *The Manufacture of News*. London: Constable.

Rosen, J. (2000) 'Questions and Answers About Public Journalism', *Journalism Studies*, (1)4:: 679–82.

Rosenfeld, L. and Morville, P. ([1998]2002) *Information Architecture for the World Wide*

Web, 2nd edn. Sebastopol, CA: O'Reilly and Associates.

Rozenberg, J. (2004) *Privacy and the Press*. Oxford: Oxford University Press.

Rowson, M. (2000) 'Seriously Funny', *Index on Censorship*, 6: 23–9.

Rubenstein, S.M. (1992) 'The Flow and Ebb of US Libel Law', *British Journalism Review*, 3(3): 47–56.

Rusbridger, A. (1997a) 'The Freedom of the Press and Other Platitudes', in Stephenson, H. (ed.) (2001) *Media Voices: The James Cameron Memorial Lectures*. London: Politicos, pp. 146–280.

Rusbridger, A. (1997b) 'Why Are We the Libel Capital of the World?' *British Journalism Review*, 8(3): 25–31.

Rusbridger, A. (2000) 'No More Ghostly Voices', *Guardian*, 15 July, p. 20.

Sadler, P. (2001) *National Security and the D Notice System*. Aldershot: Ashgate.

Said, E.W. (1978) *Orientalism*. London: Penguin Books.

Safire, W. (1993) *Safire's New Political Dictionary: The Definitive Guide to the New Language of Politics*, 3rd edn. New York: Random House.

Sahlins, M. (1985) *Islands of History*. Chicago: University of Chicago Press.

Sampson, A. (1996) 'The Crisis at the Heart of Our Media', *British Journalism Review*, 7(3): 42–56.

Sanders, K. (2003) *Ethics and Journalism*. London: Sage.

Sardar, Z. (1999) *Orientalism*. Buckingham: Open University Press.

Saussure de, F. (1974) *Course in General Linguistics*. London: Collins.

Schechter, D. (1997) *The More you Watch The Less You Know*. New York: Seven Stories Press.

Schement, J. (1998) 'Through Americans: Minorities and the New Media', in Garmer, A. (ed.) *Investing in Diversity: Advancing Opportunities for Minorities and the Media*. Washington, DC: Aspen Institute, pp. 87–124.

Schiffrin, D. (1996) *Approaches to Discourse*. Oxford: Blackwell.

Schirato, T. and Webb, J. (2003) *Understanding Globalisation*. London: Sage.

Schlesinger, P. (1987) *Putting Reality Together*. London: Methuen.

Schlesinger, P. (1989) 'From Production to Propaganda?' *Media, Culture and Society*, 11: 283–306.

Schlesinger, P. (1990) 'Rethinking the Sociology of Journalism: Source Strategies and the Limits of Media Centrism', in Ferguson, M. (ed.) *Public Communication: The New Imperatives*. Thousand Oaks, CA: Sage.

Schlesinger, P. (1991) *Media, State and Nation*. London: Sage.

Schlosser, E. (2002) *Fast Food Nation: What the All American Meal Is Doing to the World*. London: Penguin.

Schudson, M. (1978) *Discovering the News: A Social History of the American Newspaper*. New York: Banc Books.

Schudson, M. (1989) 'The Sociology of News Production', in Berkowitz, D. (ed.) (1997) *Social Meanings of News: A Reader*. Thousand Oaks, CA: Sage, pp. 7–22.

Schudson, M. (1992) 'Watergate: A Study in Mythology', *Columbia Journalism Review*, May/June 1992. http://archives.cjr.org/year/92/3/watergate.asp.

Semetko, H. and Valkenburg, P. (2000) 'Framing European Politics: Content Analysis of Press and Television News', *Journal of Communication*, 50(2): 93–109.

Sennitt, A. (2002) 'This Is LDN'. available at: http://www.rnw.nl/realradio/features/html/bbcldn020301.html.

Seymour-Ure, C. (1991) *The British Press and Broadcasting since 1945*. Oxford: Basil Blackwell.

Seymour-Ure, C. (2001) 'What Future for the British Political Cartoon?' *Journalism Studies*, 3(2): 333–55.

353

Seymour-Ure, C. (2003) *Prime Ministers and the Media: Issues of Power and Control.* Oxford: Blackwell.

Shannon, R. (2001) *A Press Free and Responsible: Self-regulation and the Press Complaints Commission 1991–2001.* London: John Murray.

Shapley, O. (1996) *Broadcasting a Life: The Autobiography of Olive Shapley,* Scarlet Press.

Shawcross, W. (1992) *Rupert Murdoch: Ringmaster of the Information Circus.* London: Chatto and Windus.

Shepard, A. (1994) 'The Gospel of Public Journalism', *American Journalism Review,* September: 28–34.

Shiple, J. (2003) 'Why's Information architecture so important?' available at: http://hotwired.lycos.com/webmonkey/98/28/indexOa.html.

Shoemaker, P.J. (1991a) 'A New Gatekeeping Model', in Berkowitz, D. (ed.) *Social Meanings of News: A Reader.* Thousand Oaks, CA: Sage, pp. 57–62.

Shoemaker, P.J. (1991b) 'Gatekeeping', in Tumber, H. (1999) (ed.) *News: A Reader.* Oxford: Oxford University Press.

Shoemaker, P. and Reese, S. (1996) *Mediating the Message: Theories of Influence on Mass Media Content.* White Plains, NY: Longman.

Shrimsley, B. (2003) 'Columns! The Good, the Bad, the Best', *British Journal Review,* 14(3): 23–30.

Silvester, C. (ed.) *The Penguin Book of Columnists.* London: Penguin Books.

Simpson, J. (2002) *News from No Man's Land: Reporting the World.* London: Macmillan.

Skillset (2002) *Journalists at Work: Their Views on Training, Recruitment and Conditions.* London: The Journalism Training Forum.

Smallman, A. (1996) 'Telling the Editorial from the Adverts', *Press Gazette,* 10 May, p. 11.

Smith, A. (ed.) (1974a) *British Broadcasting.* Newton Abbott: David and Charles.

Smith, A. (ed.) (1974b) *The British Press since the War.* Newton Abbott: David and Charles.

Smith, C. (1999) Lecture delivered to the Royal Television Society, Cambridge, 17 September.

Snoddy, R. (1993) *The Good, the Bad and the Unacceptable: The Hard News about the British Press.* London: Faber and Faber.

Snow, N. (2004) 'Brainscrubbing: The Failures of US Public Diplomacy after 9/11', in Miller, D. (ed.) *Tell Me Lies: Propaganda and Media Distortion in the Attack on Iraq.* London: Pluto Press, pp. 52–62.

Spark, D. (2000) *Investigative Reporting: A Study in Technique.* Oxford: Focal Press.

Sparks, C. (1999) 'The Press', in Stokes, J. and Reading, A. (eds) *The Media in Britain: Current Debates and Developments.* Houndsmills: Macmillan, pp. 41–60.

Sparks, C. and Tulloch, J. (2000) *Tabloid Tales: Global Debates over Media Standards.* Lanham, MD: Rowman and Littlefield.

Sparrow, A. (2003) *Obscure Scribblers: A History of Parliamentary Journalism.* London: Politicos.

Splichal, S. and Sparks, C. (1994) *Journalists for the 21st Century.* Norwood, NJ: Ablex.

Sreberny, A. (2000) 'Media and Diasporic Consciousness: An Exploration among Iranians in London', in Cottle, S. (ed.) *Ethnic Minorities and the Media.* Buckingham: Open University Press, pp. 179–96.

Starck, N. (2004a) 'Writes of Passage', doctoral thesis, Flinders University, Australia.

Starck, N. (2004b) 'Posthumous Reflections: The Newspaper Obituary as the First Verdict of History', paper presented to the annual conference of the Association for Journalism Education. London, 10 September.

Stephenson, H. (1998) 'Tickle the Public: Consumerism Rules', in Bromley, M. and Stephenson, H. (eds) *Sex, Lies and Democracy: The Press and the Public.* New York: Longman.

Stepp, C. (2000) 'Reader Friendly', *American Journalism Review*, July/August: 23–35.

Stevens, J. (2001) 'Where Are the New Storytellers?', in De Wolk, R. *Introduction to Online Journalism*. Boston: Allyn and Bacon.

Stevens, M. (2002) 'Small Camera, Big Vision', *UK Press Gazette*, 9 September.

Stevenson, W. (2000) 'The BBC in the Future', in *e-britannia*. Luton: University of Luton Press, pp. 121–7.

Storey, J. (1993) *An Introductory Guide to Cultural Theory and Popular Culture*. Hemel Hempstead: Harvester Wheatsheaf.

Straw, J. (1999) 'Wanted: One Bold Editor', *British Journalism Review*, 10(1): 29–34.

Sullivan, D. (2003) 'Google Throws Hat into the Contextual Advertising Ring', 4 March. http://jearchenginewatch.com/jereport/print.php/34721_2183531.

Taylor, J. (2000) 'Problems in Photojournalism: Realism, the Nature of News and the Humanitarian Narrative', *Journalism Studies*, 1(1): 129–43.

Taylor, P.M. (1995) *Munitions of the Mind: A History of Propaganda from the Ancient World to the Present Era*. Manchester: Manchester University Press.

Taylor, P.M. (2003) '"We Know Where You Are": Psychological Operations Media During Enduring Freedom', in Thussu, D.K. and Freedman, D. (eds) *War and the Media: Reporting Conflict 24/7*. London: Sage, pp. 101–13.

Taylor, S.J. (1992) *Shock! Horror! The Tabloids in Action*. London: Black Swan Books.

Tdorovich, L. (1997) 'Deep Throat Suspects' (June 13) http://www.washingtonpost.com/wp-srv/national/longterm/watergate/deept.htm.

Tench, D. (2004) 'You Can't Print That', the *Guardian*, 5 January. http://media.guardian.co.uk/mediaguardian/story/0,7558,1115966,00.html.

Thatcher, M. (1993) 'Margaret Thatcher's Analysis and Policy Prescriptions', in Franklin, B. (ed.) (2001) *British Television Policy: A Reader*. London: Routledge, pp. 50–3.

Thatcher, M. (1995) *The Downing Street Years*. London: HarperCollins.

The Broadcasting Act 1990 (1990) London: HMSO.

The Communications Act 2003 (2003) available at ww.legislation.hmso.gov.uk/acts/acts2003.

The Joint Industry Committee for Regional Press Research (JICREG), http://www.jicreg.co.uk (accessed 21 April 2004).

The Newspaper Society (2004) www.newspapersoc.org.uk/home.html.

Thelan, G., Kaplan, J. and Bradley, D. (2003) 'Convergence', *Journalism Studies*, 4(4): 513.

Thompson, H.S. (1971) *Fear and Loathing in Las Vegas: A Savage Journey into the Heart of the American Dream*. New York: The Modern Library.

Tibawi, A.L. (1964) *English Speaking Orientalists*. London: Luzac.

Timms, D. (2004) 'Record numbers follow Olympics via web and interactive TV'. 20 August, *Guardian Unlimited*, available at: http://media.guardian.co.uk/broadcast/story/0..1287620.00.html.

Tindale, C.W. (1999) *Acts of Arguing: A Rhetorical Model of Argument*. New York: SUNY Press.

Titscher, S., Meyer, M., Wodak, R. and Vetter, E. (2000) *Methods of Text and Discourse Analysis*. London: Sage.

Tomlin, R.S., Forrest, L. Pu, M.M. and Kim, M.H. (1997) 'Discourse Semantics', in Dijk, T.A. van (ed.) *Discourse as Structure and Process*. London: Sage, pp. 63–111.

Tracey, M. (1998) *The Decline and Fall of Public Service Broadcasting*. Oxford: Oxford University Press.

Tracy, M. (1995) 'Non-Fiction Television', in Smith, A. (ed.) *Television: An International History*. Oxford: Oxford University Press, pp. 118–47.

Truss, L. (2003) *Eats, Shoots and Leaves: The Zero Tolerance Approach to Punctuation*. London: Profile.

355

Tuchman, G. (1972) 'Objectivity as a Strategic Ritual: An Examination of Newsmen's Notions of Objectivity', *American Journal of Sociology*, 77(4): 660–70.

Tuchman, G. (1973) 'Making News by Doing Work: Routinizing the Unexpected', in Berkowitz, D. (ed.) (1997) *Social Meanings of News: A Text Reader*. London: Sage.

Tuchman, G. (1983) 'Consciousness Industries and the Production of Culture', *Journal of Communication*, 33: 330–41.

Tucker, A.H. (1992) *Social Stylistics: Syntactic Variation in British Newspapers*. Berlin: Mouton de Gruyter.

Tulloch, J. (1998) 'Managing the Press in a Medium-sized European Power', in M. Bromley, and H. Stephenson (eds) *Sex, Lies and Democracy: The Press and the Public*. New York: Longman.

Tumber, H. (1982) *Television and the Riots*. London: BFI.

Tumber, H. (ed.) (1999) *News: A Reader*. Oxford: Oxford University Press.

Tumber, H. and Prentoulis, M. (2003) 'Journalists Under Fire: Subcultures, Objectivity and Emotional Literacy', in Thussu, D.K. and Freedman, D. (eds) *War and the Media: Reporting Conflict 24/7*. London: Sage, pp. 215–30.

Tunstall, J. (1971) *Journalists at Work*. London: Constable.

Tunstall, J. (1977) 'Letters to the Editor, Royal Commission on the Press', in *Studies on the Press*. London: HMSO, pp. 203–48.

Tunstall, J. (1983) *The Media in Britain*. London: Constable.

Tunstall, J. (1996) *Newspaper Power: The New National Press in Britain*. Oxford: Clarendon Press.

Tunstall, J. and Palmer, M. (1991) *Media Moguls*. London: Routledge.

Turnbull, M. (1988) *The Spy Catcher Trial*. London: Heinemann.

Ursell, G. (2003) 'Creating Value and Valuing Creation in Contemporary UK Television: or Dumbing Down the Workforce', *Journalism Studies*, 4(1): 31–46.

van Dijk, T.A. (ed.) (1991) *Racism and the Press*. London: Routledge.

van Dijk, T.A. (ed.) (1997) *Discourse as Structure and Process*. London: Sage.

van Dijk, T.A. (1988a) *News as Discourse*. Willsdale, NJ: Lawrence Erlbaum Associates.

van Dijk, T.A. (ed.) (2000) 'New(s) Racism', in S. Cottle (ed.), *Ethnic Minorities and the Media*, pp.33–49. Buckingham: Open University Press.

Van den Bergh, P. (1998) 'The Business of Freelance Journalism: Some Advice from an Old Friend', in Franklin, B. and Murphy, D. (eds) *Making the Local News*. London: Routledge.

Vick, D.W. and Macpherson, L. (1997) 'An Opportunity Lost: The United Kingdom's Failed Reform of Defamation Law', *Federal Communications Law Journal*, 49(3). http://www.law.indiana.edu/fclj/pubs/v49/no3/vick.html.

Vincent, D. (1998) *The Culture of Secrecy: Britain 1832–1998*. Oxford: Oxford University Press.

Vološinov, V. N. ([1929]1973) *Marxism and the Philosophy of Language* (trans. Matejka, L. and Titunik, I.R.). Cambridge, MA: Harvard University Press.

Wahl-Jorgensen, K. (2001) 'Letters to the Editor as a Forum for Public Deliberation: Modes of Publicity and Democratic Debate', *Critical Studies in Mass Communications*, 18(3): 303–20.

Wahl-Jorgensen, K. (2002) 'Understanding the Conditions for Public Discourse: Four Rules for Selecting Letters to the Editor', *Journalism Studies*, 3(1): 69–81.

Wakeham, Lord (1998) 'Can Self-regulation Achieve More than the Law?' *Wynne Baxter Lecture* 15 May, http://www.pcc.org.uk/press/detail.asp?id=30.

Walker, D. (2003) 'Journalists "Most Protect Whistleblowers"' (19 July) http://news.bbc.co.uk/1/hi/uk_politics/3076813.stm.

Ward, M. (2002) *Journalism Online*. Oxford: Focal Press.

Warren, S. and Brandeis, L. (1890) 'The Right to Privacy', *Harvard Law Review* 4.

Waterhouse, K. (1993) *Waterhouse on Newspaper Style*. London: Penguin.

Waters, M. (1995) *Globalisation*. London: Routledge.

Watson, J. (1998) *Media Communication: An Introduction to Theory and Process*. Basingstoke, Macmillan.

Weaver, D. (ed.) (1998) *The Global Journalist*. Cresskill, NJ: Hampton Press.

Weaver, D., Graber, D., McCombs, M. and Eyal, C. (eds) (1981) *Media Agenda-setting in a Presidential Election: Issues, Images and Interest*. New York: Praeger Publishers.

Weaver, D.H. and Wilhoit, G.C. (1991) *The American Journalist: A Portrait of US News People and Their Work*. Bloomington, IN: Indiana University Press.

Weaver, D.H. and Wilhoit, G.C. (1996) *The American Journalist in the 1990s*. Mahwah, New Jersey: Lawrence Erlbaum Associates.

Weiner, J.H. (1969) *The War of the Unstamped: The Movement to Repeal the British Newspaper Tax 1830–6*. Ithaca, NY: Cornell University Press.

Weiss, G. and Wodak, R. (2003) *Critical Discourse Analysis: Theory and Interdisciplinarity*. London: Palgrave.

Welch, D. (1993) *The Third Reich: Politics and Propaganda*. London and New York: Routledge.

Wells, M. (2004) 'Serious Shows Turn Off Viewers', *Guardian*, 22 April, p. 9.

Welsh, T. and Greenwood, W. (2003) *McNae's Essential Law for Journalists*, 17th edn. London: LexisNexis.

Whately, R. (1848) *Elements of Logic*, 9th edn. London: Longmans.

Whitaker, R. (2004) 'How Could He Have Got It So Wrong?' *Independent*, 1 February.

White, D.M. (1950) 'The "Gatekeeper": A Case Study in the Selection of News', in Berkowitz, D. (ed.) *Social Meanings of News: A Reader*. Thousand Oaks, CA: Sage, pp. 63–71.

Whittaker, J. (2000) *Producing for the Web*. London: Routledge.

Whittaker, R. (2004) 'How Could He Have Got It So Wrong?' *Independent*, 1 February.

Wilby, P. and Conroy, A. (1999) *The Radio Handbook*. London and New York, Routledge.

Willcock, J. (1999) 'BT Threatened to Pull Ads after Newspaper Article, Tribunal Told', the *Independent*, 22 September.

Williams, A. and Kerr, J. (2004) 'Editor Steps Down', *Daily Mirror*, 15 May, p. 5.

Williams, H. (2002) 'Beware the Silly Season', *Guardian Unlimited* (31 July) http://www.guardian.co.uk/silly/story/0,10821,766668,00.html (accessed 31 March 2004).

Wilson, J. (1996) *Understanding Journalism: A Guide to Issues*. London: Routledge.

Winston, B. (1995) *Claiming the Real: The Documentary Film Revisited*. London: British Film Institute.

Winston, B. (2001) 'Towards Tabloidisation? Glasgow Revisited 1975–2001', *Journalism Studies*, 3(1): 5–20.

Wise, R. (2000) *Multimedia: A Critical Introduction*. London: Routledge.

Wober, J.M. (2004) 'Top People Write to *The Times*', *British Journalism Review*, 15(2): 49–54.

Wodak, R., De Cillia, R., Reisigl, M. and Liebhart, K. (1999) *The Discursive Construction of National Identity*. Edinburgh: Edinburgh University Press.

Wodak, R. and Iedema, R. (eds) (1999) 'Organisational Discourses', Special Issue of *Discourse and Society* 10(1).

Wodak, R. and Meyer, M. (eds) (2001) *Methods of Critical Discourse Analysis*. London: Sage.

Wolfe, T. (1977) *The New Journalism*. London: Picador.

Wolff, M. (2004) 'And Then There Was Murdoch', *Media Guardian*, 5 January.

Woods, L.A. and Kroger, R.O. (2000) *Doing Discourse Analysis: Methods for Studying Action in Talk and Text*. Thousand Oaks, CA: Sage.

Woolmar, C. (1990) *Censorship*. London: Wayland Books.

Worcester, R. (1998) 'Demographics and Values: What the British Public Reads and What It Thinks about its Newspapers', in Bromley, M. and Stephenson, H. (eds) *Sex, Lies and Democracy: The Press and the Public*. London: Longman, pp. 39–48.

Yorke, I. (2000) *Television News*, Oxford: Focal Press.

Web References

ABC (Australia) www.auditbureau.org.au/index.html#.

ABC Electronic http://www.abc.org.uk (accessed 26 October 2003).

ABC (USA) www.accessabc.com.

ABC/VFD (Britain) www.abc.org.uk.

Barnicoat, T. and Bazalgette, P. (no date) 'Endemol UK: Response to the Consultation on Media Ownership Rules', www.culture.gov.uk/PDF/media_own_endemol.PDF (accessed 13 July 2004).

BBC http://www.bbc.co.uk.

BBC Online http://www.bbc.co.uk/ (accessed 21 July 2003).

BBC Online (2003) 'Journalists "should name sources"' (18 July) http://news.bbc.co.uk/1/hi/uk_politics/3076337.stm (accessed 5 November 2003).

BBC Online (2003) 'Want to be a press baron? Read this first' (21 November) http://news.bbc.co.uk/1/hi/magazine/3225990.stm (accessed 5 January 2004).

BBC Producers' Guidance http://www.bbc.co.uk/info/policies/producer guides/.

BECTU http://www.bectu.org.uk/news/bbc/nb0098.html.

Blogger http://www.blogger.com/ (accessed 16 September 2003).

Broadband http://www.bbc.co.uk/broadband/info/whatis.shtml (accessed 16 September 2003).

Byrne, C. (2003) 'Sun's Yelland in Shock Departure', (13 January) *Guardian Unlimited* http://media.guardian.co.uk/presspublishing/story/0,7495,873980,00.html (accessed 1 July 2004).

Campaign against Official Secrecy http://www.cryptome.org/.

Campaign for Freedom of Information http://www.cfoi.org.uk.

Campaign for Press and Broadcasting Freedom http://www.cpbf.org.uk/.

CAP, A One-stop-shop for all Advertising Complaints www.cap.org.uk/news/view_announcements.asp?ann_id+27 (accessed 14 June 2004).

CERN http://public.web.cern.ch/public/index.html (accessed 21 July 2003).

Collins CoBuild http://titania.cobuild.collins.co.uk/form.html.

The Communications Act www.legislation.hmso.gov.uk/acts/acts2003.

Cozens, C. (2004) 'Guardian Agrees £50m for Relaunch', *Guardian Unlimited*, 29 June http://media.guardian.co.uk/site/story/0,14173,1249915,00.html (accessed 3 July 2004).

Croad, E. (2003) 'Blogs Bring Personal View of War' (27 March) *dotJournalism* http://www.journalism.co.uk/news/story607.html (accessed 16 September 2003).

D Notices www.dnotice.org.uk/system.htm.

Defence, Press and Broadcasting Advisory Committee http://www.dnotice.org.uk/.

De La Mare, P. (1997) http://www.dotprint.com/fgen/genlist.htm (21 April) (accessed 30 September 2003).

Dijk, T.A. van (no date) From Text Grammar to Critical Discourse Analysis www.discourse-in-society.org/beliar-e.htm (accessed 2 July 2003).

DTI (2004) *Enterprise Act 2002: Public Interest Intervention in Media Mergers. Guidance on the Operation of the Public Interest Merger Provisions Relating to Newspaper and Other Media Mergers* http://www.dti.gov.uk/ccp/topics2/guide/ukmediaguide.pdf.

EuroAccessibility Consortium http://www.euroaccessibility.org/ (accessed 30 June 2004).

Ezzard, J. (2003) '500 Years of History Ends for Fleet St' (24 September) 'http://media.guardian.co.uk/presspublishing/story/0,7495,1048274,00.html (accessed 7 January 2004).

Findlaw http://caselaw.lp.findlaw.com/data/constitution/amendment01/06.html.

First Amendment Center http://www.firstamendmentcenter.org.

Fleetwood, B. (1999) 'The Broken Wall: How Newspapers Are Selling their Credibility to Advertisers', *Washington Monthly*, September http://www.washingtonmonthly.com. The *Guardian* http://www.guardian.co.uk.

Guardian Unlimited http://www.guardian.co.uk/weblogarticle/0,6799,394059,00.html (accessed 16 September 2003).

Hightower, J. (2004) 'The People's Media Reaches More People than FOX Does' *CommonDreams* 15 June www.commondreams.org/views04/0615-14.htm, (accessed 21 June 2004).

Human Rights http://www.echr.coe.int/Eng/EDocs/HistoricalBackground.htm#book1.

Hutton (2004) *Report of the Inquiry into the Circumstances Surrounding the Death of Dr David Kelly*, CMG, London: The Stationery Office. HC247 at http://www.the-hutton-inquiry.org.uk.

International Federation of Journalists http://www.ifj.org/default.asp?Issue=FREELANCEandLanguage=EN (accessed 22 October 2003).

Internet2 http://www.internet2.edu/about/aboutinternet2.html (accessed 21 July 2003).

Internet Society http://www.isoc.org/internet/ (accessed 21 July 2003).

ITC Advertising Standards Code http://www.ofcom.org.uk/codes_guidelines/broadcasting/?a=87101 (accessed 14 June 2004).

Janeway, Michael (2000) Fall Forum 2000 Keynote Address http://www.tcg.org/Denver/keynote.html (accessed 14 June 2004).

The Jargon Dictionary http://info.astrian.net/jargon/terms/s/shovelware.html (accessed 21 July 2003).

Joint Industry Committee for Regional Press Research (JICREG) http://www.jicreg.co.uk/ (accessed 21 April 2004).

Kiss, J. (2004) 'E-publications Stand up and Get Counted', *Journalism*, 15 June 2004 www.journalism.co.uk/news/story946.shtml (accessed 6 July 2004).

The Living Internet http://livinginternet.com/?w/wi_lee.htm (accessed 21 July 2003).

Lobster http://www.lobster-magazine.co.uk/.

McIntosh, N. (2003) 'Start Here: Setting up a Website' (25 September) *Guardian Unlimited* http://www.guardian.co.uk/online/story/0,,1048698,00.html (accessed 3 October 2004).

McNay, M. (2004) 'Neither Pedantic Nor Wild?' *Guardian Unlimited* http://www.guardian.co.uk/styleguide/article/0,5817,181311,00.html (accessed 14 January 2004).

Media Info (2004) 'Claim: As TV Fragments, Newspapers Are Last Mass Medium', 23 January http://www.mediainfo.com/eandp/departments/business /article_display.jsp?vnu_content_id=2075708 (accessed 14 June 2004).

Meek, C. (2003) 'Internet is a Boon for Freelancers', (14 October) *dotJournalism* http://www.journalism.co.uk/news/story60.html (accessed 22 October 2003).

Meek, C. (2004) 'Photo Opportunities Wasted', (1 July) *dotJournalism* http://www.journalism.co.uk/news/story968.shtml (accessed 4 July 2004).

Military City (2003) 'Media Embed Ground Rules' www.militarycity.con/iraq/1631270.html, (accessed 30 May 2003).

Miller, D. (2003) 'Embed with the Military' *Scoop Opinion* 12 Apri www.scoop.co.nz/mason/stories/HL0304/S00126.htm (accessed 30 May 2003).

MORI http://www.mori.com/ (accessed 21 April 2004).

National Readership Survey http://www.nrs.co.uk/ (accessed 21 April 2004).

National Union of Journalists http://www.nuj.org.uk/front/inner.php?docid=55 (accessed 22 October 2003).

Naughton, J. (2003) 'The Genius of Blogging' (23 February) *The Observer* http://observer.guardian.co.uk/business/story/0,6903,900841,00.html (accessed 16 September 2003).

Neil Report (2004) *The BBC's Journalism After Hutton; The Report of the Neil Review Team* at http://www.bbc.co.uk/info/policies/neil_report.

The Newspaper Society http://www.newspapersoc.org.uk/home.html (accessed 21 April 2004).

Nielsen, J. 'Usability 10' (25 August 2003) http://www.useit.com/alertbox/20030825.html (accessed 16 September 2003).

Nielsen, J. 'Why You Only Need to Test with 5 Users' (19 March 2003) http://www.useit.com/alertbox/20000319.html (accessed 16 September 2003).

Nielsen//NetRatings http://www.netratings.com/ (accessed 26 October 2003).

Nielsen Norman Group (2003) http://www.nngroup.com/reports/ (accessed 16 September 2003).

Nua.com http://www.nua.ie/surveys/ (accessed 21 July 2003).

Number 10 Website http://www.Number-10.gov.UK.

OFCOM http://www.ofcom.org.uk.

OFCOM (www.ofcom.org.uk/codes_guidelines/broadcasting/tv/psb_review/reports).

OFCOM (2004a) *Ofcom publishes guidance on media mergers public interest test*, press release May 7 http://www.ofcom.org.uk/media_office/latest_news/nr1_20040507.

OFCOM (2004b) *Ofcom guidance for the public interest test for media mergers* http://www.ofcom.org.uk/codes_guidelines/broadcasting/media_mergers/.

OJD (France) www.diffusion-controle.com/fr/index.php.

OJD (Spain) www.ojd.es.

PACT (2004) *Latest terms of trade documents and trust letters* www.pact.co.uk/news/art_dtl.asp?art_id=2013 (accessed 13 July 2004).

Pax, S. (2003) 'Where is Raed?' http://www.dear_raed.blogspot.com (accessed 16 September 2003).

Perrone, J. (2004) 'What is a weblog?' (20 May) *Guardian Unlimited* http://www.guardian.co.uk/weblogarticle/0,6799,394059,00.html (accessed 3 October 2004).

The Press Association (2003) http://www.pa.press.net/about_pa/about_pa.html (accessed 10 November 2003).

Presswise http://www.presswise.org.uk/.

Prospects (no date) *Broadcast... As It Is* www.prospects.ac.uk (accessed 13 July 2004).

Pryor, L. (1999) 'Old Media Firms Dig a Grave with Shovelware' http://www.ojr.org/ojr/technology/1017969861.php (posted 9 April 1999, changed 4 April 2002, accessed 21 July 2003).

Radio Authority http://www.radioauthority.org.uk.

The Radio Authority Advertising and Sponsorship Code,.

http://www.ofcom.org.uk/codes_guidelines/broadcasting/radio/codes/adv_sponsorship_

code.pdf (accessed 14 June 2004).

Radio Joint Audience Research www.rajar.co.uk.

Raynsford, J. (2003) 'Blogging: The New Journalism?' (25 March) *dotJournalism* http://www.journalism.co.uk/features/story604.html (accessed 16 September 2003).

Royal National Institute of the Blind http://www.rnib.org.uk/xpedio/groups/public/documents/code/public_rnib001951.hcsp (accessed 30 June 2004).

Schofield, J. (2003) 'Decorators with Keyboards', *Guardian Unlimited*, 17 July http://www.guardian.co.uk/online/story/0,3605,999218,00.html (accessed 30 June 2004).

searchNetworking.com (2004) http://searchnetworking.techtarget.com/sDefinition/0,,sid7_gci211634,00.html (last updated 12 July 2004) (accessed 13 September 2004).

SearchWebServices.com http://searchwebservices.techtarget.com/ (accessed 21 July 2003).

Sennitt, A. (2002) 'This is LDN', http://www.rnw.nl/realradio/features/html/bbcldn020301.html.

Shiple, J. 'Why's Information Architecture So Important?' http://hotwired.lycos.com/webmonkey/98/28/index0a.html (accessed 16 September 2003).

Sochats, K. and Robins, B. (2002) 'Web Portals: History and Direction' http://ltl13.exp.sis.pitt.edu/Website/Webresume/WebPortalPaper/WebPortals.htm (accessed 23 July 2003).

Stephen Lawrence Inquiry (1999) www.archive.official-documents.co.uk/document/cm42/4262/sli-00.htm.

Sullivan, D. (2003) 'Google Throws Hat into the Contextual Advertising Ring' (4 March) Search Engine Watch http://searchenginewatch.com/sereport/print.php/34721_2183531 (accessed 22 September 2004).

Talking Cities http://www.talkingcities.co.uk/london_pages/sights_alpha3.htm (accessed 7 January 2004).

Tata Institute of Fundamental Research http://www.ecom.tifr.res.in/~mehul/portals/define.html (accessed 23 July 2003).

Thompson, J. (2003) 'Online Subs Counted in Print Circulation' (6 November) *dotJournalism* http://www.journalism.co.uk/news/story755.html (accessed 7 November 2003).

The Times Online (2003) *The Times Style and Usage Guide* (January) http://www.timesonline.co.uk/section/0,,2941,00.html (accessed 14 January 2004).

Timms, D. (2004) 'Record Numbers Follow Olympics via Web and Interactive TV' (20 August) *Guardian Unlimited*. http://media.guardian.co.uk/broadcast/story/0,,1287620,00.html (accessed 7 September 2004).

Todorovich, L. (1997) 'Deep Throat Suspects' (June 13) http://www.washingtonpost.com/wp-srv/national/longterm/watergate/deept.htm (accessed 5 November 2003).

Travis, A. (2004) 'Public Supports Privacy Law for Stars in Backlash against Beckham Story' (21 April) *Guardian Unlimited* http://www.guardian.co.uk/uk_news/story/0,3604,1197047,00.html (accessed 22 April 2004).

Walker, D. (2003) 'Journalists "Must Protect Whistleblowers"' (19 July) http://news.bbc.co.uk/1/hi/uk_politics/3076813.stm (accessed 5 November 2003).

Watergate http://www.bbc.co.uk/crime/caseclosed/watergate.shtml.

Webopedia http://www.webopedia.com/TERM/S/snailmail.html (accessed 23 July 2003).

Williams, H. (2002) 'Beware the Silly Season' (31 July) *Guardian Unlimited* http://www.guardian.co.uk/silly/story/0,10821,766668,00.html (accessed 31 March 2004).

World Wide Web Consortium http://www.w3.org/Consortium/ (accessed 21 July 2003).

Word Reference.com http://www.wordreference.com/english/definition.asp?en=cybercaf%E9. (accessed 16 September 2003).

362